Skill Set

Strategies for Reading and Writing

Skill Set

Strategies for Reading and Writing

Lucia Engkent

OXFORD
UNIVERSITY PRESS

OXFORD
UNIVERSITY PRESS

70 Wynford Drive, Don Mills, Ontario M3C 1J9
www.oup.com/ca

Oxford University Press is a department of the University of Oxford.
It furthers the University's objective of excellence in research, scholarship,
and education by publishing worldwide in

Oxford   New York

Auckland   Bangkok   Buenos Aires   Cape Town   Chennai
Dar es Salaam   Delhi   Hong Kong   Istanbul   Karachi   Kolkata
Kuala Lumpur   Madrid   Melbourne   Mexico City   Mumbai   Nairobi
São Paulo   Shanghai   Taipei   Tokyo   Toronto

Oxford is a trade mark of Oxford University Press
in the UK and in certain other countries

Published in Canada
by Oxford University Press

Copyright © Oxford University Press Canada 2007

Library and Archives Canada Cataloguing in Publication

Engkent, Lucia Pietrusiak, 1955–
Skill set : strategies for reading and writing / Lucia Engkent.

Includes index.
ISBN-13: 978-0-19-542307-5
ISBN-10: 0-19-542307-0

1. English language—Composition and exercises. 2. College readers.
3. English language—Grammar—Textbooks. I. Title.

PE1408.E484 2001   428   C2006-906699-X

Cover image: design pics/firstlight.com

Cover design: Andrea Katwaroo

This book is printed on permanent (acid-free) paper ∞.

Printed in Canada

Contents

Part 2   Reading Selections

Introduction

For the Instructor

This text is intended for developmental English and advanced English as a second language (ESL) classes. It was developed in a non-credit college course for students who had not achieved the required reading and writing skills for the credit English course. The students in this course were of different backgrounds and mixed abilities: some were native speakers of English who were reluctant readers, some were newly arrived international students who had university degrees from their native countries, and some were immigrants who had spent many years in the Canadian school system and spoke English fluently. Some of the material was also tested in ESL academic preparation classes.

Although some institutions have separate streams for ESL students and native speakers, at this level the two groups have enough in common to allow them to be taught together. Even some of the grammatical errors are similar. Instructors see incorrect verb forms, article and preposition errors, difficulty with complex sentence structures, and misuse of vocabulary. Reluctant readers struggle with the more complex vocabulary and structures of academic English.

Skill set is very much the product of classwork. It focuses on the problems generally seen in the writing of students in the developmental English course. The exercises address problems these students have, such as distinguishing general and specific points in order to write supporting statements in paragraphs. Some of the sample paragraphs and essays were generated from student writing assignments. In addition, many of the sentences used for error correction in unit 7 are taken from student writing samples.

Organization of the text

This book is designed to let instructors skip around from section to section as needed. It is organized so that smaller units (vocabulary and sentences) are discussed before larger units (paragraphs and essays), but that does not mean units have to be tackled in that order. The material is organized by skill areas, such as constructing complex sentences and writing topic sentences, so you can focus on the weaknesses your students have.

It is important to remember that students do not come to a course like this with a blank slate. They have been introduced to the writing process and essay structure. They do not have to master sentence structure before they move on to paragraphs, and they may even chafe at working on paragraph structure when they want to write essays.

You may wish to move on to the unit on paragraphs (unit 4) after a brief introduction to writing (unit 1) and then work on grammar (units 3 and 7) and vocabulary (unit 2) in bits as students practise writing paragraphs and then essays. You can draw from unit 6, "Rhetorical skills," as you assign different types of writing tasks. You can do a different reading each week, in any order you wish, according to your curriculum, your students' needs, and your own tastes.

Paragraphs and essays

Students are given a chance to work on independent paragraphs before they move to the essay. This allows them to practise their skills in shorter writing assignments before they progress to the essay. The focus is on the basic academic skills of making points and supporting them.

Some educators argue against teaching the five-paragraph essay since it is not "real world" writing. However, it is a useful pedagogical structure that teaches the skills students need for all kinds of writing—the ability to organize thoughts, present ideas, and support them. Whether they have to write a cover letter for a job or a business report, they still have to introduce a topic, divide their arguments into well-structured body paragraphs, and write a conclusion—just as they do in an essay. Students who are struggling with writing benefit from having a well-defined structure to follow. Moreover, students developing their writing skills by composing five-paragraph essays are no different from musicians practising scales or computer programmers working with non-commercial languages. Classwork does not have to be exactly like "real life" work to be successful and fruitful.

Readings

Reading and writing go hand in hand. It is not enough to add some readings to a writing text as an afterthought. Students who have weak writing skills often have weak reading skills, and this must be addressed. Good reading comprehension is paramount—no instructor would deny that as skills are ranked, understanding the main idea of a newspaper article is surely more important than being able to fix a comma splice. Furthermore, to become good writers, students need to read more in order to learn about the written language—its structures and vocabulary.

It is essential to test students' reading ability with comprehension questions, paraphrasing, and summarizing. Otherwise, it is easy to miss students' reading problems.

The ten non-fiction articles and five fiction pieces in this text serve several functions. First, they give students an opportunity to improve their reading skills and their vocabulary. Second, students are asked to look at sentence, paragraph, and essay structures in the readings so that they can carry over what they learned about grammar and writing into their reading. They can see different writing styles at work. Third, the readings provide the students with interesting subjects to discuss and write about.

The non-fiction readings are mostly in journalistic style. These articles are accessible and interesting to students. The one true academic reading shows students the difference in style and challenges them with more difficult vocabulary and structure. The sample paragraphs and essays show the academic style students are expected to use in essay writing.

Almost all of the readings are Canadian. Three of them are not contemporary; they show language and culture of another time. Some of the non-fiction articles are about technology and the issues of modern life. Some present opposing points of view. For instance, "Free to drive" by Margaret Wente is accompanied by "Letters to the editor" both agreeing and disagreeing with her opinion.

There are five fiction readings included—four short stories and one excerpt from a novel. It is important to include fiction in students' reading diet because they sometimes have difficulty understanding the difference between fiction and non-fiction. Moreover, fiction is good for capturing and exercising the imagination.

In addition to the typical comprehension questions, discussion topics, and assignment suggestions, the readings are accompanied by vocabulary study and notes on structure and technique. These are meant to make students more conscious of the language as they read. They can apply what they learned about vocabulary and sentence structure to actual words and sentences in the reading.

Vocabulary study

In developmental English courses, building vocabulary is crucial. Spoken English uses a much smaller range of words, so reluctant readers have limited exposure to less common words and need more guidance to learn the patterns that can help them make connections between words. Thus, this text has work on collocations, parts of speech, and common roots and affixes.

Grammar

Grammar can be a contentious issue. Instructors all agree that grammar instruction is necessary, but there is so much to learn and practise that the areas to focus on must be carefully chosen. Moreover, exercises may have little carry-over to actual writing assignments; some students excel at grammar exercises but make errors on the same points in their writing. Error correction and the construction of complex sentences are two areas that are more like real writing work. In this text, the sentences used for error correction are taken from actual student writing.

Assignments

Assignments are left open-ended so that you can tailor them to your class needs. For example, if your class is still working on paragraph structure when you do a particular reading, your assignments will focus on paragraphs. If you are working on reports or research essays, you can choose a topic for students to explore in such an assignment. You may want to specify length and format.

Answer key

Answers to most of the exercises can be found in the back. Exercises with answers readily available in the dictionary and more open-ended exercises do not have answers given.

Acknowledgements

This material was class-tested at Seneca College in Toronto and at Renison College at the University of Waterloo. Thank you to my students—their work provided the base for some of the examples and exercises. I would also like to acknowledge the support of my colleagues, especially Patricia Parsons and Don Roberts at Seneca and Dara Lane, Christine Morgan, and Tanya Missere-Mihas at Renison. The helpful suggestions of the anonymous reviewers are also appreciated.

And as usual, a big thank you to my family, who always gets drafted into reading, commenting, and sometimes even contributing—my husband, Garry, and my children, David, Susan, and Emily. Emily's essays on treeplanting and 'A' students are especially appreciated.

Lucia Engkent

Part 1

Skill Development

Writing Skills

One of the first steps to becoming a good writer is recognizing the difference between speaking and writing. Even though the written system is fundamentally based on spoken language, the differences can be quite marked. Most important, you can learn the written language only by reading. If you read little, chances are that your writing will be at the wrong level of language—it will be just a written-down version of speech.

In some languages, the differences between the written and spoken forms are dramatic. For example, Mandarin and Cantonese are both "Chinese," but a speaker of one cannot understand the other. Each can, however, write a note to the other because the written languages are practically the same.

In English, the differences lie in both vocabulary and sentence structure, with the everyday spoken language being more limited than the written. This is just a generalization, however, since there is a wide variety of spoken and written forms. A casual conversation differs from a formal speech, while a text message sent on your cellphone is written language but is more like the spoken form.

In spoken English, you use tone of voice, gestures, and context to get your meaning across. You can get away with calling something a "thingamajig," for example, if you can point to the item in question. You can get immediate feedback if your communication is unsuccessful—ranging from the bewildered look on the listener's face to direct questions such as "What do you mean?"

In written English, you have no such back-up system. Your meaning must be clear from the outset. You must anticipate what your readers need to know. You have to use precise vocabulary. (Imagine reading instructions for a new digital camera that tell you to "hook that dangly piece to the thingy over there.") The vocabulary of English has been estimated at anywhere from half a million words to a million words, depending on how words are counted. Some of the words are technical terms known to few people. Most English words are not used in everyday speech but only encountered in the written form.

You speak mainly in simple sentences, but in writing you use longer, more complex sentences. You can layer meaning with clauses. Your attention span is greater when you read than when you listen, and you can go back and check meaning, so you can handle complexity better in written form. Academic English, the language of essay writing, is even more sophisticated. For your English course, you need to be able to produce this level of language. It will be useful to you in the work world in both business and technical writing.

Addressing Audience and Purpose

Your first job as a writer is to consider why you are writing (your purpose) and who your reader is (your audience). You may write to inform, persuade, or entertain your readers. The purpose of a technical manual is to give information. A novel or short story entertains and perhaps along the way informs and enlightens its readers. Academic essays are arguments—presenting ideas to explain them and persuade the reader of their soundness.

What you write has to be tailored to your audience, so you need to know who will be reading your document. Imagine telling someone how to use a new portable music player—instructions to your technophobic grandparents would be very different from instructions to your techno-savvy classmate. Recipe directions for an experienced cook would be different from those for a novice. You might write an essay about traditions in your native country, but you need to say enough to make your essay clear to readers who may never have visited that country or are not familiar with the traditions. For instance, some students even say "in my country" without ever identifying the country for the reader.

The information you give and the words you use will vary depending on your audience and purpose:

> That patient is suffering from separation anxiety disorder, but I think it is developing into full-fledged agoraphobia. I'd like to try cognitive behavioural therapy. (audience: another psychologist; purpose: to give information for a treatment program)

> It's okay, sweetie. Don't cry. Your mama will be back soon. (audience: small child; purpose: to reassure and calm the child)

Knowing what your audience knows and needs to know is not easy. It can be especially difficult if your audience is broad, but keep in mind that you cannot follow your document around to explain it, so it is better to give too much information than too little.

The writing you do in school is artificial in that it is not communication of new information. You are writing to a teacher or professor who is an expert on the subject. Your essay on sibling rivalry is not going to tell your psychology professor much that he or she does not know; however, it will tell the professor how well you have learned the required material, researched the topic, and expressed your ideas. Sometimes you may be tempted to leave out information that you know the professors have, but it may be required for the logical links in your argument.

In a composition class, your primary audience is your instructor, and you must satisfy his or her requirements in order to earn a good grade. Some instructors are sticklers for grammar, going as far as failing a paper for a single run-on sentence. Other instructors are more laid-back, looking for clarity more than perfection. Some instructors prefer students to take writing assignments seriously and do not appreciate humour or satire. Some assign personal, creative writing tasks. Others make students practise a more formal and objective academic style to pave the way for business and technical writing. Some like a conversational style; others prefer a more traditional one. However, no matter what style they prefer, all good writing instructors should make their expectations clear.

You may be tempted to throw up your hands in frustration if your English instructor prefers a style very different from the one your last instructor did, but remember that the same thing applies in the work world. Supervisors often vary in their expectations, and you may have to relearn how to do a job for a different boss.

When writing and reading, consider who the intended audience of a piece is. For example, the reading "Helpless" by Karen von Hahn (page 274) seems to be addressed to the sales clerks and servers she has encountered in the past, but it is actually meant for people in general.

> For the writing in your English course, your audience is your instructor, and your purpose is to show the instructor what you have learned, how you can connect ideas, and how well you express those ideas.

The Principles of Good Writing

Whatever the type of writing, whatever the audience and purpose, the qualities of good writing remain the same. Documents should be legible, clear, and concise. They should engage the reader.

Clarity

Above all, written communication must be clear to the reader. Otherwise, it does not succeed as communication and is essentially worthless. When you speak, you have immediate feedback for your words because of your interaction with your audience. As a writer, you cannot follow your document around to every reader to make sure that is it understood. Clear, simple language is always preferable to overly ornate, complicated language. Just remember that simple does not mean overly simplistic.

To achieve clarity, you must choose your words carefully. You cannot just point to something if you forget the name of it. You can't get away with imprecise words like "stuff" and "whatever." The vocabulary of the written language is much larger than that of everyday spoken language, and these words are needed to ensure precision and clarity. You can get by with fewer words in your everyday speech, but for good writing you need an arsenal of words. You also need to use the vocabulary correctly.

It is difficult for writers to evaluate the clarity of their own writing. They may not know they are using words incorrectly. They may be relying on references that may not be clear to their audience. One way to improve clarity is to let a document sit for a while and come back to it with fresh eyes. Many writers have looked over something they have written and asked themselves, "What was I thinking?" Getting a second opinion is also vital. That is why published works go through several readers and editors.

A piece of writing can follow basic grammar rules and be technically "correct" yet not be clear:

> Cars come in many forms as perceived by a viewer.
> In the past century, cars have contributed to many criteria
> of human development. To view cars as an advantage is
> a benchmark, but to view them as a disadvantage is a
> learning curve. Owning a luxury car can be an advantage
> and disadvantage.

> We are pleased to announce the birth of Jonathan Edward.
> Weighing 6 lbs. 12 oz., he is the first on either side of his
> family, which now spans four and five generations,
> respectively, around the world.

In academic writing, clarity depends on support. Essay writing hinges on making points and supporting them with examples and explanations. This support is crucial to the clarity of the points.

Content

Writing is judged by what it has to say. In English class, your writing is evaluated by the strength of your argument—the logic of your conclusions, the support for the points, the suitability of the examples. Instructors may disagree with your point of view, but as long as the argument is sound and well expressed, they will not give you a low mark.

Writers build on what other writers say. The more you read, the easier you will find it to come up with ideas for your essays. For example, as you read newspaper stories of accounts of gang violence and the editorials and comments of people discussing the issue, you will get a better understanding of the complexity of the problem. When you write an essay suggesting ways to tackle the problem, your ideas will be founded on this strong understanding.

Conciseness

Unless you are writing a novel, conciseness is valued in writing. Business and technical communication must be short and to the point. No one likes to read more than they have to, unless they are reading for pleasure. Wordiness frustrates readers; it not only causes readers to lose interest but also confuses them.

You can make your writing economical by eliminating unnecessary repetition, using complex sentences instead of many short sentences, choosing precise vocabulary instead of descriptive phrases (for instance, saying "widow" instead of "woman whose husband died"), and eliminating unnecessary phrases.

Students faced with a required length for an essay assignment may pad their writing because they don't know what to say. This is always a mistake. Writing instructors know when you are padding and will not consider such an essay to be high-quality writing.

You can see examples of wordy writing and practise editing for conciseness in the exercises on page 235.

Coherence

Because written communication lacks the visual cues that speakers rely on to let listeners follow the flow of ideas, it needs to be more structured. Logical order and transition signals are essential for coherence. Coherence is explained in unit 4 on paragraph skills.

Correctness

Writing should be correct, that is, free of grammatical, spelling, and punctuation errors. Sometimes these errors are serious—they impede comprehension. Some are minor; readers can understand what is meant, but they may get annoyed, and their impression of the writer's ability and even credibility will be negatively affected.

While perfection is impossible to attain, and even professional writers make spelling and grammatical errors, it is important to strive for some degree of standard English. If you have trouble with spelling, first memorize words that are used frequently. Use all the tools available to you, such as dictionaries and spell checkers. Above all, recognize that your poor spelling is a problem and strive to improve.

As for grammar, again, you cannot achieve perfection, especially since rules change over time and even experts can disagree over correctness. For instance, the caution against not ending an English sentence with a preposition is actually based on a mistaken reference to Latin grammar. Winston Churchill famously said, "That is a rule up with which I will not put" to show the absurdity of that stricture.

Concentrate on the most important aspects of grammar. For example, students with English as a second language (ESL) always have trouble with articles and prepositions because much of the usage is idiomatic. However, verb forms are fairly straightforward and vital to the comprehension of sentences, so students should be sure to learn the rules and use them. They should also pay attention to common slips—such as the −s ending on third person singular verbs (e.g., "he walks").

Expression

Good writing is a pleasure to read. The vocabulary is interesting, and the sentence length and structure is varied. English offers such a treasure trove of words and expressions; the most successful writers are those who can use that vocabulary effectively. That does not mean that you should stuff your sentences with the most multi-syllabic words you can find but rather that you should choose the appropriate word to express whatever you want to say. Good prose is simple and straightforward but not simplistic.

Writing Personally and Impersonally

A personal voice in writing is important and indeed unavoidable, but many documents in business and technical writing have to be less personal and more objective. Because of long years of practice with compositions in English class, you may be able to handle personal writing more easily. You are probably used to personal assignments like "What I did on my summer vacation" but may have more difficulty with topics like "Why vacations are necessary for a healthy workforce." Therefore, as a college student, you should practise writing impersonally so that you can be prepared for the work world. For instance, you might have to produce a business letter that represents the company viewpoint instead of your own.

One way of looking at impersonal writing is that it means writing in the third person (*he, she, they*) instead of the first person (*I*). It also means being objective, looking at something academically. For example, instead of arguing that an increase in tuition fees is wrong because you cannot afford it, you can argue that the government should pay more because public spending on post-secondary education is an investment in society. You use more passive voice in impersonal writing, but keep in mind that too much passive bogs down the passage and makes it difficult to follow.

Student writers often overuse *I* in their essays, coming up with such phrases as "In my opinion, I personally think that . . ." If you say, "SUVs are a waste of money," that is clearly your point of view, and you don't need to say, "I think SUVs are a waste of money." Moreover, from a grammatical point of view, a sentence such as "I think that the college should lower its parking rates" has the emphasis on the main clause "I think." You can use "I think" and "in my opinion" in your essay when you need to emphasize that this is your point of view, but use such expressions sparingly—only when you really need the emphasis.

Unless you say otherwise, your writing is your opinion. If you say, "Many people think SUVs are safe vehicles," you are distancing yourself from that idea; the reader expects the next sentence to express a "but" idea that shows your viewpoint. You can see instances of this in the readings. For example, Linda McQuaig (page 293) starts her essay "The tobacco industry and its supporters have long insisted that smoking is simply a matter of 'individual choice.' They note that the dangers of smoking are well-known . . . But cigarettes are in a class by themselves when it comes to their sheer killing power." This last sentence is her opinion; the first two statements are not.

You need to develop a sense of when personal writing is appropriate. Instructors will indicate whether an essay should be personal or impersonal by the assignment question. For example, "Would you want to be married?" is a personal question, but "Discuss the benefits of marriage" indicates that a less personal response would be appropriate.

Even in an impersonal essay, you are giving your opinion and speaking from your experience. You can give personal examples, but make sure that they are appropriate and need to be expressed personally. Sometimes they are general examples that could apply to anyone. For example, if you are arguing that students cannot afford an increase in tuition fees, a personal example would be "I was so poor that I lived on macaroni and cheese. I had a friend who lived on his version of 'tomato soup,' which was boiled water flavoured with ketchup." In an academic essay, you might say, "Students can't even afford food. They are forced to go to food banks or live on macaroni and cheese or boiled water flavoured with ketchup."

Remember that personal writing is not wrong. You need to be able to write both personally and impersonally, but usually you need more practice in the latter. Notice also that it is a matter of degree; you can make something more or less personal. Moreover, it is possible to take impersonal writing too far. Governments and businesses use this style when they want to obscure who actually performed an action.

You will read examples of both personal and impersonal writing in this text, in both sample paragraphs and essays and the readings. Check the sample essays beginning on page 174 for an example of two treatments of the same topic.

> **To make writing less personal and more objective:**
> * use the third person (*he, she, they*);
> * use the passive voice (but judiciously—do not overuse the passive);
> * make general statements that apply to many people.

Exercise 1.1

Rewrite the following personal statements to make them impersonal. You will have to generalize:

Example: Now that my kids have left home and I'm approaching retirement, I'd prefer to move to a bungalow. It would be easier to keep a smaller house, and I wouldn't have to subject my arthritic knees to stair-climbing.

For empty-nesters approaching retirement, a bungalow is a good choice of house. The smaller size makes it easier to keep clean, and the lack of stairs makes it kinder to arthritic knees.

1. I like driving on the highway. I don't have to worry about so many distractions. The traffic is all travelling in the same direction, so I only have to worry about lane-changers and the occasional traffic jam.

2. My friend wants a tattoo, but I think it's a mistake. She'll regret it when she gets older. She may no longer have the same interests, and the tattoo may not look as good later when the ink fades and her skin changes with age.

3. To cut down on my food preparation time, I often cook big batches of food on the weekend and freeze it. My family particularly enjoys the chili, stews, and spaghetti sauce. I find that some soups also freeze well.

4. I like showers better than baths. The running water feels invigorating on my skin. Showers are refreshing and get me ready for my day.

5. I don't think children should have TVs and computers in their bedrooms. In my opinion, they are too distracting. I wouldn't do my homework if I could play electronic games instead. I would just stay in my room and never talk to my parents and siblings.

Exercise 1.2

High school graduates have to make many decisions—which school to go to, which program to study. As college students, they must decide whether to live at their parents' home, on campus, or in accommodations shared with other students. How to travel to school is another decision.

Take one of the decisions you made recently and give three reasons for your choice. Then rewrite the paragraph from an impersonal point of view.

Example: When I went to college, I decided to give up my car and rely on public transit. First, I would have good bus service from my apartment to the campus. Not having to pay for gas, insurance, parking, and maintenance would help my meagre student budget considerably. I could go partying without worrying about driving home.

College students often find it more practical to give up driving their own vehicles. Campuses are generally well served by public transit. The costs of gas, insurance, parking, and maintenance take a huge bite out of a meagre student budget. Students can even enjoy the student lifestyle with less worry about driving home safely.

Using Appropriate Style

Every language has different styles and varieties. In spoken language, dialects and accents vary considerably. For example, in everyday conversation, Australians use a variety of English very different from the one Canadians use. Their accents are different, and the slang expressions can vary significantly from those of Canadians. However, since written English is more standardized than spoken English, essays written by Australians would not differ greatly from those written by Canadians.

Written language has forms different from those of spoken language even though writing is based on spoken language. It is not just a written-down version of speech. Generally, it has a larger range of vocabulary and more complex sentence structure. Yet some forms of writing, such as informal notes and text messaging, are closer to spoken language in form than to most types of writing.

Just as spoken language varies depending on the audience and situation (for example, people speak less formally to friends than to co-workers), written language can be conversational, as in a letter to a friend, or more formal, as in a business report. The term "academic writing" is generally used to refer to the style expected in essays and reports in college and university. While compositions in high school and ESL classes may be informal and personal, you need to graduate to the more formal and impersonal academic style because it is similar to the one used in business and technical writing.

It is also possible to write too formally. However, this is not a common problem among college and undergraduate students. It is more often seen in the writing of professionals and academics who use jargon and complex expressions, often obscuring what they mean. For instance, a business executive may write "at this point in time" instead of using a simpler word such as "now."

North American society has moved toward greater informality. Casual work dress has replaced business suits in many occupations. People rarely use a title and surname, preferring to address business associates by their first name. Written communication has also seen a lessening in formality. For example, newspaper articles are more casual today. You can see this difference by comparing "The strange forces behind the Richard hockey riot" (page 304), which was written 50 years ago, to any of the other articles in this text or articles in current newspapers and magazines. In addition, business letters written decades ago show many outdated formal expressions, such as "I am in receipt of your letter dated the 24th of June."

Here is an example of different styles of language used to describe the same incident:

Conversational English

> Well, the thing is, the guys did a real good job on that project. They busted their butts getting all the info together. And they figured out all the stuff that could come up. Like, let's say, the power went out, they'd have this back-up plan all set to go. And they made this list of people to call, you know, if you had some sorta problem. [67 words]

Academic English

> The team did a commendable job on that project. They all worked diligently to assemble the required information. They planned for contingencies such as power blackouts and prepared an emergency contact list. [32 words]

Notice that conversational language uses more words, but the words are shorter.

The writing style used in this textbook varies. Explanations are written in a semi-formal style to make them more accessible to you, the reader. The use of *you* is necessary because directions are being given. The sample paragraphs and essays are in a slightly more formal style—in the style you might be required to produce in your English class. Many of the readings in the text are in a less formal, journalistic style. You can learn from reading all kinds of styles. Moreover, your instructor should give you direction as to which type of writing style you are expected to use for assignments.

Conversational English	*Academic English*
• regional (different dialects, accents)	• standardized
• mostly spoken but also written to friends (letters, e-mail, chat messages) and in dialogue in novels and short stories	• mostly written but also in formal speeches
• immediate feedback so speaker knows what the listener needs to understand	• writer must anticipate what reader knows and what questions reader will have
• meaning from gestures, tone of voice	• meaning from punctuation, use of space
• use of visuals from situation, scene	• some use of visuals from pictures, graphics
• personal (use of *I* and *you*)	• less personal, more detached and objective
• *you* for people in general	• focus on third person (*he, she, they*)
	• more use of passive voice to depersonalize
• imprecise words (*stuff, thing*)	• precise vocabulary for clarity
• very limited vocabulary (~2,000 words)	• huge vocabulary in use (10,000–20,000 words and more; English has the largest vocabulary—about 500,000 words.)
• Basic English has only 800 words.	
• conversational markers (*let's see, well now, you know*)	• use of transition markers to show relationship of ideas (moreover, however)
• short, simple sentences	• longer, more complicated sentences
• use of slang, colloquialisms	• little idiomatic language
• contractions to show speech forms (*don't, gonna, would've*)	• contractions used rarely
• sentences starting with co-ordinate conjunctions (*and, or, but, yet, so, for, nor*)	• use of conjunctive adverbs (*however, nevertheless, furthermore*)
• conversations can meander, digress; ideas may not be fully explained or completed.	• in long, structured paragraphs; with logical sequence; ideas supported and explained; with introductions and conclusions
• repetition, interruptions	• more development, less repetition
• shorthand among friends, relatives referring to common experiences	• reference to other works of literature, film, history, current events

Understanding the Use of *You*

In modern English, *you* is used for both the person being addressed directly (in writing, this would be the reader) and for people in general:

> You should check your assignment over carefully before you hand it in.

> In that neighbourhood, you can hear the sound of airplanes flying into the airport.

The use of *you* has become common in many forms of writing, such as newspaper and magazine articles, but you should avoid it in your essay writing. Since academic writing is impersonal, you should not address your reader directly. As for the other use of *you* to mean *people*, this usage is conversational style and, again, not suitable for essays. For instance, instead of saying, "You should brush your teeth three times a day," you could say, "It is important to brush teeth three times a day" or "People should brush their teeth three times a day." Sometimes, students run into problems with the *you* form because they switch references:

> When those children grow up, they will be very surprised to see that life is hard, and you have to do things for yourself. If you don't baby your child, they will grow up to be adults who can think for themselves.

These sentences are confusing because the *you* in the first sentence refers to the children, but the *you* in the second sentence refers to the parents. Moreover, the writer switches between *you* and *they* for the same people.

Remember that command sentences, also known as imperatives, are also considered to be *you* sentences. A statement like "Consider the differences between these two types of students" actually has an implied subject *you*, the person doing the action.

In textbooks like this one, *you* is used to address the readers—the students—directly. In journalistic writing, *you* is often used to give a more casual, friendlier tone. Because writing today is generally less formal, *you* is used frequently, and many students find it almost impossible to avoid. It is worth practising, however. While some instructors may accept a conversational tone in your essays, most do not accept the use of *you* in academic writing.

Exercise 1.3

Rewrite the following sentences to eliminate *you*:

Example: You need to see the student advisor to change your timetable.

Possible rewrites: Timetable changes must be approved by the student advisor.

Students should see their advisor to change their timetable.

1. The smallest problem with a luxury car will cost you a lot of money because the parts are harder to find and you have to pay the person for his or her time.

2. In order the pass the test, you must memorize the rules and road signs in the driver's handbook.

3. You can be successful at college if you attend class, pay attention to the instructor, and do your homework.

4. You need to spring-clean and de-clutter. Get rid of clothes you no longer wear.

5. You can see teenagers hanging around the mall with nothing to do.

Understanding the Writing Process

Essentially, there are three stages to the writing process: planning, writing, and editing. These stages can be broken down into smaller steps. For instance, planning includes choosing a topic, brainstorming, and outlining. Several drafts may be written in the second stage. Editing includes making both major revisions and minor corrections.

Writers do not always progress from one stage to the next in an organized fashion. Working on a computer allows writers to go back and forth in their writing, changing their plans and editing as they write, until they are satisfied with the final product. However, students often benefit from following a more orderly process. They may skimp on the planning stage, not thinking enough about what they want to say and how they want to say it. They also tend to give the editing stage short shrift. They look for obvious mistakes they have made but are reluctant to toss out or rework full sentences, especially sentences they have sweated over. Of course, students sometimes do not have the luxury of time for their assignments. When they have to write an essay in class, they have to get words on paper fast.

Planning

Choosing a topic is generally the first step in the planning process. How much choice you have depends on your instructor and the nature of the assignment. Although students sometimes grumble about the choice of topics and say that they want to choose their own topic, students given complete freedom to choose a topic often produce a less satisfactory essay. Instructors generally tailor topics to the needs and interests of their students and relate them to the readings and discussions in the course.

You often have to narrow your topic down from the question asked. Most topics cover a broad range of ideas. For example, a topic might be "Discuss one of the problems that second-generation immigrants face." Or you might be given a choice whether to disagree or agree with a statement.

If you cannot decide among a selection of topics, it might be a good idea to do some brainstorming on two or more of the topics. If you jot down some ideas in point form, you will be able to see which topic you have more to say on. Pick the topic you are most comfortable with and find the easiest.

You can see brainstorming and outlining on specific topics in unit 5.

Writing

As you write your first draft, follow your outline and make any necessary changes. At this point, you do not have to worry about perfection. You can correct spelling and grammatical errors in the editing stage. Essentially, you want to get your ideas down in the proper place. Remember to support your ideas with explanations and examples. Academic writing is all about making points and supporting them. You can see how this is done in units 4, 5, and 6.

Editing

Editing involves making both major changes and minor corrections to your draft. You may want to revise what you have said, changing parts of the essay around and taking out sections. Do not hesitate to delete what does not work in your essay—even if you feel you worked hard to get the sentences written. One difference between professional writers and student writers is that professionals tinker with the wording until they are satisfied with it.

Remember that you have to proofread carefully. It is better if you do this after the essay sits for a day so that you can view it with fresh eyes. This is impossible to do with an in-class writing assignment, but if you do not leave take-home writing assignments until the last minute, you will see what a difference it makes to let your writing rest a bit.

Unit 7 gives you a chance to practise your editing skills.

Good writing
- is clear and concise;
- fits the audience and purpose;
- has something interesting to say;
- has correct grammar, spelling, and punctuation;
- uses a variety of words and sentence structures.

Academic-style English
- is used for school essays and carries over to business and technical reports;
- is impersonal and objective (no *I* or *you*);
- is structured with developed paragraphs;
- has points made and, above all, supported;
- uses precise vocabulary and longer, more complex sentences;
- does not use contractions, slang, or conversational expressions.

Vocabulary Skills

Words and expressions are the building blocks of language. Grammar tells you how the words fit together, but without words there is no meaning. Having a large vocabulary at your command makes you a better reader and writer. You can increase your vocabulary through wide and attentive reading, but an understanding of how words work will also help you. You need to be able to identify the basic parts of speech and differentiate between nouns, verbs, adjectives, and adverbs. When you learn new words, you should learn about their usage—grammatical and stylistic. Words fit into patterns—how they relate to words with similar meanings, words with similar roots, and words that tend to appear together. Moreover, many grammar mistakes in writing are actually vocabulary errors. For example, you might use the wrong preposition with a verb ("gambles in" instead of "gambles on," for instance), but there is no grammar rule that explains this; it is a rule of collocation. In other words, the words just tend to go together in English, and these patterns are learned over time with each vocabulary item.

The English language offers its users the largest vocabulary of any language. English is like a huge stewing pot into which many ingredients have been added. The base is a Germanic language brought to England by the Anglo-Saxon tribes 1,500 years ago. Added to that are Norse words and structures brought by Viking raiders who settled on the west coast of England. The most significant addition was Norman French because it practically doubled the vocabulary of Anglo-Saxon English. The 1066 invasion by William the Conqueror meant that for many years the nobility spoke French while the common people spoke English. The Norman French words gradually blended into the Anglo-Saxon base so that we have many synonyms such as *help*, which has an English base, and *aid* from French. Later on, English, like other European languages, acquired technical and scientific words with roots in Greek and Latin, words like *television*, *microscope*, and *psychology*. This mongrel background of English also makes the spelling system seem chaotic since words from different languages may follow different spelling conventions.

Written language uses a richer vocabulary than spoken language. It is possible to speak basic English and get your meaning across with less than 1,000 words (using phrasal verbs such as *hand out* instead of *distribute*, for example), and most of our everyday, conversational English has a limited vocabulary of around 2,000 words. In contrast, educated people know around 20,000 words. It is estimated that English has more than 500,000 words; some counts reach as high as one million. These are some of the most widely quoted figures, but it is difficult to estimate vocabulary size because we can argue over what counts as a word. For example, the word *jerk* can refer to both the act of pulling and a stupid person, so should it be counted as two different words? Usually, the decision is made by lexicographers who can count the number of entries in their dictionaries. Another difficulty is the number of technical terms and the words from different varieties of English. It is certain that in everyday speech, people only use a small fraction of the words they actually know. The rest of the words mainly appear in written language. As a result, people who read little learn fewer words.

It is important that writers take advantage of this richness of vocabulary. First of all, it is necessary for accuracy. People speaking English can get away with imprecise words like *stuff* and *thingamajig* because they can point to the object in question and determine whether the listener understands. However, writing requires precision of vocabulary to achieve clarity.

In addition, you can keep your readers' interest by varying the words you use. A passage that repeats the same word again and again can become tedious. You can use a thesaurus (a dictionary of synonyms and antonyms) to remind yourself of other words you can use for a concept, but you must keep in mind that synonyms may have similar meanings in one context, but they are not always interchangeable. For example, you can tell someone to either *concentrate* or *focus* on an assignment, but *concentrate* is also used in chemistry to talk about concentrations in solutions and *focus* is used for cameras.

In order to increase the size of your vocabulary, you must understand the basics of how words are used and formed, be able to use reference tools, and find patterns and connections so that you can learn words in groups and not individually. Your brain stores words with connections to other words. Reading a variety of texts will expose you to a wide range of words and their uses.

Recognizing Parts of Speech

Words are labelled according to their class or part of speech, which denotes the function that they have in a sentence. The traditional divisions of parts of speech are nouns, pronouns, verbs, adjectives, adverbs, conjunctions, prepositions, and interjections. Nouns, verbs, adjectives, and adverbs are sometimes called content words, while words like conjunctions and prepositions are function words—they have a grammatical meaning in the sentence but carry little lexical meaning. Increasing your vocabulary means increasing the number of content words you know.

The part of speech label figures prominently in dictionary entries because it is so important. As you work on expanding your vocabulary, you need a sense of the different parts of speech so that you can learn new words in various forms. For example, if you study the word *reciprocate*, which is a verb, you can also learn the corresponding noun (*reciprocity*) and adjective (*reciprocal*).

It is important to be able to distinguish nouns, verbs, adjectives, and adverbs in a sentence:

> He will <u>succeed</u> this time. [verb]

> His <u>success</u> depends on the amount of effort he puts in. [noun]

> He was considered a <u>successful</u> man. [adjective]

> He <u>successfully</u> turned that company around. [adverb]

Sometimes the form of the word is the same, but the function differs:

> I need a <u>light</u>. [noun]

> Could you please <u>light</u> the fire? [verb]

> It's so warm outside that all we need is a <u>light</u> jacket. [adjective]

Understanding parts of speech can help you build your vocabulary and avoid grammar mistakes such as the following:

> He is a violence man. [He is a <u>violent</u> man—adjective, not noun, required]

> He lacks of the skills necessary for the job. [He lacks the skills necessary . . . —the preposition only goes with the noun *lack* (as in "the lack of skills") and not with the verb (as in "he lacks the skills").]

An intensive and extensive knowledge of grammatical terminology is not necessary for writing grammatical English, but you should have a basic sense of the different parts of speech to guide you in sentence construction and in vocabulary building.

Nouns

Nouns and verbs are fundamental to a sentence. Nouns are essentially the names of persons, places, things, animals, and ideas. Examples of nouns are *girl*, *house*, *desk*, *cow*, and *beauty*.

Concrete nouns refer to things you can touch, such as *stone*, *chair*, and *eggs*, while **abstract nouns** name emotions and qualities, such as *love*, *truth*, and *success*.

Proper nouns are specific names and are capitalized (*Tom*, *Vancouver*, *the Bible*, *Saskatchewan*, *Mr Smith*).

Collective nouns refer to a group of people and things but are singular, such as *staff*, *team*, and *herd*.

Compound nouns are two words that are used together as a unit. Different parts of speech can be combined. For example: *girlfriend*, *bookcase*, *boom box*, *lunch break*, *slip-knot*, *mini-bar*. The unit can be two separate words, hyphenated, or one word. It is often difficult to tell how a compound should be written; dictionaries might disagree, more than one form might be acceptable, and the compound may evolve from a two-word combination to a single word. For example, *web page* is gradually becoming *webpage*. Consult a recent Canadian dictionary if you need an authoritative source of information.

Uncountable nouns are not generally pluralized or used with indefinite articles (*a*, *an*). They include liquids (*milk*, *water*), gases (*air*, *helium*), things that are in grains (*sand*, *salt*), and abstract qualities (*beauty*, *truth*). Some tricky uncountable nouns are *advice*, *clothing*, *equipment*, *furniture*, *information*, *mail*, *paper*, *news*, *research*, *software*, *time*, and *work*.

Sometimes a noun can have both an uncountable and countable usage:

> She had a lot of <u>work</u> to do for her assignment. She still had to go to the museum to view the <u>works</u> of arts.

> We don't have much <u>time</u> to do this project. We have to check everything three <u>times</u>.

> I need more <u>paper</u>. I have to write a <u>paper</u> on *Othello*.

Some uncountable nouns have an expression that can be used when you want a countable item. For example, you can ask for "a piece of advice" or eat "a slice (or a loaf) of bread." Luggage cannot be counted, but bags and suitcases can. You cannot count furniture, but you can count individual pieces like chairs and tables. You cannot count paper, but you can count individual pieces or sheets. You cannot say that you have "much works" to do, but you can have many tasks, chores, or jobs.

Pronouns take the place of nouns and refer to them:

> I, me, my, mine, myself
> you, your, yours, yourself
> he, she, it, him, her, his, hers, its, himself, herself, itself
> we, us, our, ours, ourselves
> they, them, their, theirs, themselves

Position

Nouns are crucial to a sentence. They tell what is being talked about. Nouns can be the subject of the sentence, the object of the verb, or the object in a prepositional phrase:

> The **secretary** [subject] hid the **key** [direct object] behind the **mirror** [object in a prepositional phrase].

Nouns appear after determiners (*a, an, the, this, that, these, those, my, your, his, her, its, our, their*):

> the house, a boy, his book, their names, this boat, that restaurant

Adjectives may come in between the determiner and the noun:

> the old house, the red-haired boy, his only book, their former names, this expensive boat

Plural forms

Nouns can be singular (meaning *one*) or plural (*more than one*). For most nouns, an *–s* is added to make the plural form:

> book/books, holiday/holidays, computer/computers, year/years

Nouns that end in *–s, –sh, –ch,* or *–x* have an *–es* plural ending:

> box/boxes, bus/buses, church/churches, kiss/kisses, wish/wishes, watch/watches

Nouns that end in *–y* not preceded by a vowel have an *–ies* plural ending:

> story/stories (but storey/storeys), spy/spies

Nouns that end in –*f* or –*fe* end in –*ves* in the plural:

> knife/knives, half/halves, wife/wives

Some nouns that end in –*o* take an –*es* ending:

> hero/heroes, potato/potatoes (but studio/studios)

Irregular plurals

Words that have the same form for singular and plural:

> deer, fish, moose, sheep, shrimp

Plural forms ending in –*en*:

> child/children, man/men, woman/women, ox/oxen

Words from Latin and Greek that use Latin and Greek plurals (these are gradually being replaced by the –*s* plural of English):

> criterion/criteria
> datum/data (the singular form is rarely used now)
> medium/media
> phenomenon/phenomena
> appendix/appendices
> thesis/theses, analysis/analyses

Plural nouns with no singular form:

> clothes, scissors, pants, trousers

If you are not sure of the plural form of a noun, look it up in the dictionary.

Some common noun suffixes

–ance, –ence	alliance, difference, nuisance, silence
–er, –or	actor, escalator, instructor, inventor, teacher, traveller
–dom	freedom, kingdom, martyrdom, wisdom
–ism	feminism, heroism, plagiarism, realism
–ist	artist, cyclist, finalist, racist, typist
–ity	capability, fatality, inability, mortality, respectability
–ment	document, enjoyment, entertainment, judgment
–ness	goodness, happiness, kindness, prettiness, sadness
–sion, –tion	celebration, fusion, nation, orientation, permission

Exercise 2.1

Identify the nouns in the following list:

song	forest	likelihood
popular	darken	folder
good	shadow	national
Paris	understand	byway
future	wilderness	Tanya
dreamer	take	beauty
careful	die	hardship
upon	naysayer	repetitive

Exercise 2.2

Give the noun form of the following words (e.g., decide – decision). Note that some nouns have the same spelling as the verb or adjective form:

1. competent (adj.)

2. enrich (v.)

3. speak (v.)

4. wealthy (adj.)

5. succeed (v.)

6. real (adj.)

7. invite (v.)

8. willing (adj.)

9. deny (v.)

10. contribute (v.)

Exercise 2.3

Identify the nouns in the following sentences:

1. Canadian coins are struck in the mint in Winnipeg, Manitoba. Queen Elizabeth II's portrait appears on the obverse, the "heads" side of each coin.

2. The one-cent coin, commonly called a "penny," is a copper coin. It shows the main symbol of Canada—the maple leaf. The maple tree grows in most of Canada, but the sugar maple, from which maple syrup is made, is not found west of Manitoba.

3. The nickel, the five-cent piece, has a beaver on its reverse. The beaver is an important symbol of Canada because early European explorers and fur traders came in search of beaver pelts, which were in demand to make men's hats in Europe.

Exercise 2.3 – *continued*

4. The picture on the 10-cent piece, the dime, is the fishing schooner *Bluenose*, a ship from Lunenburg, Nova Scotia, which was famous for never having lost a race. Although it later sank in the Caribbean, the government of Nova Scotia runs the *Bluenose II*, a replica, which serves as a tourist attraction.

5. The reverse of the quarter, the 25-cent coin, shows a caribou, an animal that lives in Canada's north. The caribou is an ungulate (hoofed mammal) similar to moose, elk, and deer.

6. Canada introduced a one-dollar coin in 1987 because coins last longer than bills and because costs for vending machines, parking meters, and bus fares had increased so that it was no longer practical to use smaller denomination coins. The coin depicts a loon, a Canadian water bird known for its haunting cry, and thus the coin acquired the nickname "loonie."

7. The two-dollar coin was first struck in 1996, and the two-dollar bill was phased out. It is now commonly called a "toonie" (from "two" and "loonie"). It is Canada's first bi-metallic coin, with an outer ring of nickel and an inner ring of aluminum bronze. It bears the image of a polar bear.

8. The blue five-dollar bill shows Sir Wilfrid Laurier, Canada's first French-Canadian prime minister. The reverse depicts children at play—children playing hockey on an outdoor rink, a child tobogganing, and a child learning to skate. The quote is from the famous Canadian story "The hockey sweater" by Roch Carrier: "The winters of my childhood were long, long seasons. We lived in three places—the school, the church, and the skating rink, but our real life was on the skating rink."

9. A portrait of Sir John A. Macdonald appears on the purple 10-dollar bill. He was Canada's first prime minister, starting with Confederation in 1867. The theme is remembrance and peacekeeping. The back shows a Remembrance Day ceremony at a war memorial, a peacekeeper, poppies (flowers symbolic of Remembrance Day, 11 November), and an excerpt from the poem "In Flanders fields" by John McCrae.

10. The green 20-dollar bill is probably the most common bill in circulation. It has a portrait of Queen Elizabeth II on the front. The back has the theme arts and culture and shows Haida sculpture by Bill Reid. The quote is from the novel *The hidden mountain* by French-Canadian writer Gabrielle Roy: "Could we ever know each other in the slightest without the arts?"

Verbs

Verbs are words that describe actions (*jump, swim, wave*) or states (*be, seem, signify*). Like nouns, they are crucial to a sentence. Verb tenses are discussed in unit 3 as part of sentence structure.

Verb forms

English verb structures are less complicated and have fewer forms than those of most other European languages. English verbs have only three regular verb endings: *−s, −ing, −ed*. The base form of the verb is the infinitive without *to* (e.g., *make, seem, wear*), and it is used to make the simple present tense.

To make the different forms of the verb, you need to know three main parts:

Base	Past tense	Past participle
walk	walked	walked
study	studied	studied
run	ran	run
swim	swam	swum

While regular verbs use the *−ed* ending for the past forms, irregular verbs vary. Check your dictionary for the past tense and past participle of irregular verbs.

Auxiliary verbs

The verb in a sentence may be more than one word. For example, the auxiliary (helping) verbs *be* and *have* form part of the verb in the perfect and continuous tenses. Modal verbs (e.g., *could, should, may, would*) can also be part of the verb:

> The group is travelling to the exhibition by bus.

> I have been to Paris many times.

> She could have gotten more work done.

The verbs *be, do, have,* and *will* can be verbs on their own or can function as auxiliary verbs:

> Even though he is late, he is going to the competition.

> I do enough work around here. I do not wish to take on more.

> She has no money. She hasn't received her student loan yet.

Active and passive

The auxiliary verb *be* is used with the past participle to make the passive voice:

> The ball <u>was hit</u> hard to left field, but it <u>was caught</u>.

In the active voice, the subject of the sentence is the one doing the action, while in the passive voice the subject of the sentence is the receiver of the action:

> I <u>signed</u> the receipt, but she <u>did not give</u> me a copy. [active]

> The receipt <u>was signed</u> but I <u>was not given</u> a copy. [passive]

Phrasal verbs

Some verbs are completed by one or two adverbial particles, commonly known as prepositions:

> She <u>slept in</u> and missed class, so then she <u>fell behind</u> and had trouble <u>catching up</u>.

> I <u>got up</u> at noon, but I was still tired.

Verbals

Words that are based on verbs but do not function as main verbs are called verbals. These include participles, infinitives, and gerunds.

Verb forms that act as adjectives are called **participles**. **Active participles** end in *–ing* and show that the person is doing something, while **passive participles** end in *–ed* and show that something is being done to someone:

> The man <u>balancing</u> the bottles is a lawyer by trade, not a juggler.

> The <u>elected</u> officials were sworn in on Tuesday.

An **infinitive** is the simple, base form of the verb, with or without *to*:

> He seemed <u>to shrink</u> before my eyes.

> I need another computer program <u>to do</u> the editing.

> She wanted <u>to reorganize</u> the whole department.

Gerunds end in *–ing* and act as nouns:

> <u>Waiting around</u> is more difficult than doing something.

<u>Dancing</u> is great exercise.

I recommend <u>taking</u> the bus instead.

One of the trickier aspects of English is figuring out whether a verb takes the infinitive or the gerund to complete the idea. Note these examples:

I <u>intend to leave</u> next Thursday. I <u>suggest taking</u> the train.

I <u>enjoy playing</u> the piano. I <u>want to take</u> more lessons.

Sometimes a verb takes both forms, but a different meaning is expressed:

He stopped <u>talking</u> and listened to the odd noise.

He ran into some old friends downtown, so he stopped <u>to talk</u>.

There is no definitive grammar rule that explains why some verbs require the gerund and some the infinitive. It is more idiomatic usage than grammar, but sometimes hypothetical, unfulfilled ideas tend to be expressed with the infinitive, while real happenings tend to be found with the gerund:

I <u>hope to complete</u> a marathon this year. (hypothetical, a wish)

I <u>enjoyed running</u> the marathon. (actually happened)

This problem of infinitive versus gerund causes particular difficulty for ESL students. Lists of the different verbs for these structures are given in unit 7. As you develop your vocabulary, note which forms are required with each verb—whether a verb takes a direct object (this type of verb is called *transitive*), whether a certain preposition follows the verb (as in *rely <u>on</u>*), as well as whether it takes the gerund or the infinitive. These aspects of language should be considered part of vocabulary since there are few grammar rules to guide such usage.

Affixes that make verbs

be– bejewel, belittle, bewitch
en– enable, endanger, enjoy, enlarge, envision
–en blacken, lighten, soften, toughen
–ate activate, discriminate, motivate
–fy identify, notify, signify, solidify, unify, verify
–ize idealize, maximize, realize, recognize, sympathize

Exercise 2.4

Identify the verbs and verbals in these sentences:

1. When we go to the cottage in the winter, we have to leave the car at the main road and ski or snowshoe in, carrying everything in backpacks.

2. When we were children, my father made a skating rink in the backyard every winter. He flooded the yard with water and carefully groomed the ice. We skated every day and had neighbourhood pick-up hockey games.

3. Mike broke his arm in the hockey game when the defenceman bodychecked him. He crashed into the boards at an awkward angle.

4. Dean got tired of his children spending beautiful summer days glued to the TV and video games. He started building a tree house in the backyard and soon had his children sawing and hammering alongside him.

5. After several tries, David finally managed to get up on the waterskis. He held on while he was pulled around the island. He completed a circuit before he let go of the tow-rope.

6. I love the bike paths in my neighbourhood. I go biking almost every day in the summer, and I don't worry about the traffic.

7. The boarders are enjoying the special park area the city set up, so they petitioned for more dedicated skateboarding areas.

8. On our canoe trip, we portaged several times, but the portages were not long and we didn't have much to carry.

9. The figure skater fell on her double Axel and never quite recovered. She finished her routine disappointed in her performance.

10. They swam across the lake while he rowed next to them to make sure boaters did not come too close.

Exercise 2.5

Give the verb form of the following words (e.g., sign – signify):

1. description (n.)
2. evasive (adj.)
3. inspirational (adj.)
4. facilitator (n.)
5. white (adj.)
6. threat (n.)
7. authority (n.)
8. defiant (adj.)
9. pursuit (n.)
10. expansion (n.)

Adjectives

Essentially, adjectives describe nouns. They usually appear before the noun in English, as in these examples:

> brown dress, tall man, close escape, unparalleled beauty, questionable actions

They also appear after the verb *to be* and other verbs that describe the state of something:

> The hat is red. The air feels stuffy. The noise was deafening.

Several adjectives can be used together. A comma is used between them if they are describing a similar attribute (in other words, if an *and* sounds right):

> the big brown hen

> the typical French-Canadian house

> an itsy-bitsy, teeny-weeny, yellow polka-dot bikini

Sometimes nouns work as adjectives, as do verbals like active (*–ing* verbals) or passive (*–ed* verbals) participles:

> library book, welcoming committee, elected officials

Phrases can be used as a unit to describe a noun; they are usually hyphenated:

> His stick-in-the-mud attitude annoys me.

> It's a ten-year-old car, so it often requires repairs.

Note that these adjective phrases are used in the singular:

> I wouldn't touch him with a <u>ten-foot pole</u>. [not "ten-feet"]

Determiners, which include qualifiers and articles, are a subclass of adjectives that are considered function words:

> a, an, the, this, that, these, those

Comparative and superlative forms

Different forms of the adjective are used to make comparisons. For comparing one thing to another, the comparative form is used. It is formed by adding an *–er* ending to words of one or two syllables. For longer words, *more* appears before the adjective:

> She is <u>taller</u> than I am, but I have <u>longer</u> legs because I have a <u>shorter</u> torso.

> That is the <u>more expensive</u> of the two options.

The superlative form is used when the comparison is between one thing and two or more. It is formed with the *–est* ending or the addition of *most* before the adjective:

> He was the <u>brightest</u> child in the class.

> Of the three options, that is the <u>most cost-effective</u>.

> That is the <u>most ridiculous</u> idea I have ever heard.

Less and *least* are used as the opposite of *more* and *most*:

> She is <u>less experienced</u> than I am.

> They were <u>the least prepared</u> team in the competition.

Adjective suffixes

–able, –ible	able to, suitable for	acceptable, capable, flexible
–en	made of	golden, wooden
–ful	full of	awful, beautiful, grateful, powerful
–ic, –ical	relating to	classical, comic, musical, public
–ive	tending to	descriptive, pensive, sensitive
–less	without	careless, worthless
–ous, –ose	quality, state	grandiose, mountainous, poisonous, verbose
–worthy	worthy of	seaworthy, trustworthy
–y	having, being like	funny, sunny, hairy

Exercise 2.6

Give the adjective form of the following words (e.g., wonder –
wonderful). There may be more than one form, and the adjective may
have the same form as the word given:

1. mist (n.)
2. comedy (n.)
3. operate (v.)
4. force (n.)
5. experiment (v.)

6. accept (v.)
7. stress (n.)
8. disaster (n.)
9. science (n.)
10. publicity (n.)

Exercise 2.7

Match the adjectives in the list to a noun below:

brute, extensive, frantic, heartfelt, jagged, limited, masked, secret,
tempting, tough

1. _____ ballot
2. _____ force
3. _____ haste
4. _____ hole
5. _____ intruder

6. _____ offer
7. _____ opponent
8. _____ sympathy
9. _____ visibility
10 _____ vocabulary

Exercise 2.8

Fill in the blanks with suitable adjectives:

1. The _____ house was _____ and _____.
2. Several _____ children played around the _____ park.
3. The _____ robots completed the _____ work.
4. A _____ hat lay on the _____, _____ ground.
5. A _____ _____ toy was the last item at the
   _____ auction.

Adverbs

Adverbs explain how, when, or where something is done:

He closed the door <u>quickly</u>.

<u>Yesterday</u> we met in the boardroom.

We like to eat lunch <u>nearby</u>.

Some adverbs are formed from adjectives, with the addition of the suffix *−ly*:

carefully, quickly, realistically, slowly

Adjectives that end in *−ly* (such as *friendly*, *lonely*, *miserly*) do not have an adverb form:

The dog was friendly. The dog wagged his tail in a friendly way.

Adverbs that are not formed from an adjective are mostly function words and include many different kinds of adverbs:

time: now, then, yesterday, never

place: there, here, nearby

Some adverbs are intensifiers:

very, quite, highly, rarely

Exercise 2.9

Give the adverb form of the following words (e.g., careful − carefully):

1. simple (adj.)
2. real (adj.)
3. true (adj.)
4. signify (v.)
5. uneasy (adj.)

6. brutality (n.)
7. haze (n.)
8. absurd (adj.)
9. frequent (n.)
10. evidence (n.)

Exercise 2.10

Add adjectives and adverbs to the following sentences:

1. The man walked down the block.
2. The deer ran away.
3. The mother took her children to the park.
4. The car sped down the street.
5. The machine emitted smoke.

Reviewing parts of speech

Exercise 2.11

Decide which type of word goes in each blank—a noun, verb, adjective, or adverb. After you have labelled each blank, fill in appropriate words to fit the sentence:

1. A _____ book lay on the _____, next to the black _____.
2. The student _____ his homework. He went back to his _____ to get it.
3. The _____ couple _____ around the park watching the _____ at play.
4. Jack _____ placed the _____ top back on the _____.
5. The _____ music _____ the people pay attention.

Exercise 2.12

Fill in the blanks in the following chart, where possible:

Noun	Verb	Adjective	Adverb
		advisory	
agreement			
	anger		
			beautifully
		developmental	
	encourage		
excess			
		high	
			legally
	perform		
			pitifully
	risk		
		soft	
vision			
		wise	

Exercise 2.12 – *continued*

Use words from the chart to fill in the blanks in the following sentences:

1. He received a medal because of his _____ actions in the battle.

2. She gave him good _____; it was a shame he didn't follow it.

3. His foolish actions _____ his team.

4. She _____ a society where women would make most of the decisions.

5. Their _____ attempts at fixing the problem caused disaster.

6. They sorted out all the _____ matters and felt that they could go through with the transaction.

7. An _____ amount of water spilled out of the tank, making for a _____ situation.

8. Her voice was _____, but her words were _____.

9. They _____ that the operation was too _____ to be _____ by the rookies.

10. The unbelievable achievement of the team was praised _____.

Using Dictionaries

A dictionary is the most useful reference tool you can own. Whether you have a portable electronic version or a paperback book, consult your dictionary often to help expand your vocabulary. Get to know your dictionary. Read the introduction and familiarize yourself with the abbreviations and pronunciation key used.

A typical dictionary entry gives the pronunciation, part of speech label, and derivative forms, as well as the definition. It may also give the etymology—the origin and history of the word. For example, here is the entry for *heritage* in *The Canadian Oxford dictionary*:

> **herit·age** /ˈherɪtɪdʒ/ *noun* **1a** things such as works of art, cultural achievements and folklore that have been passed on from earlier generations. **b** a nation's buildings,

monuments, countryside, etc., esp. when regarded as worthy of preservation. **c** (*attrib.*) esp. *Cdn.* designating a building, site, river, etc. significant for its historic, architectural, or environmental value and which is protected from alteration, development, etc. by the government. **2** that which is or may be inherited. **3** inherited circumstances, benefits, etc. (*a heritage of violence*). **4** *Bible* **a** the ancient Israelites. **b** the Church. [Middle English from Old French (as HERITABLE)]

It is a good idea to have more than one dictionary. A smaller, more portable paperback is handy to carry around, while a hardcover dictionary usually covers more words. A thesaurus (dictionary of synonyms and antonyms) is a useful tool for writing assignments. Idiom dictionaries are often particularly interesting to ESL students who find the range of English expressions bewildering. Etymological dictionaries give word histories for those who like to study words and expressions.

The best way to choose a dictionary in a bookstore is to "test drive" a few. Look up the same words in several dictionaries and compare the entries. Look up common words that may have many definitions (such as *set* and *like*) and more academic words (*enumerate, repatriate*). Check for the clarity of the definition and how much information is given. Make sure the pronunciation guide is easy to use. Look for a clear, legible typeface and a format that is easy to handle. Check the date of the dictionary to make sure it is a recent edition, not just a reprint. Check for current slang (words like *bling, geek*, and *diss*) to see if the dictionary is up-to-date.

An obvious question is how to find a word in a dictionary if you do not know how to spell it. One technique is to concentrate on the beginning of the word. Even electronic dictionaries that guess at your word work much better if the first few letters are correct. Get to know possible letter combinations for sounds. For instance an *s* sound could be spelled with an *s*, a *c*, or a *ps*. Use a smaller dictionary if you want a relatively common word because you will have fewer entries to search.

Dictionaries can help speed up the vocabulary learning process. You can learn new words without consulting a dictionary, but you need to read it or hear it many times to learn the meaning from the context. A dictionary tells you the range of meanings and the different forms. Dictionaries can also be fun to browse through. Serendipity can play a part in your learning as you find new and interesting words.

Electronic dictionaries

Electronic dictionaries come in several different forms. Some print dictionaries include a CD-ROM version that you can load onto your computer. ESL students frequently use hand-held electronic translation dictionaries.

In addition, you can find several dictionaries on the Internet, ranging from electronic versions of established print dictionaries to democratic free-form dictionaries that let users contribute to and vote for definitions, such as UrbanDictionary.com. These electronic formats have improved to the extent that they can offer much information as well as example sentences. Electronic dictionaries allow you to hear the pronunciation of words, often in both American and British English. Computer graphics and animation also enliven the definitions.

Despite the advantages of electronic formats, you should still practise using a book form dictionary. For one thing, schools that do allow students to use dictionaries for writing tests usually limit them to printed forms. After all, hand-held devices can be more than dictionaries: they can hold text in memory and serve as a communication device. Because educators want to control the possibility of cheating on tests, they often do not allow electronic dictionaries.

Electronic dictionaries' ease of use can also be a disadvantage. ESL students rely on them in class and may become too dependent, looking up every unfamiliar word. As a result, they do not learn to guess meaning from context. Sometimes they are so busy punching words into their dictionary that they miss what the instructor is saying.

Here is the entry for *heritage* from an Oxford on-line dictionary, *AskOxford*:

> **heritage**
> · **noun 1** property that is or may be inherited; an inheritance.
> **2** valued things such as historic buildings that have been passed down from previous generations. **3** before another noun relating to things of historic or cultural value that are worthy of preservation.
> — ORIGIN Old French, from *hériter* "inherit."

From AskOxford.com, www. askoxford.com. By permission of Oxford University Press, Inc.

Bilingual dictionaries

ESL students generally use bilingual dictionaries that translate to and from their native language and English. Beginning students find these invaluable, but advanced students should also use all-English dictionaries so that they are not constantly translating from their native language. Moreover, a bilingual dictionary may just give lists of words with little explanation as to how the words are used and how they differ in meaning. Here is the entry for *heritage* in *The Oxford–Hachette French dictionary*:

> **heritage** /ˈherɪtɪdʒ / *n* **1** †sout (inheritance) héritage *m*;
> **2** (cultural) patrimoine *m*

ESL dictionaries

ESL dictionaries, often called "learner's dictionaries," are useful tools for anyone trying to learn more about the language. These reference books give more information about usage, often providing example sentences. For instance, entries may show whether a noun is uncountable and what preposition generally follows a specific verb. The definitions are written in simpler English; ESL students using regular English dictionaries often find that they do not understand all the words in the definition and thus are forced into an endless circle of looking up words in the definitions. ESL dictionaries often have fewer entries than a regular English dictionary, so some of the less common words will not be covered, but the entries are more informative.

The *Oxford advanced learner's dictionary* defines *heritage* as:

> **heri·tage** /ˈherɪtɪdʒ/ *noun* [usually sing.] the history, traditions and qualities that a country or society has had for many years and that are considered an important part of its character: *Spain's rich cultural heritage* ◊ *The building is part of our national heritage.*

Reproduced by permission of Oxford University Press. From *Oxford Advanced Learner's Dictionary 7th edition* © Oxford University Press 2005.

Thesauruses

Thesauruses (or *thesauri*) are dictionaries of synonyms and antonyms. Some have word lists according to category, while others are in dictionary format, giving lists of synonyms and antonyms instead of definitions. Here is the entry for *heritage* from *The Oxford Canadian thesaurus*:

> **heritage** ▶ noun **1** *they stole his heritage* INHERITANCE, birthright, patrimony; legacy, bequest. **2** *Canada's cultural heritage* TRADITION, history, past, background, culture, customs. **3** *his Greek heritage* ANCESTRY, lineage, descent, extraction, parentage, roots, background, heredity.

From *Oxford Canadian thesaurus*, edited by Robert Pontisso. Copyright © 2004 Oxford University Press Canada. Reprinted by permission of the publisher.

Thesauruses have to be used carefully. Some students try to pump up their writing by slotting in synonyms from a thesaurus, but even though words may have some similar meanings in common, their usage can be quite different. Students should use a thesaurus to remind them of the words they are familiar with but cannot quite call to mind when composing.

Collocation dictionaries

Collocation dictionaries are not as well-known, but they are useful in showing how words are used and with which words they are used. Entries for a noun typically show which adjectives and verbs are usually found with that noun. Entries for a verb include a list of adverbs and prepositions that accompany it.

For example, here is the entry for *heritage* in the *Oxford collocations dictionary for students of English*:

> **heritage** *noun*
>   • ADJ. rich | **natural** | **common, national** *Folk songs are part of our common heritage.*| **architectural, artistic, cultural, historical, literary**
>   • VERB + HERITAGE **have** *The city has an exceptionally rich heritage of historic buildings.* | **preserve, protect** *protecting our heritage of wild plants*
>   • HERITAGE + NOUN **centre, museum, site**

Reproduced by permission of Oxford University Press © Oxford University Press 2002.

Activity 2.1

In groups, compare the dictionary entries for *heritage* given in the preceding sections. Compare the information given and how it is presented. Decide which entries are most useful to you. Look up the same word in your own dictionaries. If you have a variety of dictionaries in the class, look up some other words to compare the different dictionaries.

Dictionary challenges
Dictionary Look-up: Have your teacher say a word aloud. Try to figure out the spelling and then look the word up in the dictionary. Students can race to be the first to find the entry.

Stump the Teacher: Choose words from the dictionary that you think your teacher does not know and see how many he or she can define.

Dictionary activity
1.   Look through the introduction to your dictionary. Locate the pronunciation key and the list of abbreviations used. What usage labels does the dictionary use? What is a headword? How does the dictionary treat alternate spellings? What is a derivative?
2.   Use your dictionary to find out the pronunciation of these words. Write down the pronunciation code and check the key to see what the symbols mean:

> albeit
> asphalt
> ceilidh
> chalet
> detritus

draught
hyperbole
phlegm
poignant
viscous
ascertain

3. Write down the definition of these words:

    colloquialism
    Generation X
    rubric
    blinkered
    sequester
    precipice
    fatigues

4. Use your dictionary to find the difference between these pairs or groups of words:

    affect/effect
    cite/sight/site
    complement/compliment
    principal/principle
    stationary/stationery

5. See how your dictionary handles words that are numbers. Find these terms in your dictionary and write down the definitions:

    24/7
    4 x 4
    911

6. Find the simple past tense and the past participle of these verbs:

    forbid
    kneel
    sneak
    swing
    undergo

7. Find out if these nouns are countable or uncountable:

    reprimand
    advice
    architecture
    argument
    cold turkey

8. Find the plural forms for these words:

> storey
> moose
> scarf
> series
> appendix

9. Look up these abbreviations and acronyms. Write down the long form:

> DIY
> A/C
> CEO
> B and B
> RSVP

10. Find the following idioms in the dictionary and write down their meanings:

> in the altogether
> with no strings attached
> let the cat out of the bag
> put your best foot forward
> draw a blank

Mastering Spelling

English spelling is not only difficult, it can be downright maddening because it is not consistent with the pronunciation of words. For instance, the *—ough* combination can have many different pronunciations, as seen in the words *cough*, *through*, and *although*. This does not mean you should just give up. English spelling does have patterns that can be learned, and there are tools to help you. Some words you will just have to memorize.

Because English has absorbed so many words from different languages, it has also acquired spelling features of the words. Moreover, the Latin alphabet it uses is ill-suited to the sounds of a Germanic language like English. Some scientific and technical terms are based on Greek words, which has another alphabet. To make things more complicated, pronunciation has altered over the years, while spelling has not changed as much. For example, the "silent" *k* in words like *knight* used to be pronounced.

English spelling is an obvious target for reformers. They argue that it is chaotic and unnecessarily difficult to learn. Counter-arguments include the fact that a phonetically based spelling system (one based on sounds) would hide some semantic relationships (those based on meaning). For example, the words *sign* and *signify* are related (both come from the Latin *signus* for *sign*), but their kinship would not be as evident if *sign* were spelled *sine*.

Whether you are for or against English spelling reform, the fact remains that your responsibility as a writer is to spell the words as they are currently accepted. In the world outside the classroom, spelling is also important. A misspelled document reflects badly on its author. Some people are poor spellers, and they have to work at it much harder than other people. Even avid readers can be bad at spelling.

Tips for improving your spelling:

- Learn basic spelling rules and patterns (some are given below).
- Recognize common letter combinations (e.g., –ought).
- Learn standard prefixes and suffixes.
- Learn common Greek and Latin root words.
- Use mnemonic devices to help you remember spelling (e.g., "The principal is your pal.").
- Use a dictionary. (If you have trouble locating the word, concentrate on getting the first few letters right. Try possible alternate spelling combinations. For example, if the word starts with an s sound, try looking under s, c, and ps.)
- Use a computer spell checker, but do not rely on it to catch all your errors.
- Proofread your work carefully, looking especially for words you have trouble with.
- Make a list of words you often misspell and practise them by writing them out several times.
- Go over any spelling mistakes when you get writing assignments back.
- Have someone give you a spelling quiz to see if you have learned the words on your list.

The silent e

Many words end in a silent —e, which generally serves as a sign to show how the previous vowel is pronounced. This pronunciation is sometimes called the "long" vowel, pronounced the same as the vowel's name. Compare these examples:

> mat/mate
> bid/bide
> bit/bite
> bad/bade
> hop/hope
> rip/ripe

This silent *e* is dropped when endings with a vowel are added to the base word but kept if the ending begins with a consonant. In contrast, words that end in a single consonant coming after a single vowel have that consonant doubled if the final syllable is stressed. This helps distinguish between such words as *dining* (eating) and *dinning* (loud noise). Note that verbs that end in *–e* may go to a double letter form in the past participle if the pronunciation changes, such as in *bite/bitten* and *write/written*.

Base word	+s	+ed	+ing	with affixes
hope	hopes	hoped	hoping	hopeful
hop	hops	hopped	hopping	hopper
file	files	filed	filing	
fill	fills	filled	filling	filler

Exercise 2.13

Add the ending to the following base words:

1. smile + ing
2. tile + ed
3. require + ment
4. fade + s
5. wade + ing
6. complete + ed
7. comprise + ing
8. shade + s
9. settle + ed
10. erode + ing

Doubling consonants

If a word ends in a single vowel and single consonant and this last syllable is stressed, the final consonant is doubled before the endings:

fit + ed = fitted
begin + ing = beginning
develop + ment = development [last syllable not stressed]

Sometimes the American spelling of a word has a single consonant whereas Canadian spelling has a double consonant, as in *traveled* versus *travelled*.

Exercise 2.14

Add the ending to the following base words:

1. wed + ing
2. wait + ed
3. dream + less
4. dip + ed
5. control + ed
6. chug + ing
7. occur + ence
8. keep + ing
9. grunt + ed
10. drip + ing

Words with –y

The *–y* ending often creates problems for spelling. Look at the word forms below. How are they grouped? Which words give you trouble? Think of ways to help you remember the spelling.

> study, studies, studying, studied
> muddy, muddies, muddying, muddied
> ready, readies, readying, readied
>
> die, dies, dying, died
> dye, dyes, dyeing, dyed
> notify, notifies, notifying, notified
> try, tries, trying, tried
>
> lay, lays, laying, laid
> play, plays, playing, played
> portray, portrays, portraying, portrayed
> stay, stays, staying, stayed
> day, daily
>
> enjoy, enjoys, enjoying, enjoyed
> boy, boys

Words with *ei* or *ie*

In elementary school we learned the rule "Write *i* before *e* except after *c* or when sounded as *a*, as in *neighbour* and *weigh*." This rule helps, but it does not cover all the cases. If the sound is a short *e* or a long *i*, the *ei* is often the correct spelling (as in *their* or *height*). The *ie* spelling is generally more common than *ei*. Exceptions include *caffeine* and *protein*.

Activity 2.2

Decide which words in the list follow the rules above. Can you think of ways to help you remember the words that do not?

beige	caffeine	chief
believe	ceiling	conceive
counterfeit	piece	shield
either	receive	veil
freight	reign	weight
friend	retrieve	weird
heir	seize	yield
leisure	sheik	

Greek letters

Some of the trickiest words to spell come from Greek, which uses a different alphabet, some letters of which are familiar from their use in mathematics (such as *pi* π). While some Greek letters have an obvious one-to-one correspondence with the Roman alphabet used for English (such as *alpha* α and *a*), other Greek letters are represented by two-letter combinations in English. For instance, the *ps* combination found in words like *psychology* is from the Greek letter *psi* ψ. The letter combination *ph* sounds like an *f* in English words, but its use shows us the word is from Greek, from the letter *phi* φ.

Etymology (the historical sources of a word) can help you figure out the pronunciation of *ch* in English. Greek words (which are often scientific or technical words) have the *ch* pronounced like a *k* sound because it comes from the Greek letter *chi* χ. This explains the common short form *Xmas* for *Christmas* because the letter *chi* looks like an *x*. If the word is a common, simple one and does not have typical Greek spelling combinations, it is probably a true English word in which the *ch* is pronounced as in *church* and *chicken*. French words (like *chef* and *champagne*) have the *ch* pronounced like *sh*, but these are less common.

If you know you are dealing with a scientific or technical term, expect that it might have the Greek spelling patterns. Here are some examples of words from Greek:

> chronology, chaos, psychology
> philosophy, photography, phonetics
> psychiatrist, psyche, psychic

Words often confused

Many spelling mistakes occur because different words sound alike. Here are some common ones that cause spelling problems:

> accept: receive
> except: not
>
> > She couldn't <u>accept</u> the fact that we wanted all the T-shirts <u>except</u> for that one.
>
> advice: noun form
> advise: verb form
>
> > I <u>advise</u> you not to take his <u>advice</u>.
>
> affect: verb
> effect: usually a noun
>
> > He studied the <u>effects</u> of pollution on the wetlands and found that global warming <u>affects</u> the ecology.

are: form of verb *to be*
our: belonging to us
hour: 60 minutes

> We are late. Our class started an hour ago.

brake: what stops a vehicle
break: stoppage

> I need a break. This assignment is very difficult.

> He hit the brakes as he was going around the curve.

choose: verb
choice: noun
chose: past tense of verb

> He didn't want to choose, but he finally chose the blue one. He was happy with his choice.

cite: to reference
sight: ability to see, something you see
site: a place

> The students had to cite the websites they used for their project in their bibliography.

> She lost her sight in an accident when she was four years old.

complement: verb, to go well with something
compliment: something positive said about someone or something

> She gave me a nice compliment, saying that my dress complements my skin tone.

desert: arid land with little vegetation
dessert: something sweet at the end of a meal

> Camels are the best transportation in the desert.

> Anything with chocolate is a good choice for dessert.

does: part of the verb *to do*
dose: how much medication you get

> Does he know the correct dose of those painkillers?

hear: to listen
here: not there

> Did you <u>hear</u> that funny noise over <u>here</u>?

hole: empty space
whole: entire, all of something

> You need to fill in the <u>whole</u> <u>hole</u> with plaster.

incidence: the rate of something
incident: a happening

> The <u>incidence</u> of related <u>incidents</u> is rising.

it's: it is, it has
its: possessive, belonging to it

> <u>It's</u> funny when the dog chases <u>its</u> tail.

knew: past tense of *to know*
new: not old

> I asked her if she <u>knew</u> any <u>new</u> jokes.

know: have information about something
no: not yes
now: at this time

> <u>No</u>, I don't <u>know</u> if we can go <u>now</u>.

later: not now
latter: the second of two, not the former

> Of those choices, the <u>latter</u> is better.

> I'll see you <u>later</u>.

loose: not tight
lose: to be unable to find something

> That bathing suit is so <u>loose</u> that you are going to <u>lose</u> it in the water.

passed: to have gone by, to have succeeded in a test
past: previous time

> I <u>passed</u> my driving test and my lifeguard certificate in the <u>past</u> two weeks.

patience: being able to wait for something
patients: whom a doctor tends to

> The <u>patients</u> in the hospital must have a lot of <u>patience</u> now that it is so understaffed.

peace: calm, not war
piece: a part of something

> They prayed for world <u>peace</u>.

> Could you give me a <u>piece</u> of paper?

personal: belonging to a person
personnel: human resources

> She hired her <u>personal</u> secretary through the <u>personnel</u> department.

plain: simple, not fancy
plane: airplane, also to smooth a surface

> I'd rather have my cake <u>plain</u>.

> It's so much better to travel by <u>plane</u>.

principal: most important, person in charge of a school
principle: a basic rule

> The <u>principal</u> of the high school said it was a matter of <u>principle</u>.

presence: being somewhere
presents: gifts

> Her <u>presence</u> was required at the party for the opening of the <u>presents</u>.

quiet: little or no noise
quite: rather

Although it was <u>quiet</u> in the house, it was <u>quite</u> hot.

right: correct, not wrong
rite: ceremony
write: to put words on paper

That's <u>right</u>. Joanne can <u>write</u> a description of the religious <u>rite</u> for her assignment.

scene: a part of a play or movie, a place where something is happening
seen: past participle of *to see*

I haven't yet <u>seen</u> that <u>scene</u> of the play in rehearsal.

stationary: in one spot
stationery: writing supplies

I exercise on a <u>stationary</u> bicycle.

We ran out of letterhead paper, so I had to call the <u>stationery</u> store.

than: comparative
then: adverb of time

<u>Then</u> I learned that he was faster <u>than</u> I am.

their: belonging to them
there: adverb, like *here*
they're: they are

<u>They're</u> waiting for <u>their</u> luggage to arrive over <u>there</u> in the lounge area.

though: although
thought: past tense of think and noun form

<u>Though</u> Kim <u>thought</u> she could make it, she missed the beginning.

to: preposition
too: also, and used with other words such as *much* and *few* to show excess
two: the number after *one*

> I'd like <u>two</u> cards <u>too</u>, please.

> I gave the report <u>to</u> the manager.

> The company showed <u>too</u> little growth to satisfy the stockholders.

threw: past tense of *to throw*
through: preposition

> He <u>threw</u> the ball <u>through</u> the window.

weak: feeble, not strong
week: seven days

> By the end of the <u>week</u>, he was feeling very <u>weak</u> and sick.

wear: put on clothes
were: past tense of *to be*
where: in which place
we're: we are

> <u>Where</u> are you going? You <u>were</u> just out.

> <u>We're</u> going to the mall because we have nothing to <u>wear</u> for the dance.

weather: climate
whether: if

> <u>Whether</u> we go on the hike or not will depend on the <u>weather</u>.

which: question word
witch: a woman who is believed to have magical powers

> There were several women dressed as <u>witches</u> at the Halloween dance. <u>Which</u> one was Joan?

who's: who is, who has
whose: possessive, belonging to whom

Who's been eating my porridge? Whose shoes are these?

woman: singular
women: plural

The three women met with another woman to have lunch.

you're: you are
your: belonging to you

You're going to get your jacket wet.

Exercise 2.15

Choose the correct word to complete the sentence:

1. _____ [Whose/Who's] backpack is this?

2. She says she doesn't believe in _____ [woman's, women's] liberation.

3. Jenna _____ [does, dose] not want to _____ [choose, choice, chose] the colours right now.

4. _____ [Your, You're] kidding. I can't believe you _____ [though, thought] he had given you a _____ [complement, compliment].

5. Tighten this bolt. It's much too _____ [loose, lose].

6. The temperature _____ [affects, effects] the result _____ [weather, whether] or not you change that setting.

7. I've run out of _____ [patience, patients] with him. I want a new lab partner.

8. _____ [We're, Were, Where, Wear] you planning on reviewing the _____ [scene, seen] with the actors before the dress rehearsal?

9. I need _____ [to, too, two] collect _____ [to, too, two] more gems to finish this level of the game.

10. He _____ [passed, past] my house an hour ago, so he should be _____ [their, there, they're] by now.

Exercise 2.16

In pairs, give each other a spelling test of words from the list below. Make a study list of the words you have trouble with:

a lot	descendant	pastime	changeable
accommodate	develop	phenomenon	chosen
accomplish	development	precede	column
accumulate	dining	preference	coming
achievement	embarrassed	prejudice	committee
acknowledge	emphasize	prevalent	competitive
aggravate	entrance	religion	foreign
all right	environment	repetition	forty
almost	especially	restaurant	fourth
analyze	exaggerate	rhythm	government
answer	exercise	schedule	grammar
apartment	fascinate	secretary	height
apology	February	seize	humorous
appropriate	immediately	separate	proceed
argument	indispensable	sincerely	professor
athlete	interesting	speak	pronunciation
beginning	knowledge	speech	receive
believe	license	studying	recommend
business	manoeuvre	succeed	relevant
calendar	marriage	surprise	religion
conscience	necessary	technique	Tuesday
conscientious	noticeable	temperature	usually
convenience	occasion	thorough	vacuum
convenient	occur	tragedy	Wednesday
criticism	occurred	tries	writing
definitely	opinion	truly	written
dependent	parallel	cemetery	

Recognizing Roots and Affixes

Words can be formed from root words from Greek and Latin. For example, the Greek word *phone* for sound is found in English words like *telephone* (sound from far away), *microphone* (small sound), and *phonetics* (the study of speech sounds). An affix is a group of letters attached to the front or end of a word to change its meaning. There are two kinds of affixes—prefixes and suffixes. Prefixes go before the word. A prefix can make a word negative, such as in *clear* and *unclear*. Suffixes go at the end of the word, changing its part of speech. The suffix *–ify* is a verb ending, as shown in the word *beautify* compared to the noun *beauty*. Common suffixes like these are listed in the first section of this unit, "Recognizing parts of speech."

Knowing some common root words and prefixes and suffixes can help you figure out the meaning of unfamiliar words, especially those in science and technology. Learning these word forms can help you expand your vocabulary.

Prefixes may change their spelling slightly depending on the first letter of the root word. For example, the negative prefix *in–* becomes *im–* before *b*, *p*, or *m* (*impossible*, *impenetrable*) and *ir–* before *r* (*irrefutable*). *Sub–* (under) can also appear as *sub–*, *suc–*, *suf–*, *sug–*, *sup–*, and *sus–* (as in *sustainable*). These spelling changes depend on phonetic rules. In other words, the sound (and therefore spelling) is adjusted to make the word easier to pronounce. For example, *irreplaceable* is easier to say than *inreplaceable*.

Negative prefixes

Many different prefixes are used to change a word to a negative or opposite meaning. The most common of these prefixes are *in–* and *un–*.

Note that the prefix *in–* can also mean *in*, as in the word *inhale*. This may cause confusion as in the word *inflammable*, which means that something is likely to go up "in flames," not that it will not burn. Therefore, to avoid such confusion, warning signs are likely to say *flammable* and *nonflammable*. Other words where the *in–* prefix is not negative include: *inbred*, *incorporate*, *indent*, *indrawn*, *inform*, *input*, and *inspire*.

It is also important not to confuse *anti–* (against) with *ante–* (before), which appears in words like *antebellum* (before the war) and *antenatal* (before birth).

a–	without, not	apolitical, atypical
an–	without (before vowels)	anarchy, anaemia, anonymous
ant–	against, opposed to (before vowels)	antacid, Antarctic, antonym
anti–	against, opposed to	antibiotic, antifreeze, antiperspirant
contra–	against	contraceptive, contradict, contravention
counter–	against, opposite	counter-clockwise, counterproductive
de–	away from	debug, decriminalize, de-ice, deplane
dis–	absence, apart	dishonest, dislike, disreputable
dys–	bad, difficult	dyslexic, dysfunctional
in–	not	inanimate, inconsiderate, insufficient
il–	not (before *l*)	illegitimate, illegal, illogical
im–	not (before *b*, *p*, *m*)	imbalance, immobile, impolite
ir–	not (before *r*)	irrefutable, irreplaceable

mal-	bad, badly	malformed, malnourished
mis-	wrong, badly	misspell, mistake, misunderstand, mistreat
non-	not	nonconformist, nondescript, non-fiction
pseud(o)-	false	pseudonym, pseudo-science
un-	not	undesirable, unimpressed, unthinkable

In addition, some English words, such as *bad, evil, ill,* and *wrong,* are attached to other words, usually with a hyphen, to create negatives and opposites: *bad-tempered, bad-mouth, evildoer, ill-treatment, ill-advised, wrong-headed.* The suffix *–less* can also make words negative (*careless, faithless*).

Exercise 2.17

By adding or deleting prefixes, give the opposite of the following words:

able	competent	grateful	quote
ability	continue	hero	readable
active	discolour	implausible	regular
addictive	divisible	informed	renewable
amoral	excusable	interesting	represent
argument	favourable	justified	successful
appetizing	finite	literate	toxic
audible	flexible	malnutrition	unworthy
believable	forgettable	manage	usable
behave	formal	patient	visible
classified	function	practice	wise

Prefixes of size and quantity

ambi-	both	ambiguous, ambivalent
bi-, bin-	two	bicycle, bilingual, binoculars
cent-	hundred	centigrade, centipede, century
dec-, deca-	ten	decathlon, decibel, decimate
di-	two	diode, dioxide
hyper-	over	hyperactive, hyperbole
macro-	large	macrocosm, macroeconomics
mega-	great	megabyte, megacity, megalomania
micro-	small	microbe, microbiology, microfibre
mill-	thousand	millennium, millisecond
mono-	one	monogamy, monologue

multi–	many	multi-faceted, multiplex
omni–	all	omnipotent, omniscient
pan–	all	Pan-American, pandemic, pandemonium
poly–	many	polyglot, polygamous, polygon
quasi–	partly	quasi-intellectual, quasi-professional
semi–	half	semi-detached, semi-sweet
tri–	three	trio, triangle
ultra–	beyond	ultra-conservative, ultrasound
uni–	one	unicorn, unification

Other number prefixes include *duo–* (two), *quarto–* (four), *quint–* (five), *hept–* (six), *sept–* (seven), *octo–* (eight), and *nono–* (nine).

Exercise 2.18

Match the word on the right with the correct definition on the left:

1. ambidextrous _____
2. bigamist _____
3. centennial _____
4. decade _____
5. hypersensitive _____
6. mega-mall _____
7. millipede _____
8. monologue _____
9. monotheism _____
10. multilingual _____
11. multimedia _____
12. panacea _____
13. triathlete _____
14. triplicate _____
15. unicycle _____

a) being able to use both the right and the left hand (usually for writing)

b) belief in one god

c) cure-all

d) huge shopping mall

e) insect with many legs (possibly a thousand)

f) long speech spoken by one actor in a play

g) one-hundred-year anniversary

h) period of 10 years

i) single-wheeled cycle often used by acrobats

j) someone who competes in three events (running, swimming, biking)

k) someone who gets married when he or she still has a legal spouse

l) speaking many languages

m) three copies of something

n) too sensitive to something

o) using more than one medium of expression, such as audio and video

Prefixes of location and direction

ante–	before	antedate, antechamber, anterior
circum–	around	circumference, circumstance, circumvent
co– (com/n/l/r/)	together	cooperate, connect, co-worker
ex–	out	exit, explode, exhale
in– (il–, im–, ir–)	in	incision, imprison
inter–	between	interfere, interrupt, interview
intra–, intro–	within	intravenous, introduce
peri–	around	perimeter, peripheral, periscope
pre–	before	predict, pre-emptive, preview
post–	after	postpartum, post-secondary
re–, retro–	again	recite, retrograde, return
sub–	under	subliminal, subtitle, subzero
super–, sur–	above	superior, supreme, surcharge
syn–, sym–	with	symphony, symposium, synchronize
trans–	across	transform, translate, transportation

Exercise 2.19

Match the word on the right with the correct definition on the left:

1. antenatal _____
2. circumpolar _____
3. collaborate _____
4. excise _____
5. inhale _____
6. intermingle _____
7. intramural _____
8. postdate _____
9. post-graduate _____
10. prehistoric _____
11. renovation _____
12. submarine _____

a) around or near one of the earth's poles
b) before recorded history
c) boat that goes under the sea
d) breathe in
e) cut out
f) make like new again
g) man who is superior to all others
h) mix together
i) musicians playing with others in a group
j) related to before a birth
k) studies undertaken after graduating with a university degree

Exercise 2.19 – *continued*

13. superman _____

14. symphony _____

15. transit _____

l) system to move people across town

m) taking part within a school's walls, especially sports

n) to give a later date

o) work together with someone

Greek and Latin roots and affixes

arch	first, chief	hierarchy, monarch
audi, audit	hear	audio tape, audition
auto	self	automobile, autobiography
ben, bene	good	beneficial, benign
bibl, biblio	book	bibliography, Bible
bio	life	biology, biometrics
chron	time	anachronism, chronology, synchronize
corp	body	corporal punishment, incorporate
dic, dict	speak	contradict, dictation, predict
doc, doct	teach	doctor, indoctrinate
eu	good	euphemism, euthanasia
fac, fact	make, do	faculty, manufacture
graph, gram	write	biography, graphology
liter	letter	literal, literate
log, logy	word	meteorology, logistics
man, manu	hand	manager, manicure, manually
mis, mit	send	admit, commission, missive
phil	love	philosophy, Philadelphia
phon	sound	phonetics, symphony, telephone
scrib, script	write	describe, prescription, subscript
son	sound	sonogram, sonorous
spect	look	inspect, spectacles, spectator
spir	breathe	inspiration, expire
tele	far	telecommute, telegraph
ven	come	venue, convention
vid, vis	see	audiovisual, revise, videotape
voc, vok	call	evocative, vocal, vocation

Activity 2.3

Discuss the meaning of the underlined words by using the meanings of the roots and affixes, and make a list of related forms (such as an adjective form related to a noun) where possible:

1. Magellan led the first <u>circumnavigation</u> of the globe.

2. Jan is a marine <u>biologist</u> who specializes in the <u>vocalizations</u> of dolphins.

3. Don't worry. That was just a <u>sonic</u> boom from a jet.

4. He pronounced his <u>dictum</u>, and everyone obeyed.

5. He's a true <u>bibliophile</u>; he has crammed bookshelves into every room.

6. The <u>corpse</u> was discovered in the <u>factory</u>.

7. The <u>transmission</u> was unclear because of the static.

8. The <u>philanthropist</u> was a <u>benefactor</u> for many worthwhile charities.

9. The <u>eulogy</u> was so stirring that many of the mourners broke down in tears.

10. He asked the professor if he could <u>audit</u> the course.

Recognizing Collocation

Some words go together, and some do not. The word *collocation* refers to probable word combinations. For example, *say*, *speak*, and *tell* mean almost the same thing, but while we can say, "I'll tell you a secret," we would not say, "I'll speak a secret" or "I'll say a secret." We "speak a language"—but "say a word." We say *native language* and *mother tongue* but not generally *mother language*.

Collocation can include adjectives that go with nouns (*antique furniture* but not *ancient furniture*), verbs that go with nouns (*offer advice* but not *award advice*), prepositions, or particles that complete verbs (*depend on* someone but not *depend for* someone), and noun combinations (*time management* but not *price management*).

Collocations are likely word combinations. They can be shown statistically by using concordances (tools that show the occurrence of words in texts). For example, if you apply a computer analysis to a body of text, you can see each time a certain word is used and what words occur with it. Even if they are unfamiliar with the concept of collocation, native speakers of a language are likely to feel that certain word combinations sound better than others.

Some dictionaries, such as ESL dictionaries, list collocations in their word entries. You can even get a whole dictionary of collocations, such as the *Oxford collocations dictionary for students of English*. ESL students often do not know such collocations and use unlikely word combinations that may be grammatical but do not sound right to native speakers. For example, we cannot *borrow a hand*, but we can *lend a hand*. Native speakers of English who have weaker vocabulary skills may also make incorrect word choices.

Collocation errors are more likely to occur when ESL learners translate from their native language. A bilingual dictionary shows words that have the same meaning in one context but may not give much information on how to use the word.

To learn collocations, you must pay attention to how words are used and look for common word combinations. It is important to get a sense of which words sound right together. You can test your ability to spot collocations in the following exercises.

Exercise 2.20

In the following list of verb + noun combinations, cross out the unlikely ones, leaving the collocations. There may be more than one collocation in each entry, and the expressions do not have to mean the same thing:

Example: take a course, ~~study a course~~, ~~get a course~~, complete a course

1. make a test, take a test, work a test, follow a test

2. ask a request, make a request, want a request, grant a request

3. conduct research, make research, carry out research, hold on research

4. drop a hint, take a hint, see a hint, have a hint

5. lose experience, make experience, collect experience, lack experience, acquire experience

6. run up a debt, sell a debt, make a debt, settle a debt

7. do a method, adopt a method, work a method, follow a method

8. follow a reason, give a reason, take a reason, hold a reason

9. show a risk, follow a risk, run a risk, make a risk

10. gain support, take support, run support, provide support

Exercise 2.21

Match the word in the left column with one in the right column to complete a collocation:

Adjective	Noun
border	attack
calculated	hesitation
daring	material
hazardous	matter
momentary	patrol
reasonable	rain
subtle	reminder
torrential	request
urgent	risk
weak	tea

Activity 2.4

Create a collocation chain with noun phrases. The first person starts with a combination of two nouns such as library book, and the next person must give a combination that starts with the second word, such as book club.

You can practise more with collocations in the editing exercise on correcting collocations (page 210).

Understanding Connotation

It is not enough to the know the meaning of a word; you must know its connotation—the emotional impact it makes. For example, the word *murder* is much stronger than the word *kill*. A person is complimented when he is called *generous* but insulted when he is called a *spendthrift*.

Words have a lot of power and should be used carefully. Make sure you understand the connotation of the words you use in your writing. As you expand your vocabulary, pay attention to the connotation of the new words and expressions. Some dictionaries will give you such information.

Activity 2.5

Consider the connotation of the following groups of words. Do they have the same meaning? Which are positive, and which are negative? Which are stronger? If you are not familiar with the words, look them up in your dictionary:

1. house, home
2. cheap, inexpensive
3. thrifty, stingy
4. arrogant, confident
5. mentally ill, crazy
6. bachelor, spinster
7. old geezer, senior citizen
8. frank, blunt, candid, tactless
9. classic car, jalopy
10. handyman's special, dump, fixer-upper
11. laugh lines, wrinkles
12. beggar, panhandler
13. unemployed, between jobs, on pogey
14. secretive, sneaky
15. slender, thin, slim, anorexic, skinny, scrawny, emaciated, svelte

Activity 2.6

In groups, make your own lists of words and expressions similar to those in the preceding activity. Think of words and expressions with similar meanings but different connotations.

Using Synonyms and Antonyms

Synonyms are words that have similar meanings, while antonyms are words that have opposite meanings. However, it is important to remember that even though two words may be synonyms, they are not interchangeable. There may be slight differences of meaning, connotation, or collocation.

Using synonyms and antonyms allows you to make your writing more interesting. English offers such a rich vocabulary that it is a waste to repeat the same word again and again. For instance, instead of using the word *car* over and over again in a paragraph, you could use synonyms like *automobile* and *vehicle* to vary your vocabulary.

Thesauruses, books of synonyms and antonyms, are useful tools for reminding a writer of other possible word choices. You should not just blindly choose a synonym from a thesaurus. First make sure you know how the word is used.

Exercise 2.22

Using a thesaurus, replace the underlined words or expressions with other words or expressions that have similar meanings:

1. The stranger's act of kindness <u>astonished</u> the beggar who was <u>accustomed</u> to abuse.

2. Samson's <u>riddle</u> was <u>baffling</u> to everyone who tried to solve it.

3. Every day, newspapers warn their <u>readers</u> about some health <u>hazard</u> related to common foods. After a while, people become <u>sceptical</u>.

4. Even though the lovers <u>quarrelled</u> <u>constantly</u>, they usually made up <u>quickly</u>.

5. They set out on their <u>journey</u> with high <u>hopes</u> of a <u>reconciliation</u>.

6. He made a <u>rookie</u> <u>error</u> by expecting his <u>staff</u> to correct the problem.

7. The old <u>building</u> was <u>deteriorating</u> <u>rapidly</u>, and there was no <u>hope</u> of saving it.

8. The long <u>commute</u> proved <u>too much</u> for them, so they <u>downsized</u> and moved into a condo.

9. The <u>onlookers</u> were <u>afraid of</u> getting involved, but one finally called 911.

10. They <u>strolled</u> through the park, <u>watching</u> the children at play.

Understanding Idioms

An idiom is an expression in which the figurative meaning is different from the literal meaning. *Figurative* means that the whole expression gives a picture (think of a figure) that is different from the meaning of the individual words (the word *literal* is related to the word *letter*; think of it as letter by letter or word by word). For example, the idiom *let the cat out of the bag* does not literally refer to a cat and a bag; it means *reveal a secret*.

Idioms are generally more conversational in style. For example, "Same-sex marriage is a political hot potato for the Conservatives" is more informal than "Same-sex marriage is a controversial issue for the Conservatives." You can use some idioms in formal, academic essays, but use them judiciously. If there is another, more standard way to express the same meaning, use that if you want to be more formal. The more idiomatic language you use, the more conversational your writing becomes.

Activity 2.7

Here are some more examples of idioms. In groups, discuss the meaning of the idiom, and rewrite the sentence replacing the idiom with other words:

1. If we don't find the bug in this program soon, we are going to <u>be up the creek without a paddle</u>.

2. I didn't want to make the announcement yet, but as usual Mark <u>jumped the gun</u>.

3. Of course, she copied his essay. She was <u>caught red-handed</u>.

4. I can't afford to go to restaurants every day for lunch, so I <u>brown bag</u> it.

5. She was all set to bring up the problems from last year, but I told her it was best to <u>let sleeping dogs lie</u>.

6. Tomas was not expecting an inheritance because he's the <u>black sheep of the family</u>.

7. Whenever her mother starts lecturing her, it <u>goes in one ear and out the other</u>.

8. I can't say I'm surprised he messed up that assignment. He's <u>not the sharpest knife in the drawer</u>.

9. I'm not going to tell him. I don't want to be the one <u>in hot water</u>.

10. I can't eat anything right now. I have an oral presentation to make next class, and I've got <u>butterflies in my stomach</u>.

Activity 2.8

In small groups, make a list of 10 idioms that you know. Compare it to the other groups' lists, looking for common ones. Which ones would be most useful for ESL students to learn?

Using Jargon

Jargon is technical language, such as medical terminology, legalese, and computer terms. The word often has a negative connotation because it is extended to mean wording that is not clear. Writers are often told to avoid jargon, but it actually depends on the audience. If the intended readers or listeners have the right background to understand the technical language, then jargon is not only appropriate, it is necessary. It allows the professionals within that group to communicate effectively and concisely. For example, a doctor can tell another doctor that a patient has a *subcutaneous haematoma* but would tell the patient that it is a *bruise*. Avoid using jargon if your audience would not understand the words.

Some words start out as jargon and move into common usage. Computer terms like *input* and *output* are now used for non-computer purposes.

Exercise 2.23

Identify the fields these groups of words come from:

1. IV, contusion, ICU, carcinoma, septicemia
2. plaintiff, subpoena, writ, affidavit, pro bono
3. boot, blog, mouseover, CPU, data compression
4. escrow, tenancy in common, lien, title search, assumable mortgage
5. vehicle trespass, B&E, a.k.a., complaint, disorderly conduct

---

Recognizing Colloquialisms and Slang

The words you use should be appropriate to the situation. An essay, a job application letter, and a business report all call for more formal writing than an e-mail message to a friend or a creative writing composition. Language can range in levels of writing from very informal through semi-formal to formal styles. Language style can be compared to clothing style. Just as you would not wear jeans and a T-shirt to a wedding or a job interview, you would not write an informal, chatty e-mail full of slang to a prospective employer.

North American society has moved towards more informality. For instance, in the 1950s men generally wore suits and hats, and women wore gloves and skirts. Today, "casual Friday" attire often becomes the style for the whole workweek. The same move to informality can be seen in writing. Business letters used to be much more formal in tone with phrases such as "I remain respectively yours." Most of the writing we see today, such as newspaper columns, is written in a more casual, conversational style.

Colloquialism is a word used to describe informal, conversational language. A word like *kid*, for example, may be marked "colloquial" or "informal" in the dictionary. This means that it is not suitable for more formal speaking or writing situations. In an academic essay, it would be more appropriate to use *children* instead of *kids*.

Slang goes one step further than colloquialism. Slang is a type of language common in casual speech. It is characteristic of a group. Teenagers have their own slang, as do rap musicians and computer geeks. Slang changes over time. In the 1920s, young people would say something really good was *the cat's pyjamas* or *the bee's knees*. In the 1950s, they would describe it as *neato* or *swell*, then *groovy* in the sixties. At the end of the twentieth century, teens used *awesome* and words like *bad*, *sick*, and *wicked* to describe something that was in fact very good. Slang also varies regionally: A British teenager is more likely to say "Brilliant!" whereas a Canadian might say "Sweet!" Slang should not be used in academic writing and should be avoided by ESL learners because it can be considered rude and offensive.

Obscenity is another kind of language that is more common in spoken language than in written. Again, attitudes have changed. In 1939, audiences were shocked when Rhett Butler said to Scarlett O'Hara, "Frankly, my dear, I don't give a damn" in the film *Gone with the wind*. Today, movies are filled with profanity, and the "f-word" may appear in almost every line of dialogue. Newspapers are a good guide as to what is generally accepted in a society. If the word appears in print in a general publication, it is not considered truly offensive. Remember that academic writing is more formal, and therefore more proper, than newspaper writing.

Overly formal, stuffy language is also not appropriate in most situations. A real estate agent talking about the *purveyance of a domicile* instead of the *sale of a house* would confuse and put off most clients. Remember that the primary purpose of writing is to give information clearly and concisely. Write to communicate, not to impress.

Exercise 2.24

Rewrite the sentences to replace the underlined slang words and expressions with more formal ones:

1. When the plane flew low overhead, we all <u>hit the deck</u> even though there was no danger.
2. When his boss reassigned the project, Jamal <u>freaked out</u>.
3. When we wanted to add a casino night to the fundraising plans, he <u>nixed</u> the idea.
4. He's so worried about the project that he's a <u>basket case</u>.
5. They spent the day <u>goofing off</u> and fell behind schedule.
6. She's always <u>mooching</u> fries from everyone at lunch but will never buy her own.
7. I need <u>the 411</u> on the whole situation.

Exercise 2.24 – *continued*

8. He was <u>all doom and gloom</u> about the agency's chances of winning that contract and staying profitable.

9. Coming off the roller coaster, he stumbled, turned green, and <u>tossed his cookies</u>.

10. He <u>did squat</u> on this project, so he doesn't deserve credit.

Studying Vocabulary

Although you will not have a chance to look up every unfamiliar word you come across in your reading, it is a good idea to make a vocabulary list for any reading you study in class. Look up unfamiliar words in the dictionary. Write them in your notebook, along with a definition and any other useful information (part of speech, irregular forms, usage label, synonyms, collocations). Even if you do not go back and memorize this information, the fact that you have gone through the effort of writing it down means that you will remember it better. If you just look up a word in the dictionary and continue with your reading, you will not retain it as well.

Expanding vocabulary:

- Read a lot to increase your exposure to words and how they are used.
- Read a variety of types of material (newspapers, books, websites), on different topics, to widen the fields of words you encounter.
- Pay attention to the language when you read. Look out for new words.
- Try to guess the meaning of words from the context and notice how they are used and which words accompany them.
- Use a dictionary to find out more about unfamiliar words.
- Keep a notebook for vocabulary you encounter. Writing down notes on the word will help you remember it better. Notes can include grammar and usage notes, such as the part of speech and the collocation. Write down the phrase or sentence the word appeared in.
- Learn words in groups. For example, if you use a dictionary to look up the meaning of an unfamiliar word, check out the derivatives, collocates, and any synonyms or antonyms given. Make sure you understand differences in usage.
- The more you read, the more you will encounter the words, and then you will understand them better.

Unit 3

Sentence Writing Skills

Words are combined to make sentences, and sentences are combined to make paragraphs. In turn, the paragraphs form parts of essays, reports, letters, and any other forms of writing. The sentence is the basic unit of grammar—writing is judged grammatical or not based on the formation of the sentences. Sentences are also the most important structure for meaning, so it is important to get sentences formed correctly.

The parts of speech and word formation were reviewed in unit 2. Unit 3 is essentially the grammar chapter. "Grammar" is sometimes thought of as a dirty word by both students and teachers. It brings to mind nitpicking and endless drill and practice. On the other hand, some people enjoy talking about grammar rules and actually doing practice exercises. They may find it easier than the composition part of writing class.

Students who need to improve their writing can benefit from a review of grammar rules. It can be an eye-opening exercise for native speakers who are not accustomed to looking at English in that way. ESL students, on the other hand, may be quite comfortable talking about the use of verb tenses and uncountable nouns. They may excel at grammar tests but have trouble writing grammatical sentences in their essays. Even though they may have spent years studying grammar rules, sometimes it helps to look at the structure of English in different ways.

Questions about grammar are not simple, black-and-white questions. Grammar, like other aspects of language, evolves and changes over time. For instance, the relative pronoun *whom* is dying in English, as is the subjunctive structure in conditionals (e.g., "if I *were* a rich man"). Moreover, what is considered acceptable in casual speech may be considered incorrect in standard academic writing. For example, we may say, "Here's the books you ordered" or "Everyone should pick their courses now." Written English tends to be more "correct" than speech.

As for grammar terminology, you may already be familiar with it, or it may be unfamiliar jargon to you. Knowing these terms is not essential for you in order to construct a good sentence, but the proper vocabulary makes it easier to explain grammar rules. Moreover, terminology can vary. For instance, "continuous" verb tenses are also called "progressive." Do not worry about memorizing the terms, but try to get a feel for the structures they describe.

This unit offers a quick review of the major parts of a sentence at a fairly basic level. It is not meant to be a comprehensive look at grammar. (If you need to know more, consult a grammar book such as *The Oxford practice grammar*.) The explanations focus on the fundamental structures of the language so that you can recognize what is behind common errors and fix them. The exercises give you more examples and allow you to practise and discuss the rules. More practice can be had in unit 7, which deals with editing and correcting errors.

Understanding Basic Sentence Structure

Essentially, a sentence starts with a capital letter and ends with a period (or question mark or exclamation mark). It is important for the reader to be able to tell where each sentence begins and ends. Especially when writing by hand, you need to make the sentence boundaries clear. Capital letters should be easily distinguishable from small letters, even if you use block printing, and a period should be easily distinguishable from a comma. Thus, the primary consideration is that a sentence should look like a sentence.

A sentence needs a subject and a predicate to qualify as a sentence. The subject is what you are talking about, and the predicate is what you are saying about it. The subject is a noun or a pronoun along with any modifiers. The predicate is the verb along with objects and their modifiers.

Here are some basic sentence patterns:

John fled. [subject + intransitive verb]

They opened the package. [subject + transitive verb + direct object]

Ahmed gave her a ring. [subject + verb + indirect object + direct object]

Yuki is an architect. [subject + linking verb + predicate noun or adjective]

She painted the room blue. [subject + verb + direct object + objective complement]

The house is over there. [subject + verb + adverbial]

The subject is a noun, noun phrase, or noun clause. A subject cannot appear in a prepositional phrase. A subject can be a compound subject, containing two or more nouns joined with *and*:

The <u>house</u> on the corner is slated for demolition. [single word subject: the noun *corner* is in a prepositional phrase and cannot be the subject]

<u>Walking to school</u> is one of the ways I get my exercise. [noun phrase as subject]

<u>That he ruined the day for his family</u> did not seem to enter his mind. [noun clause as subject]

<u>Jack,</u> <u>Amir,</u> <u>and</u> <u>Tim</u> enjoyed the pumpkin pie. [compound subject]

Verbs can be more than one word—auxiliary verbs along with the main verb. In a sentence, the predicate can include more than one verb:

He <u>should have been</u> more careful. He <u>could have been</u> <u>electrocuted</u>.

The children <u>ran</u>, <u>skipped</u>, and <u>hopped</u> across the field.

It is useful to be able to identify the core sentence—the basic parts without any modifiers. These basic parts include the subject and verb. Then you can tell if you have a grammatical sentence or not. Here are some example sentences with the core parts underlined:

Yesterday <u>I</u> <u>paid</u> all my <u>bills</u> on-line.

My <u>brother</u> <u>fixed</u> the door <u>handle</u> with a screwdriver.

Screaming in fright, <u>Lynn</u> <u>ran</u> down the street.

The <u>*Bluenose*</u>, a fishing schooner from Lunenburg, Nova Scotia, <u>is</u> the <u>ship</u> depicted on the Canadian dime.

Sentences that are in the imperative mood—in other words, commands—look like one-word sentences, but the implied subject is *you*:

Stop!   [You] Stop!

Take a chair.   [You] Take a chair.

The minimum for a sentence is a subject and a verb. The subject and verb are also the basis of any sentence.

Exercise 3.1

For the following sentences, identify the subject, verb, and objects to get the core sentence:

1. Strolling through the park, Peter whistled a cheerful tune.

2. Surprisingly, my brother's soccer team, which had an abysmal record, won the game.

3. On Saturday night we went to the theatre to see an amateur production of *The importance of being earnest*.

4. With her new promotion, she can indulge her expensive tastes as she redecorates.

5. One of the band members has decided to leave the group to pursue a career as a rapper.

6. His friend Tony is throwing the bachelor party.

7. I lost my book. Can I borrow yours?

8. My neighbour signed for my package but forgot to tell me he had it.

9. His flight leaves at eight. He hasn't even packed yet.

10. I don't know when we'll be back.

Understanding Verb Forms

Verb endings (*–ing* and *–ed*) and auxiliary verbs (*be, have, will*) are used to make the different tenses:

Simple present: She walks to work every day.

Simple past: She walked to work yesterday.

Future: She will walk to work tomorrow.

Present continuous: She is walking to work right now.

Past continuous: She was walking to work when I saw her.

Future continuous: She will be walking to work from now on.

Present perfect: She has walked to work many times, but usually she takes the bus.

Past perfect: She <u>had walked</u> to work before he called to offer her a ride.

Future perfect: She <u>will have walked</u> to work by the time I can pick her up.

Present perfect continuous: She <u>has been walking</u> to work since the bus strike started.

Past perfect continuous: She <u>had been walking</u> to work before she decided to buy a car.

Future perfect continuous: She <u>will</u> <u>have</u> <u>been</u> <u>walking</u> to work for two years by the time she gets a car.

Present events

To express general facts, you use the simple present tense (as in this sentence). To describe actions that are occurring now (as in this clause), use present continuous (also called present progressive). To express past ideas that are relevant to the present, use the present perfect tense or present perfect continuous.

The earth is round. The sky is blue. Astronomers are people who study stars.

I am studying Japanese as a third language, and I am finding the classes interesting.

Ellen has lived in Edmonton for six years. [This means that she still lives in Edmonton, in contrast to "Ellen lived in Edmonton for six years."]

Past events

Actions that happened in the past and are complete are described with the simple past tense. Actions that took place over a period of time are expressed with the past continuous. Actions that occurred before another past action are in the past perfect:

I tried to learn how to play the bagpipes, but I stopped taking lessons.

Naomi was cleaning up the mess when her supervisor walked in.

He had studied Arabic for several years before he went to Egypt.

The past perfect form is used less frequently today. People have a habit of using the simple past for past actions, even if one happened beforehand:

>After he washed the car, it rained.

Future events

The simple future (with *will*) can be used for most actions that will take place in the future. The present continuous and *going to* also express future actions. The difference in meaning is slight, but the *will* form tends to be used with decisions just made, whereas the other forms refer to already decided upon events. The simple present is sometimes used for future scheduled events, often regular events:

>The band will travel by bus to Halifax.

>The band is travelling to Halifax by bus.

>The band is going to take the bus to Halifax.

>The bus leaves at nine.

The tenses you will use most in your writing are simple present, simple past, and present perfect.

Exercise 3.2

Write the correct form of the verb for the blank. More than one tense might be appropriate:

1. Tanya _____ [bring] her son along on the trip to the museum, and he _____ [behave] very well.

2. Thomas _____ [see] a skunk in the woods, but he _____ [avoid] it because his teacher _____ [warn] him about skunks.

3. We _____ [eat] eggs for breakfast every day last week.

4. Our flight _____ [leave] at ten, but we _____ [have] to get there early.

5. On Mondays and Wednesdays, the students _____ [play] soccer after class.

6. I _____ [meet] you at seven in the restaurant. Don't be late.

7. We _____ not _____ [sleep] well because it was too hot in the residence.

Exercise 3.2 – *continued*

8.   Janice _____ [enjoy] the trip to Parliament Hill because she wanted to learn more about Canadian history.

9.   How many T-shirts _____ you _____ [buy] on our visit to Chinatown? I only _____ [buy] three.

10. Jeannie _____ already _____ [see] the museum exhibit, so she _____ [go] shopping and she _____ [meet] us at 4 o'clock this afternoon.

Auxiliary verbs

An auxiliary (helping) verb must be followed by another verb. The auxiliaries *be*, *have*, and *will* are used to make several of the tenses. Other auxiliaries include *do* and the modal verbs (*may*, *might*, *can*, *could*, *should*, *would*).

The auxiliary verb determines which form of the verb follows it. If the sentence has several auxiliary verbs in a row, the last one is the main verb (underlined in the examples below):

> I should have been <u>paying</u> attention in class.

> I should have been <u>elected</u> president.

The chart reviews auxiliary verbs and how they are used:

Auxiliary	*Verb that follows*	*Used for*	*Example*
have	past participle (*-ed* ending for regular verbs)	perfect tenses	I have lived here for six months.
be (am, is, are, was, were, been, being)	present participle (*-ing* form)	continuous tenses	He is working now.
be (am, is, are, was, were, been, being)	past participle (*-ed* ending for regular verbs)	passive voice	The time was well spent.
will	base form (infinitive without *to*)	future tenses	He will speak after the dinner.
do, did	base form (infinitive without *to*)	emphasis; negatives; questions	I did call her. You did not fail. Did he see them?
modal verbs (can, could, may, might, should, would, etc.)	base form (infinitive without *to*)	to express possibility, probability, conditions, etc.	They can walk there. She might be late. I would ask first.

The verbs *be*, *have*, *do*, and *will* can also be used as simple verbs without another verb:

> Richard is a hard worker.

> They have 50 dollars to spend on the gift.

> He did the dishes right after dinner.

> She was exhausted, but she willed her eyes to stay open.

Modal verbs, however, can never be used alone. They must be followed by a verb, and it must be in the bare infinitive form:

> They should redo the whole project. They can get the funding.

Furthermore, the *–ing* form of the verb is not a complete verb, so it cannot be used without an auxiliary as the verb in a sentence.

It is important to remember these verb patterns to avoid errors such as "I have saw" or "he can going." If you make these types of mistakes, check your verb forms over before you hand in your work.

Exercise 3.3

Choose which form of the verb should be used in the sentence:

1. He could not have _____ [be, being, been] waiting in the store. I would _____ [have, having, had] seen him.

2. Jamal was _____ [wait, waiting, waited] a long time before the clerk finally served him.

3. She had _____ [wrote, writing, written] several versions of the essay before she was finally happy with one.

4. I might _____ [be, being, been] able to help you with that problem. I can _____ [contact, contacts, contacting] my brother-in-law. He is a paralegal.

5. The problem could have been _____ [solve, solving, solved] without violence.

6. Anneliese should _____ [has, have, having, had] complained earlier. It's _____ [be, been, being] so long now that it's harder to prove.

7. They will _____ [take, taking, took] the package along and pass it on to her sister.

Exercise 3.3 – *continued*

8. She may _____ [be, been, being] promoted when Richard leaves.

9. Didn't you _____ [follow, followed, following] that explanation? It could have _____ [be, been, being] shorter, but it was fairly clear.

10. She could have _____ [reads, read, reading] those chapters before the class. She had enough time.

Transitive and intransitive verbs

A transitive verb requires a direct object to complete it. For example, the verbs *see*, *deny*, and *have* are incomplete without an object:

> I saw five whales.

> He denied the accusation.

> I have change for a twenty.

Many verbs can be used both transitively and intransitively:

> Michael spread the fertilizer over the lawn. [transitive]

> The fire spread quickly. [intransitive]

> She likes to read. [intransitive]

> I read the newspaper with breakfast. [transitive]

In dictionaries, verbs are generally marked as "transitive" and "intransitive." Check to see which abbreviations your dictionary uses for these two words.

Exercise 3.4

Determine whether these verbs are transitive or intransitive by deciding whether the sentences are correct or not as they stand. If you need an object to complete the verb, then the verb is transitive. Fill in the blanks with an appropriate object, where necessary:

1. Heather saw _____ last week.

2. They ate _____ late yesterday.

3. He rejected _____.

Exercise 3.4 – *continued*

4. She swam _____ quickly.

5. Melanie caught _____ last week.

6. Ivan told her _____.

7. His actions irritated _____.

8. Jon whistled _____ and the dog came.

9. The songs included _____.

10. She bought _____ at the mall.

Exercise 3.5

For these transitive verbs, identify collocations by choosing which nouns could complete it (an article may be necessary):

1. slam: bicycle, brakes, door, laundry, thought

2. pronounce: idea, name, language, word

3. install: alarm, birds, locks, software, table, umbrella

4. throw: ball, bank account, fireplace, party, pottery

5. review: account, health, jungle, notes, visitor

6. watch: children, impact, television, time

7. drive: anger, ball, computer, house, truck, whistle

8. elevate: leg, memory, position, theory

9. expect: honesty, lottery, meal, promotion, person, reward

10. skip: class, dog, law, meal, rope, train

11. access: car, information, person, room, trouble

12. bear: burden, fruit, hate, lateness, wisdom

13. wipe: counter, flow, glasses, match, meal, tears, window

14. make: break-up, children, date, dinner, mistake

15. report: accident, crime, life, person, walk

Using Active and Passive Voice

In an active sentence, the grammatical subject does the action of the verb:

James threw the stick past his dog, but his dog ignored it.

In the passive voice, the subject is acted upon. You can make a sentence passive by moving the object before the verb to become the subject:

Anita painted the landscape. [active]

The landscape was painted by Anita. [passive]

For the passive voice, a form of the verb *to be* is used (*is, am, are*), and the main verb is in the past participle form, which ends in *−ed* for regular verbs. There may also be modal verbs in the structure (*will be, would be, may be*) or other verb forms (*have been, is being*):

The show will be cancelled if it rains.

The painting could have been forged.

The documents were shredded accidentally.

The active voice is preferred because it is easier for readers to understand, but the passive is useful when you want to de-emphasize who or what did the action. It is therefore common in technical writing. For example, lab reports are often written in the passive because it does not really matter who did the action:

The water was heated to the boiling point, and the solution was added.

The company was founded in 1845.

The parade was postponed because of the accident.

Some students have problems with the passive voice. They may form it incorrectly, not using the auxiliary *to be* or not using the past participle *−ed* verb form:

Canadians do not prepared for a terrorist attack. [incorrect]

Canadians are not prepared for a terrorist attack.

They may write a passive sentence when an active would be more appropriate:

The donations were recorded in the red notebook by John. [awkward]

John recorded the donations in the red notebook.

Another mistake is using verbs that are not normally found in the passive voice, such as intransitive verbs, and verbs that express state. Verbs that are commonly incorrectly made passive include *become*, *belong*, *depend*, *exist*, *lack*, *occur*, and *happen*:

> The mistake is happened because he was not paying attention. [incorrect]
>
> The mistake happened because he was not paying attention.

Exercise 3.6

Determine whether the following sentences are active or passive:

1. She bought all her textbooks on-line.
2. The manager corrected the mistakes and reprimanded the staff.
3. The car bomb exploded, killing five.
4. The interview was scheduled for 11:15.
5. His story was not believed by anyone.
6. The lawyer advised her client to stay quiet.
7. Finally, the winner was chosen.
8. He was reported to the police.
9. I can't remember the last time we spoke.
10. No one ate the casserole. It must have tasted terrible.
11. Amanda won the race in a record time.
12. Everyone enjoyed the concert.
13. The game was lost by a slim margin.
14. She left the package unopened.
15. He was surprised by the amount of money collected.

Go back over the sentences and decide whether the voice can easily be switched. If so, make active sentences passive and passive sentences active (you may have to add an agent doing the action). Discuss how well the sentence works in active and in passive voice. Explore different ways of expressing the same idea in active and passive. For example, #3 could be restated as "Five people were killed when the car bomb exploded."

Showing Singular and Plural

Both verb and noun forms are determined by the concept of singular (to show one thing or one person) and plural (more than one). Students need to make sure they understand the difference so they can put the *s*'s in the right place. Although the basic concept is simple, some cases can be confusing, and this is an area where many grammatical errors are made in sentences. For instance, ESL students may make errors such as "a teapots" or "John walk," and native speakers make agreement errors such as "one of the engineers were."

Unlike most European languages, which have many word endings, English has the *–s* ending doing triple duty: it is used to show plural nouns, possessive nouns, and third person singular verbs. For possessive forms, the *–s* is used with an apostrophe. This can be very confusing for people learning English as a second language and even to native speakers of the language:

> The <u>computers</u> were down because of a virus. [plural noun— more than one computer]

> The <u>clown's</u> nose fell off. [possessive—the nose belonging to the clown]

> Jennifer <u>walks</u> to school every day. [third person singular verb form]

Most nouns in English have an *–s* added to them to show plural, with an *–es* ending if the original word ends in an *s*-like sound:

> bike/bikes, pie/pies, box/boxes, job/jobs, patient/patients, church/churches

Plural nouns, including irregular plurals, are discussed in unit 2 (page 22).

The determiners *a, an, another, each, every, this,* and *that* are singular:

> I want another folder. This one is all bent.

> Each of these rooms is too small.

The determiners *these* and *those* are plural:

> Have you checked over these results? This one looks off.

> I need some of those bigger envelopes. Where are they?

Words that end in *–one, –thing,* and *–body* (*everyone, anybody*) are singular:

> Is anybody home? Nobody is there. Everybody has gone. Something is missing.

The verb form has to agree in person and number with the subject. Most regular verb forms do not vary for singular and plural (e.g., *she waited*, *they waited*; *I sleep*, *we sleep*), but agreement is important for irregular verbs (which include the forms of the modal *be*, thus affecting passive and continuous verb forms) and in the simple present tense when the third person singular has an −*s* ending:

> He has a cottage on Lake Huron, while his parents have one further east.

> Laura bikes to work every day, but she wants to buy a car.

In order to get the proper verb form, you have to identify the subject. In the following examples, the subject is underlined once and the verb is underlined twice:

> One of the children is not coming.

> Kevin and Tom are cousins.

> The books in the hallway are donations for the charity book sale.

Showing singular and plural with subject/verb agreement and pronoun reference is a messy problem for writers in English. The main problem is that if the writer chooses an unspecified third person singular reference, he (or *he or she* or *he/she*) gets into a pronoun problem. Traditionally, *he* has been considered correct grammatically, but it is seen as sexist because it excludes females. In speech (and in some literature with authors as exalted as Charles Dickens), the *they* form is often used:

> A student should make sure they choose the right courses.

This usage is so pervasive that even when the sex is obvious, the *they* turns up:

> The woman who wins the top model competition will get a contract with a prestigious agency, and they will get a chance to travel all over the world. [should be *she*]

You can get away with the *they* usage in casual speech, but remember that academic writing should be grammatically correct, so you need to find a solution to this problem. You can use *he or she* if you only need the reference once or twice, but a whole paragraph of *he or she* can be very tedious. Do not use *he/she*—it is not an actual word. Neither is *s/he*, which is an attempt at coining a new term. You can choose to alternate *he* and *she*, but you cannot do it in a single paragraph. In other words, do not give the person a sex change midway through a paragraph. One of the simplest things is to play it safe and avoid the problem by using a plural form:

> Students should make sure they choose the right courses.

The plural form does not always work out. For example, sometimes it is necessary to make one reference singular and one plural to avoid confusing pronouns:

> Parents should raise their children so that they learn financial responsibility.

> Parents should raise their child so that he or she learns financial responsibility.

It is important to stay consistent, however. Do not switch from singular to plural unnecessarily:

> Finally, a spoiled child is often rude. Children who always receive all they want without thinking of anybody else rarely show appreciation and say "thank you."

Exercise 3.7

Choose the correct word form for the sentence (if both are possible grammatically, choose the more likely):

1. One of the car/cars broke down during the trip.

2. An apple/apples a day is/are recommended.

3. What I don't understand is/are why she has/have two of them.

4. The member/members of the school band is/are excused from the test.

5. All dog/dogs in the park should be on a leash/leashes.

6. A few of the poster/posters are left; we can sell them at the flea market/markets.

7. Emma take/takes dance/dances lesson/lessons every Tuesday/Tuesdays.

8. She corrected all the error/errors in the essay.

9. Several piece/pieces were missing. Each is/are hard to replace.

10. There were many mistake/mistakes, but they were not major one/ones.

Showing Possession

Possession means that something belongs to someone or something. This relationship is generally shown with possessive pronouns (*my, your, his, her, its, our, their, whose*) or an apostrophe and an *s* attached to a singular noun. After plural nouns that end in *s*, possession is shown by an apostrophe alone, without the *s*:

> <u>My</u> mother is coming to visit along with <u>my</u> sister and <u>her</u> husband.

> The <u>accountants'</u> report criticized <u>Elizabeth's</u> handling of the books.

> The Martins are staying at the <u>Johnsons'</u> condo in Florida.

> The <u>children's</u> toys were left all over the floor.

Sometimes you will see names that end in *s* with just an apostrophe and no added *s*, just like plural nouns, as in *Moses' mother*. However, it is preferable to add *'s*, as in *James's book*.

Other possessive pronouns are not used before nouns. These include *mine, hers, yours, theirs,* and *ours*. They do not have apostrophes:

> This is not my bike. That one over there is <u>mine</u>.

> They paid off the mortgage, so the house is now officially <u>theirs</u>.

> Whose shoes are these? I thought they were <u>yours</u>.

Possession is also shown with an *of* phrase. This is used for things and to indicate the source of something:

> the mouth of the river

> the model of the car

> the author of the book

Sometimes this type of relationship (with objects, not persons) is expressed with an adjective. This adjective may be a noun functioning as an adjective:

> the river mouth

> the car model

Students who mistakenly add apostrophes to plurals may have trouble distinguishing possessive and plural forms. If there are two nouns in a row and the first one ends in an *s*, it is likely that the first noun is possessive. One way to check is to replace the word with a possessive pronoun (*his, her, its, their*); if the sentence makes sense with the substitution, the word in question is likely a possessive form:

> Peter's [his] mother brought all the dishes [~~their~~] home.

> The instructor lost the students' [their] exam papers.

Another mix-up is with the homophones *its/it's* and *whose/who's*. *It's* is a contracted form of *it is* or *it has*, while *who's* is a contraction of *who is* or *who has*. If the non-contracted form works in the sentence, there should be an apostrophe. *Its* and *whose* are the possessive pronouns:

> It's [it is] time to figure out who's [who is] going to the conference.

> Whose car is that? [who does the car belong to?—possessive]

> It's [it is] funny to see the dog chasing its tail. [the tail belongs to the dog]

Since contractions are generally not used in academic writing, you can avoid using *it's* and *who's*.

Exercise 3.8

Identify the words showing possession and add any necessary apostrophes:

1. Its a question of responsibility, but he should not ignore Peters involvement.

2. Her glasses broke when Tims brother stepped on them.

3. The childrens bedtime was moved up, and their nap time was shortened.

4. There were many videos, CDs, and DVDs at Megans garage sale.

5. Murphys Law says that if something can go wrong, it will.

6. I couldn't decide which curtains to buy, but I finally picked the ones with green stripes.

Exercise 3.8 – *continued*

7. The boys boat started sinking, but they made it to shore. They even rescued their belongings.

8. On Tuesdays we meet for lunch and discuss the students progress.

9. We need our own sleeping bags, but the tents are provided by the excursion company.

10. Ians car broke down, so we missed our rendezvous with the tour guides.

Using Determiners

Determiners are words that come before a noun to identify which person, place, or thing is being talked about. Determiners include articles (*a, an, the*), demonstratives (*this, that, these, those*), possessive forms (*my, your, his, her, its, our, their*), relative pronouns (*which, whose, what*), and indefinite determiners (*few, many, more, several, some*).

You do not have to learn the different terminology as long as you can use determiners correctly. One problem area (singular versus plural) is discussed above. Relative pronouns are discussed on page 95. The use of articles can be troublesome, especially for ESL students. The usage is often idiomatic and different from the way articles are used in other languages.

The articles in English are *a, an,* and *the. A* and *an* are indefinite articles. They have the meaning of "one," so they are not used for plural forms. *The* is a definite article and is used with both singular and plurals.

Generally, the first time a noun is introduced, the indefinite article is used, but once the reader knows which thing is being referred to, a definite article is used to refer to something specifically:

> I picked an apple off the tree. [one apple] The apple was red and juicy. [specifically, the apple I picked] I like apples. [apples in general] The apples in my uncle's orchard are especially good. [specific apples]

A is used before consonants, and *an* is used before vowel sounds. This usage depends on how the initial sound is pronounced, so both *a* and *an* appear before *h* and *u*:

> a walk, a school, a book, a car, a dish, a fairy tale, a lovely scene

> an article, an elephant, an island, an octopus, an ugly hat

an umbrella, a university, a hero, an hour

a/an herb (depending on individual pronunciation)

Remember that indefinite articles (*a*, *an*) cannot be used with uncountable nouns (introduced in unit 2, page 20). Quantifiers such as *many* and *few* are used with countable nouns; uncountable nouns take *much*, *some*, and *little*:

I have little money left, but you can have a few dollars.

He didn't have much concrete information, but he had many contacts to recommend.

Proper names, such as the names of countries and institutions, may have articles in their name depending on the other words used in the name. For example, a country name has no article if it is plain (Canada, Russia, China), but an article is used when another noun like *republic*, *states*, or *union* is found in the name (the Dominion of Canada, the Soviet Union, the Republic of China). University names have an article if the word "university" appears first: the University of Toronto, but York University.

Exercise 3.9

Fill in the blanks with articles or other determiners where required:

1. I met several people on _____ trip. _____ student I met on the bus is going to _____ University of Ottawa. She wants to become bilingual, but _____ French is quite weak, so she's working with _____ tutor. She eventually wants to study _____ law, and she thinks _____ bilingualism is _____ asset for any profession.

2. They've decided to arrange _____ picnic for _____ park's anniversary. They are going to hire _____ clowns and _____ magicians. _____ neighbourhood high school band is going to perform in _____ band shell during _____ afternoon, and _____ local bands are going to play _____ more modern music in the evening. _____ food vendors will sell everything from _____ hot dogs to _____ ice cream.

3. We had _____ wonderful trip to Halifax. We visited _____ museum at _____ Pier 21. It told the story of European immigrants who disembarked at _____ pier. Many travelled by _____ train to _____ final destinations. I even found _____ name of _____ ship that _____ family came to Canada on. We also took _____ trip on _____ *Bluenose*

Exercise 3.9 – *continued*

replica ship. I love any kind of _____ sailboat, so _____ tall
ship was _____ real thrill. We saw _____ display about
_____ *Titanic* at _____ Maritime Museum of _____
Atlantic. Many of _____ *Titanic* victims are buried in _____
Halifax. _____ story of _____ 1917 Halifax explosion was
really astonishing. _____ munitions ship blew up in _____
harbour, levelling _____ entire downtown area, killing two
thousand people and injuring nine thousand.

4. After _____ weeks of looking, I finally found _____ apartment.
   It's on _____ Baker Street, near _____ university. I'll be able
   to walk to _____ class, but I can take _____ bus when
   _____ weather is bad. It's _____ two-bedroom apartment.
   I'm going to share with _____ cousin. It's in _____ high-rise
   building, on _____ seventh floor. _____ living room is really
   nice because it has _____ picture window with _____ view of
   _____ river. We have some furniture from our parents, and we
   can get _____ few pieces from _____ garage sales or
   _____ thrift shop. I can't wait to have _____ own place.

5. _____ attitude is _____ most important factor in determining
   how well _____ student succeeds. All learning depends on how
   much someone wants to learn because that desire will translate
   into _____ effort. That desire must be real—not just _____
   wish like "I wish I could speak English well." _____ real
   motivation means that _____ student will seek out _____
   opportunities to practise, will work on _____ exercises with
   _____ persistence, and will read to find out more. _____
   motivated student will read _____ novels in English, will find
   _____ English-speaking friends, and will watch _____ movies
   and _____ television to improve _____ language skills. In
   _____ other words, _____ student will carry _____
   learning into _____ leisure time.

Using Prepositional Phrases

Prepositional phrases are a frequent add-in to the basic sentence structure.
Most specify time or place (when or where); some show the manner—how
something was done. They are formed with a preposition followed by a
noun phrase (a noun with articles and adjectives if required):

in the house

at school

with the red hat

in five minutes

in a sloppy way

Prepositions:

about, above, across, after, against, along, among, around, at, before, behind, below, beneath, beside, between, by, down, during, except, for, from, in, inside, into, near, next to, of, off, on, onto, out of, outside, over, past, through, to, under, until, up, up on, with, within, without

Notice how the prepositional phrases (underlined in the sentences below) add meaning to the sentence:

The girl threw the ball.

After her brother's taunt, the girl from next door threw the ball into the street.

Jack sat in the back of the bus to avoid the family with the crying baby.

Being able to identify prepositional phrases is important because by eliminating these phrases from the mix, you can isolate the subject and verb and check to see whether the sentence is grammatical. A grammatical subject never appears in a prepositional phrase:

One of the soldiers was killed. [the subject is *one*, not *soldiers*]

The members of the choir were tired after the long rehearsals. [the subject is *members*, not *choir*]

Prepositions themselves pose problems for both people learning English as a second language and native speakers. The basic meanings are relatively straightforward, but they combine with verbs to make idiomatic combinations. Some verbs are completed by a specific preposition. For instance, we say *to rely on* and *to contend with* someone or something. Phrasal verbs are two and three-part verbs that are completed with prepositions (technically distinguished as particles, but they are essentially the same words). For

example, we say someone is *getting by* on a reduced income and that someone is trying *to catch up*. Unfortunately, there are few rules that can help. One
is that *up* usually adds the meaning of *completely* or *elaborately* (e.g., *dress* versus *dress up*). Most of these combinations, however, are idiomatic and must
be learned individually. A good dictionary includes phrasal verbs and gives
the prepositions that go with the verbs.

Exercise 3.10

Underline the prepositional phrases in the following sentences:

1. Some of the best dinosaur fossils can be found at the Royal
   Tyrrell Museum in the Badlands area near Drumheller, Alberta.

2. In Quebec City, you can visit the Plains of Abraham, the site of
   the 1759 battle where the English forces defeated the French,
   putting Canada under the control of the British.

3. Because of the popularity of the book *Anne of Green Gables*, one
   of the most popular tourist attractions in Prince Edward Island is
   the house that inspired the novel.

4. The corner of Portage and Main is the downtown heart of
   Winnipeg and is considered the windiest intersection.

5. Sainte-Marie among the Hurons is a recreated seventeenth-
   century Jesuit mission headquarters in Midland, Ontario.

6. Victoria, the capital of British Columbia, is located on Vancouver
   Island, whereas Vancouver is on the mainland and is a much
   larger city.

7. Niagara Falls is not the highest waterfall in the world, but the
   Horseshoe Falls, on the Canadian side of the border, is the
   world's largest by volume of water.

8. Nunavut is a new territory created in 1999. Once a part of the
   Northwest Territories, it is unusual because it has an aboriginal
   government, and Inuktitut is one of the official languages.

9. The Marine Museum of the Atlantic in Halifax, Nova Scotia, has
   exhibits on the 1917 Halifax explosion and the response of
   Halifax to the sinking of the *Titanic* in 1912.

10. The Bay of Fundy has the highest tides in the world, which rise at
    a rate of six to eight feet in height in an hour.

Exercise 3.11

Fill in the blanks with an appropriate preposition to complete the prepositional phrase:

1. Chris plays road hockey _____ the summer to keep his skills sharp _____ his regular games _____ ice _____ the winter.

2. We went to see the Blue Jays play _____ Friday night. We had seats _____ the highest part _____ the stadium _____ the nosebleed section.

3. I found an apartment _____ my sister's house, and it's convenient _____ work, too. I'm looking forward to spending more time playing _____ my nephews. They like going _____ the park and hanging _____ the monkey bars.

4. Marcus likes to laze _____ the couch _____ Sunday afternoons watching his favourite teams _____ television.

5. The shortstop hit the ball _____ _____ the park _____ his second home run _____ the game.

6. I love to swim _____ the early morning _____ the cottage. I can dive _____ the end _____ the dock. In a few strokes, I can swim _____ the bay _____ the small beach.

7. If you look _____ the bookshelf _____ the door, you'll find the slang dictionary _____ the top shelf _____ the other dictionaries.

8. The students play soccer _____ the park _____ class _____ Wednesday afternoons. _____ the time they finish the game, it's getting dark.

9. Ling and Albert are planning a destination wedding. It will take place _____ a resort _____ the island of St. Lucia.

10. I can't find the key. I looked _____ the hook, _____ my purse, _____ the desk, and even _____ the junk drawer. I checked _____ the desk to see if it had fallen.

Exercise 3.12

Add prepositional phrases to the following sentences:

1. The house was demolished.

2. The students are studying quietly.

3. The wall needs to be painted.

Exercise 3.12 – *continued*

4. The band performed.

5. The rugby team won the game.

6. The movie is playing.

7. The children are running.

8. I fell.

9. The man drove.

10. Anna is studying Japanese.

Using Co-ordinate Conjunctions

The co-ordinate conjunctions are *and, or, but, for, so, nor,* and *yet.* They are used for joining sentences or parts of sentences:

> Jesse <u>and</u> Kate were putting up new drywall.

> We arrived tired <u>yet</u> happy.

> They topped the pizza with pepperoni, mushrooms, <u>and</u> green pepper.

> Marcus wanted to take fencing lessons, <u>but</u> he could not afford the gear.

> You could see the Friday show <u>or</u> go to the matinee.

Punctuation of co-ordinate conjunctions can be tricky. A comma does not come before these conjunctions unless there is a full sentence afterwards:

> Martha installed a firewall and changed the passwords.

> Martha installed a firewall, and Silvia changed the passwords.

When a list of items is given, a comma is optional before the *and*. British English favours using this "serial" comma, while American style tends to leave it out. Canadians, as usual, are in the middle. If you do opt to use a serial comma, use it consistently:

> Rob topped his hamburger with mustard, ketchup, and relish.

> OR: Rob topped his hamburger with mustard, ketchup and relish.

In conversational style, sentences often begin with a co-ordinate conjunction, but this should be avoided in academic writing. Technically, it is not grammatical. It is acceptable for less formal writing, but the language in your essays should be more "correct":

> Students can be more comfortable taking on-line courses. They can work in a homey atmosphere, at ease in their favourite chair. And they don't have to get dressed up. And they can even work in their pyjamas. So they can enjoy the course more.

> Students can be more comfortable taking on-line courses. They can work in a homey atmosphere, at ease in their favourite chair. In addition, they don't have to get dressed up and can even work in their pyjamas. Therefore, they can enjoy the course more. [preferable for academic writing]

Exercise 3.13

Make the two sentences into one, using co-ordinate conjunctions and eliminating unnecessary words:

1. Peter had to get the transmission fixed. He had to get the brakes fixed.

2. Zach thought he passed his driver's test. He had to book another one.

3. Kate plays the piano. She plays the guitar.

4. My uncle was killed in a motorcycle accident. My mother won't allow me to get a motorcycle.

5. Erin's brother is an engineer. Erin's brother-in-law is an engineer.

6. Melissa could go to the University of Calgary. Melissa could go the University of Alberta.

7. Ben thought he had a job on the oil rig. The job fell through.

8. We thought of holding my parents' anniversary party on a dinner cruise boat. We thought of holding my parents' anniversary party in the revolving restaurant.

9. Christine was supposed to pick Jim up at the train station. She forgot.

10. Suji couldn't understand the formula. She read the chapter again.

Parallel structure

When using co-ordinate conjunctions, you must ensure that each sentence part that you join has essentially the same grammatical structure. This is called parallel structure.

Martha likes dancing and to sing. [not parallel—gerund *dancing* linked with infinitive *to sing*]

Martha likes dancing and singing. [parallel]

Martha likes to dance and sing. [parallel]

Martha likes to dance but hates to swim. [parallel]

Martha likes to dance, but Dimitry prefers to sit on the side. [parallel]

The structures being joined can be single words, phrases, or full clauses. Sometimes the structures are in a series of elements. Again, the joined elements must have the same basic grammatical structure:

On their vacation trip, they wanted to sit on a beach, eat great food, and they hoped to visit family. [not parallel]

On their vacation trip, they wanted to sit on a beach, eat great food, and visit family. [parallel]

Ensuring parallelism can be difficult. You have to figure out what parts of the sentence are being linked. You can put them in a list to see if everything has the same structure and fits the sentence:

When Eli lost his keys, he looked | under the desk,
 | beside the filing cabinet,
and | checked under the sofa
 | cushions

before he finally found them in his coat pocket. [not parallel]

When you line up the elements and check them with the head of the phrase, you can see that "he looked under the bed" and "he looked beside the filing cabinet" are both grammatical, whereas "he looked checked under the sofa cushions" does not work.

When Eli lost his keys, he looked | under the desk,
 | beside the filing cabinet,
and | under the sofa cushions

before he finally found them in his coat pocket. [parallel with three prepositional phrases]

Parallel structure is especially important in thesis statements where three elements are often linked to show the three ideas explored in the body paragraphs. You can practise parallel structure with thesis statements in unit 5.

Exercise 3.14

For each list, choose which item is not parallel:

Example: washing dishes
  setting the table
  to pour the drinks [not parallel]

1. a good plot
   interesting characters
   kept the audience's attention
   exciting special effects

2. worried
   in a bad mood
   tired
   frustrated
   hungry

3. strolling through the park
   running around the track
   rollerblading down the path
   walk around the block

4. made some appetizers
   put the beer in the fridge
   set the table
   tidy the living room

5. tour the Parliament buildings
   the bike paths around the city
   visit the National Gallery
   shop in the Byward Market

Exercise 3.15

Fill in the blank with a phrase that will fit the sentence and have parallel structure:

1. Marie topped the pizza with tomatoes, sausage, _____, and onions.

2. I was born in Edmonton, raised in Vancouver, and later _____.

3. College students can be high school graduates, mature students, and _____.

4. Her presentation was clear, concise, and _____.

5. To be successful, college students should attend class, manage their time, and _____.

Exercise 3.16

Correct errors in parallel structure:

1. Before the snow falls, we have to rake the leaves, plants some bulbs, and the mulch has to be spread.

2. At the cottage, Martin spends time on the lake canoeing, in his sailboat, and waterskiing.

3. An ideal job would have good financial compensation, a good work environment, and the co-workers have to be friendly.

4. For the make-over, her hair was coloured, cut, and a straightener was used.

5. The movie was R-rated because of excessive violence, the characters swore a lot, and nudity.

Writing Noun Clauses

Clauses are parts of complex sentences and have both a noun and a verb. Noun clauses can function as both subjects and objects:

> His behaviour was inexcusable. [noun subject]

> What he did was inexcusable. [noun clause subject]

> I understood his apology. [noun object]

> I understood that he was sorry. [noun clause object]

Words that may begin noun clauses:

> that, if, whether, when, where, what, why, how, who, whom, which, whose

Here are some examples of noun clauses:

> She asked <u>whether I could come</u>.
>
> They wondered <u>if it would rain</u>.
>
> The school accepts <u>whoever wants to attend</u>.
>
> I don't understand <u>how they fixed it</u>.
>
> <u>Who will win the race</u> is a mystery.

Many noun clauses begin with *that* (never *which*), but if the clause comes after the verb, the *that* can be eliminated if the sentence is clear without it:

> She realized [that] he was late.

Noun clauses that function as subjects should be relatively short. English doesn't like top-heavy sentences requiring the reader to wait for a long time to come to the verb because these sentences are more difficult to understand. They can be revised by using an *it* phrase:

> That we could still negotiate a fair deal after so many false starts is amazing. [awkward but grammatical]
>
> It is amazing that we could still negotiate a fair deal after so many false starts. [better]

Exercise 3.17

Construct a sentence with a noun clause to express the two ideas in one sentence, changing the wording where necessary:

Example: He was late. It was surprising.

> It was surprising that he was late. OR That he was late was surprising.

1. I was upset. The trip to Europe was cancelled just when my parents agreed to fund the trip.
2. Juan made so much progress in his English skills. His tutor was pleased.
3. The students were relieved. The assignment due date was extended.
4. She broke the world record in high jump. It was astonishing.
5. He came second in the class. It was a big surprise to her.

Exercise 3.18

Complete the noun clause to fit the blank:

1. She asked whether _____.

2. That _____ was disappointing.

3. How _____ was Jane's main concern.

4. He didn't understand why _____.

5. Whoever _____ is fine with me.

Writing Adjective Clauses

A clause is, in effect, another sentence added into a sentence since it has both a subject and a verb. Adjective clauses, also called relative clauses, describe a noun and are introduced by relative pronouns (*who, whom, what, when, which, why, that*):

> The woman who led that protest march is Jamie's cousin.

> The reason that I am so tired is that I stayed up all night finishing that essay.

> The cottage road, which is not paved, is impassable in the winter.

> The DVD that he ordered is not available anymore.

Adding clauses to sentences is a good way to give extra information to a sentence without changing its main idea or focus. For example, if you want to identify someone but you do not want that identification to be the main idea of the sentence, you can use an adjective clause:

> My friend Liz, who went to Europe with me, is travelling to New Zealand this summer.

As in noun clauses, the *that* is sometimes eliminated if the meaning is clear:

> The reason [that] I am so tired is that I stayed up all night finishing that essay.

> The DVD [that] he ordered is not available anymore.

The relative pronoun *whom* is the correct form when the pronoun refers to the object of the verb or of the preposition. However, it is dying out in English usage. In conversation and informal writing it is almost never used, but it is more common in academic writing:

> The woman whom I met last week is a set designer.

> The woman who I met last week is a set designer. [commonly heard but not acceptable in academic English]

Punctuation is important in sentences that contain adjective clauses. Commas around the clause signal that the information is extra, that taking out the clause will not affect the meaning of the sentence. If there are no commas, the clause is essential to the meaning because it restricts who or what is being spoken about. In grammar terms, the first case is called a non-restrictive or non-defining adjective clause, while the latter case is a restrictive or defining adjective clause:

> The Class 2B students, who failed the test, have to attend a tutorial. [non-restrictive clause showing that all the students in Class 2B failed]

> The Class 2B students who failed the test have to attend a tutorial. [restrictive clause—only some of the students in Class 2B failed]

Exercise 3.19

Identify the relative clauses in the following sentences:

1. The students who were in the joint program have to sign up for some extra projects.

2. The students who are in the joint program have to sign up for the class Prof. Harris teaches.

3. Janice, whom I taught last year, is planning to be a teacher herself.

4. The company where she worked part-time in high school offered her a scholarship for college.

5. The pumpkin pie I baked won first prize, but my apple pie was such a disaster that I didn't even enter it.

Exercise 3.20

Combine the following sentences using relative clauses. Change the word order as necessary:

Example: We got married in the church. The church is being torn down.

The church where we got married is being torn down.

OR   The church that is being torn down is the place where we were married.

1. I worked at the company part-time as a student. The company offered me a full-time position when I graduated.

2. The students forgot to do their assignment. The students had to stay after class.

3. The singers were trained in Europe. The singers were most familiar with classical tradition.

4. The professor wrote the textbook for the course. The textbook is very expensive.

5. We are meeting at a restaurant. The restaurant is on campus, next to the biology building.

6. Children come to the community pool to learn to swim. Their ages range from seven to 12.

7. Some people keep exotic pets such as tarantulas, rattlesnakes, and piranhas. These people want to be different and prefer to live dangerously.

8. Wendy likes bargains. She is on a tight budget. She goes to used book stores and thrift shops.

9. In winter, bad weather can make driving extremely dangerous. Bad weather includes snowstorms, whiteouts, freezing rain, and hail.

10. Digital television is replacing the old-fashioned analog medium. Digital is characterized by clearer picture quality.

Writing Adverb Clauses

Adverb clauses (often called subordinate clauses) modify whole sentences and, like adverbs, tell when, where, why, or how something was done. They are introduced by subordinate conjunctions:

He studied hard for the test. He didn't get a passing grade.

<u>Although</u> he studied for the test, he didn't get a passing grade.

> Marie was late for the interview. The car broke down.
>
> Marie was late for the interview <u>because</u> the car broke down.

The adverb clause that begins with the conjunction is also called a subordinate or dependent clause, and the other half of the sentence is the main or independent clause. The clause is dependent because it cannot stand on its own; it depends on the main clause to make a complete sentence:

> Although he studied for the test. [incomplete sentence]
> He didn't get a passing grade. [complete]
>
> Because the car broke down. [incomplete sentence]
> Marie was late for the interview. [complete]

Here are the main subordinate conjunctions:

> after, although, as, because, before, even though, if, since, unless, until, when, where, whereas, whether, while

For most sentences, the subordinate clause can come either before or after the main clause:

> <u>If</u> you remove the cover first, it is easier to access the parts.
>
> It is easier to access the different parts <u>if</u> you remove the cover first.

Note the punctuation. In the two sentences above, a comma separates the two clauses in the first one. The reader needs to know when one clause ends and the other begins. If the subordinate clause is second, the subordinate conjunction tells the reader that a new clause is starting, so the comma is unnecessary. Note also that there is no comma after the conjunction:

> Although, he was tired of hearing her complaints, he finished the job. [incorrect]

Often you have a choice whether to use a co-ordinate or subordinate conjunction. Some express the same meanings:

> <u>Although</u> Takeshi hates playing golf, he never misses the company golf day.
>
> Takeshi hates playing golf, <u>but</u> he never misses the company golf day.

(Note, however, that English does not allow both these conjunctions at the same time. "<u>Although</u> Takeshi hates playing golf, <u>but</u> he never misses the company golf day" is incorrect.)

A sentence with a co-ordinate conjunction is considered a compound sentence; both clauses have the same weight. A sentence constructed with a subordinate conjunction is considered a complex sentence. It allows you to express different levels of meaning. What is expressed in the subordinate clause is the less important (subordinate) idea; the main idea is in the main clause. For example, in an essay supporting school uniforms, you could say:

> Although school uniforms are often hideous, it is comforting to know that everyone is dressed the same and your style can't be found wanting.

The writer is acknowledging the lack of fashion in uniforms but is stressing the positive side (the idea that is in the main clause). If the sentence was flipped, it could be used in an essay discussing the disadvantages of uniforms:

> Although it can be comforting to know that everyone is dressed the same, it must be acknowledged that school uniforms are truly hideous.

This technique is discussed in "Conceding a point", page 204.

You can write a sentence with more than one subordinate clause, as long as you have a main clause to make it a grammatical sentence. But do not overload your sentence:

> While he was waiting for the train, wondering if it would ever come, he looked through a magazine because he was very bored, but even though the articles were interesting, he could not concentrate on the information given, as his thoughts kept coming back to the mistakes he had made in the job interview.

Note the differences between *although* and *even though*. They have the same basic meaning, but *even though* is stronger, showing a contrast that is surprising:

> Although he had done his training, he could not complete the marathon.

> Even though he had trained hard for months, he could not complete the marathon.

Remember that *even though* is always two words. And the word *though* by itself is conversational style and not suited to essay writing.

Conjunctive adverbs (also called adverbial connectives) such as *however*, *therefore*, and *nevertheless* are often confused for subordinate conjunctions:

> He couldn't figure out how to install the sink, therefore he finally read the instructions. [incorrect]

> He couldn't figure out how to install the sink, so he finally read the instructions.

> Because he couldn't figure out how to install the sink, he finally read the instructions.

> He couldn't figure out how to install the sink; therefore, he finally read the instructions.

A conjunction can join two sentences together, while a conjunctive adverb is primarily an adverb. To join two sentences with a conjunctive adverb, you need to add something that will make the connection grammatical, such as a semi-colon.

Conjunctive adverbs generally function as transition signals (listed on page 140). It is relatively easy to distinguish adverbs from conjunctions—an adverb can appear in different places in the sentence; a conjunction cannot:

> Gillian wanted to buy a modern house in the suburbs; <u>however</u>, Roy preferred an old fixer-upper downtown.

> Gillian wanted to buy a modern house in the suburbs. Roy, <u>however</u>, preferred an old fixer-upper downtown.

> Gillian wanted to buy a modern house in the suburbs. Roy preferred an old fixer-upper downtown, <u>however</u>.

> <u>While</u> Gillian wanted to buy a modern house in the suburbs, Roy preferred an old fixer-upper downtown.

> Gillian wanted to buy a modern house in the suburbs <u>while</u> Roy preferred an old fixer-upper downtown.

Notice that the subordinate conjunction *while* can only appear at the beginning of a subordinate clause, but the adverbial *however* can appear at the beginning, in the middle, or at the end of a sentence.

Exercise 3.21

Join the following pairs of sentences with a subordinate conjunction:

Example: I tried to install the wireless router. My system crashed.

> When I tried to install the wireless router, my system crashed.

1. Tim Horton had a hand in starting the business that bears his name. Laura Secord had nothing to do with the candy-making business.

2. The candy store was named after Laura Secord. The founder wanted a Canadian heroine as a trademark.

3. The Canadian flag is such a recognized symbol today. It did not have an easy road to design and official acceptance in 1965.

4. The first explorers came to Canada seeking a route to the Orient. They came back for the valuable fish and furs.

5. British Columbia agreed to join Canada. A railroad would be built to connect it with the eastern provinces.

6. The Canadian Pacific Railway took many years to complete. It was so difficult to build through the rock of the Canadian Shield in Central Canada and the mountain ranges in British Columbia.

7. The United Empire Loyalists came north to Canada after the American Revolution. They wanted to remain British subjects.

8. Lacrosse is one of Canada's national sports. It is not very popular, especially when compared to hockey.

9. Tommy Douglas became a member of Parliament. He wanted to introduce the same reforms to Canada that he brought to Saskatchewan.

10. The Acadians were expelled from Nova Scotia. They settled in Louisiana.

Using Participles and Gerunds

A verb that ends in *–ing* can be many things. It may be part of a verb in one of the continuous tenses:

> Jamie was skating with David when she fell.

> Amanda is learning to skate.

It may be a gerund, a verbal that functions as a noun. In a sentence, a gerund can be both a subject and an object:

> Wishing is not enough.

> He hates waiting.

These gerunds can be completed by objects and modifiers:

> Seeing the whales up close was an amazing experience.

> Running up the stairs is good exercise.

> She enjoys walking alone.

Verbals that end in *–ing* can also be participles, which function as adjectives:

> Running water does not freeze readily.

> The boys running around the room are my nephews.

The *–ing* form is in the active voice, while the *–ed* participles are used to express the passive:

> Some politicians would like to see an elected Senate.

> I love freshly baked bread.

Gerund phrases should not be confused with participial phrases. Both gerunds and participles end in *–ing*, but gerunds act as nouns while participles act as adjectives:

> The woman watching the dancers is a talent scout. [participle describing the woman]

> Watching the dancers is a good way to learn the choreography. [gerund phrase as grammatical subject]

Another tricky part of understanding and using gerunds is distinguishing the verbs that take gerunds and those that take infinitives (the *to* form of the verb):

> I enjoy walking in the park.

> I want to walk in the park.

See page 225 for a list of such verbs and exercises.

A common mistake that students make when they try to use a gerund phrase as a subject is that they add a preposition:

> By working all night is a bad way to write an essay. [incorrect]

> Working all night is a bad way to write an essay. [correct]

> By working all night, she finished the essay. [correct—the *by* phrase is not the grammatical subject]

Exercise 3.22

Here are some *–ing* phrases that could be used as gerund phrases or participle phrases. Write two sentences for each—one using the phrase as a gerund and one as a participle:

Example: running around the track

> I love running around the track. [gerund]

> Running around the track, I am often joined by a friendly dog. [participle]

1. sleeping in the corner
2. skating around the rink
3. driving down the street
4. dancing every day
5. reading novels
6. confronting a burglar
7. talking on a cellphone
8. watching DVDs
9. shopping for shoes
10. cheating at poker

Reducing Clauses to Phrases

When two clauses have the same subject, one clause can sometimes be reduced to make a phrase:

> Gillian, who is the former president of the club, stayed on to help her successor deal with the firings.

> Gillian, the former president of the club, stayed on to help her successor deal with the firings.

> While they were going over the lesson, the students discovered a new problem.
>
> While going over the lesson, the students discovered a new problem.
>
> Going over the lesson, the students discovered a new problem.

If the clauses have different subjects, this type of reduction cannot be made:

> While the students were listening to the lecture, the lights went out.
>
> While listening to the lecture, the lights went out. [incorrect]

In these examples, note the changes:

> We ordered the meal for the group before we went to the restaurant.
>
> We ordered the meal for the group before going to the restaurant.
>
> The movie was sold out although it got bad reviews.
>
> The movie was sold out, despite having got bad reviews.

Exercise 3.23

In the following sentences, reduce the underlined clauses to phrases where possible:

1. When he was touring the house, Marc noticed that it needed a lot of work.

2. The house, which was located in a prime downtown area, had large rooms and original wood panelling that needed to be stripped.

3. The powder room, which was tucked under the stairway, had pink tiles and 1970s fixtures.

4. Because he had worked for his father's construction company, he had the skills to do most of the work himself.

5. He particularly liked the stained glass, which was almost 100 years old.

6. Elena, who was Marc's wife, was reluctant to take on the project because she didn't want to live in a construction zone for years.

Exercise 3.23 – *continued*

7. <u>Although she was handy with power tools and a paint brush,</u> she preferred a place that required less work.

8. <u>Because they both had demanding jobs,</u> she wanted to have relaxing weekends, not more work.

9. <u>If they did the work themselves,</u> they could afford to live downtown.

10. <u>After they weighed all the pros and cons,</u> they put in an offer on the house.

Combining Sentences

When you use a co-ordinate conjunction, you create a compound sentence. When you use other clauses, you create a complex sentence. Sentences without clauses are called simple sentences. Simple sentences are more common in spoken English. In your writing, it is important to have a variety of sentence structures. It makes your writing more interesting to read and improves the flow of ideas. It lets you add information to a sentence without losing the focus of the main clause. It also makes your writing more sophisticated at the higher level more suited to college and university work. A paragraph that contains only simple sentences sounds simplistic.

A clause is, in effect, another sentence added to a sentence. Clauses are different from phrases because they have the structure of a full grammatical sentence with a noun and a verb:

> <u>Because he wanted to revise the whole paper,</u> he threw out his drafts. [clause]
>
> The student <u>who foolishly threw out his drafts</u> wanted to revise the whole paper. [clause]
>
> <u>Wanting to revise the whole paper,</u> he foolishly threw out his drafts. [phrase]

Noun clauses work as subjects and objects, adjective clauses describe nouns, and adverb clauses use subordinate clauses such as *although* and *because*.

Exercise 3.24

Use phrases and clauses to write one or two concise sentences incorporating the ideas in the groups of sentences below:

Example: The five-dollar bill celebrates children at play.
There are different pictures of winter sport on the reverse side.
Children are shown playing hockey.
A child learning to skate is also depicted.
There is a picture of a toboggan.
There is a quotation from "The hockey sweater."
"The hockey sweater" is a famous short story.
"The hockey sweater" was written by Roch Carrier.

The five-dollar bill celebrates winter sport, with pictures of hockey, skating, and tobogganing and a quotation from "The hockey sweater", a famous short story by Roch Carrier.

1. Queen Victoria chose Ottawa to be the capital of Canada.
   She made the decision in 1857.
   In 1857 Ottawa was known as Bytown.
   Bytown was a small lumber town.
   Bytown's location was advantageous.
   It was farther from the American border.
   The other towns considered were all close to the border.
   It was on the border between French and English Canada.
   Bytown also had a picturesque bluff.
   The bluff was a good location for the Parliament Buildings.

2. The Hudson's Bay Company is Canada's oldest corporation.
   It started in 1670.
   It started with a land grant from King Charles II.
   The king's cousin was Prince Rupert.
   Prince Rupert and his associates started the corporation.
   The corporation controlled the fur trade in the area around Hudson Bay.
   The area of the land grant was the drainage area of rivers flowing into Hudson Bay
   This land grant gave the corporation control of 40 per cent of the current area of Canada.

3. In the 1930s, the most famous Canadian was Grey Owl.
   He is considered Canada's first conservationist.
   He wrote books and lectured about saving the wilderness and the beaver.
   He died in 1938.
   After his death, newspapers told his real story.

Exercise 3.24 – *continued*

He said he was an Indian.
He was actually an Englishman named Archie Belaney.
Belaney came to Canada as a teenager.
He was in love with the idea of living in the wilderness.
He dyed his hair.
He darkened his skin.
He made up stories about his past.

4. The Confederation Bridge was opened in May 1997.
   It stretches from New Brunswick to Prince Edward Island.
   It is often referred to as the "fixed link."
   It is 12.9 km long.
   It is the longest bridge over ice-covered salt water.
   It carries two lanes of traffic.
   Travellers pay a toll on leaving Prince Edward Island.
   They can go by the bridge or by ferry.

5. The Dionne Quints were five identical twin girls.
   The Dionne Quints were born in 1934.
   1934 was in the midst of the Great Depression.
   They were born in Corbeil, Ontario.
   Their parents were poor French-Canadian farmers.
   Their birth and survival was considered a miracle.
   The Ontario government took the girls away from their parents.
   They were installed in a special hospital.
   People could come and see the girls in "Quintland."
   They were the country's biggest tourist attraction.

6. The building of the transcontinental railway led to the creation of
   Canada.
   British Columbia would only join the confederation if a railway were
   built.
   The railway was promised in the 1860s
   The railway was completed in 1885.
   It was difficult to build.
   There were many political battles.
   It was very expensive.
   The areas in the Canadian Shield and the Rocky Mountains were
   particularly difficult.

7. Marilyn Bell was the first person to swim across Lake Ontario.
   She was 16 years old.
   An American swimmer was offered $10,000 to swim across
   Lake Ontario.

Exercise 3.24 – *continued*

Bell was asked to compete against her by a rival newspaper.
Bell was not offered any prize beforehand.
It took her 21 hours.
She had to fight high waves, eels, and oil spills.

8. Nunavut is a new territory.
It was created in 1999.
It was originally part of the Northwest Territories.
Its population is about 28,000.
Its population is 85 per cent Inuit.
The Inuit language is Inuktitut.
Inuktitut is one of the official languages of Nunavut.

Recognizing Fragments and Run-on Sentences

Remember that a sentence must have a subject and a verb. A sentence fragment is an incomplete sentence:

Going whale-watching off Vancouver Island.

When I dug for dinosaur fossils in Drumheller.

The actor who was chosen for the lead role.

The small red brick house down the street.

To fix a sentence fragment, you need to find out what is missing and supply it:

Going whale-watching off Vancouver Island was an incredible experience.

When I dug for dinosaur fossils in Drumheller, I relived my childhood dream of being an paleontologist.

The actor who was chosen for the lead role had to leave the production.

The small red brick house down the street is for sale.

A run-on sentence, on the other hand, is essentially too much sentence:

> The models walked the runway they showed the clothes.

One kind of run-on sentence is a comma splice, in which a comma incorrectly divides the sentences:

> Polar bears live in the Arctic, they need the ice to live on.

Sometimes sentences can be considered run-on if they contain too many clauses—even though they are grammatical:

> When the waitress took the order, which was difficult to do because of the noise of the hockey game, which was the final game of the season, so the hockey fans were out in full force and full voice, she misunderstood the customers' orders, and the kitchen prepared the wrong food, so the customers were angry and complained to the manager, who blamed the kitchen staff, but the waitress admitted she could not hear the order very well, so new meals were prepared on the house.

There are essentially three ways to fix run-on sentences: make two sentences, use a semi-colon, or add a conjunction:

> The play had sold out its run was extended. [incorrect]

> The play had sold out, its run was extended. [incorrect, comma splice]

> The play had sold out. Its run was extended. [correct, two separate sentences]

> The play had sold out; its run was extended. [correct, semi-colon]

> The play had sold out, <u>so</u> its run was extended. [correct, co-ordinate conjunction]

> <u>Because</u> the play had sold out, its run was extended. [correct, subordinate conjunction]

Exercise 3.25

Decide whether the following sentences are fragments, run-ons, or correct sentences. Fix the fragments and run-ons:

1. Watching a soccer game on Sunday afternoon.

2. The goalkeeper came out to handle the ball the attacker managed to get a kick in to score a goal.

3. They managed another goal on a penalty kick, however the game was already lost.

4. Although they had been division champions. They could not get past the powerhouse teams.

5. I like to watch the children play soccer. Because they all travel in a bunch following the ball.

6. She has become addicted to reality shows on television, she especially likes the ones where she can vote on who is the most talented.

7. Eating snacks in front of the television set and not exercising.

8. My children love to watch nature documentaries, which are a lot better than a steady diet of cartoons and music videos.

8. Infomercials, usually shown after one o'clock in the morning, advertising a useless array of products.

10. Those infomercials, however, attract a large number of customers who cannot resist the sales pitch.

Using Punctuation and Capitalization

Punctuation is an important part of sentence structure. Readers rely on capital letters and end punctuation to tell them where sentences begin and end. Commas show the different parts of a sentence. Because sentences in academic English are more complex, the punctuation is crucial to the reader's ability to follow the sentence.

End punctuation

The end of a sentence is marked by a period, question mark, or exclamation mark. In essay writing, almost all of your sentences will end with a period. You should have very few questions and no exclamations at all.

Sentences should not end with three dots (an ellipsis mark). It gives the impression that the writer is not committed to the sentence and is just trailing off. (Ellipsis marks are properly used in academic writing in quotations to show that some words have been left out.)

Periods are also used with some abbreviations, such as shortened words (Prof. for Professor) and university degrees (M.B.A.). Initialisms (abbreviations formed from the first letter of words, such as ESL for English as a second language) and acronyms (like initialisms but pronounced as words, such as AIDS for acquired immune deficiency syndrome) rarely have periods between the letters. Check your dictionary if you are unsure of the usage.

Space

Leaving space is a part of writing properly. It contributes to the readability of the document. A text that is too jammed with words is harder to read. Your résumé, for example, should have enough white space to make it attractive and readable.

There should be no space between the end of the word and the punctuation. A comma, for example, should never appear at the beginning of the next line, no matter how squished your words are at the end of the line.

In the old days of typewriters, typists were taught to leave two spaces at the end of a sentence. This is no longer the convention since people use computers and proportional fonts; one space is sufficient.

Space is also important to show the beginning and end of paragraphs. Generally, paragraphs are indented with five spaces, or a half-inch tab space. Block-style paragraphing uses no indent but rather a blank line between paragraphs. Readers should be able to easily see where a new paragraph starts.

Proper margins are important for all your documents—leave an inch on each side. Use left justification with a ragged right margin so that you will not have gaps in your lines of text or have to deal with hyphenation. Double space assignments so that your instructor has room for corrections and comments.

Commas

Commas are placed in sentences, mainly to separate different parts of the sentence. Commas generally appear:

- after initial adverbs: Thankfully, we hailed the rescue team.

- between items in a list: We ate roast beef, mashed potatoes, green peas, and corn. OR We ate roast beef, mashed potatoes, green peas and corn.

- after adverb clauses: Because it was raining, we cancelled the picnic.

- before clauses introduced by co-ordinate conjunctions: I took a nap, and then we left.

- before and after modifying phrases or clauses: John, who is this year's president, gave a welcome speech.

The second example in the list above shows the optional use of a serial comma, a comma before the *and* in a list of several items (discussed on page 89).

Commas appear in lists of adjectives where the two adjectives have a similar function and could be replaced with an *and*:

> She told a strange, sad story about a beautiful Mexican dancer.

A missing comma can change the whole sentence:

> Students come to class to learn not to have fun.

> Students come to class to learn, not to have fun.

Commas are often inappropriately placed at breath stops in a sentence, such as between a subject and a verb, especially if the subject is long and complex. Other common comma errors include putting commas after *although* and *such as*.

Exercise 3.26

Insert periods, commas, and capital letters where needed in the following paragraph:

> cleaning out my grandmother's cluttered musty old house after she died was a monumental task like many old people who had lived through unspeakable war and famine she was an incurable hoarder she kept old newspapers plastic bags and cardboard boxes she didn't trash out-of-date calendars she just tacked up a new one in a different spot on the wall we found new clothes that had been saved for a special occasion and never used her husband's clothes still hung in the closet even though he had passed away a dozen years earlier in the cold cellar were jars of pickled food that must have been 20 years old two full-size freezers were crammed with food some of the packages were many years old she felt safe with all her possessions and never wanted to let anything go

Apostrophes

There seems to be an epidemic of apostrophe overuse and misuse today, not only in students' writing but also on printed signs and even in some published works. Some people incorrectly bestow apostrophes on words ending in *s* and between *nt* letter combinations. As a result, we see miswritten words such as "chair's" and even "he wan't's."

Misplaced apostrophes can cause readers to be confused as well as annoyed as the meaning of the apostrophe is lost:

> The drill sergeant called the recruits names. [he called them names, mocking them]

> The drill sergeant called the recruits' names. [he called their names out]

> Were in trouble now. [should be "We're in trouble now."]

Essentially, apostrophes are used for contractions and possessive forms.

A contraction is a shortened form of words, such as *he isn't* for *he is not*. An apostrophe takes the place of dropped letters in a contraction. For example, in verbs contracted with *not*, the apostrophe replaces the *o* (*isn't*, *doesn't*, *can't*). The auxiliary verbs *be*, *have*, and *will* are sometimes contracted: *I'm going*, *they've noticed*, *she'll see*, *I could've done it*. Apostrophes can also show dropped numbers as in "The radio station played hits from the '70s." They are **not** used in non-contracted verbs (*she tries*, *he listens*). Do not confuse the verb form *lets* ("he lets me take the car") with the contracted form *let's* (*let us*, as in "let's go").

Possessives are words that show that something belongs to something else (e.g., *Jim's car*, *the students' pet rabbit*). The possession can be a loose relationship, as in such phrases as *a day's work* or *a summer's day*. If you have trouble distinguishing possessive forms, see the section "Showing possession" in this unit (page 81).

Apostrophes are **not** used before most plurals (*many ways*, *two different techniques*). The few exceptions are plurals when an *–s* alone would be confusing:

> He got all A's and B's on his report card.

> She dots her i's with circles.

Sometimes you might see apostrophes used in plurals of shortened words (e.g., *reno's* for *renovations*) and of number and letter combinations, but these are unnecessary:

> He ordered CDs of hits from the 1960s and 1970s.

> They booked two limos for transportation to the prom.

Exercise 3.27

Insert apostrophes where needed in the following sentences:

1. Susans brother has been living in his grandfathers house to help take care of him. Hes missed some classes but hes planning to make them up with night classes. The universitys on-line program lets him follow many different options.

2. Lets go to the Johnsons cottage this weekend. Weve had an open invitation for ages. Ill just give them a call to see if its okay. Itll be good to get away, and if we dont go now, who knows when well be able to get away?

3. James always listens to his teachers instructions because he knows how important following instructions is to getting good marks.

4. Unlike his siblings, hes willing to take over his fathers business selling antiques.

5. The students work needed to be completely redone. I dont know why there were so many mistakes.

Colons

Colons (:) are used to show illustration of an idea. They can be used to introduce a sentence or a list. They should not be used after *are* or *such as* because those words are not at the end of the sentence:

> The pizza dough requires few ingredients: flour, water, sugar, salt, oil, and yeast.

> My favourite sports are: soccer, swimming, and squash. [incorrect—colon is unnecessary]

> There was only one thing left to do: He had to contact his friend's parents to let them know what happened. [correct; the capital on *he* is optional]

Semi-colons

Semi-colons (;) are used between two related sentences and to distinguish items in a complex list where commas are needed:

> The soccer game was exciting to watch; the teams had each been previous champions.

> Dave was the strongest member of the team; however, he was let go because he could not get along with anyone.

> Canadian coins show a number of national symbols: the maple leaves on the penny; the beaver, the animal that brought many Europeans to Canada, on the nickel; the dime's *Bluenose*, a famous racing schooner from Nova Scotia; the caribou on the quarter; the loon on the dollar coin; and the polar bear on the two-dollar coin.

Quotation marks

Quotation marks ("..." or '...') are used to show that you are using someone's exact words:

> Jo Pavlov shows how hard it is for her to admit her failing when she says, "I can't believe I just typed that. I can't believe I'm saying these things out loud. My dirty secret shame."
> (page 269)

For a quote appearing within a quote, you should use quotation marks different from the ones you used for the main quote (e.g., double quotation marks instead of single):

> Sidney Katz shows the racial taunts Rocket Richard endured when he says, "Inspector William Minogue, who, as police officer in charge of the Forum, frequently hears opposing players calling Richard 'French pea soup' or 'dirty French bastard' as they skate past." (page 306)

Quotation marks are also used around the titles of short stories and articles, while the titles of the books or newspapers are printed in italics. For example, "Helpless" was one of Karen von Hahn's columns in *The Globe and Mail*; it is reprinted in *Skill set*. (In some citation styles, underlining is used instead of italics; underlining and italics are considered equivalent.)

Hyphens and dashes

A hyphen is used within a word (such as *co-author* and *self-discipline*), while a dash is used between words in a sentence. Some words have two accepted spellings—with a hyphen and without. Sometimes the word loses the hyphen over time. For instance, the word *e-mail* is now often written *email*. Check your dictionary if you are not sure of the spelling.

If a word cannot fit on a line, a hyphen is used to break the word into two parts. The hyphen must appear between syllables (syllable breaks are shown in dictionaries). You will see this use of the hyphen in publications because the text is written with full justification (both the right and left margins form straight lines). If words were not split, there would be annoying white spaces in the lines. You can avoid this use of the hyphen by simply writing the whole word on the next line. Use only left justification with a ragged right margin in your writing.

A parenthetical dash is used to set words off from the rest of the sentence. These words can be extra information or a comment. The same function can often be met by parentheses (round brackets) or commas, which can set off a clause or phrase that is not part of the main idea—but the dash gives more emphasis. Notice the usage of each in this section.

A parenthetical dash is also called an "em dash" (because of typesetting—it is the same width as the letter *M*). There should be no space before or after the dash.

While a hyphen can be found on a standard keyboard, dashes are not. Word processing programs can be set up to replace two typed hyphens with a long dash. Otherwise, it is a symbol that can be inserted, along with the "en dash." The en dash is used with numbers such as dates (e.g., 1947–63) and is the width of the letter *N*, thus not as wide as the em dash.

Capitalization

Capital letters appear at the beginning of sentences and on proper nouns (official names):

> Maria is planning a trip to Saskatoon to visit her grandmother.

> Actually, Mr Burton earned his M.B.A. at the Haskayne School of Business at the University of Calgary.

The names of school subjects are capitalized if they are official titles but not if they are general subject names:

> I'd like to take another biology course. Here's an interesting one—BIOL 130, Introductory Cell Biology.

The capital letter has been dropping from such common phrases as "French fries," but properly they should have a capital.

The use of capitals in the titles of books or articles mentioned in a text depends on the style used. In MLA style, for example, the title of this book would be written *Skill Set*, and Sidney Katz's article (page 304) would be "The Strange Forces behind the Richard Hockey Riot," with the first and all other words capitalized (except prepositions and articles). In APA and Oxford style, the titles would be *Skill set* and "The strange forces behind the Richard hockey riot," with only the first word and any proper nouns capitalized.

Exercise 3.28

Capitalize the words that need capital letters in the following sentences:

1. jillian decided to take a psychology course from the continuing education department.

2. do you want to order chinese food or pizza? I have a coupon from marco's pizza.

Exercise 3.28 – *continued*

3. sir john a. macdonald was canada's first prime minister. his picture is on the ten dollar bill.

4. john mccrae wrote the poem "in flanders fields", which is on the back of the bill.

5. remembrance day honours canada's war dead. a minute of silence commemorates the end of world war I at 11 a.m. on november 11.

Exercise 3.29

Add capitalization and punctuation where necessary:

1. mr peterson requested the review of the department because of its poor performance the manager thought it was unnecessary

2. shakespeares play romeo and juliet tells the story of two teenagers in love in sixteenth century italy its a tragic tale because the lovers are from two feuding families

3. i dont know what to buy as a gift for joannes baby shower shes having twin boys

4. if youre worried about fitting the course into your schedule why dont you take it online

5. lets take the train to montreal so we dont have to worry about driving and parking the citys subway system which is called the metro is an efficient way to get around town

6. a man who grew up not having to do housework is less likely to help his wife out around the house

7. to bake a cake you need to assemble the following ingredients butter sugar eggs flour baking powder salt buttermilk baking soda and vanilla

8. i asked him to leave me a copy of the report but he forgot he finally e-mailed it to me and i had to print out a copy

9. we went over every word of the report however we missed several errors so it didnt look very good when we gave it to the supervisor

10. she asked whether i could take over her shift on saturday night i wanted to go to jacks party so i said no

Paragraph Writing Skills

Essay writing is essentially presenting ideas and supporting them. It is argument in the broader sense of the word. Paragraphs are the building blocks of essays—if you can write a good paragraph, you can write a good essay. A paragraph may even stand as a mini-essay on its own as an independent, developed paragraph.

The first criterion for a paragraph is that it clearly looks like one. Students sometimes get sloppy and do not leave proper spacing in their writing, but readers depend on the space to see where each paragraph begins and ends. Usually, a paragraph begins with an indentation and may end in the middle of a line. In publications, the first paragraph after a title or subtitle is not generally indented. In business writing, block style is common: paragraphs are not indented, but a blank line appears between paragraphs. Indenting the beginning of paragraphs is the most common style for student writing. Whichever style is used, it should allow the reader to distinguish the paragraphs easily.

Length is often an issue in writing for school because students are concerned that their writing meets assignment criteria. Modern writing favours shorter paragraphs. Newspapers and magazines have short, undeveloped paragraphs, often just a sentence or two, because the print is in narrow columns and long blocks of unbroken text are difficult to read. Modern novels have a lot of dialogue, and the convention is to start a new paragraph with each new speaker, so there are many short paragraphs. Academic writing, however, favours longer paragraphs, though not as long as in the past. For instance, books written 100 years ago have paragraphs that can go on for more than a page. Because of the influence of television and the Internet, today's readers lack the attention span to digest that much unbroken text. The paragraph length that you are reading now (about 100 to 150 words) is typical of academic, business, and technical writing today. A single-paragraph writing assignment may extend to over 200 words.

Essays, reports, and letters are divided into paragraphs. A paragraph is a unit of meaning, as is a sentence. Each paragraph puts forth an idea and supports it. What is in a paragraph depends on the function it serves. It may introduce or conclude an essay; it may be a definition, description, or comparison. The same criteria for a good paragraph apply no matter what its function.

Most academic-style paragraphs start with a topic sentence, which introduces the main idea and is usually the first sentence. The rest of the paragraph is essentially composed of arguments supporting the idea in the topic sentence, with supporting details supplied to prove those arguments. Remember that the main task of academic writing is to put forth an idea and to support it. Writers must connect the dots for the reader, showing the relationship between the ideas in the sentences.

Independent Paragraphs

Sometimes students are required to write single paragraphs for assignments. These independent paragraphs tend to be longer than the paragraphs that would appear in an essay or report. They may have eight to 12 sentences and range from about 150 to 200 words. They begin with a topic sentence, have perhaps three supported points, and end with a concluding sentence. In essence, they are a shorter version of an essay, and they allow students to practise the basics of making arguments and supporting them before moving on to the complexity of a longer piece of writing.

Here is a typical outline for an independent, developed paragraph:

Topic sentence

    Elaboration of topic sentence (if necessary)

Point 1

    Support (explanation, example, illustration)

Point 2

    Support (explanation, example, illustration)

Point 3

    Support (explanation, example, illustration)

Concluding sentence

This is not the only way to develop a paragraph, but it is one way that will lead you to success and help you to build your essay writing skills.

Here are examples of developed paragraphs following this pattern. The word count is included to show you typical length:

Students should take notes when they are attending lectures or reading. Note-taking is a skill they can develop in their high school years and is especially vital in college and university. First, by the very act of writing, they are engaging in active, not just passive, learning. Research has shown that students retain less if they only listen or read, but by writing and talking about the material, they retain it better because these actions require more of the brain. In addition, note-taking requires students to process the information. Because they cannot write down every word, they have to choose the most important points, paraphrase, and summarize information. Even if the notes are lost, the action of note-taking means that the material is better understood and more firmly fixed in the brain. In addition, college and university classes rely on the lecture to transmit information. The professor might have a different take on the subject than is offered in the textbook and only explain it in class. Finally, students can use the notes they have taken for review for tests and exams. It is easier to reread notes than to reread the whole textbook. Thus, note-taking is a valuable practice for students. [203 words]

Campus residence is a good choice of accommodation for first-year students. First, it can be economical. Apartments and houses often have to be leased for a full year, while students pay for residence only for the months they are in school. They can also save on the cost of transportation and utilities. In addition, living on campus is convenient. Students do not waste time travelling to and from school. The campus facilities are close at hand and are often open long hours and during the weekend. Finally, residence offers students the chance to socialize and learn to live with other students, who may have very different backgrounds. Often long-term friendships develop. Students who meet as floor-mates may decide to share off-campus housing in later school years. Students starting at a new school in a new city can make the campus residence their home away from home. [144 words]

Although undeniably convenient, residence may not be the best choice of accommodation for students. First, it can be expensive. Students sharing a house or an apartment can often find a cheaper place to live. If the students know how to cook, homemade food is also less expensive and more nutritious than eating in the cafeteria with a meal plan. Furthermore, living off campus allows students a chance to escape from school. A residential neighbourhood can offer many different amenities and a chance to interact with non-students. Students can also escape the noise and partying often found in a residence. They can study in peace and quiet away from the escapades of young people revelling in their freedom away from parents. Although students often choose residence for first year, many prefer living off campus once they are established in the new city. [143 words]

Activity 4.1

Analyze the structure of the paragraphs above. Identify the three points and the support for each.

Writing Topic Sentences

In academic writing, the topic sentence gives the main idea of the paragraph. Generally, it appears at the beginning of the paragraph, although it can be in the middle or at the end of a paragraph and may even be implied and not directly stated. A topic sentence should state a supportable idea that can be explored in the body of the paragraph. It makes a claim that should be proved or explored in the rest of the paragraph. All the other sentences in that paragraph should relate to the topic sentence; these sentences are more specific than the topic sentence, which is quite general.

Topic sentences are particularly important in expository paragraphs that argue or explain an idea. They are found in the body paragraphs of the essay but not in the introduction or conclusion. Narrative paragraphs and process descriptions may open with the first event or step, and so they might not have a topic sentence introducing the paragraph. In an essay, the topic sentences of the body paragraphs take their cue from the thesis statement. (See page 168 for practice on this.)

A good topic sentence should tell the reader what to expect in the paragraph. For example, for a paragraph that starts, "Editing is an important step in writing an essay," the reader will expect that the paragraph shows why editing is so important. The topic sentence also limits the paragraph—all the sentences should fit under the umbrella of the topic sentence. This is called unity. For example, 'Students should brainstorm their topic first' would not fit in the paragraph about editing.

A well–written topic sentence serves as a guideline for the writer, so instructors often insist that students start with a topic sentence. Practising writing topic sentences will also help students write better thesis statements for their essays. The main difference between a thesis statement and a topic sentence is that a thesis statement gives the main idea of an essay while a topic sentence introduces just a paragraph.

It is good practice to put the topic sentence first because this structure is the most common and easiest for student writers. The topic sentence should be a supportable idea, not a fact or opinion, and it should state an idea that can be explained in a single paragraph, so it is neither too broad nor too narrow.

A topic sentence should state the main idea, not announce it:

> This paragraph is about the injustice faced by the part-time worker. [announcement]
>
> The part-time worker faces much injustice. [better]

> I will talk about the differences between bus and car travel. [announcement]
>
> Travelling by bus is a different experience from travelling by car. [better]

Because it limits what can be dealt with in one paragraph, a topic sentence should not be too broad:

> Young people face many problems in today's society. [too broad]
>
> Businesses often discriminate against teenagers. [better, more specific]

> Alcohol hurts many people. [too broad]
>
> Fetal alcohol syndrome affects social development. [better]

A topic sentence should not be too narrow:

> Electronic books are not good to take to the beach.
> [too narrow]
>
> Electronic books are less convenient than the paper format. [better]

> Students can improve their mental arithmetic while working a cash register. [narrow]
>
> Students can learn practical skills at their part-time job. [better]

In most academic writing, a topic sentence should be a supportable idea—a judgment made about an idea, not a straight fact:

> Many high school students have part-time jobs. [fact]
>
> Part-time jobs have many benefits for high school students. [better]
>
> Electronic books are read on a computer screen instead of on paper. [fact]
>
> It would be hard to get avid readers to give up paper books for electronic formats. [better]

A topic sentence should have one main idea, not two:

> The key to success in college is attending class and taking notes. [two ideas]
>
> The key to success in college is attending class. [better]
>
> Electronic books are more convenient and cheaper than paper books. [two ideas]
>
> Electronic books are more convenient than paper books. [better]

Avoid using a *because* idea in your topic sentence; it makes your sentence too specific:

> Smoking should be prohibited in restaurants because it creates unhealthy work conditions for servers. [too limited]
>
> Smoking should be prohibited in restaurants. [better]

Do not overload your topic sentence:

> With on-line shopping, you can have the convenience of staying at home, surfing as much as you want among the websites, looking for the item you want, comparing prices, and reading posted reviews. [overloaded]
>
> With on-line shopping, you can have the convenience of staying at home. [better]

Exercise 4.1

For each of the following sentences, state whether it would make a good topic sentence. If it would not, explain why. Is it too narrow, too broad, or a simple fact? Suggest alternatives for the poor topic sentences:

1. A dictionary is a reference tool that gives definitions of words.

2. A dictionary is a useful reference tool for all students.

3. Parents have to ensure that their children grow up to be responsible adults.

4. I will explain how Asian parents run their adult children's lives.

5. A multi-function printer can print, copy, scan, and fax documents.

6. Survival swimming skills should be taught to all students.

7. Public transit consists of buses, trains, subways, and streetcars.

8. Students learning English should read children's fairy tale books.

9. Today's young people don't vote because they are not that interested in following politics.

10. Today, portable music players are small devices with the capacity to hold thousands of songs in digital format.

Exercise 4.2

A good topic sentence can stand on its own; readers can immediately see what the paragraph is about. For example, full noun references should be used. Here are some actual topic sentences from students' paragraph writing assignments. Which ones are unclear? Which ones are good topic sentences?

1. Everything goes well in my life, there are lots of goals in my future.

2. One talent I wish I had is musical ability.

3. It's the computer.

4. The computer is the most important invention of the twentieth century.

5. Information from the Internet always has to be taken with a grain of salt.

6. Today, many kinds of stuff make us more and more smart.

Exercise 4.2 – *continued*

7. Modern politicians must look good on television.

8. The following criteria are important.

9. The advantages of this way are staying at home, you can surf as much as you want among the websites, looking for the item you want, comparing prices, reading advice from the people who already had their experience with it, but at the same time buying something on-line costs you extra for shipping and delivering, and, of course, you have many problems if you are not satisfied with the product and would like to return it.

10. There are some big-box stores in cities nowadays where people can go shopping in different departments for different stuff.

11. Big-box stores are superior to smaller, independent stores because they have better prices.

12. I would like to start off by explaining why this premise is often correct.

13. Yes, a lot of teams get good results because of trash-talking.

14. Trash-talking is an effective strategy in sports.

15. To give in need is to give indeed.

Exercise 4.3

From the following groups of sentences, choose the one that would make an appropriate topic sentence for the other sentences in the group:

1. a) Doing the assigned readings before class is essential for success in university.
    b) If you have not read the assigned reading, the lecture will mean little to you.
    c) When you do the reading at home, you can look up words or concepts you find difficult.
    d) You learn the material more easily through repeated exposure—from both reading and listening.

2. a) Parents give their children an allowance and let them choose how to spend it.
    b) Children are encouraged to try different activities to see where their interests and talents lie.

Exercise 4.3 – *continued*

   c) Canadian parents raise their children to be independent as adults.

   d) Children are encouraged to make their own decisions, starting with choosing what to wear when they are preschoolers.

3. a) Novels allow students to exercise their imagination, picturing characters and settings in their mind.

   b) High school students need to read more novels in their English courses.

   c) Novels expose students to other worlds and times, broadening their view of life.

   d) Students develop good reading skills by following a long, involved story.

4. a) Just like a fish that cannot comprehend what water is, people cannot really understand their culture unless they experience another one.

   b) If students see people who live with far less, they will learn to appreciate what they have.

   c) Students can improve their communication skills while travelling even if they do not speak other languages.

   d) Travelling abroad is a vital part of education.

5. a) The various meanings of words are explained in dictionary entries.

   b) Dictionaries are useful tools for students.

   c) Students can check their spelling by consulting a dictionary.

   d) Useful grammatical information is given in word entries.

Exercise 4.4

The following paragraphs lack topic sentences (and concluding sentences). Choose the best topic sentence from the choices given:

1. _____ First, students must really want to study the particular subject. If they are forced to take a course they do not like, they will not do as well. On the other hand, a liking for a subject fosters an interest that will motivate students to do extra reading and learn all they can. In addition, students need motivation to stick to the work when it is difficult. It is human nature to do only what is easy, but course work can be very difficult, and only the most motivated students persevere.

Exercise 4.4 – *continued*

Finally, motivation means that students have their eyes on the ultimate goal—a diploma, certificate, or degree. They understand the big picture and can see how everything fits together. They are more likely to put up with the parts of the program that they do not like as much. They are willing to make sacrifices to achieve their goal.
a) Finishing a college program is very difficult.
b) The most important factor in academic success is motivation.
c) If students enjoy a subject, they will read more about it.
d) Sometimes college students have to take compulsory courses that they do not like.

2. _____ If children have too many organized activities, they have no downtime to relax. They need time to goof off and just be kids. Secondly, they should not be dependent on others to entertain them. Boredom can spur children on to create their own games. For example, a large cardboard box can become the castle in a game of medieval knights. Furthermore, when children play games that are not controlled by adults, they learn to compromise and negotiate with others. There is no adult intervening to tell them how to play or how to interact.
a) Children are often bored.
b) Our modern technological society is not good for children.
c) Parents hate it when their children complain about being bored.
d) Children need free, unstructured time.

3. _____ Hoarders are obsessive about collecting things. Some of these items might be quite useless. For example, some people keep every flyer that is delivered to their house or every plastic bag they bring home from shopping. Hoarders cannot bear to throw things out. They are emotionally attached to their collections and feel like a part of them is being ripped away. Finally, hoarding is clearly an illness because sufferers cannot live normal lives. Their homes become huge messes that are unsanitary and unsafe. One famous hoarder, Langley Collyer, died in 1947 when some of the mountains of junk in his home fell on top of him. It took a month to find him because literally tons of stuff had to be removed from the house to clear the way.
a) Everybody likes to collect things.
b) Excessive hoarding is a psychological disorder.
c) People today don't know how to properly clean their homes.
d) Our society produces too much stuff.

Exercise 4.4 – *continued*

4. _____ Euchre is played with two teams of two, so it provides a good social grouping. Working with a partner fosters both cooperation and competition. The games are short, so partners can switch and not be stuck with someone for a long time. Because players only get five cards each, the hands are played quickly and require less concentration, unlike Bridge. Therefore, players can chat more during the games. Euchre offers the right balance of challenge and fun.
   a) Euchre is a difficult card game to play, but it is a lot of fun.
   b) Bridge is too difficult a card game to enjoy.
   c) Euchre is one of the best card games for social interaction.
   d) Playing cards is a good way to spend time with others.

5. _____ The music puts them in their own little world, with its own soundtrack. The earbuds or headphones prevent them from hearing what is going on around them and act as a signal to other people—"do not disturb." People are less likely to start a conversation or offer a bit of small talk to people with music players.
   a) Portable music players are one more way that people cut themselves off from personal contact.
   b) Today, many people walk around with portable music players.
   c) Teenagers today are going to suffer hearing loss because of their music players.
   d) MP3 players are a great way to carry music around all day.

Activity 4.2

Here are several topic sentences on the same general topic. Discuss how they differ. What would each paragraph say? How is the focus different? In pairs, generate more topic sentences on this subject. Choose one topic sentence, and write a paragraph completing it:

(Note: *Empty nesters* are parents whose children have grown up and left home, and *boomerang children* are those who leave as adults but come back at some time to live with their parents again.)

1. Boomerang children must make adjustments to their lifestyle in order to live with their parents.

2. Empty nesters should downsize their homes once their children leave to prevent them from returning.

Activity 4.2 – *continued*

3. Adult children who live with their parents should contribute financially to the household.

4. Adult children who still live at home must take on more responsibility for household chores.

5. Parents with boomerang children should not treat them as children.

6. Many college and university graduates are forced to return to their parents' home.

Activity 4.3

In groups, generate three topic sentences for possible paragraphs in each of the following subject areas:

1. A problem that needs to be addressed at your school (such as parking or the registration process)

2. Benefits of sport

3. Pets

4. Driver's licences

5. Video games

Making Points

The topic sentence introduces the main idea that is being put forth in the paragraph. That main idea is argued with several points. In the paragraph below, three arguments (marked in boldface) support the idea that teenagers are the main movie-goers:

> Teenagers are the most desirable market for movie producers. They are more likely than other age groups to spend their entertainment dollar on the cinema. **First, teenagers go to the movies as their main social activity.** They are old enough to go out on their own but too young for other social activities such as bar-hopping. They even go to see movies they are not that interested in simply because their friends are going, and they might see a movie more than once. **Moreover, teenagers prefer the theatre as a more enjoyable environment for movies.**

They get out from under their parents' watchful eyes and get the full effects of a large screen and superior sound system. Their parents, on the other hand, often prefer to cocoon at home and wait for the DVD. **Finally, teenagers have disposable income.** They often have allowances and part-time jobs but do not have to pay for rent or tuition, unlike college and university students. It is not surprising that so many movies today are aimed at teenagers' tastes.

The points made should relate directly to the topic sentence and should have the same focus. The points should be supportable yet more specific than the topic sentence. For example, for the topic sentence "Part-time jobs can be very beneficial to students," your points should say **why** part-time jobs are good and should focus on the students' point of view, not the employers' or the parents'. Consider the following sentences as points for this topic sentence:

> **Topic: Part-time jobs can be very beneficial to students.**
> a)   Students generally work at low-wage jobs as servers in restaurants. [does not show a benefit]
> b)   Students can gain many benefits from part-time jobs. [just repeats the main idea of the topic sentence]
> c)   Employers can pay students less money. [a benefit for employers, not students]
> d)   Students can learn useful skills on the job.
> e)   Students have to learn to manage their time efficiently to balance both work and school. [a requirement, not a benefit]
> f)   Part-time jobs are an important source of income for students.
> g)   Handling customers is an important part of many entry jobs. [related to a benefit but not the actual benefit]
> h)   Students eventually have to enter the work world. [does not show the connection to part-time jobs]
> i)   Students who work gain valuable work experience.
> j)   It is difficult for students to afford tuition and the cost of living. [shows the reason why students need money but does not focus on benefits of working]

Sentences d, f, and i give the reasons why part-time jobs are useful. Each of these points would be supported with examples and explanations, as shown in the next section on supporting points.

Exercise 4.5

For the topic sentence, choose three sentences that would make the best points for that paragraph:

Cooking a meal from scratch is a worthwhile skill to acquire.

a) Cooking is a lost skill.

b) Home-cooked meals are more nutritious.

c) People eat too much junk food.

d) Cooking at home is less expensive than eating out.

e) Many prepared foods are available in grocery stores.

f) Few people can cook today.

g) Cooking is useful for entertaining and impressing guests.

h) Cooking is not very difficult to learn.

i) Sometimes people buy prepared foods and pretend they have cooked them.

j) People can just reheat frozen foods in a microwave oven.

Supporting Points

When you make a point, you have to support it. Support means giving the reader examples or explanations to make that point clear and to convince the reader of its validity. The supporting sentences are more specific than the point they are supporting.

Here are two kinds of support for a statement:

> Documents must be written for the intended audience. [argument]

> The level of vocabulary and the background given should reflect the knowledge the proposed reader has about the subject. [explanation]

> For example, a computer user manual should have simple instructions with no jargon. [example]

Consider again the suggested outline for an independent, developed paragraph:

Topic sentence

> Elaboration of topic sentence (if necessary)

Point 1

> Support (explanation, example, illustration)

Point 2

> Support (explanation, example, illustration)

Point 3

> Support (explanation, example, illustration)

Concluding sentence

For the topic sentence "Canadians can do much to reduce environmental harm in their everyday practices," here are three possible points:

1. First, they can reduce the amount of garbage they produce.

2. Canadians can also limit their use of resources.

3. They can safeguard the water supply.

In a developed paragraph, points such as these generally have from one to three sentences in support. For this example on the environment, a reader would expect that each of these three points be followed by statements that explain how Canadians can do this. Discuss how this is accomplished in the following paragraph outline:

> Canadians can do much to reduce environmental harm in their everyday practices.

> First, they can reduce the amount of garbage they produce.

>> They can choose products with less packaging, such as bulk food items.

>> They can redirect items that they don't need, such as clothing, to recycling depots rather than throwing them into the garbage.

Canadians can also limit their use of resources.

> Driving smaller cars instead of SUVs reduces the amount of gasoline burned.

> They can use less electricity by converting to energy-saving appliances and by shutting off unnecessary lights.

Finally, they can safeguard the water supply.

> They should use water wisely, not watering their lawn unnecessarily or washing their cars excessively.

> They should not pour toxic waste down the toilet, sink, or sewer.

All Canadians must do their part to protect the environment.

Add a third supporting statement to each of the three arguments.

Exercise 4.6

Choose the sentence or group of sentences (a, b, or c) that makes the best support for the argument:

Topic sentence: Punctuality is important to success in college.

1. First, when students arrive on time for class, they create a good impression.
   a) They are less likely to miss important information and tests, and so their marks will be higher.
   b) They impress the teacher. The teacher will be quite satisfied with the impression the students make.
   c) They show that they are interested in the class and are prepared to work hard. Teachers are more likely to give breaks to such hardworking students.

2. In addition, students who are late often miss important information.
   a) A lot of important information is given at the beginning of class, and latecomers will lose out. That will result in a lower mark.
   b) For example, they may not get the feedback from the last assignment, which is often handed back first in class. They will also miss the explanation for that day's lesson.
   c) Sometimes there is a pop quiz at the beginning of class. Latecomers who miss it will get a mark of zero.

Exercise 4.6 – *continued*

3. Finally, late students miss out on time given for tests and assignments.
   a) They show that they don't care about the test, so the instructor is less likely to take their work seriously.
   b) These students get a lower mark if they do not complete a test. Sometimes they might even miss a test entirely since pop quizzes are often given at the beginning of class.
   c) Tests are very important, and students need to pass these tests to pass the course. Every test mark counts and can make the difference between passing and failing the course.

Exercise 4.7

Choose the sentence or group of sentences (a, b, or c) that makes the best support for the argument:

Topic sentence: When considering entry-level positions, college graduates should not limit their consideration to salary alone.

1. One important consideration is the skills the position requires.
   a) Graduates want to use the skills they have been taught in school and to develop new ones. For example, a marketing student who has learned to prepare copy wants to practise that skill on an actual campaign.
   b) College students acquire many practical skills. Sometimes these are useful for their everyday life. Sometimes they don't learn the skills well enough. Then they have problems in their jobs. Companies expect that students have learned all the required skills. That is what a diploma means.
   c) Students learn many skills in college. Some jobs require a number of different skills. For example, they learn the skills they need for the job.

2. Another criterion for choosing a position is the possibility of advancement.
   a) When employees advance to more senior positions, they get more money, so they can pay off their student loans.
   b) Graduates might get stuck in entry-level jobs. They may be forced to work for bad bosses who make employees do useless tasks, take the credit for their employees' work, or delegate tasks unevenly or unrealistically.

Exercise 4.7 – *continued*

    c) Graduates are prepared to take entry-level jobs to get their foot in the door, but they do not want to be stuck there for years. A large company that has many levels of employment might offer more opportunities for promotion through the ranks.

3. A third criterion for choosing a job is the work environment.

    a) In addition to salary, the benefits are an important consideration. Also, people must think about the location, the ease of transportation, and the hours.

    b) The environment is very important to our lives, and we should be careful not to pollute it. Workplace pollution policies can be very effective if all the employees believe in them.

    c) Although it is difficult to learn about future working conditions beforehand, candidates can get a sense of the company's work environment from the interview. For instance, they will most likely meet their immediate supervisor, who will set the tone of the place.

Exercise 4.8

Academic writing moves from general to more specific statements. Pick the most general from the statements below:

1. a) College students do not have parents shepherding them through their schedules.

    b) College students have to become self-sufficient when they strike out on their own.

    c) College students have to prepare their own meals.

    d) College students have to be responsible for rent, utilities, and transportation.

2. a) She won our neighbourhood Monopoly challenge.

    b) She is good at all sorts of games.

    c) She cleaned us all out in poker last night.

    d) I remember her as the leader of the children in the playground.

3. a) Smoking impairs your ability to breathe.

    b) Smoking is bad for your health.

    c) Smoking can lead to lung disease.

    d) Smoking makes your breath stink.

Exercise 4.8 – *continued*

4. a) Contract work can lead to abuse of workers.
   b) Contract workers often receive no benefits.
   c) Contract workers have no job stability.
   d) Contract workers get paid less for the same work.

5. a) Some people put clothes on their pets.
   b) Some people sleep with their pets.
   c) Some people treat their pets like people.
   d) Some people pamper pets with spa treatments or doggie daycare.

Exercise 4.9

For the following pairs of sentences, write "For example" or "For instance" in the blank if the second sentence is indeed an example that helps you understand the first sentence. Remember that an example is more specific. If the second sentence is not an example, determine whether it is an explanation or simply a repetition of the idea in the first sentence:

1. Some tattoos show the qualities that people admire. _____, they may choose a Chinese character for 'serenity' or 'joy'.

2. Many parents solve their children's problems, which does not help their children's self-confidence. _____, when the children grow up, they depend on other people to solve their problems.

3. Public transit has several advantages. _____, less polluting exhaust is produced by buses or trains than by individual vehicles.

4. Unlike private schools, public schools set the stage for a tolerant society. _____, children learn to be more accepting of others in public school.

5. Gardening is a good way to teach children about nature. _____, they can be outdoors in the natural world.

Exercise 4.10

Write a supporting statement, such as an explanation or example, for the a, b, and c statements:

1. Many students prefer to attend community college rather than university.
   a) First, college is less expensive.
   b) Second, college students have practical hands-on learning.
   c) Third, a college education leads directly to specific jobs.

2. The baby-boomer style of parenting has several drawbacks.
   a) First, parents give their children too many material things.
   b) Second, parents organize too much of their children's time.
   c) Third, parents don't discipline their children enough.

Exercise 4.11

In pairs or small groups, write one or two sentences to support each of these general statements. Compare your answers with your classmates':

1. Students need good study habits to succeed in college. (What habits?)

2. Job candidates need to prepare for an interview. (How?)

3. Hiking in the wilderness can be dangerous. (Why?)

4. Board games can teach children valuable skills. (What skills?)

5. Students can furnish their first apartment very cheaply. (How?)

6. Fashionable clothes are often impractical and uncomfortable. (Give examples.)

7. Cellphones are useful in emergencies. (Give examples.)

8. Superstitions can cause people to change their regular routine. (How?)

9. Dictionaries provide more than just the definition of a word. (What else do they give?)

10. Students can use word processing programs to improve their writing. (How?)

Writing Concluding Sentences

If you are writing a single-paragraph writing assignment, your paragraph should have a concluding sentence to tie it all up. Generally, the concluding sentence echoes the topic sentence—giving essentially the same main idea but not repeating it in the same words. A body paragraph in an essay or report does not necessarily need to be wrapped up in a concluding sentence. Shorter paragraphs do not need a concluding sentence because the topic sentence is probably still fresh in the reader's mind.

Note the concluding sentence (marked in boldface) in the following paragraph:

> Although working part-time can create a serious time crunch, high school students should consider the many advantages of having a job. The most important consideration is the money. Teenagers' desires for such items as cellphones and CDs can exceed their allowance. More important, however, many students must start saving for their post-secondary education, especially if they plan to study in another city, since most parents cannot afford to give their children everything they want or need. In addition, part-time jobs give students a chance to taste different kinds of work. They can find out whether they like dealing with the public, for example. This type of self-knowledge can be invaluable when choosing courses with an eye to a future career. They also learn how hard it is to work, especially in minimum-wage jobs. This gives them a greater appreciation for the work itself and for the education required to get a better job. In the workplace, students gain valuable skills, such as typing, filing, and answering the telephone. They take on responsibilities, such as being punctual, working with others, and following orders. Work experience is essential on a graduate's résumé. **Therefore, students who can handle the load should work part-time to reap the many benefits of a job.**

Exercise 4.12

Here are some topic sentences from previous exercises in this chapter. Write a concluding sentence that could complete the paragraph. You can also go back to Exercise 4.4 and write concluding sentences for those paragraphs:

1. Punctuality is an important part of success in college.

2. The baby-boomer style of parenting has several drawbacks.

Exercise 4.12 – *continued*

3. Many students prefer to attend community college rather than university.

4. When considering entry-level positions, college graduates should not limit their consideration to salary alone.

5. Cooking a meal from scratch is a worthwhile skill to acquire.

6. Part-time jobs can be very beneficial to students.

Achieving Unity

A paragraph should have unity—it should have one main idea. The topic sentence sets out this main idea, and all the other sentences should fit under the umbrella of the topic sentence. For example, a paragraph that begins 'Part-time jobs can be very beneficial to students' should only have sentences that explain why part-time jobs are good for students. It should not contain sentences that give the disadvantages of working or explain how to find a job.

Exercise 4.13

Identify the two sentences that do not fit in this paragraph:

ESL students can benefit from reading children's fairy tales. First, reading is the best way to improve general language skills because it exposes students to both language and ideas. The simpler vocabulary and sentence structure of children's books make them accessible to ESL students and allow them to build their reading skills gradually. Modern novels are also good reading practice because students have to follow a complex plot with a variety of characters. Secondly, fairy tales are part of the culture, and ESL students need to be familiar with these stories to understand references in film and other literature. For example, psychology books may refer to a person exhibiting a Cinderella complex. The characters are well-known and can appear in movies, in modern novels, or even in newspaper articles. For instance, a politician's situation might be described as "the emperor's new clothes," a reference to a story by Hans Christian Andersen. Andersen was a Dane who had an unhappy childhood but gained a measure of fame with the stories he wrote. Furthermore, the fantastical worlds of magic, witches, and elves can be entertaining. The popularity of these tales has survived over centuries to modern incarnations such as the Harry Potter books. Rather than dismissing fairy tales as juvenile reading, ESL students should seek them out as supplemental reading.

Exercise 4.14

Choose which sentences would fit under the topic sentence:

The economics of professional sport is detrimental to the fan base.

1. Games often start later in the evening so that they can be broadcast in the more lucrative prime-time spots even though that is often too late for younger viewers.

2. Violence should be better controlled in games so that it doesn't set a bad example for children.

3. The pace of baseball is too slow for fans accustomed to fast action.

4. Free agents switch teams as they chase bigger salaries, so fans have trouble staying loyal to certain players.

5. Games are paused so that broadcasters can insert commercial breaks.

6. Professional athletes often sign multi-million-dollar endorsement contracts.

7. High salaries of players are often reflected in higher ticket prices.

8. Athletes demand higher salaries not because they need the money but because it is part of a competition—the best-paid athlete is considered the best athlete.

9. Games are less interesting to watch when the team with all the high-priced talent is generally the one that wins.

10. Fans of small-market teams are often in danger of losing their teams to bigger cities.

Using Transition Signals

Writers need to help readers follow the development of their ideas. To this end, they use transition markers or signals—words and expressions that introduce a sentence to show how the sentence relates to other sentences. For example, a phrase such as *for example* tells readers that the sentence is an example of the point made in the previous sentence. Just like signals on a car tell the drivers behind where the driver is going, the signals in a paragraph tell readers where the ideas are going so they can follow them.

Here are some common transition signals:

> **Addition:** also, finally, first, furthermore, in addition, moreover, next, second

Cause and effect: accordingly, as a result, consequently, therefore, thus

Comparison: likewise, similarly

Contrast: however, in contrast, instead, nevertheless, on the contrary, on the other hand, otherwise

Emphasis or clarity: in fact, indeed, in other words, of course, that is

Special features or examples: for example, for instance, in particular, mainly, specifically

Summary: in brief, in closing, in conclusion, in short, on the whole, to conclude, to summarize

Time relations: afterwards, at that time, earlier, in the meantime, lately, later, meanwhile, now, then

Most of these expressions function as adverbs and are sometimes called conjunctive adverbs or adverbial connectors. It is important to distinguish them from conjunctions such as *although* and *but* so that you join sentences correctly. (This grammar point is discussed in "Writing adverb clauses" in unit 2, and Exercise 7.23 gives you a chance to practise.)

Here are some examples of transition signals at work. Note that in the following pairs of sentences, the second pair includes a transition signal, making it easier to follow the meaning:

I went through the paper files to scan the older documents into the system. I weeded out the out-of-date papers and checked the accuracy of the information in the system.

I went through the paper files to scan the older documents into the system. At the same time, I weeded out the out-of-date papers and checked the accuracy of the information in the system.

Essay writing helps students develop their thinking skills. They have to understand the relationship between a general idea and a specific example.

Essay writing helps students develop their thinking skills. For instance, they have to understand the relationship between a general idea and a specific example.

Smokers should have the right to decide whether they poison their own bodies or not. They cannot make that choice for the others whom they affect with second-hand smoke.

Smokers should have the right to decide whether they poison their own bodies or not. However, they cannot make that choice for the others whom they affect with second-hand smoke.

Exercise 4.15

Write an appropriate transition signal in each blank:

1. Computer games can give children an opportunity to exercise their problem-solving skills. _____, in a strategy game, children have to work through different scenarios to make the most advantageous move.

2. Many drivers exhibit unnecessary aggressive behaviour on the highway. Some tailgate trying to make other drivers speed up or move out of the way. _____, some drivers weave in and out of lanes looking for any space to advance.

3. Disney movies often have 'happily ever after' endings even when the source material is a tragedy. _____, in the Hans Christian Andersen story 'The little mermaid', the mermaid dies at the end, while in the Disney cartoon she marries the prince.

4. We worked together to paint the room efficiently: Jack used the roller to cover the large surfaces. _____ I used a brush to cut in around the trim and the corners.

5. I missed the class when our instructor taught us how to do a summary. _____, I did not do well on the summary test.

6. The Canadian team was considered a favourite for the championship. _____, the odds changed when a few of the top players were injured.

7. The United States is the most powerful country in the world. _____, it is understandable that many underdog countries feel resentment towards Americans.

8. The story of Laura Secord warning the British troops of an American attack includes many myths. _____, one version says she led a cow through the swamp.

9. A post-secondary education costs students thousands of dollars. _____, graduates can expect greater income.

Exercise 4.15 – *continued*

10. Reading children's books is good reading practice because the stories have simpler ideas, structures, and vocabulary. _____, children's books teach about the culture.

11. First, he went to the bank to withdraw some cash. _____ he went to bargain with the person selling the bike.

12. As prime minister, Lester B. Pearson had a minority government. _____, he managed to bring in major changes such as national health care and a new Canadian flag.

13. New immigrants can survive Canadian winters better if they dress properly. _____, they should invest in a warm coat and waterproof boots.

14. Personal music players can lead to hearing damage. _____, ear buds direct sound right into delicate ear drums.

15. Modern technology is supposed to improve communication between people. _____, people tend to e-mail strangers across the world rather than actually talk to their next-door neighbour.

Achieving Coherence

The sentences in a paragraph must fit together in a logical, coherent manner. The word *cohere* means "to stick together." Coherence is achieved by the order of the sentences, by the use of transition signals to show the reader how the ideas connect, by the use of pronouns to refer back to nouns in a previous sentence, and by the repetition of words and ideas.

Readers can follow a paragraph better when the ideas are in an order they are familiar with. For instance, a paragraph describing the history of something would most likely be in chronological order.

Another way to achieve coherence is through the use of transition signals, like *for example* and *in addition*. The use of these signals is shown in the previous section.

Pronouns refer to a specific noun and help to link sentences:

> Andrew had to get his project approved. It [refers to the project] was an orientation film in which he [Andrew] needed to interview first-year students. They [the students] would discuss the problems they had faced.

Demonstrative pronouns (such as *this* and *these*) also help to link sentences:

> Fairy tales, folk tales, and myths are important parts of children's books. **These stories** teach a cultural heritage that is built upon in other kinds of literature.

Remember that in English, an indefinite article is usually used the first time something is mentioned, and then a definite article is used. This grammatical structure also helps readers follow the ideas:

> We wrote **a report** at the end of our project. **The report** summarized our problems and how we overcame them.

Repeating key words, or using synonyms to refer to them, is another way to ensure coherence in a paragraph:

> Luxury **cars** are a waste of money. While these **vehicles** are comfortable and well-made, they are too expensive to purchase, maintain, and insure. Drivers really just need a car to get them safely from point A to point B. The powerful engine of a **luxury car** is useless when a driver is stuck in a traffic jam or restricted by speed limits.

Exercise 4.16

A test of a coherent paragraph is to take it apart into individual sentences and see if someone can put it back in the right order. Label the following sentences in each blank: TS (topic sentence), P (point), SS (supporting sentence), and CS (concluding sentence). There are three points, each supported with two sentences. Decide on the best order for the sentences and add transition markers for the final version:

_____College students moving into an apartment or a house should use just a cellphone and not bother with a land line.

_____The cost of a cellphone is comparable.

_____Monthly fees are similar, and students can get the plan that suits their usage level.

_____Since students may move more than once a year, they can avoid the high cost of getting new land-line hook-ups each time.

_____Convenience is an important consideration.

_____Students can keep the phone with them at all times, which is especially important since students are rarely at home.

Exercise 4.16 – *continued*

_____Instead of changing their phone numbers each time they move, cellphone users can keep their own individual numbers.

_____With students having individual phones, potential roommate problems can be avoided.

_____There will be no arguing over how to split the phone bill and which long-distance charges belong to which person.

_____Cellphone users can have their own voice mail and not depend on their roommates to pass on messages.

_____Even though there are disadvantages such as poor reception, cellphones are a better choice for most students.

Sample Paragraphs

Examine the paragraphs below, reviewing the features of a good paragraph as you read. Compare the topic sentence and concluding sentence of each. Identify the points made to prove the main idea and the specific examples or explanations used to support the points. Identify transition signals and other methods used to achieve coherence.

> We should choose our career path based on our own interests and talents rather than on a job's earning potential. One reason is that we spend a large part of our lives at work, and it is wrong to waste precious hours doing something we do not enjoy. Second, if we choose a career in an area where we are talented, we will probably achieve more. For example, an accountant who wishes she had followed her passion for music will probably not be as successful in her job as someone who actually enjoys working with numbers. Finally, the job market is unpredictable, and people can change careers frequently in their lives. We cannot predict where the jobs will be when we finish school. For example, a degree in computer programming used to be considered a guaranteed ticket to economic success, but with the high-tech bust, many programmers found themselves unemployed and forced to reinvent themselves in other fields. Liberal arts degrees, even in such dismissed fields as philosophy, can lead to lucrative careers in business, where analytical and communication skills are valued. High school graduates should follow their passions when they choose a career.

Shopping is more than a necessary chore; it is a good way to spend leisure time. First, instead of sitting at home in front of the TV, shoppers get exercise walking around the stores. Shopping can also be a social activity, a bonding experience. For example, young women enjoy getting together to survey the new merchandise and serve as each other's fashion consultants. Thirdly, living in our material world requires education. Savvy consumers have to learn about products and prices. Spending time in a mall allows shoppers to comparison-shop and to get information from different salespeople. Finally, and most important, shopping is fun. Shoppers can gaze at colourful displays, watch other shoppers, stop for a coffee or a snack, listen to mall music, and imagine how all the high-tech goodies and trendy clothes will make their lives better. It is no wonder that so many people today view shopping as a pleasant pastime.

People who choose to spend their free time shopping are misguided. Shopping is the curse of the modern consumer world, not a leisure activity. First, buying merchandise is stressful. Shoppers have to choose how to spend their hard-earned dollars on a bewildering array of items, including various models with practically imperceptible differences. Getting the best price requires hard work, patience, and good luck. While some people argue that shopping is good exercise, the benefits are negligible. Instead of a brisk walk in fresh air, shoppers meander about the aisles, spending much of their time standing around looking at items or waiting for service. Moreover, malls and stores are crowded, noisy places. Worst of all, the fact that so many people spend so much time shopping shows that our society has degraded to the lowest level of materialism. We care more about buying things than spending time with our family and friends in worthwhile pursuits. The evils of shopping cannot be avoided, but the activity should be limited to buying the bare necessities.

Family dinner

The following paragraphs are all on the same topic—the family meal. Read the paragraphs and examine the structure and language of each paragraph. Look at the main idea in the topic sentence, and identify the points made and the supporting sentences. Determine the approach of each paragraph. For example, is the paragraph discussing causes, effects, or solutions? Is it descriptive? Is it a comparison? Does it describe a process? Can you determine what topic question might have generated the paragraph? Determine the style of each paragraph—is it personal, conversational, or academic?

Compare the paragraphs. See how the same information can be given differently for a different purpose. You can also compare these paragraphs to an essay on the same topic on page 158.

A) The shared family meal is yet another casualty of the hectic modern lifestyle. We don't seem to have the time to sit down to dinner together. One reason is our complicated schedules. Children's after-school and evening hours are filled with sports and music lessons. When they reach the teenage years, these activities are replaced by part-time jobs. Parents not only work long hours, but their return home may also be delayed because of a long commute. As a result, family members often eat separately. Moreover, a sit-down meal requires time to prepare and to consume. People don't want to devote that much time to what they consider a simple act of fuelling their bodies. Finally, many don't have the culinary skills to make nutritious and appealing meals. They rely on restaurant take-out and processed foods from the supermarket. It is not surprising that suppliers of ready-to-eat food are doing such good business, and it does not look like this trend will reverse itself any time soon. Family dining is obviously a thing of the past.

B) As our family sat down to Thanksgiving dinner, I enjoyed the sight of the gathering of the clan for the traditional meal. The whole extended family, all seventeen of us, came dressed in Sunday best. My grandfather sported his favourite bow-tie, and the younger girl cousins had new dresses to show off. The main table was set with the best linen, china, and crystal, and the centrepiece of gourds and autumn foliage proclaimed the season. The children's table was at the end of the formal dining table, but it looked festive even with the orange polyester tablecloth and everyday dishes. After saying grace, we passed the dishes around the table. Everyone had contributed to the meal: Grandma had cooked the turkey, and Grandpa had carved it. Uncle Garth had brought his special wild cranberry sauce. Aunt Judy's vegetable medley tempted even the most determined of broccoli haters. My mother's pumpkin pie topped with dollops of whipped cream was the traditional dessert. It was a scene played out every year, but I never got tired of it.

C) A shared meal is an important family ritual, worth nurturing and keeping alive even in the fast-paced lives of the twenty-first century. First, families who take the time to dine together are generally eating healthier foods. They are not gobbling down a slice of pizza before running off to a night class or music lesson. Families who value mealtime usually take care with the food itself—making sure it is nutritious and tasty. In addition, the family meal is an opportunity for learning. Children can help prepare and serve the meal, thus acquiring practical cooking skills. They can also learn social skills, such as proper table etiquette, that will serve them well in their future business lunches. Finally, a family meal is above all a time for family members to touch base and talk about what is happening in their daily lives. At the end of the school and work day, the family can sit down together and share what happened that day as they eat their evening meal. Families that eat together have stronger bonds because the shared meal is a uniting element in family life.

D) My mother always insists on a family dinner at least once a week. Us kids all want to rush off somewhere that night, but oh no, can't schedule that last-minute study and gabfest on Sunday—I have to eat with my family. More than simply showing up and stuffing our faces, however, we have to cooperate in both making and cleaning up the food. As long as I don't have to do dishes! I can't stand getting my fingers all pruney. During the dinner we have to talk: "How was your day?" "You know already, Mom. I spent two hours peeling potatoes." "Anything new with your friends?" "I don't know—I couldn't see them tonight." By the end, however, we always end up talking animatedly about politics or news stories. I get half my Current Events quiz answers from Sunday night. I find I know more cooking than my friends and feel immensely superior when I exclaim "What? You've *never* peeled a potato?"

E) Over the past three generations, the eating habits of Canadians have changed dramatically. In the past, mealtimes were generally regular, and families often sat down to share a meal together. Today's busy families rarely find the time to eat together; people grab a bite to eat when they can and often eat alone, sometimes taking their food to their bedrooms or eating in front of the TV. Instead of home-cooked meals, Canadians today eat more processed foods and restaurant meals. Supermarkets stock a variety of prepared foods—from frozen dinners to deli meals. The growth of fast-food restaurants shows how important they have become to family life. The types of foods Canadians eat have also changed because of the greater variety of ethnic food available. They used to have very conservative tastes, sticking to the food they knew from home. Now Canadians of all ethnic backgrounds consume Italian pasta, Chinese stir fries, Greek souvlaki, Thai noodles, Tex-Mex tacos, and Middle Eastern hummus. Moreover, fruits and vegetables are shipped in from all over the world, so Canadians are not restricted by what is locally in season. Our food and the way we eat it is in line with the way we prefer to live our lives.

F) Even with today's hectic lifestyle, it's possible to reap the benefits of a shared family meal. First, it's important to acknowledge the importance of the family dinner and to schedule time for it. This may mean cutting down on some activities. At the very least, Sunday dinner should be set aside as family time. Second, if the meal is planned ahead of time, it will go more smoothly. The menu should be decided on and groceries should be bought beforehand. In addition, the work should be shared. If it is up to only one person to do all the preparation, the meal does become more of a chore. Children can start helping with food preparation at a very young age— washing vegetables, for example. Working together not only lessens the workload, it allows family members to talk together and to acquire cooking skills. Furthermore, for the meal to be an important part of family life, it must be acknowledged as a time for discussion. Parents should be careful not to nag but to listen to their children's concerns. Talk about political and social issues can pass on moral values and increase awareness of current events. Proper table etiquette can be taught at the same time. Finally, the family should share clean-up responsibilities. By working, talking, and eating together, families can forge strong bonds and foster communication.

Paragraph recap

For single-paragraph writing assignments:

- start with a topic sentence that clearly delineates the main idea of your paragraph;
- give two to four arguments for that main idea;
- support each argument with explanation or examples;
- use transition signals to show the relationship between ideas;
- make sure your paragraph has unity (one main idea);
- make sure your paragraph has coherence (all the ideas flow logically);
- check your paragraph for grammar, spelling, punctuation, and style.

Essay Writing Skills

Essays are essentially arguments. The word *essay* comes from the French word meaning "to try." The writer tries to show or prove something to the reader. The audience for students' essays is their professor or teacher. The purpose is purely academic; instead of giving new information (the purpose of most written communication), student essay writers are charged with the task of showing what they have learned, synthesizing information, and explaining the thesis in a way that shows their understanding of the subject. Students are being tested on both their thinking and their communication skills, so essay writing requires logical organization of ideas.

Understanding Essay Structure

The essay structure often taught in school is the five-paragraph essay. It has an introduction, three body paragraphs, and a conclusion. Even though this type of essay is rarely seen outside the classroom, the form is adaptable to other kinds of writing. Business reports, for example, are longer than five paragraphs, but they too have an introduction, a body divided into different ideas, and a conclusion. A cover letter for a job application also shows the same structure: the first paragraph introduces the subject and states the purpose (that the writer is applying for a job), the body paragraphs each deal with a different area (education, work experience, and relevant skills, for example), and a conclusion (telling the prospective employer how to contact the applicant). And, of course, the five-paragraph essay model can be expanded to suit longer essays, which also have an introduction, body, and conclusion.

In a five-paragraph essay, the first paragraph is the introduction. It provides background for the reader, gets the reader's attention, and prepares the way for the thesis statement. The thesis gives the main argument of the essay and comes at the end of the introduction.

The thesis statement is supported in the three body paragraphs. The arguments are divided so that each paragraph has a different main idea. The body paragraphs start with a topic sentence giving the main idea of that paragraph. A good body paragraph has support for the points made, has unity (only one main idea), is coherent (the sentences flow and follow logically), and has transition markers (to signal the relationship between ideas).

The conclusion generally starts with a restatement of the thesis and goes on to give a "so what?" idea to lead the reader back out of the essay. The conclusion should not give new ideas to support the thesis. In a short essay, the conclusion should not summarize the essay because it would be too repetitive.

Sometimes this type of essay is referred to as a "hamburger essay," with the introduction and conclusion serving as the bun holding the meat of the essay (the body) together. This analogy simply tells students that the body of the essay is the most important part.

Comparing the paragraph and the essay

Unit 4 focuses on the structure of a paragraph. An independent, developed paragraph is a mini-essay. Moving from paragraph writing to essay writing is not difficult. You need to expand on ideas and to learn to write introductory and concluding paragraphs. Compare this independent paragraph and the five-paragraph essay on the same topic that follows:

> Even with the wide variety of prepared foods available today, cooking is a worthwhile skill for anyone to have. Most important, home-cooked foods are better because they are more nutritious, better-tasting, and less expensive. Processed foods contain high amounts of salt, sugar, and fat. People who cook at home have control over the ingredients. They can tailor the dishes to their family's tastes and avoid any food to which someone may be allergic. Second, being able to cook is a useful social skill. Inviting friends over for dinner is a time-honoured method of entertaining. In Canada, home-cooking has an added dimension when immigrants can share their ethnic foods with people of a different ethnic background. For example, many Canadians would love to try home-cooked Chinese food rather than the typical restaurant fare of sweet 'n sour chicken balls. Finally, knowing how to cook is an important part of self-sufficiency. As much as possible, people should be able to take care of themselves and not rely on others. Cooking is not difficult, and people who can't even boil water are pitiable. People should start learning to cook when they are children, but it's never too late to start learning. [199 words]

The Value of Home-Cooking

With the modern busy lifestyle, people seek to save time in meal preparation. They often eat out, whether at fast-food places or upscale restaurants. They buy prepared foods from the deli counter of the supermarket or frozen meals that just have to be warmed up in the microwave. As a result, cooking is becoming a lost skill. While it is possible to survive without knowing one end of a chef's knife from the other, being able to prepare a home-cooked meal is a valuable skill.

The most obvious benefit of home-cooking is the ability to control the quality of the food. Processed foods contain high amounts of sugar, salt, and additives, while fast food is high in fat. Cooks choose their own raw ingredients and control the seasonings. They can ensure the quality of the ingredients and make the dishes to their taste. This is especially important for people with allergies or restricted diets. An added benefit is the lowered cost. Cooks provide their own labour and can thus spend more on superior ingredients. The same quality of food would not be found outside of expensive restaurants.

Cooking is also a valuable social skill. Hosting a dinner party is a time-honoured method of entertaining guests. Even for casual get-togethers, it is gratifying to be able to serve food that is homemade. In the dating game, moreover, cooking is useful. It is said that the way to a man's heart is through his stomach, but women are also attracted to men who are handy in the kitchen. Parents may also expect their adult children to cook well enough to contribute to holiday dinners and to carry on their family traditions. For immigrant families, preparing ethnic foods is a way to keep their native culture alive.

Cooking can even make people feel healthier. They can feel personal satisfaction when they produce an edible meal. Self-sufficiency is a goal that people should all aim for. It is humiliating to have to admit that they cannot provide the basic necessities of life for themselves. Working at manual skills can also provide balance in our lives. For example, computer programmers who spend all their hours at a keyboard need to get in touch with natural products. Kneading bread dough can relieve stress and give different muscles a workout, reducing the risk of carpal tunnel syndrome.

These many benefits of cooking show that it is still an important skill despite the proliferation of restaurants. The younger generations should not let themselves be seduced by the amount of prepared food on the market and should carry on their family cooking skills. Parents should ensure that their sons and daughters learn to cook while they are living at home.
[454 words]

Planning an Essay

An essay requires more planning than an independent paragraph. Writers must make sure that the essay is well-balanced. For example, the three body paragraphs should be approximately the same length. Each paragraph should have different ideas with no repetition or overlap.

Writing is generally a three-stage process: planning, drafting, and editing. The planning stage includes researching, thinking about the topic, brainstorming ideas, and putting together an outline. The drafting stage is when the actual writing is done. The final stage involves rereading the draft, revising, editing, proofreading, and correcting. However, writing does not always proceed in such a clearcut way. For instance, writers may revisit the outline once they start writing because they think of a better way to organize it. People who compose on a computer may find their essay evolves from their brainstorming with less of a progression from one step to another.

Students often spend too little time in the first and third stages; they rush to get words on paper without thinking about how they want to develop their ideas, and they are too easily satisfied with what they have written, reluctant to delete sections that do not work or to proofread carefully to catch mistakes. Granted, students are often put into writing situations where they do not have the luxury of time to plan or edit. If they are required to write a 300-word essay in half an hour, they must concentrate on getting words down as quickly as possible. However, if they have practised writing an essay with the three stages, they can work more efficiently when they are under tight time constraints.

Choosing a topic

The first step is choosing a topic. Usually, teachers give their class a choice of topics, perhaps related to assigned readings or current events. Often the topics are discussed in class before students have to write about them. Students should pick the topic they are most comfortable with. They probably have choice within the topic, such as agreeing or disagreeing with a statement, or they have to narrow the topic down. If students can generate their own topic, they should do this in consultation with their instructor because it is too easy to flounder without direction.

Here are some typical essay topics:

Describe an ideal job.

How can the use of public transit be increased?

What can be done to make post-secondary education more affordable?

Why do people get tattoos?

What are the benefits of married life as opposed to remaining single?

What factors determine how well an immigrant will adapt to life in Canada?

Activity 5.1

In groups, make a list of essay topics you would like to write about.

Generating ideas

Before you start writing your essay, make sure you have enough to say. One of the best ways to do this is just to jot down point-form ideas about your topic. Look at it in different ways. For example, if you are going to write about the advantages of wearing school uniforms, jot down points about the disadvantages at the same time. As you think of the disadvantages, you may think of counter-arguments that might fit in your "pro" essay. If you are asked to come up with a solution to a problem, make sure you spend enough time considering the problem itself and the different ramifications.

Brainstorming in this manner is an efficient way to start your essay writing process, but there are other ways of doing it. People who think visually may use bubble diagrams for their points with lines to connect related ideas. Freewriting is a method in which students just write what comes into their heads and then look through the writing for an argument they can develop. Some writers ask themselves questions about a topic ("Why does this happen?" "What can this lead to?" "Who is affected?") to generate ideas. You may need to experiment to find out what works for you. Whichever method you use, it's important to think about the topic thoroughly to generate enough ideas to choose from and not just grab the first three random arguments that come to mind.

Activity 5.2

With your instructor and classmates, discuss the techniques you have found helpful for getting started with an essay or for getting past writer's block. Consider different ways of brainstorming.

From brainstorming to essay

Here you can see an essay go from topic to point-form ideas, rough organization, an outline, a draft, and finally the completed essay:

Topic: Suggest rules for cellphone etiquette.

To come up with rules for cellphone use, the writer first did some brainstorming on what is annoying about the way people use cellphones:

Things that are annoying about cellphones:
- Phones ring in class, business meetings.
- People answer their phones when they are in the middle of a conversation with someone else.
- People talk loudly on a cellphone on the bus.
- They talk about private matters that everyone can hear.
- They carry on long conversations in public places, like waiting rooms.

- People stop in the middle of the hall or stairway to talk on the phone.
- They talk in restaurants when they are with someone else.
- Cellphones ring in movies and plays.

Then the writer came up with some ideas for cellphone rules, grouping them in three areas:

- Phones should be turned off in class.
- Phones should not be allowed in business meetings.
- Cellphones should be turned off at concerts, movies, and plays.

- People should not talk loudly on a cellphone in a public space.
- People should not block hallways and stairwells talking on the phone.
- People should not have personal conversations that can be overheard.
- People should not have long conversations on buses and in waiting rooms.

- People should apologize if their phone rings when they are talking to someone.
- People should not answer the phone when they are talking to someone.
- People should not talk on the phone to someone else when they are with someone at a restaurant.

The next step was making a formal outline:

Rules for cellphone etiquette:
1. Phones should be turned off when they can disturb events (class, concerts, movies).
2. People should not treat public space as their own private area when they are talking on the phone.
3. People should give their full attention to the person they are with, not with someone on the phone.

For the draft, the writer developed and supported the ideas from the outline and wrote an introduction and a conclusion:

Cellphones can be seen all over the place. Almost all adults already own one. Cellphones are convenient and can perhaps even save your life. But they have become a nuisance as people misuse them. Cellphone users need to learn proper etiquette. They should turn off the phone entirely when it could be disruptive, they should use the phone carefully in public spaces, and they should pay more attention to the person they are with rather than the person on the phone.

Cellphone users should not leave their phone on all the time. It's very annoying to have a phone ringing when you are trying to concentrate on something. There are many places cellphones would be disruptive. In classes, in movies, at plays, in concerts, and in business meetings. People are supposed to pay attention to what's going on—not to their phone. If a phone goes off in the theatre, it can bother the actors. Even vibrating phones. So they should be turned off.

Another thing is that cellphone users should pay attention to where they are and the people around them. They don't care they have an audience. The people on the bus or the commuter train do not want to listen to one side of a half-hour conversation. They don't want to hear about someone's gall bladder operation or there shady business dealings. Moreover, people often talk loudly on the phone. They talk more loudly than they would talk to someone sitting next to them, so they disturb everybody around them. Sometimes people stop in the middle of a crowded hallway or staircase to talk to someone on there phone. This can cause traffic problems and be really irritating. Cellphone users need to be more considerate of the people around them.

Finally, people need to remember that the person they are with is more important then the person on the phone. Sometimes you can see people sitting in a restaurant talking on a cellphone and ignoring the other person at the table. This is really rude. And if you answer a phone call when you are talking to someone, it tell the person they are not as important. If people really need to take an important call, they should apologize to the person they are with and keep the call brief.

These are three ways people can use cellphones better. To make for better social interaction. Actually, cellphones haven't been around so long. And maybe people still have to get the hang of using them properly and politely. We need to educate people to think of others when they use their phones.

Revising and proofreading the draft, the writer reduced the wordiness and conversational phrasing and corrected spelling errors. Compare the two versions:

Rules for Cellphone Use

Cellphones have become ubiquitous. So many adults already own one that companies searching for a new market are now designing them for young children. While cellphones are a convenient tool, and can perhaps even be life-saving in emergencies, they also have become a nuisance as people misuse them. Cellphone users need to learn proper etiquette: turning off the phone entirely when it could be disruptive, using the phone judiciously in public spaces, and giving the person they are talking to priority over the person on the phone.

Cellphone users should realize that they should not leave their phones on at all times. A ringing phone can often disturb other people. In classes, at movies, plays, and concerts, and in business meetings, people are required to be attentive to the entertainment or business at hand. For example, the actors on stage can be totally thrown off their stride by the sound of phones ringing in the audience. Cellphones should be turned off completely at any such event because even vibrating phones can be disruptive.

Second, cellphone users should always be aware when they are in shared, public spaces. They sometimes seem to forget, or do not care, that they have an audience. The people on the bus or the commuter train do not want to listen to one side of a half-hour conversation detailing someone's gall bladder operation or shady business dealings. Moreover, people often talk loudly on the phone, more loudly than they would talk to someone sitting next to them, thus disturbing those around them. In addition, stopping to use the phone in a crowded hallway or staircase can cause traffic problems and irritate others. Cellphone users need to be more considerate of the people around them.

Finally, people need to acknowledge that the person they are interacting with is more important than anyone calling. It is very rude to have a cellphone conversation in a restaurant while ignoring the other person at the table. Interrupting a conversation to answer a phone tells the first person that he or she is not as important as the caller. If people really need to take an important call, they should apologize to the person they are with and keep the call brief.

These three guidelines of cellphone etiquette can make for smoother social interaction. Cellphones are a relatively new invention, and perhaps people still have to get the hang of using them properly. We need to educate people to think of others when they use their phones.

Writing an Outline

Outlines can help keep you on track. This is especially important for in-class essay writing because if you run out of time, the instructor will be able to see where you wanted to go. Outlines can be very detailed or very simple. A basic outline for a five-paragraph essay would have the thesis and the three topic sentences. You can also include the supporting points.

Here is an example of an outline, followed by the full essay:

Thesis: Family meal lets people share food, learn good behaviour, and spend time together.

1. Eating together:
    *   home-cooked, more nutritious food
    *   eating slowly
    *   variety of foods
    *   traditional foods

2. Good behaviour:
    *   table etiquette
    *   sharing chores

3. Time to talk:
    *   news to share about the day
    *   current events

The Family Meal

In today's hectic lifestyle, meals have become little more than pit stops. People grab something on the run, often fast food or processed foods, and rarely take the time to sit down and enjoy a meal together with the most important people in their lives—their families. However busy their lives become, they should take the time to gather together for meals. The family meal provides people with an opportunity to share food, learn good behaviour, and spend time together.

A meal is primarily about the food, and a shared family meal offers many benefits. The food is generally healthier, since it is more likely to be home-cooked. It is usually consumed more slowly—which is also good for the digestive system. Children are introduced to foods they might not eat if they are accustomed to having individual meals. Shared dinners often feature food that is traditional to the family and its ethnic culture. Moreover, children may learn how to appreciate and prepare such foods.

The family meal also offers opportunities to learn good behaviour. Children can learn proper table etiquette when they share a relaxed meal at home rather than grabbing a burger at a drive-through. These good manners will serve them well later when they are attending business lunches or wedding receptions. The meal also offers a good opportunity for family members to share the chores of preparing and serving the meal and cleaning up afterward. Children who have learned to work together in this way grow up to be more considerate and less likely to sit around expecting to be waited on.

Finally, dinnertime is a chance for families to get together and talk. Because the meal is at the end of the day, everyone will have news to share. Children can talk about what they learned at school, and parents can share events from their workday. They can talk about current events and exchange opinions. The family meal can be an occasion for enjoyable, relaxed conversation. With everyone leading such busy lives, a shared meal can be a uniting element, giving family members an opportunity to communicate with one another.

The benefits of a shared family meal are so profound that people should not eliminate it from their lives, no matter how busy they get. Modern families must take a good hard look at their schedules and take some time off from business meetings, extracurricular activities, and clubs to spend time together as a family sharing a meal. Even if they find it impossible to arrange to eat together every evening, they should schedule a family meal once a week at the very least.

You can compare this essay to paragraph C on page 147.

Activity 5.3

Here are some brainstorming notes on the topic "What factors determine how much second-generation immigrants will maintain their mother tongue?" Arrange the ideas in three paragraphs. Write a topic sentence for each paragraph. Work with a partner or in a small group:

a) whether they attend language school for their mother tongue

b) how well their parents speak English

c) the birth order (oldest child versus youngest)

d) whether they visit their parents' native country

e) whether they live with or frequently visit grandparents who do not speak English

f) whether the children live in a community where many immigrants speak that language

g) the attitude of the second generation towards the ethnic culture

h) whether they can read and write in that language

i) how useful the language is for international business or travel

j) whether the parents encourage the children to speak the language

Writing a Thesis Statement

The thesis statement is the most important sentence in the essay. It comes at the end of the introduction. A thesis statement is a complete, concise, grammatical statement that presents a supportable idea that can be explored in the scope of the essay.

A thesis statement should not be a fact:

> The size of the average family grew during the baby boom. [poor thesis]

> The baby boom had sociological, economic, and political effects in Canada. [better]

It should not present a personal opinion that cannot be argued:

> I like biking. [poor thesis]

> Biking is a fun, healthy, and socially responsible activity. [better]

It should not be too broad for the essay:

> Teenagers face many problems growing up. [poor thesis]

> Children of immigrant parents have to deal with cultural differences. [better]

It should not be too narrow:

> Second-generation immigrants may not like the potential spouse picked out by their parents. [weak]

> Second-generation immigrants may not accept the idea of a traditional arranged marriage. [better]

It should not be an announcement:

> In this essay, I am going to compare big-box stores with independent businesses. [poor thesis]

> Independent stores offer knowledgeable service, good product choice, and shopping convenience. [better]

Note that a thesis statement is a complete, concise, grammatical statement. It cannot be a fragment:

> Working at home.

> Working at home offers several advantages over working in an office. [correct]

It cannot be a question:

> What is the best way to stop teenagers from smoking?

> Anti-smoking campaigns need to be tailored to teenagers' concerns. [correct]

It cannot be a command:

> Note the differences between King Lear and Macbeth.

> Shakespeare's King Lear and Macbeth are two very different rulers. [correct]

It must be one statement, not four:

> Swimming pools in school are a good investment for three reasons. First, swimming is so important that all children should learn how to swim. Second, having pools on-site is very convenient for lessons. Third, the community can use the pool after school hours, making it a more economical use of the facility.

> Swimming pools in school are a good investment because of the need for basic swimming skills, the convenience of the on-site facility, and the potential for community use. [better]

If it includes the arguments of the body paragraphs, it must have parallel structure (see page 91 for an explanation of parallel structure):

> The family meal means that people can share food, spending time together, and they can learn good behaviour at the table. [incorrect]

> The family meal provides people with an opportunity to share food, spend time together, and learn good behaviour.

In a five-paragraph essay, the thesis statement may state the three main ideas to be discussed in the body, but in a longer essay this is not practical and a less specific thesis is presented:

> Teenagers often conflict with their parents on their social life, appearance, and household responsibilities. [good for a five-paragraph essay]

> Teenagers' relationship with their parents is often full of conflict. [good for a longer essay]

If the thesis statement lists the arguments of the body paragraphs, the thesis should be concise, with the three main ideas expressed in short phrases. Care must be taken to ensure that the sentence is grammatical, following parallel structure. In addition, the body paragraphs should explore the arguments in the same order that they are presented in the thesis statement.

Exercise 5.1

Decide whether the following sentences would make good thesis statements. If not, discuss what is wrong with them and how they could be improved:

1. This essay will show that SUVs are a waste of money.

2. Paper books cannot be fully replaced by electronic books because books are more convenient, easier on the eye, and aesthetically pleasing.

3. There are three main types of reasons why people get tattoos that will be explained here.

4. Reducing work hours enhances employee productivity, quality of life, and health.

5. What can be done about the homeless?

6. Many of today's fashions are impractical.

7. There are many unsung heroes in Canadian history.

8. Wireless connections allow people to use their laptops anywhere in the house.

9. Beauty is important.

10. This report will analyze the disadvantages of the QWERTY keyboard.

11. Before I tell you which side I support, let's review the topic first.

12. Students shouldn't be pawns in a strike.

13. There are four advantages to leasing a car rather than buying one.

14. So why should you invest in an RRSP when you are just a student?

15. Having a good credit rating will help you secure bank loans.

Exercise 5.2

These are incorrect four-sentence theses. Rewrite them into one concise, grammatical thesis statement. Take out any information that can be explained in the body paragraphs:

1. There's a lot of evidence to show that fast food is unhealthy, but people keep eating it. They like it because it's cheap. It tastes good. Fast food is very convenient.

2. People get tattoos for many reasons. One, they want to decorate their bodies. Two, they want to show that they belong to a specific group. Three, tattoos show what is important to them.

3. The QWERTY keyboard is an illogically designed system. It makes the left hand work harder. It hampers faster typing. It is more difficult to learn.

4. There are three main reasons for leasing a car. First, the monthly payments are lower. Second, you can always drive a new car after the three-year lease is over. Third, I don't have to worry about breakdowns as usually everything is covered under warranty.

5. For students who are at a loss during a teachers' strike, these are things they can do. They can read their textbook and review their notes. They should complete any assignments given before the strike so they will be up-to-date and maybe even ahead when the strike is over. They could do extra reading on the subject material to truly master it.

6. There are several basic types of TV commercial. One is the lifestyle ad where advertisers want consumers to think they will have the kind of life depicted in the commercial if they use the product. Another kind is the humorous commercial that tries to make the consumer laugh and therefore remember the product. Thirdly, there are straight information commercials that tell the consumer what he needs to know.

7. Transportation can be fixed in big cities if everyone cooperates. First, the public transit system needs to be improved to make it more convenient to use. Secondly, more goods need to be shipped by rail instead of by truck. Finally, use of personal vehicles needs to be controlled with fines or incentive programs.

Exercise 5.3

Rewrite these thesis statements so that they are concise and grammatical, with parallel structure:

1. The government should encourage young people to vote by teaching them about politics in schools, showing political news on television shows geared to them, and how easy voting is.

2. By reducing the workweek, the employment rate would be lower with more people working, productivity would go up, and more time for families and to enjoy life.

3. Parents can help their children go off to college by giving them money for tuition and living expenses, help them choose a school and program, and to encourage them when they are feeling discouraged.

4. The advantages of shopping on-line are that buyers can choose from a wide array of items, many of which may not be available in local stores, and they can do this shopping at home which is more convenient than going to the mall, and compare prices and read reviews before they buy.

5. The factors that would influence my choice of job: happiness, challenging and variety.

Activity 5.4

Write a thesis statement for the following essay topics:

1. What is the key to success in college?

2. Should second-generation immigrants be encouraged to marry within their ethnic group?

3. How do high school students benefit from a part-time job?

4. Why are extracurricular activities important in school?

5. What factors should a student consider when choosing post-secondary education?

You can also write thesis statements for the topics you generated in activity 5.1.

> **A thesis statement should**
> * answer the essay question;
> * show the point of view of the writer;
> * be one sentence;
> * be the last sentence of the introduction;
> * be concise;
> * have parallel structure.

Writing an Introduction

The function of an introduction is, of course, to introduce the topic to the reader. In a five-paragraph essay, the first paragraph is the introduction, while in a longer essay or report, the introduction may extend to several paragraphs or a whole section or unit. In an essay, the introduction generally ends with the thesis statement. The introduction leads the reader gradually to the thesis, provides any background information the reader may need, and narrows the topic.

What is actually in the introduction depends on the topic. For instance, an essay discussing solutions to a problem should have an introduction that explains the problem for the reader. In an essay discussing one side of a controversial issue, the main opposing arguments can be mentioned briefly in the introduction as a lead-in. If a reading (e.g., a book, a story, an article) is a point of departure for the essay, the point of view of the reading's author may be mentioned before the essay writer goes into his own thesis.

An introduction should not start with a thesis statement—that leaves no room to say anything else but the arguments of the essay. It should not contain a four-sentence thesis. It should catch readers' attention and prepare them for the essay. The introduction does not have to be very long; the body paragraphs should be longer.

Sample introductions

A) In an essay that discusses the effects of overwork, it would be appropriate to explain the causes first:

> Although it was once predicted that technology would result in too much leisure time for workers, the opposite seems to have happened. Instead of working fewer hours, we are working harder than ever. Downsizing has put pressure on surviving employees. Cellphones and laptops mean that workers are in contact with clients and their work at all times. As a result, stressed-out workers are showing signs of physical, mental, and social problems.

B) In an essay that explains the disadvantages of school uniforms, an introduction could establish why they are sought after:

> School uniforms are becoming increasingly popular as parents and school authorities try to rein in rebellious youth and tame the excesses of fashion. These people point to the skimpy tops girls wear and the pants falling off boys' bodies to argue that uniforms are best, that they lead to more discipline in the school. However, school uniforms will not accomplish what they want. Uniforms are impractical, uncomfortable, and unattractive.

C) This introduction establishes that starting college is both exciting and challenging before explaining the difficulties:

> Graduating from high school and going off to college is an exciting time. Students look forward to being on their own and pursuing the studies that will lead them to a career. However, many first-year students drop out when they find they cannot make the transition to college successfully. College students have to adjust to living on their own, being responsible for their studies, and coping with financial limitations.

D) In an essay that responds to a reading, it is useful to recap the author's arguments:

> In "All grown up and still in tow", Sherri Beattie argues that baby-boomer parents should let their children handle university on their own. She explains that her parents, a generation earlier, had let her muddle through on her own. While boomer parents should not interfere too much in their children's business, they should not be entirely hands-off either. Boomer parents can guide their children in their post-secondary education because they are more knowledgeable about schools, because the modern world is more complicated, and because high school graduates are not as mature as they seem.

Activity 5.5

Write an introduction (three to five sentences) for the thesis statements you generated in activity 5.4.

> **Tips for an introductory paragraph:**
> * It should gradually lead the reader to your thesis, which is the last sentence of the introduction.
> * It should give background information to the reader or prepare the way for your thesis.
> * It should not mention arguments in support of your thesis (i.e., it should not repeat statements that are in your body paragraphs).
> * It should not be longer than a body paragraph, in most cases.

Writing Body Paragraphs

A body paragraph in an essay is essentially the same as the developed paragraphs discussed in unit 4. It starts with a topic sentence giving the main idea. The rest of the paragraph has points and support. A body paragraph, however, is generally shorter than an independent paragraph, and it does not require a concluding sentence.

In an essay, the topic sentences of the body paragraphs take their cue from the thesis statement. In other words, they should relate to the thesis by taking the same idea but narrowing it down for the focus of the paragraph. The wording should be different so that the sentences are not repetitive.

> Thesis statement: Public transit is a worthwhile investment because it is good for citizens' health, finances, and quality of life.

> Topic sentence #1: Public transit leads to health benefits for the whole population.

> Topic sentence #2: Investing in a better transit infrastructure ultimately saves money for everyone.

> Topic sentence #3: Citizens' quality of life improves as more people use public transit and the number of cars on the roads decreases.

A topic sentence such as "Cars produce a lot of pollution" does not link directly to the thesis because it does not mention the benefits of transit. The reference is oblique; the readers have to make the connection rather than the writer having made it for them.

Remember that the topic sentence of each body paragraph should be clear on its own. Use nouns, not pronouns, in the first sentence of a paragraph. For example, Topic sentence #1 above cannot read "It leads to health benefits for the whole population" because the "it" cannot refer back to a noun (public transit) in the previous paragraph. Each paragraph is a new beginning, so nouns should be clearly identified.

The topic sentence sometimes links to the previous paragraph. For example, if the first body paragraph of the essay talks about the money earned at a part-time job, the second paragraph might begin "In addition to the much-needed income, part-time jobs offer an opportunity to learn new skills."

Body paragraphs in an essay do not need concluding sentences, especially concluding sentences that just repeat the topic sentence. However, you can use a concluding sentence in the paragraph if it is necessary and works well.

Activity 5.6

Write three topic sentences for each of the following thesis statements:

1. Students should pick a post-secondary program based on their interests, their skills, and the job prospects.

2. History courses are important because they teach critical thinking skills, explore life lessons, and show students about their heritage.

3. How easily immigrants adapt to their new country depends on their educational background, their language skills, and their personality.

Choose one of the topics above and write the three body paragraphs. Work with a partner or in a small group, if you wish.

Writing a Conclusion

Conclusion paragraphs are similar to introduction paragraphs. Unlike body paragraphs, they are not developed with a topic sentence, arguments, and support. Like an introduction, a conclusion should not contain ideas that support the thesis statement. The conclusion starts with a restatement of the thesis, but that is the only repetition and it should not be in the same words. In longer essays, you can write a short summary in a conclusion, but this is not advisable in a five-paragraph essay. The repetition is boring and insulting to the reader. Similar to the introduction, the conclusion should be shorter than the body paragraphs.

A conclusion can give the "so what?" idea showing the significance of what has been argued in the essay. It can offer suggestions for improvement or predict the future. It should not spring on the reader a preference or point of view because this should have been clear in the thesis statement.

A conclusion should not apologize for brevity (e.g., "These are only some of the problems teenagers face") or make new points to support the thesis. It is the last thing said to the reader, so the conclusion should have a punch.

Here are sample conclusions for the same topics as the sample introductions above:

A) With all these harmful effects of working long hours, we should make a change in our work habits. Even though cutting hours would result in lower pay, we have to value our health above anything else. We need to make sure we lead a balanced life and not work ourselves to death.

B) It is not surprising that so many students, and even their parents, despise school uniforms. Students are individuals; there is no reason to make them uniform in appearance. They are getting an education, not being enlisted in an army.

C) If students can make these adjustments to college life, they will be successful in school. Moreover, they will have gained maturity and learned to deal with responsibility. This will be as valuable as their education in their future life.

D) College and university students do need some guidance from their parents in order to make the transition to adulthood. While Beattie recommends letting students sink or swim, it would be better for parents to help them gradually adjust. Parents should, however, be aware of their children's abilities and not step in when help is not needed.

Activity 5.7

Write conclusions to go with the introductions you generated in activity 5.7.

Practising Essay Writing

Here are some brainstorming notes you can use for practice. You can work alone, with a partner, or in a group. Working with the same base allows you to compare results in the class. You can focus on different parts of the essay: the outline, the thesis, topic sentences, body paragraphs, introductions, and conclusions. For example, each group can write an introduction for the essay on immigrant assimilation and then compare the introductions to see the range of possibilities. You can add ideas or eliminate any you do not think fit your essay.

You can also start the process from scratch, coming up with essay topics and brainstorming as a class or in small groups. In addition, you can look back over this unit and develop some of the essay ideas in other activities and exercises. You can also look at the readings in part 2, all of which have essay topics as assignments.

Topic: How can at-risk students be encouraged not to drop out of high school?
a) arts courses (music, drama, art)
b) counselling
c) visits to post-secondary schools, work sites
d) speakers from the work world, former drop-outs
e) alternatives to regular courses (co-op, independent study)
f) tutoring for students who are failing
g) variety of courses, both academic and hands-on
h) extracurricular activities to engage the students

Topic: What factors determine how readily immigrants will assimilate to Canada?
a) their education level
b) their attitude to their new culture, open-mindedness
c) whether they live in an ethnic neighbourhood or not
d) their age
e) their family structure
f) whether they work with Canadians
g) whether they have immigrated reluctantly
h) how similar their native language and culture are to their new ones
i) how much they've travelled and seen other countries
j) willingness to learn

Topic: What should parents teach teenagers to prepare them for living on their own?
a) budgeting
b) cooking nutritious meals
c) keeping track of their bank and credit card statements
d) saving money on food purchases
e) cleaning rooms (bathroom, kitchen, living areas)
f) doing their own laundry
g) dealing with utilities (hydro, gas, cable)
h) dealing with emergencies such as toilets flooding and lights going out
i) how to use basic tools (hammer, screwdriver, paint brush)

Use the following structure when you divide up the points for your essay:

Outline
Thesis statement:
Topic sentence 1:
    Points for this paragraph:
Topic sentence 2:
    Points for this paragraph:
Topic sentence 3:
    Points for this paragraph:

Sample Essays

Read the following sample essays, examining the structure. Identify the thesis statement and see how the topic sentences relate to it. Look at the support given for the points made in the essay.

The Definition of Success

Many people equate success with wealth. If someone has a mansion and a fleet of luxury cars, that person must be successful. However, even though few people ever attain that degree of affluence, many can look proudly upon their many achievements. Success means making worthwhile contributions in work and in society and gaining contentment in life.

Because work is so important in human life, people need to do worthwhile work to be considered successful. It does not matter if the job is running a global corporation or cleaning the streets; all jobs contribute something to society and need doing. Some work may not pay very well, such as artistic endeavours, but it should still be recognized as valuable. Artists contribute memorable performances, written works to educate and entertain, and sculptures and paintings to satisfy the aesthetic needs of their audiences. People need to take pride in their work and do it to the best of their ability to be considered a success.

A successful life is one that also makes a mark on society. People can do this through their work but also through other achievements. Raising children to become valued members of society is a way of making a difference in the world. Having friends and helping those in need are important aspects of human existence. Human beings are social animals above all else, so lives spent in isolation cannot be considered as valuable as those that reach out to people.

Aside from what they contribute to society, people cannot be considered successful if they have not achieved some measure of contentment in their own lives. This may not involve vast sums of money or numerous possessions but just enough to have their basic needs met. Studies have shown that people in poorer countries actually have more joy in their lives than those in rich, Western countries. People who gripe and complain about every facet of their existence must be considered more failures than successes.

When people want to evaluate the success of their lives, they must look at what they have accomplished through work, through their contributions to society, and in their individual existence. A life well-lived is one that has made a mark as well as one that satisfies the person living it. People only get one chance at life—they must do what they can with the time they are given.

The Success of Fast-Food Restaurants

Since the first drive-in restaurants of the 1950s, fast food has increased in popularity so much that the industry is a dominant player in the global economy. The golden arches of McDonald's restaurants are one of the most recognized corporate symbols in the world. The industry has so much clout that it can influence political policies such as the minimum wage. Fast-food businesses are successful because they offer food that is cheap, tasty, and convenient.

Price is an important consideration in the food industry, and fast food is less expensive than other restaurant meals. A combo at Harvey's, for example, is less than five dollars, so a family can get a meal out for under 20 dollars. The industry strives to keep prices low by keeping wages low. The factory approach to meal preparation allows it to hire untrained workers willing to accept this wage. The industry has also sought to control food production costs through vertical integration, getting into the agriculture business and meat processing. The bottom line is that the low price of fast food makes it attractive to most segments of society.

The fast-food industry has mastered the art of offering food that appeals to the taste buds of human beings. High fat content is one of the main characteristics of fast food, and fat makes food taste good, despite the nutritional drawbacks. French fries, for example, are the most consumed restaurant food. Leaner, more nutritious offerings are less appealing and sell poorly. High starch, salt, and sugar content also make the food taste good and satisfy cravings.

Convenience is probably the most important consideration in the popularity of fast food. The restaurants are ubiquitous in both small towns and big cities. The main streets leading into town are often fast-food strips where McDonald's, Wendy's, Taco Bell, and Tim Horton's co-exist side by side. Fast service is a hallmark of these restaurants; the name 'fast food', after all, suggests speed. Customers can either use the drive-through or walk up to the counter and get a hot meal delivered in a couple of minutes. They do not have to cook or do dishes. With North American families struggling with overloaded schedules, the lure of quick, easy food is irresistible.

Fast-food restaurants offer inexpensive, delicious, and convenient food to a North American market that needs it. Added to these basics is the clever marketing of the industry, such as making fast food particularly appealing to children with toys and play areas. Even though consumers know that fast food is not particularly nutritious, they line up to fill their stomachs and fill the coffers of the franchise owners.

Reasons for Body Art

Many people today sport tattoos and body piercings. Although these adornments have been around for thousands of years, their current popularity is somewhat surprising since it does not result from long-standing cultural traditions. Now it is not only bikers, soldiers, sailors, and criminals who go for tattoos; middle-aged, middle-class people are also following the current fashion for such epidermal embellishment. The reasons that body art is popular stem from artistic pursuits, personal expression, and image projection.

Tattoos and body piercing can simply be viewed as another form of human decoration. Body art has its place along with make-up, hair styles, jewellery, and fashion. People want to enhance their physical attributes. A colourful tattoo is just a pretty picture—but one that is permanently inscribed on the skin. A glittering navel stud is considered sexy when a young woman has a well-toned midriff to show it off. Tattoos and piercings draw attention to the body, something people have sought to do since prehistoric times.

In addition to being attractive, body art can express various attachments. Some people have a tattoo of the name of their lover or spouse. A biker may have the name of his gang inscribed on his body. People can choose a tattoo that shows their ethnic heritage, such as a Chinese character, which might even express a concept the person admires, such as "joy" or "wisdom." The tattoo shows what the person believes in.

Tattoos and piercings also promote a certain image that young people value. They still have some shock value in society, so they are often chosen by rebellious adolescents. This is no different from earlier generations wearing long hair to antagonize their parents. Moreover, because the processes involved are painful, people might enjoy the 'tough guy' image associated with those types of body art.

The motivations behind body art vary, but it is currently very much in style. It will be interesting to see how long tattoos and piercings remain on the scene. All fashion and fads have their day. While piercings can be easily removed, leaving only a small hole, tattoos require sophisticated removal treatments. Plastic surgeons may well be busy in the future removing the indiscretions of youth, especially tattoos that have blurred or stretched along with the body.

Parenting College Students

After years of shepherding children through elementary and secondary school, parents don't want to be out of the loop when their children graduate and head off to post-secondary school. Even though the children are legally adults, they often do not have the maturity and knowledge to handle college or university on their own. Although they must let their children live their own lives, parents can play a role in helping their children through college.

First, parents can help their children choose a school and a program of study. This is a crucial decision. Students invest important years and thousands of dollars in their studies, so they need to make sure they are making a wise choice. Based on their own experience in school and in the workplace, parents can give their children information about the various schools and fields of study. Moreover, they know their children's talents and interests and can often predict what their children will find suitable. However, parents must realize this is guidance only; they should not push their children into places their children do not want to go.

Another way parents can assist their children is by giving financial support. College can be very expensive, especially if students are living away from home. While students should be encouraged to work part-time and during the summer to save money for tuition and living expenses, parents should also contribute to the education costs, depending on what they can afford. Some students may feel that the money is only a loan. Whatever the arrangement, students will find their path to education much easier with a few extra dollars in their pocket.

Finally, parents should support and encourage their children. They can show interest in their children's education by asking about their courses and professors even if they know little about the subject. If the students are living at home, their parents can provide a comfortable environment for them to study in. For students living away, parents can send "care packages" of nourishing food and little gifts. Staying in contact with the students gives them emotional support.

In conclusion, parents can assist their children without overly interfering. They can help them make a gradual transition from adolescence to adulthood, especially since the college years are too important to leave children totally on their own.

Personal versus impersonal essays

Some instructors assign personal topics to their students in an effort to engage them more in their writing. Others want students to practise writing objectively and impersonally as training for the work world. You should be able to handle both kinds of essays and to know what is called for. Your instructor should make his or her preferences clear. The question asked will also indicate whether the response should be personal. Here are two essays on the same topic, one personal and one impersonal. (See page 7 for more on writing impersonally.) Notice that the personal essay is more specific, while the impersonal one is more general and can apply to a variety of situations.

> Topic: McJob is the term coined to refer to low-paying, often menial jobs that frequently involve serving the public, based on the model of working at McDonald's. What can students learn from working in such jobs part-time and during the summers?

The Benefits of McJobs

Students often work part-time or summer jobs to pay their way through school. These positions are usually "McJobs"—low-paying labour, often involving public service. While many people disdain such menial labour, students can actually benefit from such work in more than monetary terms. They can learn time management, practical skills, and personal skills.

By working part-time, students learn to manage their precious time. First, they have to balance their school and work responsibilities. They know they cannot procrastinate with their academic assignments because they have little time to waste. Moreover, they learn to be punctual because bosses are less accepting of tardiness than even teachers are. Finally, they learn to get their work done efficiently.

There is a wide range of practical skills that can be acquired on the job. These can be carried over to other jobs or even to everyday household chores. For example, students who work as landscapers will be able to take care of their yard and garden when they become homeowners. Restaurant cooks can serve their future families good meals. Cashiers can handle money for everyday transactions. Clerks in clothing stores become adept at pressing and folding clothing.

Since so many part-time and summer jobs involve dealing with the public, student workers develop valuable people skills. They learn how to be polite and cheerful and how to listen to a complaint without flying off the handle. Because they deal with such a wide range of people, they have a better understanding of humanity. For example, a cashier in a fast-food restaurant will see people struggling to come up with a few dollars to pay for a meal. Camp counsellors learn how children develop and learn.

Part-time and summer jobs allow students to grow and acquire skills. Students have to make sure that they do not take on too many hours because their school work is still the priority. However, learning does not stop at the classroom door, and students should be open to these experiences that they may not have a chance at again. [338 words]

Topic: What have you learned from working at McJobs?

What McJobs Have Taught Me

As a student, I had my share of McJobs. I worked as a waitress, a cashier, and tour guide. Although some of my friends sneered at my jobs and chose to get into debt with student loans instead, I found that working like this was a good experience. My jobs taught me valuable skills in time management, food and drink preparation, and speaking to the public.

My work experience taught me how to use my time and energy profitably. Not only did I have to learn how to balance my studies, work hours, and social life, I learned how to get the most of my work hours. As a waitress, I learned never to go anywhere empty-handed. I had enough miles to walk without having to do them twice. If I took plates of food or drinks to the tables, I went back to the kitchen with empty plates from other tables. Even today, as I clean house, I find that I work as efficiently as I did in my days as a server, making sure I'm carrying something both coming and going.

The skills I learned in the food service industry carry over to everyday life. Sometimes I had to mix drinks, so I picked up some bartending skills that still come in useful at parties. At times I had to help the kitchen staff, so I learned to cook and plate food. I did not even know how to cook eggs before I had to help prepare breakfast at a truck stop restaurant where I worked. Plating food is all about making it look appetizing, something that is as useful at home as it is in a restaurant.

Probably the most important skills I acquired were people skills. As a waitress, I had to deal with picky customers. Serving food for a catering company took me to formal functions at embassies and government buildings where I had to contend with a demanding clientele including dignitaries such as Pierre Trudeau and René Lévesque. As a tour guide, I learned to project my voice and keep my audience interested. Because I worked in Ottawa, I had to be bilingual, so my fluency in French increased.

Even though working part-time made it difficult to spend enough time on my school work, I don't regret the hours I worked because of all I learned. I probably would have wasted more time if I didn't have jobs, and my marks would not have been much better. [412 words]

Essay checklist:
- A five-paragraph essay has an introduction, three body paragraphs, and a conclusion.
- Your thesis statement should be the last sentence of the introduction. You restate this thesis as the first sentence of your conclusion.
- Each body paragraph should start with a topic sentence that relates directly to the thesis.
- The arguments in support of your thesis are in the body paragraphs and not in the introduction or conclusion.
- Support your points with specific examples or explanation.

Rhetorical Skills

Rhetoric is the art of speaking or writing to make an argument or impress someone. Communicating effectively involves knowing the structures of language—the way words, sentences, paragraphs, and essays are put together —and the way language is manipulated to have an effect on the reader.

Writing instructors generally speak of different rhetorical forms: narration, description, definition, comparison, exposition, process description, and persuasion. Each form has its particular use in communicating ideas. For example, if you are asked to tell a story, you will use the narrative form to tell what happened. If you are asked to explain a word or idea, your rhetoric technique is definition to explain what something is. In essay writing, there is often a combination of the above modes or forms. Of course, there may be an emphasis of one form over another. Still, whichever mode you use you must make points and support them clearly and concisely.

This unit deals with the specific modes of writing. Each is explained and illustrated with sample paragraphs and short essays.

Illustrating

Essay topics assigned to students in college or university often require the writer to show and tell. This is the essence of illustrating as a rhetorical form. Instructors want the students to be able to explain an idea, a concept, a thought. Illustrating then is the ideal mode. (Many of the essays in the previous unit are such expository essays.) Often merely stating something is not enough; it requires showing.

The Hazards of Treeplanting

Every year, thousands of Canadian university and college students head north for summer jobs planting trees. Logging companies have to reforest a certain percentage of their cut land, so they subcontract to treeplanting companies. That's where the treeplanters come in. The goal of a treeplanter is simple: plant as many trees as possible. It seems, however, that everything will conspire to prevent the planter from achieving this: the weather, the bugs, and the rough living and working conditions.

Because planters spend the whole day outdoors and sleep in tents at night, they have to deal with every kind of weather condition. When they start in May, there is often snow on the ground. A spring snowstorm can crush their tents. Planters plant in the rain, during thunderstorms, and in snow, only to go home to shiver in their tents wearing every warm thing they brought. Later in the season, they have to endure the kind of searing heat that sparks forest fires.

The bug situation is like a video game in which increasing levels of difficulty bring new enemies to fight. Level 1 would be easy and relatively bug-free. Level 2 would introduce the blackflies, a few at first and then a psychotic swarm of tiny, annoying flies getting into the planter's eyes, ears, and nose. Level 3 would be blackflies and mosquitoes. New bugs are added to the mix approximately once a week. After mosquitoes, there come friendly flies, deer flies, sandflies and horseflies. Each has their own deadly weapon and method of attack. Unlucky planters have even found wasp nests with the thrust of their shovel. It's not enough to be suffering from the bites themselves; every planter is in constant danger of self-inflicted bug-swatting-related injuries.

In addition to bugs, treeplanters have larger threats from the animal world. Bears are attracted to the food and garbage around camp and become a terrifying nuisance. They are undeterred by such defensive systems as noise-makers and flares and will sometimes come right into the camp. As they work, planters try to make a lot of noise so the bears will avoid them. Other animals can threaten treeplanters. While encounters with charging moose are relatively rare, they can happen.

Dirt is a constant companion in the bush. It is inhaled, eaten, and ground into a treeplanter's flesh. A planter's hands will not be completely free of dirt until a few weeks after the return to civilization. Locals in day-off towns know how to spot a planter. A planter's shovel hand has rough calluses that prove havens for dirt and sand. Treeplanters generally go into town once a week to get a decent shower, do laundry, and pour a couple of beers down their throat to chase all that dirt they swallowed.

The job itself entails bending over to put a seedling in the ground 2,000 times a day, scrambling over obstacles and unfriendly terrain. Trees cannot be haphazardly shoved into the ground; quality is of the greatest concern to the crew boss. The plug must remain unbent and completely in mineral soil, while the tree itself must be straight, at the proper depth and spacing. A planter has to satisfy several tree-checkers as well as his or her crew boss. In a 10-hour day, allowing for breaks and bag-up times, 2,000 trees means a tree planted every 10 seconds. Good planters often plant three or four thousand a day, working quickly because the money earned depends on how many trees get planted. At eight to 10 cents a tree (depending on the terrain), a planter can make $250 a day and earn enough for tuition in the first month.

Because of the repetitive and high-impact nature of the work, planters are prone to injuries. Tendonitis strikes ankles, knees, elbows, and wrists. The numbness in the toes can last for months after planting. Bruises and scrapes are inevitable in the rocky, "slash"-covered landscape. My supervisor used to tell us that if we did not fall down at least twice a day, we were not going fast enough. Rainy or icy conditions are especially hazardous. The weight of three to four hundred trees in a planter's tree-bags makes the balancing act that much harder.

Treeplanting is no summer vacation. It is hard, miserable, competitive work, and those who enjoy it are certifiably insane. Do not go for the experience, to save the environment or to make money. In fact, do not go at all. As for me, I will be there again next year.

Giving examples

As shown in unit 3, supporting your general statements is important. Examples are commonly used as specific support. An example serves to prove your point. You do not have to give a list of supporting evidence when one judicious example will do. Of course, this example has to be relevant and fairly detailed.

The transition signals *for example* and *for instance* are generally used to introduce a sentence example:

> People can cut down on unnecessary trips with their vehicles. For example, they can walk or bicycle to the corner store.

> Students can build their readings skills gradually. They can read children's books, for instance, to develop their abilities with simpler vocabulary and sentence structure.

If you are giving a list of examples within a sentence, use the verb *include* or the phrase *such as*:

> My courses this semester include biology, psychology, and chemistry.

> I play many sports, such as baseball, tennis, and hockey.

Both *include* and *such as* tell the reader that these are only some of the examples, so do not end the sentence with *and so on, etc.*, or an ellipsis (. . .). Note that the comma appears before *such as*, not after.

Avoid launching into an unnecessary narrative mode for examples in essays. This leads to wordiness and distracts from the point you are trying to make:

> People who live in squalor have many problems. One of them is wasting time looking for things that are misplaced. For example,

> Tom has a job interview. As he is getting ready, he starts looking for a clean white shirt and a copy of his resumé. He digs through all his stuff at home but without any success. As a result, he loses time and arrives at the interview too late. Thus he lost a good chance to get a good job. [wordy]

> People who live in squalor have many problems. One of them is wasting time looking for things that are misplaced. For example, a job candidate who arrives late for his interview because he could not find a clean shirt may lose the chance at the job. [better]

Finally, do not use abbreviations such as *e.g.*, *i.e.*, and *etc.* in your paragraphs and essays. These abbreviations belong in your notes, not in your final drafts.

Assignment

Write an expository essay explaining the duties in a job that you have held.

Narrating

Story-telling is the most ancient of human arts, serving as both entertainment and a teaching tool. Researchers have shown that facts are remembered better if they are delivered in the context of a story. In other words, you may recall the facts of events better if you read them in a historical novel rather than in a history textbook.

Narration is simply telling a story, saying what happened, whether it be a true story or a fictional one. How much detail is in the story, however, depends on the audience and purpose. You may be spinning out a story of something funny that happened to you, perhaps even exaggerating for effect. You may be writing a fantastical children's story to entertain your young nephew. Or you may be relating what happened in a traffic accident for a police report, as in the following account:

> I was driving northbound on Chapel Road, going through an intersection that had no traffic lights or stop sign. A car in the southbound side was in the left turn lane. The car turned left before I cleared the intersection and hit the front of my car, on the driver's side. It pushed my car up onto the snow bank.

Here is another simple narrative:

> My treeplanting crew all know the dangers of bears. I've told them to make a lot of noise when they are out in the bush. Many of them sing as they plant trees. This bear, however,

came upon me suddenly. I was unloading the seedlings from
the back of the truck. The other crew boss had gone to check
on one of her planters. This black bear came around a thicket.
I don't know who was more surprised—the bear or me. After
a moment's hesitation, it charged at me, knocking me down.
It bit on my steel-toed boot but didn't break through to my foot.
With my free foot, I kicked it in the snout and yelled at it.
It backed off, and then charged again. I kicked it again, and it
turned back and loped off into the bush. Fortunately, I wasn't
really hurt.

Some people are gifted story-tellers, enthralling listeners and keeping
their attention. Others have trouble telling a story, confusing their audience
by skipping back and forth relating the events that happened or boring their
audience with too many unnecessary details.

It is important to keep your audience and purpose in mind. A story
for entertainment is generally longer and more detailed. A narrative that
simply states the facts of the events would be used in a business report. In
addition, how much information you give depends on what your audience already knows. For example, if you are telling what happened to
Uncle Joe when he was fishing, you do not need to give as much information to your family members, who already know Uncle Joe, as you
need to give to your friends, who may not know the personal quirks of
your extended family.

Journalistic essays often start with a narrative—an account of something
that happened to the author or someone else. The author uses the narrative
to get the reader's attention and to serve as an introduction to the topic. This
is the technique used in "All grown up and still in tow" (page 262) and
"Survive squalor and learn to tidy" (page 268). "Podless and happy to be that
way" (page 277) is an example of a narrative essay.

Be sure to make the point of your narrative clear. For example, if you
are writing a complaint letter to a company and are telling a long, involved
story of what happened, you should have an introductory paragraph that
succinctly tells what your complaint is and what action you want. The narrative can then be support for your point.

Sequence is an important consideration in narration. An audience can
follow a story better if it is told in chronological order (with the events in
the order that they occurred). Use time transition signals such as *then* and *as
a result*. The story told in "The strange forces behind the Richard hockey
riot" (page 304) is harder to follow because the author goes back and forth
in time, starting with a description of the riot but then going back to
explain what caused it. This technique is often used for dramatic purposes.
If you choose to use it, as always, remember your audience. The technique
can make your narrative more difficult for a reader to follow.

When you relate a story, it is important to keep verb tense in mind. In English, we often use the simple present tense to tell a story since it makes it more immediate. Even though Shakespeare has been dead for 400 years, we say, "Shakespeare tells the story of two lovers in *Romeo and Juliet*." The past tense is also used for narration. It is important, however, not to mix the two tenses unnecessarily. Whether you decide to tell your story in the present tense or in the past, do not switch.

Here are two versions of the same story, a well-known Aesop's fable. The first uses dialogue to spin the story out. The second is a simple reporting of events.

The North Wind and the Sun

The North Wind was a boisterous and blustering fellow. His breath blew cold and strong, and he liked to shake leaves from trees and push the waters of the sea into billowing whitecaps. In particular, he liked to wreak havoc on the people below. He would send their hats flying off their heads, tie their laundry into knots on the clothesline, and scatter important papers across the yard.

"I own the sky, and I rule the earth," he boasted.

One fall day, as the North Wind was up to his usual mischief, he came upon the Sun, who was covered behind some clouds. The North Wind blew them away so that he could see the Sun clearly.

The Sun smiled. "Thank you, North Wind. I'm sure the people down there appreciate what you have done too."

The North Wind sensed that the Sun was making fun of him with his easy smiles. And he didn't like it. "I'm stronger than you are, you know."

The Sun smiled again. "I'm sure you are, North Wind."

The Wind looked below and saw a traveller walking along the road. The man wore a heavy cloak and a wide-brimmed hat.

"We should have a competition. Do you see that man below? The one who can take his cloak off will be considered the stronger. Do you want to go first?"

"No, you can have the first go at it."

The North Wind came behind the traveller and suddenly burst forth a wintry blast. He caught the traveller unawares—momentarily. Then the man grabbed his cloak and hat tightly against his tiny frame. The North Wind twirled about and sent a powerful gust in front of the man. More determined than ever, the traveller wrapped his clothing about him.

Now, this went on for quite a while, but no matter which way the wind blew, the traveller held onto the hat and cloak for dear life. Finally, the North Wind exhausted all his tricks and withdrew.

When it was the Sun's turn, he merely kept beaming brightly, and soon the traveller felt not only the warmth but the heat of the day. The man began to remove his clothing: first his hat and then his heavy cloak. Pretty soon he was loosening his other garments.

"Sometimes," the Sun said, "gentle persuasion works better than force."

Note that the present tense is used in the next telling of the story:

> One day the North Wind and the Sun decide to have a competition to see who is the strongest. They spy a traveller below and agree that the one who is able to get the man's cloak off will be deemed the winner. The Wind blows harder and harder, but the man holds on to his cloak very tightly. Then it is the Sun's turn. As the rays of the Sun beat down on the traveller, he grows very warm and takes off his cloak. The moral is that sometimes gentle persuasion works where force does not.

Narration has direct quotation and reported speech. See page 252 for more on quoting.

Exercise 6.1

Here is another Aesop's fable, told in past tense. Rewrite it, changing it to the present tense. Or rewrite it adding details to expand the story:

> There once was a hare who wanted to race with a tortoise. He believed it would be an easy win since the tortoise crawled on all fours and carried his home on his back. The hare had powerful hind legs, and he could spring forth in great jumps and bounds. The race was unfair, of course. Surprisingly, though, the tortoise said yes to this competition. So on the day of the race, both hare and tortoise agreed that the first to reach the pond, which was across the meadow, would be the winner. The hare graciously gave his competitor a head start. In two hops, the hare caught up with the tortoise and in another two leaps he was far ahead, so far ahead that he decided to rest and take a nap. The tortoise, however, steady plodded on, one leg after another, until he passed the sleeping rabbit. By the time the hare woke up, the tortoise had reached the pond. The moral of this story is that slow and steady wins the race.

Exercise 6.2

Here is an informal, personal narrative. Write a few sentences to say what happened from the Orc's point of view or the manager's point of view (for an incident report):

> So there we were sitting front row centre for one of the preview performances of *The Lord of the Rings*. We hadn't wanted to sit that close, but there was a bit of an order mix-up and there wasn't too much choice. Anyway, even though our seats made it difficult to see everything happening on stage, especially when sections of

Exercise 6.2 – *continued*

the stage were elevated, we did get an amazing view of the action. We could have reached out and touched the actors sometimes. I did have the urge to peel the fruit sticker off the bottom of Merry's boot. But sitting in the front row was hazardous. We got lungfuls of the dry ice "smoke" and got covered in tissue paper bits in a "storm." The actors came so close to the edge of the stage sometimes that I started cringing, especially when the Orcs were doing acrobatic tumbles and the stage platforms were rising, creating an ever-changing landscape. Some had walking sticks attached to their arms; thumping the sticks made them even more menacing in their elaborate costumes. And then there was the Orc who I could see losing his balance as he teetered on the edge. Sure enough, he fell over, off the stage—landing right on top of me. It was only a few seconds before he scrambled back up, helped by another actor. Except for feeling sore in my knee and elbow, I could almost believe it didn't happen. At intermission, the actor came out in plain clothes—I would never have picked him out of a line-up—he looked sweet, not terrifying. He introduced himself, "I'm Sean, I'm the one who fell on you" and apologized sheepishly. The manager also came out, apologizing and offering a small (very small) item from the gift shop to "make up for being startled." It's too bad my wits weren't working. I should have asked for Sean's autograph, in case he ever becomes famous. At least I have a good story to tell.

Narratives
- should be in a logical order, with transition signals to help the reader follow the action;
- should give as much detail as required for the audience and purpose.

Assignments and activities

1. Write a one-paragraph account of something interesting that happened to you recently.
2. Write the story of a folk tale or fairy tale that you know. Add dialogue to make the story more detailed.
3. The instructor can divide the class into small groups of two to four students. Each group should get a transparency and start a story, writing the first sentence. The transparency should then be handed to another group to continue the story. The whole story can then be shown on the overhead projector.

Describing

Description paints a picture in the reader's mind. Sometimes you need to add description to clarify what you are talking about. Sometimes you want your audience to practically feel and sense it themselves. You may not be called upon to write a descriptive essay, but you may have to include description in other forms of writing. Remember your audience and purpose. For instance, the amount of detail you include will vary, depending on whether you are trying to entertain your audience with a story or just trying to make something clear on the way to explaining something else.

Here are some examples of descriptive paragraphs:

> Everybody needs a private place to think, dream, and just escape life. When I was younger, I spent a lot of the summer at our family cottage. It was a chalet-style building, and my bedroom was under the roof. Outside my room was a little balcony, which had a ramp that led to the rocky hill right next to our cottage. The ramp meant that I could leave my room without going through the main door of the cottage and alerting the whole family to my movements. That balcony exit was my personal escape. I didn't really get into mischief, but I liked to go out and climb to the top of the hill. It was mostly rock, but there was an indentation that provided a not-too-uncomfortable seating area. I could look down at the roof of the cottage to one side, deep into the woods on the other, and in front of me was the lake, which I could see between the trees. I often did not see any other people even though I was only a few feet from our neighbour's lot. I loved to sit there and smell the pine, feel the warm sunshine and the cooling breeze, and hear the lapping of the waves. It was my little piece of heaven.

> My roommate's brother Ammar is a giant. He's not just tall; he's also broad as a linebacker. He tends to wear clothes two sizes too big for him in a style generally seen in a rap video. His unkempt hair and perennial five o'clock shadow add to his unfriendly giant appearance. If you saw him coming down the street, you'd probably surreptitiously get a better grip on your purse or cross the road outright. However, if instead of doing either of those things, you offered him some ice cream, you'd probably end up being best friends forever and have play dates to watch Disney movies. He once came over specifically to watch *Finding Nemo* with me, while his sister rolled her eyes and stayed in her room. I don't think she appreciates his particular charms.

Look for descriptive passages in the readings in part 2. For example, in "The strange forces behind the Richard hockey riot," Maurice Richard is described as: "Thirty-four years old, five foot nine, he weighs 180 pounds and is handsome in a sullen kind of way. His intense, penetrating eyes seem to perceive everything in microscopic detail" (page 306). Discuss the techniques the authors use for description.

Some pointers to keep in mind for description:
- As with all writing, clarity is the most important feature.
- Organize your details so that your reader can follow you.
- Keep in mind your audience and purpose.
- Use adjectives and adverbs, but don't overload your sentences with them.

Assignments
1. Write a one-paragraph description of your home. It can be your current room in residence, an apartment, or your family home.
2. Write a description of an interesting person you know.
3. Describe an object (such as a can opener) for someone who has never seen one. You can pretend you are describing it for an alien from another planet.

Defining and Classifying

Sometimes in your writing, you have to explain the meaning of some terms (definition) or show how they are related to similar concepts (classification). This is not as simple as it seems. Defining is more than simply copying a definition from the dictionary. For example, you could be asked to write an essay on the meaning of success—what is it to be successful in life? Some people equate success with wealth, while others focus on achievement and others on quality of life. See the sample essay "The definition of success" on page 171. Karen von Hahn defines "help" in her essay "Helpless" (page 274).

Classification simply means that you are defining something using different categories. For example, you might write about the kinds of customers you have as a server in a restaurant or different types of marketing approaches that can be used with a product. You might be asked to write a whole paragraph or essay as definition or classification, or you might find you need just a section to make something clear to your reader. "Three kinds of drivers" is a sample of a classification essay. Another kind of classification is division, in which the different parts of one thing are described.

Here is an example of a definition paragraph:

> Narcissism is defined as self-love. The word comes from Narcissus, a character in Greek mythology who was handsome and vain. He fell in love with his own reflection in a pond, staring at it for hours, while the lovesick nymph Echo looked on and tried to call out to him. His name was given to the flower, similar to a daffodil, that tends to grow by lakes and ponds. Narcissists can be vain, like Narcissus. Mainly they think they are special and privileged and no one else in the world matters. For instance, students who interrupt the class to demand attention to their needs may be showing this kind of behaviour. Many narcissists are charming and attractive, so they get away with lording it over others. They generally have an exaggerated view of their abilities. For example, some contestants on talent shows such as "Canadian idol" often react with disbelief when informed that they have no talent. Unfortunately, many people today have a narcissistic tendency because it has been fostered by education movements in which parents and teachers have bent over backwards to foster children's self-esteem.

Three Kinds of Drivers

Driving to work or school is one of the most dangerous activities people undertake in their daily lives. The possibility of getting hurt or killed in a traffic accident is actually higher than getting killed by a terrorist, but we don't take bad driving seriously enough. The danger on the roads is largely caused by bad drivers. Three of the worst kinds of drivers are those who are over-cautious, distracted, or aggressive.

Some drivers are so scared of driving that, ironically, they create more hazards trying to be careful. Over-cautious drivers insist on going very slowly. They may go down the highway below the speed limit or the speed of traffic. It wouldn't be so bad if they restricted their movements to the slow lane, but sometimes they take the middle lane to avoid the truck traffic. If they do not know where they are going, they may crawl down a street looking at street signs or may even reverse if they miss their turn. Overly careful drivers delay making left turns, waiting for the road to be completely clear, thus causing the drivers behind them to become impatient and perhaps even do something rash such as pulling around them.

Other kinds of bad drivers are those who try to do two things at once. The most common transgression today is using a cellphone while driving. Even using a hands-free set does not prevent a driver from being distracted. Cellphone users often weave or drive more slowly. Some drivers try to consult a map while they are actually moving. Some use traffic jams to catch up on their reading, even when the traffic is stop-and-go. Other activities include eating or personal grooming, such as putting on make-up. Any of these actions distract the driver from the most important task—driving. Preoccupied drivers put everyone at risk since it only takes a split second to cause a crash.

Aggressive drivers are probably the worst kind of driver. They drive quickly and take risks because they are always in a hurry. They think the speed limit is for wusses, and they tailgate drivers in the fast lane on the expressway, even if those drivers are driving 120 km per hour in a 100 km zone. They are also annoying because they follow so closely that they have to hit the brake lights often, confusing drivers behind who think there is a traffic slowdown. These drivers have type A personalities—they do not want to be behind anyone. They weave in and out of lanes and take chances. It is only luck and the attentiveness of other drivers that save them from more accidents.

The most dangerous hazards on the road are other drivers. Careful drivers have to watch out for those who are overly careful, preoccupied, or type A personalities. They have to understand the characteristics of the drivers in order to be able to predict their behaviour on the road. Driving today requires the vigilance of other drivers.

Assignments

1. Write a paragraph defining one of these abstract terms: beauty, heroism, intelligence, leadership.
2. New words are coined every day; many come from developments in technology. Write a paragraph defining one of these terms: phishing, cookies, loonie and toonie, rap. Include information on how these words were developed.
3. What is a Canadian? Write a definition paragraph or an essay.
4. Write a classification essay on three kinds of people you encounter in your everyday life. For example, if you work as a sales clerk or restaurant server, you can describe three different kinds of customers or three kinds of supervisor.

Showing Cause and Effect

Academic essays often explain the causes or effects of something. Sometimes an essay can discuss both causes and effects, especially if there is a domino effect or a chain reaction in which one event leads to another, which in turn leads to another. For example, you could explain how trying a drug could lead to addiction and how addiction may lead eventually to crime.

Here is a sample paragraph explaining the social effects of the birth of a child:

> Everyone has cause to celebrate the birth of a child, not only the proud parents but also the whole community in which the infant is born. With the parents, a child represents the

successful union of marriage, which traditionally means a product of two committed persons, husband and wife. A child means regeneration, a continuation of family and futurity. A child brings forth hope and promise. In that vein, the larger community also benefits from bringing an infant into the world. A child needs sustenance, and from farmers to grocers, food suppliers depend on a child's need to be fed. A baby requires necessities and toys, so clothiers weave blankets and diapers and toy-makers produce rattles, blocks, and plush teddy bears for the infant. A child sometimes needs more care than parents can provide, and doctors and nurses watch over the health of the newborn. From the intangible to the tangible, from love to practical, economic concerns, a child is welcomed into society.

The following cause/effect essay is eight paragraphs long, showing you how the basic five-paragraph form can be expanded.

Causes of Modern Incivility

Complaining about other people's behaviour is nothing new in any society. Ancient Greek writings show that even in those times, people were concerned that teenagers were disrespectful and impolite. Today, people point to such phenomena as road rage, the lack of formal manners, and vulgarity on television to make their claim that incivility is on the rise. Whether people are in fact ruder today than before is debatable. However, changes in technology, politics, and society in the late twentieth century have influenced human behaviour, making people less considerate of others.

The use of new technologies such as computers is the most obvious influence on behaviour. While technology does open up new ways of communicating with our fellow beings, it also cuts us off from real human interaction. It is much easier to be rude sitting in a car or at a keyboard than it is face-to-face. In road rage incidents, aggression and violence escalate between drivers, from cutting other drivers off to obscene gestures and even physical confrontation between drivers who get out of their cars to fight. Psychologists say people feel dehumanized in their vehicles and therefore freer to act aggressively. Similarly, Internet users can send angry, obscene messages because they feel anonymous and not responsible for their actions.

Another problem is that new gadgets come into widespread use before the social rules for using them can develop. Cellphones offer convenience but also intrude on public space as people talk loudly on their phones in restaurants and let them ring in the middle of a lecture. Sometimes the use of a technology affects behaviour in other situations. People used to chatting with their family while they watch a DVD at home sometimes behave the same way in a movie theatre.

Technology has also sped up our world, making us less considerate of others. With instantaneous communication possible, people do not take the time to reflect on their words. Moreover, this hurry-up world causes stress. People have a lot of information to digest and deal with—and little time to do it. So it is perhaps not surprising that the courtesies people generally pay each other have fallen by the wayside.

The late twentieth century also brought a political shift that indicates a change in attitude that fosters selfishness. The right wing conservative viewpoint preaches lower taxes, fewer social programs, and the rightful dominance of the marketplace. This is, in effect, an every-man-for-himself philosophy. People have to be ruthless to succeed, and they cannot consider others' welfare. Consequently, they behave inconsiderately. Because people are supposed to be self-reliant, they do not need others and therefore do not respect others.

The emphasis on individual needs has many manifestations. The 1980s was called the 'me' decade. Education became child-centred, and self-esteem was promoted. Parents and teachers were encouraged to praise children so that they could grow up to be confident and content; even poor results were given good marks for effort. However, this over-emphasis on self-esteem resulted in a false sense of entitlement. People educated in this way may think too highly of themselves and may figure that they deserve special treatment, that what they want is more important than anyone else's needs.

In addition, deference to authority is less than it used to be. In traditional families, ideal children were those who were seen but not heard because parental authority was absolute. Not only do parents get less respect, but other authority figures, such as doctors, politicians, supervisors, and teachers, are also frequently challenged. Some of this is due to the media revealing the weaknesses of such figures. This lessening of deference to authority can be positive because it leads to such actions as questioning doctors and not just accepting everything they say, but it has also led to increased incivility as protestors smack cream pies into the faces of prime ministers and politicians shout at and insult each other.

Although we can find many reasons why people behave with less consideration for others today, we should not be too quick to conclude that society today is uncivil. We have to recognize other truths. First, social rules are cultural. As our world brings people with different values together, some adjustments have to be made, leading to new standards of behaviour. We must also be careful to distinguish between casual and rude. A few decades ago, people dressed up to go an airplane trip and never called an older person by a first name. Does this mean a decline of civility or merely a more relaxed style of behaviour? Finally, our society has made improvements in the way we treat those who have lesser status. Overt racism is less accepted today, and we make fewer class distinctions. Women are no longer considered the possessions of their husbands and relatives. In those respects, we can say modern behaviour is better.

You can see other examples of cause and effect writing in this text. In unit 4, paragraph A (page 147) discusses the reasons that the family meal has become less common, and paragraph C (page 147) explains the effects of having a regular meal together. "The strange forces behind the Richard hockey riot" (page 304) explains the causes of the riot. Christopher Hutsul explains one effect of overreliance on cellphones in "Disconnecting hard to do, cellphone generation finds" (page 282). Look for other examples of writers explaining either causes or effects in this text and in your other reading.

Assignments

1. In a paragraph, explain how the poor choice of a given name can affect a child.
2. In an essay, explain the reasons that young people start smoking.
3. In an essay, explain how traffic jams affect our society.

Reviewing

When you write a review, you evaluate and give your opinion of a work. You could review a book, a movie, a CD, a concert, or a product. Your review might include comparisons to similar works. You can summarize the story, but remember that your audience might not yet have seen or read it, so do not reveal too much of the plot—especially the ending. Everyone is entitled to his or her own opinion, but in academic writing this opinion must be clearly and logically supported.

Reviewing is also a base for critical literary analysis. The word *review* means to look over or look at something again. In short, reviewing is a critical evaluation or the close examination of materials. From an academic point of view, reviewing is not just a synopsis of what has been said or written, but rather it gives a perspective, or expresses an opinion, of the content. In a book review, for instance, you state the reasons for liking or for not recommending it and then back those reasons up with relevant details. For example:

> "The open window" by Saki (a pseudonym for H.H. Munro) is not as funny today as it was some 90 years ago when it gained classic status in short fiction. The characters are hackneyed stereotypes, and Saki depends on names to create the humour. For example, Framton Nuttel, the butt of the impish girl's joke, is neurotic because his name suggests personality traits. Vera—from the Latin word meaning truth but used ironically here—tells a tall tale that immediately takes him in. Certainly, the technique of significant names is a standard shortcut for many writers ever since stories were told around the fireplace, but Framton is just a bit too gullible. He may be new to this English village, but he is a grown man who has had some experience in life and in dealing with people.

Surely he could see through the little girl's scheme and be a little more accepting of the aunt, Mrs Sappleton, who appears to be the nutty one. Surely, the aunt knows her niece well enough not to believe the girl's explanation that Nuttel, who has just fled the house in terror, has a great fear of dogs. Finally, Saki's ending seems lame: it just isn't humorous.

Assignment

1. Collect some reviews from the local newspaper or the Internet. It is easy to find reviews of movies, concerts, plays, books, and restaurants. Look at the techniques used. Choose two different reviews about something you are familiar with, such as a movie you have seen. Write a paragraph on how effective the reviews are. Would they have influenced your decision to see that movie?
2. Write a brief review (about 150 words) of a book, movie, computer game, concert, or CD.

Describing Process

Process description is often found in technical writing. It is generally "how to" writing common in instruction manuals. There are two main kinds of process writing—instructional and descriptive. Instructions can be written in a list or in prose paragraphs. They are directed at the reader, and so they use *you* and command sentences. The other kind simply describes the process objectively, without giving instructions. For example, if you explain to a gardener how to plant a flower, you are giving instructions. If you give an account of how a plant grows, you are writing a process description without being instructional.

Good process writing is clear and concise. You have to give enough information for your reader to understand the process being described but not too much information. You have to know your audience. If you are describing a technical process, much will depend on how comfortable the reader is with the jargon of the field.

It is important to break the process down into the different steps. Sometimes you will have to subdivide, with some general phases of the process broken down into various steps. For example, the planning stage of essay writing includes researching and thinking about the topic, jotting down ideas, and planning an outline.

Here is an example of a set of instructions, followed by an instructional process paragraph and then a descriptive process paragraph:

How to take notes:
1. Come to class prepared, having done preliminary reading, and with tools (pen, paper).
2. Pay attention to the lecturer.

3. Write down, in point form, the main points of the lecture.
4. Listen for cues, when the lecturer stresses specific points.
5. Use short forms for common words and the terms of the field.
6. After class, review notes, making sure they will be clear later.

Note-taking is one of the skills you must learn in college, especially since you might not have learned how to do it in high school. First you have to come to class prepared. It goes without saying that you need to bring your note-taking tools, your pens and notebook, but you should also have read whatever chapters are required for that lecture. Then you will be able to follow it better. Pay attention to everything the lecturer says. Your goal is to write down the main points. To do that, you have to follow the lecturer's cues. For example, if the professor says something like "most importantly," you know that she is stressing something. Similarly, you can ignore any small talk, like the chat with students about the movies they saw on the weekend. To be efficient, use point form and abbreviations. In addition to the standard short forms, you can develop your own system. Make sure you make ones for the technical terms that are often repeated in that subject area. After class, make sure you go over your notes. If the notes are not clear, add information or rewrite illegible bits while the lecture is still fresh in your mind. If you take notes faithfully, you will remember your lectures better and have study notes ready.

Note-taking is one of the skills college students must learn since it is not usually taught in high school. Proper preparation is important. Students need to bring their tools (pen and paper) and come to class having read the required chapters in the textbook. Careful attention to the lecture is required. Professors usually stress the important points. Students need to develop their own system of point-form notes, including abbreviations for technical terms common in their field. The last step is one that many students neglect. Notes have to be cleaned up and added to after class to make sure they are legible even after the material of the lecture is no longer fresh in the mind. The act of note-taking helps students retain the information better.

Process description is also found in the description of biological or geological process:

Tsunamis 101
by Jan Dutkiewicz

Say tsunami and up pops a mental image of a single, giant wave rising out of the ocean to swallow cities whole. In reality, tsunamis (meaning "harbour wave" in Japanese) are a series of waves that start small and grow as they approach land. They are the result of oceans attempting to smooth out their surface after a disturbance.

Tsunamis are triggered by any phenomenon that causes a large part of the water's surface to rise or drop relative to normal sea level. These events are usually the result of earthquakes occurring along undersea fault lines, the cracks in the earth's crust between tectonic plates. When these plates collide or grind against each other, they can elevate, lower, or tilt major sections of the ocean floor, suddenly offsetting the level of water at the surface. The displaced water then rushes to level out, causing a tsunami. The waves travel outward in all directions from the place where the earthquake occurred, just like the ripples created when a stone is thrown into a lake.

Tsunamis can also be caused by undersea volcanic eruptions, landslides, or explosions on the surface, such as the 1917 Halifax harbour explosion that sent 10-metre-high waves crashing into the city. It has also been suggested that asteroids or other extraterrestrial bodies could cause tsunamis if they plummet into large bodies of water, but there have been no examples of this in recent history.

A popular misconception is that tsunamis are monstrous waves that scour the ocean destroying everything in their path. The displacements caused by earthquakes and other cataclysms move huge masses of water, but they do not dramatically shift the surface level. Tsunami waves travelling in the open ocean can travel hundreds of kilometres per hour, but they are usually less than one metre high and their crests can be up to a hundred kilometres apart. They can be virtually invisible from the air and, for ships, be indistinguishable from the normal movement of the ocean. It is when these waves make landfall that they achieve their destructive potential. There are stories of fishermen who had no idea that a tsunami had struck their villages because they were too far out in the ocean to see or feel any waves at all.

As the ocean becomes shallower near the coast, tsunami waves slow down, compressing and directing their energy and volume upward, some rising to amplitudes of over 50 metres and annihilating whatever they encounter. Depending on the depth and slope of the coastline, it is also possible for the tsunami waves to wash over the shore like a flood or rapid current, as they did in the widely televised video footage taken in Thailand during the recent disaster in Southeast Asia.

Generally, coasts and islands with steep fringes or surrounded by barrier reefs are safer than those with gradually rising fringes or those that are exposed to open ocean. This is because reefs can absorb much of the oncoming waves' impact and deep coastlines do not allow tsunamis to slow down and grow into deadly towers of water.

© 2005, Canadian Geographic Enterprises
http://www.cangeo.ca/tsunami/tsunamis101.asp
Jan Dutkiewicz, MBA, is a freelance writer and photographer.

For a change of pace, here is a tongue-in-cheek process essay. The style is informal and humorous. The author is actually an "A" student.

How to Be an "A" Student

An "A" student is a complex and exquisite creature. Everyone in a class knows who the "A" student is without actually having seen grades. It would be insulting to suggest that "A" studenthood could be achieved merely through class attendance, intensive studying, and solid test preparation. The most important quality in an "A" student is not the mark he or she receives, but the attitude that he or she exudes. You too can be an "A" student without having to improve your grades.

The first step in the process must be to refine your appearance. While seemingly cliché, eyeglasses have long been necessary for all true "A" students. Feel free to add pocket protectors, ink stains, and comfortable brown loafers. The object is to distinguish yourself from the rest of the class. Stylish hairdos and trendy clothes must become anathema to you; an "A" student does not care about fashion.

Research should be your next step. Not "hitting the books" in the sense of actual studying for your classes. No indeed, you must memorize the entire scripts of *Monty Python and the Holy Grail*, *Star Wars*, and *The Lord of the Rings*. A certain amount of time should be spent learning Klingon. Be ready to quote at the drop of a $150 textbook.

Furthermore, you must develop a certain eagerness in your air, brightness in your eyes, and a general imperviousness to insults. Your hand must be quick to rise in class. If you do not know the answer, go off on a completely unrelated tangent. You must use big words, the more syllables the better, regardless of your actual grasp of their meaning. If you speak with confidence, no one will call you on it.

Once you have mastered the facade, language, and countenance of the "A" student, you must then acquire the habits. You must be the first to arrive and last to leave for every class, preferably tailing the professor. Memorize your TA's office hours and become a regular at them. Put your professor's phone number on your speed-dial. Any hours that you cannot possibly fill with hassling your teachers can be spent profitably at the library. Actually reading books there is not necessary; you just need to pick up the smell of them.

When you have achieved the proper state of being, your fellow students will treat you with mingled awe and jealousy. You will no longer be invited to crazy parties or be treated with likewise undignified familiarity. On the contrary, as a NERD (Notable Education Resourcefulness Demonstrator), you can be sure that the peons will keep their distance. An "A" student is an awesome thing to behold. Once you have perfected the attitude, you can be proud to be a part of such a noble tradition.

Assignments

1. Find some process description in a textbook for one of your core courses. Look for an example of point-form instructions, prose instructions, and a prose passage that describes how something happens or is done. Jot down notes comparing the three.
2. Write a process description of a task that you are familiar with. For example, you can write about painting a room, cleaning a kitchen, making a pizza, or taking inventory.
3. Describe the process of getting a driver's licence.
4. Write a satirical essay, similar to "How to be an 'A' student." For example, you could write about spring-cleaning or making employee-of-the-month. Alternatively, you could write a serious process essay on how to become a successful student.

Making Comparisons

Comparison is an important technique in writing. Sometimes writers must compare two things to show which is preferable. Sometimes they use an analogy, a type of comparison, to explain something. The word *compare* itself is problematic because it actually means to show similarity. Writing teachers refer to "compare/contrast essays" to be precise, but common usage is just to talk about comparison with the understanding that it refers to both similarities and differences, with the stress on differences.

There is a common expression in English that says you cannot compare apples and oranges, which means you cannot compare two very different things. The two things you are writing about in a comparison essay should have some basis for comparison. It would not be logical to write an essay comparing a sock to a tree, for instance. Often a comparison essay shows a preference for one or the other. For example, in an essay comparing life in a big city to life in a small town, you would probably take a stand that one is better than the other.

It is also important to remember that in an essay, the writer does the work. It is the writer's job to make the comparison clear; the reader should not have to infer it. For example, you cannot write an essay talking about one movie and then another and then say to your reader, "As you can see, these two movies are very different." You need to show how they are different. For instance, you could say something like "The new film shows the director's growth. He uses fewer cheesy special effects and instead relies on character development."

Four-paragraph comparison essays are not recommended because they usually end up as two separate descriptions with little explicit comparison.

Comparison essays are tricky to structure. You have to make sure that your reader can follow the points without getting confused. In block form, you talk about one item, then the other, keeping the elements in the same order. In a point-by-point comparison, you go back and forth like a ping-pong ball, but you make sure that you maintain order. For example, in the comparison paragraph below, the American character is always discussed before the Canadian one, and the writer deals with both nationalities for each general idea before moving on to the next idea:

> While the American hero is the maverick forging his own way, the Canadian character has been moulded by deference to authority. This fundamental difference can be traced to the way the two countries were formed. The US started with a war, the American Revolution. Canada was born with an act of the British Parliament. The US Constitution promised its citizens "life, liberty, and the pursuit of happiness" and gave them the right to bear arms. Americans think they have the right to shoot anyone who threatens them. The Canadian Constitution espoused "peace, order, and good government." After all, how many countries have a police force, the RCMP, as a national symbol? Americans believe in every man for himself. The rich should be congratulated, and the poor should be derided, especially if they do not have health insurance. Canadians believe in a strong society. The rich should be made to feel guilty, and the poor should be helped. Everyone should benefit from health care. Americans believe that government should stay out of their face. Canadians believe that the government is there to help them. Americans put God on their money; Canadians believe that religion, like culture, is one's personal business. Americans have watched in horror as Canadians have moved to legalize gay marriage and decriminalize marijuana. Canadians have watched in horror as Americans have declared war on Iraq in the name of defeating terrorism. While this is a gross generalization of national differences, and of course not every American or Canadian thinks this way, it does reflect fundamental differences, which show no sign of disappearing. Instead, they are strengthened as liberal Americans move north to find a more peaceful life, and conservative Canadians go south to make their fortune.

Here is a sample paragraph giving similarity:

> Daffy Duck from Warner Brothers' *Looney tunes* films and Donald Duck from Walt Disney Productions are the two most recognizable cartoon ducks. Both ducks belong to the days of

the Saturday matinee where they entertained kids of all ages with their distinctive brand of humour. Both Daffy and Donald are drakes; that is, male ducks with attitude. For example, Daffy believes he should run the cartoon world of Elmer Fudd, Porky Pig, Yosemite Sam, and Bugs Bunny; Donald wants life to go smoothly—his way—or else those around him, such as his three nephews Huey, Dewey and Louey, will feel his ill-temper. And because of this attitude, the two ducks become the butt of the joke or the point in a moral lesson. The world is just too unkind to them. To illustrate, Daffy and Donald always play second fiddle to the likes of other cartoon characters, even though they may be the centrepiece of that particular episode. Daffy can only utter, "You're despicable" to Bugs Bunny when the rascally rabbit defeats the duck's ploy. Or Donald can only fume and quack in unintelligible squawks when Chip and Dale, the chipmunks, obliterate Donald's Thanksgiving dinner or Christmas tree. Nevertheless, both Daffy and Donald reflect the negative aspects of human behaviour so perfectly that they become endearing characters.

Point-by-point comparison:

There are three distinct differences between a camp and a cottage. First, the word *camp* suggests temporary quarters and roughing it in the bush, whereas the word *cottage* gives a sense of abode or home in a quaint rural setting away from the hustle and bustle of city life and a feeling of permanence. Second, a person imagines a camp to be made of canvas tents, grounded by poles, ropes, and pegs, and to have an open fire pit smouldering with twigs and dead branches and something freshly killed, now broiling on a spit. A cottage has doors that close properly, windows with glass panes to let the sunshine in and keep the bugs out, and a roof that does not sway when a gentle breeze blows. Finally, a camp brings out the rugged outdoors qualities in us. We go camping (we never go cottaging); we make camp in the wilderness, and we do without if we forgot to stow it in a backpack. A cottage is a home away from home, still with all the comforts of home: satellite TV, a microwave oven, a fridge, and an Internet connection. The term *cottage*, therefore, is more fitting for a summer house than *camp*.

Block style comparison:

There are three distinct differences between the concept of a camp and a cottage. The word *camp* suggests temporary quarters and roughing it in the bush. We imagine a camp to be made up of canvas tents, grounded by poles, ropes, and pegs, and to have an open fire pit smouldering with twigs and dead branches and something freshly killed, now broiling on a makeshift spit. A camp brings out the rugged outdoors qualities in us. We go camping; we make camp in the wilderness, and we do without if we forgot to stow it in a backpack. On the other hand, the word *cottage* gives a sense of abode or home in a quaint rural setting away from the hustle and bustle of city life and a feeling of permanence. A cottage has doors that close properly, windows with glass panes to let the sunshine in and keep the bugs out, and a roof that does not sway when a gentle breeze blows. Moreover, a cottage is a home away from home, still with all the amenities and comforts of home: satellite TV, a microwave oven, a fridge, and an Internet connection. The term *cottage*, therefore, is more fitting for a summer house than *camp*.

The Disney Version

In recent years, fairy tales have changed considerably. Children today are more familiar with the sanitized version, the Disney version, than with the raw tellings of the Brothers Grimm or Hans Christian Andersen. The classic tales of Beauty and the Beast, Sleeping Beauty, Snow White, Cinderella, and the Little Mermaid have been transformed into politically correct, cutesy renderings. The hard edge in the originals has been so softened that they have become cotton candy. The three dramatic differences can be found in fairy tale animals, in the level of violence, and in plot resolution.

Animals, big and little, populate the world of the fairy tale and contribute to the plot, but the cartoon versions are softer and more pet-like. For example, in Disney's *Beauty and the Beast*, the 'beast' prince is a cute rendering of an animal. He has a bad temper, but his bark is worse than his bite. In the classic Brothers Grimm version, however, the petulant prince is transformed by a witch into a raging, ugly beast with little compassion for Beauty. Similarly, the little animals such as cute mice and twittering birdies become helpful domestic servants in the cartoons, helping Cinderella sew a dress and Snow White to clean the house. In the classic version, Cinderella has no use for mice, and the birds that separate the lentils from the sand are spiritual manifestations of her dead mother.

The original fairy tales are much more violent than the cartoon versions. Characters are asked to sever limbs, serve up pulsating hearts of virgins, and commit other gory acts. For example, Cinderella's stepsisters each cut off part of their foot to make the glass slipper fit. At the wedding ceremony, their eyes were pecked out by avenging birds befriended by Cinderella. In the Hans Christian Andersen version, the mermaid had to actually cut out her tongue to make herself mute. Moreover, she plotted to murder the prince's bride. The cartoon versions lack this type of violent act.

There is no blood spilled in *Cinderella*, and the stepmother is not even very wicked. While the sea witch in *The Little Mermaid* is menacing, she does not actually kill anyone.

Finally, the story lines are softer in the new cartoon versions of the old stories. Sometimes the ending is even changed. Andersen's Little Mermaid kills herself at the end of the story, while Disney's mermaid has a happily-ever-after wedding with the prince. Cinderella's stepsisters are maimed in the original, just jealous and unhappy in the cartoon. Sleeping Beauty was raped by the prince in the Grimm version but awoken with a kiss in later stories. In the story of the three little pigs, the first two pigs are eaten, and the wolf gets his due in a pot of boiling water, while modified versions have no one getting killed.

Fairy tales have changed a lot over the years. Sometimes, change is good to keep in tune with the times, but in fairy tales, politically correct retellings have made the stories insipid. The desire to make young viewers safe from the realities of life has emasculated the power of the classic stories.

Analogy

An analogy is a comparison in which a situation is compared to something well-known in order to make it clear. In the following excerpt, see how the writer uses an analogy to help you understand an abstract concept:

> Canada has been described as a patchwork quilt of cultures, religions, etc., and is justly praised for making this work. But to continue the analogy, a patchwork quilt needs a backing to hold it together, and our public schools play part of this role. They provide all of our children the opportunity to interact with people from very different religious and cultural backgrounds, thus providing an opportunity to develop tolerance and understanding. (Wayne Cook. 2005. "The religious schools dilemma." *Toronto Star* 20 January: A20)

The basic analogy here is that a quilt is stitched together with separate pieces of fabric, just as Canada is a country of different ethnic groups. In a quilt, you can see the individual pieces. Canada has also been compared to a mosaic in which individual pieces are also visible. In comparison, the United States has been referred to as a "melting pot" because its ethnic groups have been all stirred together and come out as one entity—American. Discuss these comparisons. Are they valid today?

Here is another analogy:

> The English language is like a huge pot of stew. Old English, or Anglo-Saxon as it is known, is the base, a Germanic language. To this base many ingredients have been added. Words from Old Norse were brought to England by the Viking

invaders. When William the Conqueror won the Battle of Hastings in 1066, he became the first of many kings of England who did not speak English. Their language, Norman French, gradually blended in with English, changing some its structures and practically doubling its vocabulary. Another ingredient added to this stew was the huge vocabulary based on Latin and Greek words, used mainly for scientific and technical terms. As these ingredients cook in the stew, they become less distinct and the flavours blend together.

Assignments

Write a paragraph or an essay comparing:
* two places you have lived or visited
* two schools or two education systems
* two vehicles, computers, or two items you have contemplated purchasing
* two people you know

Persuading

Most essays are a type of argument because you are putting forth ideas and supporting them, but when you are arguing a controversial issue, you need a persuasive argument. Unlike a quarrel, in which you have an emotional dispute with someone, a persuasive essay offers reasoning. You try to make someone understand your point of view or to move someone to an action that you recommend. You must be objective, logical, and forthright to win your case. You must connect and support your ideas.

Why We Need to Pay Taxes

Canadians often grumble about paying taxes. They think the government is picking their pockets and wasting their money. They maintain that they pay too much and look longingly south of the border at the lower tax rates. They claim businesses are better run than the government—even when shown evidence of corruption and wastefulness in large corporations. They ignore the fact that Canada is an expensive country to run because it is a huge area with a small population. Most important, however, they do not realize that the services Canadians get with their tax money are an important and sound investment.

Taxes fund vital social services such as health, education, and welfare that all people benefit from, either directly or indirectly. For example, higher education levels mean better trained workers for the whole society. Schools train our doctors, architects, plumbers, and barbers. Business costs are reduced when graduates have the skills to do the job and do not need extensive training. Welfare for the less fortunate lessens the gap between the rich and the poor, an inequity that can lead to social problems such as crime. Governments that invest in recreation services for children will have a fitter populace and therefore save money on health care.

Second, taxes mean that the costs are shared by society and are therefore not an unreasonable burden for individuals. In the past, when individual citizens paid doctor and hospital bills, not only did Canadians have a lower health standard but also a terrible debt load. The few dollars contributed in a tax bill to pay for medical care eases a burden that could bankrupt an individual. Moreover, many families would not be able to send their children to school if they had to pay thousands of dollars a year for their education. In addition, the cost is borne by those who can most afford it, since taxes are generally tied to income.

Furthermore, systems that are funded by taxes rather than user fees have lower administrative costs. Privately run agencies have overhead costs. For example, they have to compete with other companies for the business and thus need to spend on advertising. User fees require middlemen and collection services. For example, in the American system of health insurance from employers, billions of dollars are wasted in administration. Governments just have to worry about covering costs, not about making profits to satisfy investors.

Canadians should just realize how costly the alternatives are and pay their tax bill without so much grumbling. Of course, this doesn't mean allowing government spending to get out of hand. Canadians need to be informed voters just as they need to be informed consumers.

Technology and Children

Technology devotees are not satisfied with having made adults hooked on technology; now they are marketing their products to younger and younger consumers. TV programs have been designed for small babies. Children start playing video games and computer programs as preschoolers. Elementary school children have cellphones and PDAs. Although parents today are eager to buy their children the latest in electronic gadgetry, they should stop and think about the ramifications. A dependence on technology can prevent children from developing properly.

The more time children spend with electronic gadgets, the less healthy they are. If they go outside after school, they play, run, and jump. They get fresh air and sunshine and lots of exercise. If they plunk themselves down in front of a TV or computer screen, they are straining their eyes and not exercising their bodies. Moreover, TV watching may be accompanied by snacking on junk food. In addition, kids plugged into personal music players are destroying their hearing.

Children's creativity is also restricted by television and computers. While a reader has to exercise his brain to imagine the world described in a book, a TV watcher is passive. Artwork done on a computer is limited by the restrictions of the program. Children need to get physical with their creations—to feel the clay between their fingers, to hold the pencil or paint brush. Today's children "interact" with electronic toys that "talk" and move, while in the past they would have built a fort from a cardboard box and acted out scenes with handmade puppets.

Social development is also retarded in our electronic world. Even though the Internet and cellphones are supposed to make communication easier, they actually replace face-to-face interaction. Children do not play with children in the neighbourhood; they send e-mail to strangers around the world. They talk on a cellphone instead of talking to the person they are sitting next to. Their portable music players transport them to another space, not the one they are physically in. Today's children are growing up less able to communicate with people directly.

Even though technology is supposed to be making this a better world, it is hurting our children. While it is impossible to stop the technological advances, wise parents should limit the time their children spend with electronic gadgetry. It is important to let them experience the real world first. Then they will appreciate and understand their technology better.

Most of the essays in the reading section (part 2) argue for a point of view. As you read, pay attention to the author's thesis and see how it is argued. It is especially useful to read opposing viewpoints on specific issues. The readings "Free to drive" (page 286) and "Was court right to back suits against Big Tobacco?" (page 293) offer an opportunity to look at opposing views.

Logical fallacies

In argument, the term "logical fallacy" is used to explain a mistake in reasoning. Sometimes a fallacy is an unfair or improper method of arguing. Other times, it is a flaw in the process. There are some common logical fallacies:

Against the person: Instead of focusing on the idea, the writer mocks the person:

> You shouldn't listen to such an idiot. Even using all his fingers, he can't count to 10.

Circular argument: The writer goes in circles rather than advancing the reasoning:

> This idea is good because it is fitting. There's nothing bad about a good idea when you know it is right.

Appeal to force: The writer becomes angry and threatens the opponent with harm:

> If you know what's good for you, do as I say. I have a third-degree black belt in karate.

Hasty generalization: The writer uses only one piece of evidence and draws a grand conclusion:

> Don't expand the welfare system. I know a panhandler downtown making 100 dollars a day. These people are making a decent living off the streets.

Appeal to pity: The writer makes the opponent feel sorry for him:

> Sir, I broke my arm in a fall when I helped my sick grandmother to the hospital for emergency surgery today, so can I have an extension on my essay that was due yesterday?

Faulty chronological reasoning: The writer draws a relation between one incident and another illogically:

> His grades started slipping when he moved to the new apartment.

Non sequitur: One idea does not logically follow another:

> Instead of frowning all the time, smiling wins friends. Many people are afraid of the dentist.

Make sure that your arguments are sound when you are writing a persuasive essay. Do not fall into any of the traps of logical fallacy.

Conceding a point

In spoken language, when you are having a discussion over an issue or arguing points of view, you often agree with the other person's arguments but add a counter-argument. It is a "yes, but" strategy. Writers do the same thing when they concede a point but focus on what they perceive to be a stronger argument.

One reason writing is so difficult is that you have to see your work from the reader's point of view and imagine what is going on in your reader's head. What you are saying may be perfectly obvious to you, but it may not be clear to the reader, so it is important that your arguments follow logically. Moreover, if there is a strong argument against your point of view, it is like the elephant in the room—there is no sense ignoring it. Your persuasive essay can become stronger if you anticipate and acknowledge some of the obvious counter-arguments.

One of the easiest ways to make a concession in your argument is to use an *although* statement:

> Although computers have many educational benefits, they stifle children's creativity.

> Although computers may limit children's interaction with their immediate surroundings, they open up the whole world for their exploration.

Note that the first sentence is against computers, while the second sentence is for them. The main idea is in the main clause. By using a subordinate clause, you are saying that the statement in the subordinate clause is less important (therefore subordinate) to the idea in the main clause. Make sure that the idea you want to emphasize is in the main clause.

When you read, watch out for words like *but*, *however*, and *while*, which can signal a concession:

> The tobacco industry and its supporters have long insisted that smoking is simply a matter of "individual choice.". . . But cigarettes are in a class by themselves when it comes to their sheer killing power. (Linda McQuaig, page 293)

> While it is true that governments sometimes waste money, so do businesses.

You do not have to mention all the counter-arguments in your essay, but if there is one that stands out as an obvious choice, concede it.

Qualifying statements

A good argument has to be reasonable, and so it must acknowledge that the world is not black or white, all or nothing. When you write an essay, you have to choose your words with care so as not to alienate your readers. You do not want to overstate your case.

Readers can accept qualified statements better than absolute statements. In the following statements, the first is absolute while the second is qualified and therefore easier to accept:

> Women do well at language-related tasks while men are good at spatial tasks.
> Women generally do better at language-related tasks while men tend to perform better on spatial tasks.

> All smokers develop lung cancer.
> Smokers have a higher risk of developing lung cancer.

Avoid using words like *all*, *always*, and *never*. They are rarely true. Instead, use *often*, *some*, and *many*:

> All teenagers work part-time. [not true]

> Many teenagers work part-time. [better]

Modal verbs (e.g., *may, might, could*) are another way to qualify statements:

> She is the best film editor in the world.

> She may be the best film editor in the world.

Verbs such as *seem* and *tend* can also make statements less absolute:

> He has no knowledge of physics.

> He seems to lack knowledge of physics.

Remember also that the simple present tense expresses the idea of a general statement, so it does not need additions to express the idea of a common occurrence. Students sometimes try to show the idea of generality by using a future tense or adding *always*:

> First-year students always find it difficult to make the adjustment from high school.

> First-year students will find it difficult to make the adjustment from high school.

> First-year students find it difficult to make the adjustment from high school. [better]

Be careful not to overuse qualifying statements. You still have to take a stand. You do not want to appear wishy-washy and uncommitted.

Activity

Identify the qualifying words and expressions used in the persuasive essays in this text. You can look at the sample essays in this chapter, "Why we need to pay taxes" and "Technology and children," and the readings "Free to drive" (page 286) and "Was court right to back suits against Big Tobacco?" (page 293). You can also look for concessions at the same time.

Assignment

Write a persuasive essay on one of the current issues in the news. For example, take a stand on safe injection sites for drug users, year-round schooling, or stem cell research.

Editing and Proofreading Skills

Word formation, grammatical structures, and mechanics are reviewed in units 2 and 3. This unit gives you further practice, mostly in error correction. The sentences show common errors. They are based on errors that were actually made by students in writing classes. Some of the students were learning English as a second language; some were native speakers of English.

Correcting Vocabulary Errors

Exercise 7.1 Word choice

These sentences are based on errors made when students mixed up one word for another, made a poor word choice, or even invented a word. Some of these are tricky, so you may want to work with a partner. Many of the words sound similar to the right words. Change the underlined word for one that fits the meaning of the sentence:

1. Students going to college have to go through a <u>transformation</u> period while they learn how to live on their own.

2. None of the <u>tellers</u> in the clothing store approached me offering help.

3. Harriet Tubman is known for her <u>outrageous</u> contribution to freeing African-American slaves.

4. The blast of the Halifax explosion killed more than 1,600 people; some were <u>incarcerated</u>.

5. I chose to study Rocket Richard because he <u>peeked</u> my interest.

6. Louis Riel was <u>trialed</u> for treason.

7. This assignment was <u>uneasy</u> at first.

Exercise 7.1 Word choice – *continued*

8. Students need to <u>thrive</u> for improvement.

9. He was caught <u>making</u> a crime and had to do community service.

10. The author <u>narrated</u> a story of his youth, when he fell in love.

11. The problems we faced made the whole trip <u>unjoyable</u>.

12. Through the <u>event</u> of researching Sir Wilfrid Laurier, I came to realize how much he contributed to our country.

13. At McDonald's, I was in charge of <u>sanity</u>. I had to make sure everything was clean and disinfected.

14. They were asked why they took the car, but they did not have a <u>sensitive</u> answer.

15. The author is <u>implementing</u> that the problem is the government's fault.

16. People who choose luxury cars often just want to show off their <u>richness</u>.

17. The plumber could not find the <u>issue</u> with the toilet.

18. I feel very <u>stressful</u> when I have to take an exam.

19. People choose their friends by their <u>outlook</u>.

20. Students need to develop good reading <u>habitats</u>.

Exercise 7.2 Word differences

Choose the better word to fit the blank. Explain your answer and discuss the meaning difference in class:

1. Mother Teresa is <u>famous/notorious</u> for helping the poor in India.

2. I didn't want to <u>disrupt/disturb</u> him when he was so busy with his family problems.

3. At <u>last/finally</u>, tuition fees should be lowered because education is a social investment.

4. Jessica felt <u>ashamed/shameful</u> when he pointed out her mistakes.

5. She accepted the compliment <u>gracefully/graciously</u>.

6. My parents are <u>intolerable/intolerant</u> of the liberal dating practices in North America.

Exercise 7.2 Word differences – *continued*

7. My writing still has many <u>shortages/shortcomings</u>.

8. The children were taught to be <u>respectful/respective</u> of their elders.

9. Their assignment was to <u>disapprove/disprove</u> the theory.

10. They are having trouble <u>adapting/adopting</u> to Canadian winters.

11. Students need to have the <u>wish/desire</u> to learn.

12. Cellphones with cameras are now very <u>famous/popular</u>.

13. Don and Kate bicker <u>continually/continuously</u> but have stayed married for 30 years.

14. She chooses to <u>donate/pay</u> money to local charities, especially those that benefit children.

15. I have <u>learned/studied</u> French for 10 years, but I still don't speak it well.

Exercise 7.3 Word choice

Replace the underlined phrase with a word that means the same thing (you might need to make slight changes to the sentence to make the word fit):

1. Teenagers should have a <u>time that they must come in by at night</u>.

2. The <u>man whose wife died</u> found it difficult to participate in the planned social activities.

3. The food was <u>not able to be eaten</u> because it had sat out for too long.

4. She admired his <u>quality of being on time</u>.

5. Parents should never give in to their children's <u>fits of frustration and anger</u> in stores when they don't get what they want.

6. I always plan family parties with <u>the woman who is married to my brother</u> because we have similar tastes.

7. I need a better job to pay for my <u>school fees for college</u>.

8. Part of the employees' salary goes into a <u>plan to give them money when they retire</u>.

9. After the plane crash, many children became <u>children with no parents</u>.

Exercise 7.3 Word choice – *continued*

10. The years of <u>time with no rain</u> ruined the economy of the prairie region.

11. The <u>man who had two wives</u> hid his two lives well.

12. Silvia has been working as a social worker for a <u>period of ten years</u>.

13. He got a job as a <u>person who drives other people around in a limousine</u>.

14. Nada prefers to use a bike <u>that stays in one place</u> rather than exercising outside.

15. When he was a kid, he got in trouble for <u>stealing things from stores</u>.

Exercise 7.4 Collocation

Correct collocation and vocabulary errors, changing the sentence structure where necessary:

1. I came to Canada to have an opportunity to exercise my English.

2. People must earn money to support their lives, so sometimes they have no choice but to take a menial job.

3. I feel accomplished when I get my assignments done early.

4. If someone's passport is missing or robbed, he or she can't show his or her identity.

5. If they can't be given good treatment, their illness will be heavier.

6. They went over all the specs to make sure they would pick a good choice.

7. The time the bread takes to bake depends on what size holder is used for the bread.

8. Even when the neighbours complained, he would not turn down the voice on the stereo.

9. In high school, students were sponge fed by the teachers.

10. I lost my book as a result of someone stealing me.

Exercise 7.5 Parts of speech

Correct the errors in parts of speech:

1. Although Canada is a safety country and the criminal rate is dropping, many people seem worry about dangerous on the streets.

2. Because of its extremely cold, only a handful of people want to visit Antarctica.

3. The Montreal Canadiens loss the game because of Rocket Richard's absent.

4. More trees and flowers can beauty our city. It's importance to develop more parks.

5. They should response to the question. It really wasn't worthy $150.

6. In the future, they'll be able to find a better job with the value experience they've gained.

7. People can easy find news on the Internet, but they have to be sure of the sources of information.

8. Because they want to success, they have to proceed very careful.

9. In recently years, many people go abroad to work or studying.

10. Immigrants might have to change their customs and believes to fit in with the cultural surrounding them.

11. Another definitely thing students should do is to do the reading before class.

12. Students can improve their reading comprehend by practice more. They will become more confidence.

13. One certainly thing high schools should do is offering specific writing and reading courses to students.

14. Although the man was death, his spirit was still felt to be in that place.

15. Canada is an immigration country. People gradual adapt to the new culture.

Exercise 7.6 Spelling

Correct any errors:

1. I went threw the chapter and hilighted the main points, so studing will be much easier.

2. It's important for the enviorment that we reduce the amount of polution we create.

Exercise 7.6 Spelling – *continued*

3. They're was a problem with the salade, so I threw it into the garbage.

4. The police pulled him over for driving wrecklessly, but after he attacked them, he ended up spending the nite in gaol.

5. When we were kids, we idlized Superman and Batman, so we whore caypse and ran around the house.

6. After the accident, my car was a right-off, so the wreckers took it away.

7. The immigrants' education level will often determine weather or not they adopt to the society easily.

8. If the punishment were more sever, may be fewer people would run red lites.

9. Cloths that you don't where anymore should be recycled as donations to charity.

10. Eating a nutrisious, well ballenced diet definately keeps the body healthy.

Exercise 7.7 One word or two?

Some of the following sentences contain errors in which one word should actually be two words (or three) or vice versa. For instance, students often write *a lot* incorrectly as one word, and they confuse *apart* and *a part*. Correct any of these mistakes (you might have to change the spelling a bit):

1. They're on sale now for $5.99 apiece, but I already bought three and don't need anymore.

2. Jill and her sister look a like, but they have very different personalities.

3. It was quiet on the downtown street. I saw a lone man infront of the department store display.

4. Exercise should be apart of everyday life. Even a walk around the neighbourhood can be beneficial.

5. He raced a head of the pack and then had to wait a while for the rest to catch up.

Exercise 7.7 One word or two? – *continued*

6. I don't have alot of time to get the reports all together. I'd like a bit more time.

7. She read the instructions a loud and then took the pieces apart to start again.

8. Once in awhile I like to put a side all my work and go for a walk alone to clear my head.

9. I couldn't get ahold of him atall. Eventhough he has voicemail, he has not activated the service.

10. They need an other chance to do the work. It's altogether a new project with these new specifications.

11. She couldn't figure out what was amiss. It wasn't like him to duck her calls. It was all so strange.

12. She doesn't like staying a lone. On the otherhand, she doesn't get a long with her family.

13. They couldn't complete the installation themselves. Never the less, they won third prize.

14. We decided to take the video camera to record the results. Further more, it was away to backup the data.

15. It may be a question of preparation. We need to get the tools already before we begin.

16. She was taken aback when he asked her a bout her age.

17. She had a faraway look in her eye as she watched the children play out side the window.

18. Now a days, people rely on technology far too much. They can't do things themselves.

19. Inspite of the distance, she wanted to go to her son's university to see what he was upto.

20. I cannot see the downside for that proposal. It seems like it would work well in our case.

Troublesome words

It is important to learn how words are used in sentences, to recognize word patterns. For instance, a verb might need a direct object or a specific preposition after it. The following words are those that often show up in grammatical errors. They are especially problematic for ESL students. The example sentences show the common patterns for these words.

Study the patterns and discuss them in class. Then correct the errors in the exercise below:

afford

The verb *afford* is a transitive verb, so it takes a direct object. It is generally used with *can*, *could*, and *be able to*. It can also be followed by an infinitive. It is not used in the passive voice.

> I can't afford a Gucci bag, so I have to be satisfied with a knock-off.

> They can't afford to lose another day on that project.

agree

Agree is often followed by *with*, plus a person or a noun referring to some sort of decision or plan.

> I agree with the basic proposal, but I think we should change the timeline.

> She usually agrees with him, but this time she put her foot down.

> They agreed to postpone the conference.

compare

The prepositions *to* and *with* are often used with the verb *compare*. A frequent error is using the active participle *comparing* instead of the passive participle *compared*. *Comparing* has to refer to whoever or whatever is making the comparison, while *compared* refers to what is actually in the comparison.

> Compared to the deluxe model, this one is a better buy. Those features are unnecessary.

> She put together a chart comparing the features of the two cars.

concern

The verb *concern* refers to someone being affected or worried about something. The person is the object of the verb and so is generally described with the passive participle *concerned*.

> This letter concerns his habitual lateness.

> The teachers are concerned about his lack of progress.

convenient/convenience

Convenient must refer to something quite specific. A person or a life cannot be described as convenient.

> The meeting time wasn't convenient for everyone on the committee.

easy/difficult

The common ESL error with *easy* and *difficult* (and their synonyms) is using these adjectives to describe the person rather than the task.

> It is easy to follow his argument. His essay is very clear.

> Learning a new language is difficult, but practice makes it easier.

even

Even is an adverb used to strengthen or intensify. It is used just before the surprising part of a statement. *Even though* is stronger than *although* but is used in the same way. A common ESL error is to use *even* as a conjunction, but it cannot stand alone in that position—it must have an accompanying conjunction to make *even though*, *even if*, or *even when*.

> Even John was pleased with the results.

> I even got my nails done.

> I couldn't even see the stitching; it was so fine.

> She started working even faster when the bell rang.

> Even if the mini-skirt does come back into fashion, I wouldn't be caught dead wearing one.

> Even though Monica spent a fortune on her outfit, she didn't look half as good as Rachel.

Alter the following sentences by adding the word *even*. See how many positions *even* will fit in each sentence. You might have to make slight alterations to the sentence:

1. If Fred had notified us a day earlier, I would have been able to fix the problem with less effort.
2. Although Fatima couldn't see the alterations, she approved the new design as a better choice.
3. I had to follow the template, so I couldn't use Jamie's suggestions.

4. If I raised the hemline and took in the seams, the dress wouldn't look better.

5. If Martine had been able to slow the spread of the rumour a little bit, it wouldn't have meant a decrease in the stock price.

hardly, scarcely, barely

Hardly is not the adverb form of the adjective *hard*; instead, it is a synonym of *scarcely* and *barely*.

I could hardly hear him. [I heard him only a bit.]

We have scarcely any money left.

spend

Spend is used with money or time.

They spent days on the project, but that didn't show in the results.

I spent 50 dollars on the purse.

How much did you spend on your vacation?

suppose

Suppose means to think. In the passive voice, it shows expectation. In the past of the passive, it shows something should have happened but didn't. Students who leave off the *d* in the past participle are confused by the pronunciation since the sound of the *d* disappears next to the *t* of *to*.

I suppose that he could have misplaced the file.

Remember that you are supposed to change those figures to metric.

I was supposed to pick him up at four, but I forgot.

used to

Native speakers often do not write the *d* on *used to* because of the pronunciation. ESL learners have trouble keeping the two *used to* expressions separate, in both form and meaning: A past action is expressed with *used* plus the infinitive, while *used to* in the passive voice with a gerund expresses the idea of being accustomed to something.

I used a credit card to open this door. [the verb *to use* in its basic meaning]

A credit card can be used to open this door. [passive construction with the verb *to use*]

I used to work long hours, but now I have a new job. [past action]

I'm used to working long hours, so I don't mind my new shifts. [I am accustomed to working long hours.]

Exercise 7.8 Troublesome words

Correct any errors in the following sentences:

1. I've been saving my money, but I still cannot afford buying a new car.

2. I'm concerning about my business with this strike.

3. Comparing to my sister, I lack musical ability.

4. Clothes, toys, or cars are spent too much money on.

5. I suppose to meet him at four, but the bus was late.

6. She use to be his assistant, so she knows a lot about the development of the project.

7. The presentation of the food is another area they should concern about.

8. Even he had contacted us earlier, we would not have been able to fix the problem.

9. My life is very convenient now that I have a laptop.

10. Cellphones are easily to make contact with others.

11. Experts concerned children would lose social skills if they spend too much time with computers.

12. That new car cannot be afforded unless we take on extra hours.

13. He worked hardly on his manuscript, but he barely got anything accomplished.

14. She used to living in Regina, but she moved to Edmonton for a job.

15. I didn't understand what he was saying even he spoke more slowly.

Correcting Grammar Errors

Exercise 7.9 Determiners

Correct any errors:

1. Marilyn Bell was a first person to swim across the Lake Ontario.

2. There are many ways to access information through Internet.

3. Many of students have trouble writing essays. They need to take it one step at the time.

4. Pete is considering going to University of British Columbia or Simon Fraser University.

5. Diana was a most popular and famous woman in the world in the 1980s.

6. Meaning of a gift can be misinterpreted and can cause problems in relationship.

7. He could be success if he took program seriously.

8. The honesty is one of most important traits she is looking for in a man.

9. James wants to be doctor, but he is discouraged because it requires many years of study.

10. The book on the table belongs to the student who usually comes in late.

Exercise 7.10 Countable and uncountable nouns

Correct any errors:

1. I gave him an advice, but he refused to take it. He went ahead and bought the furnitures on delayed payments.

2. They suffered several setbacks in their plans. They didn't have the informations they needed at the start.

3. The teacher gave us many homework to do, but I got a head start on learning my vocabularies.

4. I bought new luggages for the trip—two suitcases and a rolling duffle bag.

5. She did not return the money but instead used them.

Exercise 7.10 Countable and uncountable nouns – *continued*

6. He restored the car. It's a real beauty now, but it took him a lot of time to do.

7. Many people who live on the street are addicted to alcohols and drugs.

8. The rehabilitation program gave them happiness and hopes.

9. Now that she has finished her assignment, she has another work to do.

10. I don't have the time or money to take on that project.

11. Students have troubles with their reading and writing tasks.

12. Tattoos are like make-up, clothes, and jewelleries; they decorate the body.

13. I need to stop at the grocery store. I have to buy a bread, a milk, a cheese, and some fish. [be specific]

14. The graduate students do many researches. The studies are often funded by pharmaceutical companies.

15. I asked him for an information package about the company.

Exercise 7.11 Verb tense and form

Correct any errors:

1. I selected those articles that can be helpful for my assignment since I have no previous experience with this kind of research. After I have found several articles, I looked for a website.

2. After work, employees will have more time to relax, loose up their muscles from their hard workday, and just made themselves at home.

3. When I started high school, I have been going to ESL to catch up on my English skills. Now in college I still think I need more practice.

4. If children are not teached the difference between right and wrong, they might don't pay attention to their behaviour.

5. Her parents never attend university, unlike the baby-boomer parents. They didn't know much about the schools and the procedures.

Exercise 7.11 Verb tense and form – *continued*

6. Managing money can be very difficult for college students. If they are used to spend their money freely, then when it was time to live on their own, budgeting will be a hard task to accomplish.

7. The change in organization makes people working more to get the same amount accomplish.

8. If I had finished the project on time, I would not lost so many marks. Now I have to make sure I will do a good job on the final research assignment or I will not have passing the course.

9. People did not take transit because they don't want to wait for buses, hates the overcrowding, and prefer the convenience of a car.

10. I love go camping. I particulary liked canoe trips. I don't even mind portaging.

11. Teachers can make reading groups to let the students to have more chance to read.

12. I'm not use to the new system yet, but I think it will helped management to pinpoint problems more quickly.

13. First, I decide to go to the bank because I didn't have any cash. But when I arrive at the bank, I found that I had forgot my bank card.

14. She has had many interesting experiences: She has been bungee jumping in Australia, she has dancing in a Parisian cabaret, and she seen the fall of the Berlin Wall.

15. If I won a million dollars in the lottery, I will still want a job. I would want to use the knowledge I learned in school, and I would still needing to earn money for when I run through the lottery money.

Exercise 7.12 Active and passive voice

Correct any errors:

1. An accident was happened on the highway, so I was late for class.

2. I happened to see Jill at the cafeteria, so I didn't have to call her.

3. People often get misleading by salespeople. They buy something they will regret later.

4. People are fear the threat of terrorism even though more people are suffered from cancer and heart disease.

Exercise 7.12 Active and passive voice – *continued*

5. I'm afraid I've worried him now. I didn't think he would be taken the news so hard.

6. I was hurried to meet my friends. The traffic jam made me late.

7. It was rained yesterday, so the barbecue was rescheduled.

8. People can easily find news on the Internet. With just a few clicks, the information could be appeared on the screen.

9. If I practise enough, my skills will be improved, but I don't think I will make the NHL.

10. Children should assigned some simple housework. Chores need to be share by all family members.

11. Students can also be benefit from playing video games. These games are improve problem-solving skills.

12. Extras like designer jeans should be buy by the teenagers themselves; the parents shouldn't have to bankrupt themselves to be keep up with their children's demands.

13. In China, a family only allows to have one child. The reduced family size puts more attention on those children as they have two parents and four grandparents all focused on them.

14. The Parliament buildings were build in the early 1860s, before Canada became an official country.

15. Christmas is a time of year to celebrate. Families get together, and gifts are exchange.

Verbs expressing emotion

The verbs used to describe emotions can be confusing in English. There are two basic patterns: In one, the person experiencing the feeling is the grammatical subject of the sentence. In the other, the stimulus (the thing causing the feeling) is the subject and the person feeling the emotion is the direct object of the verb. Sometimes these verbs have a similar meaning but follow a different sentence pattern:

> I fear snakes. [the person is the grammatical subject]

> Snakes frighten me. [the person is the grammatical object]

> Hal enjoys jogging.

> A walk in the park would please them.

The verbs that take the person as the grammatical object cause problems for students, especially those learning English as a second language. They create incorrect sentences such as "I am exciting about the field trip" or "I am interesting in the lab work." Because the person experiencing the emotion is the object of the verb, a passive construction is used to describe the person. To really understand the mistake in the participle, you have to go back to the root verb. This is shown in the pattern in the following examples:

> Astronomy interests me.
>
> Astronomy is interesting.
>
> I am interested in astronomy.
>
> This grammar lesson confuses me.
>
> This grammar lesson is confusing.
>
> I am confused by this grammar lesson.

Here are some verbs that follow the same pattern, with the person as the grammatical object:

amuse	depress	horrify	puzzle
annoy	disgust	impress	satisfy
appal	disappoint	insult	scare
bewilder	encourage	interest	shock
bore	excite	irritate	surprise
bother	fascinate	mislead	thrill
charm	flatter	offend	
confuse	frighten	please	

In contrast, here are some verbs for which the person is the grammatical subject:

> admire, enjoy, fear, hate, like, love, miss, not mind, prefer, regret, resent, respect, trust

Example sentences:

> I enjoy a walk in the park. A walk in the park is enjoyable.
>
> I don't mind waiting.
>
> He regrets breaking up with her.

Exercise 7.13

Choose the correct form of the verb to complete the sentence:

1. I get _____ [confused, confusing] whenever he talks about the long-term financial prospects.

2. She is _____ [frightened, frightening] because he is stalking her.

3. My mother was _____ [pleasing, pleased] that my sister and I could plan the trip without arguing.

4. The test results were _____ [disappointing, disappointed], but the questions had been _____ [misleading, misled], so it's no wonder we did poorly.

5. Yuri was _____ [offending, offended] by what his supervisor said.

6. The mess in the kitchen was _____ [disgusting, disgusted]. It _____ [bothering, bothered] me that they could live like that.

7. I found the book very _____ [interesting, interested], but I was _____ [shocking, shocked] by the ending.

8. My roommate had many _____ [annoyed, annoying] habits. I was _____ [relieving, relieved] when he decided to move.

9. I was _____ [flattering, flattered] when she chose me for the promotion.

10. The work is _____ [satisfying, satisfied], and my supervisors are _____ [encouraging, encouraged].

Exercise 7.14

Correct any errors:

1. She admired the skill with which he built the deck and was pleasing with the result.

2. Pooja found the questions confused, so she's relieved to have passed the mid-term.

3. She was surprised that they threw her a birthday party.

Exercise 7.14 – *continued*

4. I don't mind waiting. I'll just read my book. I'm at an excited part—the hero is frightening the bad guys so they will give up their pursuit.

5. I resent his interference. He knows it, and he's trying to charm me into agreeing to the plan.

6. He felt worry about the evaluation, even though his supervisor always seems satisfying with his work.

7. His behaviour was appalling. I can't respect him anymore.

8. I like to talk to her because she's an interested person. She has travelled widely.

9. The party was really boring. There was too much shop talk. I found it annoyed.

10. That dress is not very flattered. I felt insulted that she chose it for me.

Gerunds and infinitives

The –*ing* forms of the verb when used as nouns are called *gerunds*, as in "Seeing is believing." The base form of the verb preceded by *to* is called an *infinitive*, as in "He didn't know what to do." Both these types of words are called *verbals*. When a verbal follows another form, it could be either the gerund or the infinitive. It depends on the first verb; there is no definitive grammar rule to explain which verbal is used. ESL students, especially, have to memorize each usage. Sometimes verbs can be completed by either a gerund or an infinitive, and sometimes the two expressions have different meanings. Here are some examples:

I appreciated seeing the plans beforehand because they failed to notify us of the changes.

After attempting to get a role in the production, he now says he dislikes acting in plays.

He prefers directing. He prefers to direct plays. [no meaning difference]

I remembered to take the medicine. I remembered taking the medicine. [different meanings]

Note that the infinitive is also used to express the *in order to* idea, where *in order* can often be left out:

> He quit school [in order] to go to Hollywood.

> I whistled [in order] to attract his attention.

Verbs that take gerunds:

appreciate	dislike	keep	recommend
anticipate	dread	like	remember
avoid	enjoy	mind	resent
begin	escape	miss	resume
cease	fear	postpone	risk
consider	finish	practise	start
continue	forget	prefer	stop
delay	hate	quit	suggest
deny	involve	recall	try

Verbs that take infinitives:

afford	fail	need	start
appear	forget	neglect	stop
attempt	hate	plan	think
begin	hope	prefer	threaten
choose	intend	pretend	try
continue	learn	promise	want
dare	like	remain	wish
decide	live	remember	
expect	long	seem	

Exercise 7.15 Gerunds or infinitives

Choose the correct form of the verb to complete the sentence:

1. I enjoy _____ [taking, to take] a walk after dinner.

2. He intends _____ [waiting, to wait] until she returns even though he'll miss _____ [seeing, to see] the concert.

3. The director threatened _____ [firing, to fire] the whole division.

4. The farmer suggested _____ [taking, to take] the river route to get a better view.

5. Jack happened _____ [seeing, to see] Eliza in the market, so he invited her _____ [joining, to join] us at the sports bar later.

Exercise 7.15 Gerunds or infinitives – *continued*

6. The committee decided to postpone _____ [repainting, to repaint] the clubhouse until after some much-needed renovations.

7. Remind me _____ [returning, to return] the books to the library after class.

8. He keeps _____ [telling, to tell] me to invest more money in stocks, but I don't think I can afford _____ [taking, to take] the risk.

9. They neglected _____ [taking, to take] the necessary precautions and so had to postpone _____ [redoing, to redo] the race.

10. I wanted _____ [trying, to try] the bungee jump, but Sam preferred _____ [keeping, to keep] both feet on the ground.

Exercise 7.16 Gerunds and infinitives

Correct any verb errors in the following sentences:

1. The witness denied ever to see the accused man. She remembered seeing a much taller man.

2. I hope getting a better mark next time, so I will start to study earlier.

3. She promised to be more careful next time, and she seemed to be sincere.

4. Elaine expected seeing him at 4:00, but he had delayed starting the meeting, so he was late.

5. I suggest to try another way. You should pretend agreeing with him and then fix the problem yourself.

6. I resent having to do this over again. He shouldn't have tried doing it without help in the first place.

7. She couldn't decide whether to continue seeing him or not.

8. I recommend to wait until she's older. She'll enjoy riding the roller coaster then.

9. They resumed cutting the budget after the CEO threatened firing more staff.

10. I recall asking him about it before, but he avoided to answer me.

Exercise 7.17 Prepositions

Fill in the blank with the correct preposition where necessary:

1. That new equipment isn't suitable _____ winter conditions. We'll have to replace it _____ something rated for −15.

2. I don't feel sorry _____ you. It was your fault that you weren't ready _____ the test.

3. When she puts her earphones _____ and listens _____ her MP3 player, she becomes oblivious _____ everything around her.

4. You are capable _____ much better work. You should pay attention _____ class.

5. He arrived _____ the airport too late _____ the plane. He had to wait _____ the next flight.

6. I'm not familiar _____ that brand. Is the company known _____ making good products?

7. They were grateful _____ the extra help. They were confused _____ that grammar point.

8. My apartment building is adjacent _____ the park, and I can see the baseball games _____ my window.

9. She's demanding _____ answers. She wants to talk _____ the manager.

10. I depend _____ my brother to calm the situation whenever I argue _____ my parents.

Exercise 7.18 Prepositions

Correct any preposition errors in the following sentences:

1. She's been living by her own for too long; she has a hard time getting along with people.

2. Here are some solutions about the problem. We need to choose the best one of these.

3. I can store important data at my laptop computer and retrieve it later on my convenience.

4. The family can have a conversation together in front of the dinner table.

5. If someone is acting suspiciously, bystanders should pay more attention on the behaviour.

Exercise 7.18 Prepositions – *continued*

6. Many people have a desire on a luxury car to show off to their friends.

7. Students should be given reading homework on the textbook at every week.

8. I looked up the company in the Internet, but I couldn't find enough information about it.

9. I can make my meaning clear with choosing good vocabulary.

10. This apartment is a good choice because it's quick to get to downtown from here.

Exercise 7.19 Prepositions and different parts of speech

Sometimes the use of prepositions is confusing because of the differences in parts of speech. Often the noun may have to be followed by a preposition, but the verb does not. Here are some example sentences:

John <u>influenced</u> his brother. [verb, no preposition]

John is a big <u>influence on</u> his brother. [noun + preposition]

I <u>lack</u> musical talent. [verb, no preposition]

I have a <u>lack of</u> musical talent. [noun + preposition]

Correct any errors:

1. Everybody fears of terrorist attacks, but there's no solution to the problem.

2. Immigrants come to Canada in the pursuit of a better life. At first, they make do with basic survival.

3. He shows a lack of basic arithmetic skills and absolutely no understanding the principles of physics.

4. The course emphasizes on basic first aid treatments and life-saving measures.

5. They need to learn about their colleagues' religious beliefs so they can respect them.

6. The techniques used affect on the results and should be taken into account.

Exercise 7.19 Prepositions and different parts of speech – *continued*

7. The author describes about the difficulties he faced enrolling for university. He mentions about the misunderstandings.

8. She expects of Zach to finish on time and to solve the problem.

9. They have no respect for the hard work their parents put in to earn that money.

10. The effects on the family structure are difficult to evaluate. The parents' expectations of their children are important.

11. Her desire of privacy has become obsessive. She's becoming a true hermit.

12. With the merger of the two companies, they gained of a new division to take care of the service calls.

13. One way to help homeless people is to increase of charity programs.

14. The new organization structure will have an impact on all day-to-day operations.

15. He started a new workout regime and managed a weight gain of 20 pounds.

Try rewriting the sentences above, switching from the noun to the verb form, and vice versa, where possible. For example, "Everyone has a fear of terrorist attacks" is a possible version of the first sentence.

Exercise 7.20 Possessive forms

Correct any errors:

1. I couldn't find out who's keys these are, so I took them down to the Security's Department.

2. Erin lent me her keys to the storage room's because I misplaced mines.

3. A long time ago people had large families, but nowaday's people have fewer children.

4. I didn't have a dictionary, so I borrowed Ron's. I had to go find mine later.

5. The childrens' babysitter needs a ride home if she babysits after midnight.

Exercise 7.20 Possessive forms – *continued*

6. The Johnson's house was broken into last week. They're whole place was trashed.

7. I've been sitting here watching the puppy try to chase its tail. Who's dog is it anyway?

8. Helen and Andy left there backpacks near the bandshell.

9. Sallys car was broken into, and her CDs were stolen.

10. If you don't have you're textbook, you can borrow Elizabeths, but make sure you don't mark it up because she is very fussy about her things.

Exercise 7.21 Subject/verb and pronoun agreement

Correct any errors:

1. One of the band members are from Australia. He play the trumpet.

2. Working with John and Jane were a pleasure. They are very talented.

3. On average, a book today has more than 500 pages. They take too long to read.

4. Every day, the mother goose, along with its five goslings, go across the highway. The drivers all seems to be watching out for the geese.

5. A lot of people leave the city on long weekends. The resulting traffic jams are an ordeal.

6. *Star wars* is my favourite movie, but I don't like the new trilogy. They have more special effects than heart.

7. Surveillance cameras does not help to make society secure. It only helps to capture criminals after the fact.

8. The number of candidates for the November elections have risen to 20. It should make for an interesting election.

9. If any documents are misplaced, it can be found easily if the information are stored on computers. The search functions allow quick retrieval.

10. You should buy that laptop next week. They will probably go on sale.

Exercise 7.22 Fragments and run-ons

Fix the sentence structure errors to eliminate fragments and run-on sentences:

1. She's pretending to work. But she is just playing solitaire on the computer. With time running out.

2. The preliminary steps in job hunting including writing a résumé, asking for references, and networking. Then the job hunter can start actually applying for jobs.

3. She lets Jake use the car whenever he asks. Even though he's a terrible driver. Last year he had three accidents.

4. We studied all the readings in class, however many of the students had trouble remembering the material for the test.

5. It's not hard to see what the problem is, the machine won't start because this piece is jamming it.

6. Because he had accumulated so much stuff in residence. He borrowed his parents' van when he was moving out.

7. In most cases, being your own boss and not having to answer to anyone.

8. I had to go to the bank before I could pay him back. Being in debt makes me uncomfortable.

9. He lets his employees have a say in the decision-making process, therefore their job satisfaction is high. Few of them moving on to other jobs.

10. Because of his success with the last project. He was promoted to assistant manager. After a while he was making much more money. So, he asked his girlfriend to marry him.

Exercise 7.23 Sentence structure

Correct the errors and improve the sentence structure:

1. She realized which she was late, so she called in to delay the meeting.

2. He wondered why did she not return his calls. He thought that they had hit it off.

3. Success is something that everyone wants it.

Exercise 7.23 Sentence structure – *continued*

4. I come from Saudi Arabia which its national language is Arabic.

5. By going to a fast-food restaurant, it will save time.

6. In a smaller store, you often find the staff more knowledgeable about the products and are more willing to go the extra mile to help you.

7. Pressing hard on the fountain pen, the nib broke.

8. For international students in Canada, they face difficulties with daily life.

9. Because with the fast development happening in China, there are no longer any benefits for studying abroad.

10. The manager cut the staff he reorganized the filing system and got everything to run more smoothly.

Correcting Punctuation and Capitalization

Exercise 7.24 Apostrophes

Correct errors in the sentences below by either adding, moving, or removing an apostrophe where necessary:

1. Jills brother could'n't find a job this summer, so he's visiting her in Winnipeg.

2. Many of the band members were unable to fit the extra practice's into their schedules.

3. This feature let's the user move the icon's over to align with the others.

4. Jack does'nt want to go to the Marshall's cottage next week because its too long a trip.

5. The children's playroom is alway's a mess, so shes given up on keeping it clean.

6. Whos going to the play tomorrow? We need to reserve tickets before its' too late.

7. Lets see if Fatima can join us. She know's Montreal very well. Its her hometown.

8. He like's to read comics about amazing superheroe's. He buy's them at second-hand stores.

9. Were expecting two shipment's of blue jeans—one from each of our regular supplier's.

Exercise 7.24 Apostrophes – *continued*

10. Its been a long time since Ive seen any evidence of Martins abilitie's. He let's others do all the work.

11. Each student's work is graded by teaching assistants. The professor only makes random check's.

12. Todays teenagers have a lot of disposable income, so they can buy DVD's and other luxuries.

13. The meetings are held regularly on Tuesday's in the senior's lounge.

14. The players' luggage was stored in the manager's room while they were waiting for the bus'es to arrive.

15. Thursday's lesson concern's the rampant misuse of the apostrophe in sign's and letters.

Exercise 7.25 Mechanics

Add punctuation marks and capital letters where necessary in the following sentences:

1. if i hadnt been paying attention i would have been hit by that ball

2. the japanese garden at ubc is a beautiful restful place i like to visit there on sunday afternoons

3. allison loves horror movies but i hate being scared my favourite movie is gone with the wind

4. tailgating is a traffic violation moreover it is dangerous not only can the tailgater easily hit the car ahead but drivers behind the tailgater get frustrated seeing brake lights because they do not know whether there is an actual traffic slowdown

5. like a drill sergeant steven shouted do not panic walk dont run

6. on my trip to europe i visited paris, monaco, florence, rome, venice, munich, and amsterdam i met a lot of students from different countries who were travelling on the same tour bus

7. the peoples response is predictable they wont support the new party because of its stand on social justice issues

8. i cant say whos coming to the wedding because i havent seen the latest list

9. the womens washroom was closed for maintenance so frances and lee took over the mens room

10. charless mother used to play for a ladies softball team she held a few pitching records

Editing to Improve Style

Exercise 7.26 Conversational style

Rewrite the following passages into a more academic style and correct errors:

1. I have done both the cellphone and land line thing. Let me tell you, a home phone is the way to go. I can't wait till the end of my agreement to get rid of that cellphone. Well, actually, I can't get rid of it completely. I would still have it for emergencies.

2. Look at residence for example. Residence is a licence to have fun, drink lots, and meet new people; basically a licence to party. Sounds like fun, but there are a few problems.

3. A career is something that person will be stuck with for the rest of his/her life unless they are willing to fork out the time and money on schooling again. So people should obviously choose a career wisely.

4. Well, in college it's a big difference. Now students have to budget their money well or they can get really screwed over. Which is the most important part of being on your own.

5. Parents should give help to their children when they asked you to. Otherwise, they will just yell at you for not giving them space. Sometimes they will say you're annoying and stuff like that.

6. No longer can you come home and have Moms home cooking. Welcome to fast TV dinners and a life of Kraft dinner. Now that balanced diet has been thrown out the window to provide more time for homework and studying.

7. The rich people now-a-days have mommy and daddy's moneypit to fall back on if they screw up once in university. But when poor students get in they know if they don't do well they'll be poor for years to come.

8. This guy came to do the landscaping. And he put in a new walkway. And he tore out all the old shrubs. And he made some new planting beds. But we're gonna put in the plants next spring cause we're too late in the season.

Exercise 7.27 Wordiness

Rewrite the following sentences to make them concise by eliminating repetition and unnecessary words:

Example: When large factories are built, they invariably increase road traffic, which makes neighbourhoods far more dangerous places than they were before. (21 words)

Large factories invariably increase road traffic, making neighbourhoods more dangerous. (10 words)

1. Canadian streets and public spaces should have more surveillance cameras. Having more surveillance cameras can help police.

2. The key to success or the most important factor of success in college courses is time management. Managing time in a proper and effective way is the key to success at every part of life. Students all over the world in numerous colleges are facing the same problem of not coping with time.

3. I was shopping along side with a friend of mine.

4. In college, students waste time on socializing and being with friends and waste their time on unnecessary things, such as talking on the phone, sitting in a café for hours, and lots of other things which affects their time.

5. I went to the mall that was close to where I reside. I walked into a store. It was a store only for watches. I was hoping I would definitely find what I was looking for because I spotted a store for watches.

6. Factors such as work, school, and other activities determine how much time and effort one can really put towards a relationship. To begin with, work can determine how much time someone can put into a relationship. For example, a couple where both people work a lot, less time would be put into the relationship but more effort should be put in to make up for the time.

7. Grades should reflect actual student achievement. Giving students a grade that they do not deserve does not help them later in life. When students receive a grade, it should be earned and not given to them as a favour because it is not good for their future. Students need to learn how to earn a grade, rather than receiving a grade that they do not earn. The grade they receive should reflect their actual achievement and skill level. Marks should not be given to students who do not earn them. Later on in life it will not do any good for them due to the fact that they just received a

Exercise 7.27 Wordiness – *continued*

mark instead of actually earning one. Marks should not be given to students just to do a favour for them because they would get credit for something they did not work for. Achievement should be the reason for receiving a good grade, not just being given one as a favour.

8. In our modern day society that we live in, it is understandable that materialism is equated with happiness because people are happy with material goods.

9. What I would do next time would probably be to maybe start my research earlier so I would have extra time to spare if I ran into problems finding the resources needed to complete a complete research assignment.

Exercise 7.28 "For example" narratives

Some students launch into rambling narratives when they give examples in their academic paragraphs and essays. An anecdote can make something interesting, but it can also distract from the main task at hand—proving the points made. Rewrite the examples, preferably in one sentence:

1. Some people get a tattoo to remember someone or somebody. For example, a person showed his tattoo to me. He told me this tattoo means his girlfriend's name. When he and his girlfriend fell in love, he got the tattoo. Now they broke up, but he told me he would never erase the tattoo and forget his girlfriend because this is his first love.

2. People can edit their work faster and easier. For example, a student finishes an essay. He finds some mistakes and wants to edit it. If he writes his essay by hand, he needs to write it again. If the essay is in the computer, he can edit it using the cut and paste function.

3. Students should take advantage of their free time and seize the moment while they can. For example, the teacher has just assigned homework. At the end of the class, they know that they have a spare period next. Instead of taking the right step and completing that work, they waste time on something less important.

Exercise 7.28 "For example" narratives – *continued*

4. People will chose public transit if it is made more convenient and faster than driving. For example, a business man has to get to work. There are traffic jams on the highway. The driving is all stop and go. But a train bypasses all the traffic. It moves more quickly. Moreover, the man can do work on the train.

5. Sometimes students do not take the time to study for tests and exams. For example, a student is going to have a test next week. Instead of studying for the test, that student decides to go to a party every night and pull an all-nighter the day before the test.

Exercise 7.29 General correction and revision

Rewrite the sentences to correct errors and improve style:

1. In writing, I sometimes feel difficult to express my ideas, maybe I should learn more vocabularies.

2. I am feel happy that you could give me some advise about my writing problem.

3. On holidays, people can relax themselves and enjoy.

4. The article of Terry Fox is the one interesting story. It mentioned about his livelihood since he was born until he passed away.

5. Children, in many parents eyes, are always babies. But is that means children have to be treated as a baby? I know parents care about their child so much, want them to be safed, and well protected.

6. Speak a second language is a valuable skill because we can easy to travelled on the country, easy to found a good job, and easy to learned on a new culture.

7. The lessons that we need to attend are far much interesting that what I expect before.

8. Movies, music video's and just walking down the street, we see multiple people with different markings and holes on their body.

9. Sports games are not that easy to become exciting again after commercial breaks because they get slowed down again and again.

10. Rebellious teenagers want to do whatever their parents not allow them to do.

Exercise 7.30 General correction and revision ◦

Rewrite the passages to correct errors and improve style:

1. Yesterday we went to Fairview Park Mall to go shopping. First, we went there by bus for 20 minutes. Several minutes later, we arrived and ran into the mall. Then, we visit many shops that are interesting.

2. It seems that many people don't really pay alot of attention towards getting ready to leave home and attend a new community away from friends and family. They come across alot of other things for eg. yes! I'm away from home my parents, this and that. They really just see that how important the freedom they can get after post-secondary school. But once there away from home. They then see how difficult it is to maintain it. So, therefore pay close attention to how well you can organize yourself and get things done without struggling and stressing over things that could have been done much more eaisly if you were to be smart and do them from before.

3. If a second generation immigrant has no interest in learning about their language than chances are their not going to keep it or learn it in the first place. Comparing to someone who is actually interested in their culture and language, and actually does want to learn and keep their native language.

4. In Every day life, we people get problems. Some problems can be solved; some problems cannot be solved. As someone once said "nothing is impossible." As a student we are the people have the most problem. For example, school marks; fee, and transportation. Also many more that got nothing to do with this essay.

5. If the immigrant family has a strong belief that their children should maintain the native language, they constantly remind the child to keep the language, such as reinforcing the child to speak the language.

6. Also, teenagers might be one of the reasons why cellphones are so successful than the regular phones at home. Why? Because most teenagers are on the go and barely close to home. Either their at school, out with friends or working.

7. In most horror stories the elements are easy and simple to understand, that is good because the reader must have a good idea of what is the problem and where is the fear factor, otherwise if the story is too complex to understand then the reader will have to fight his way through trying to find the scary parts, that will result into reading mystery type of story rather than a horror story.

Reading Skills

The importance of good reading skills cannot be overstated. It is impossible to become a good writer if you do not read a lot. Written English is different from the spoken variety of the language, so people who do not read much do not know the language—they are not comfortable with the complex sentence structures, the more sophisticated vocabulary, or the conventions, such as using punctuation correctly.

Languages exist in different varieties. These include dialects, such as Canadian English, Australian English, and Jamaican English. People also use different varieties of the language when they are speaking to family members as opposed to their work supervisors. The style of language they use in an e-mail to a friend is different from the style they use in a job application letter. Moreover, the vocabulary of everyday, conversational English is quite limited compared to the huge number of words used in standard written English. Spoken English uses gestures and tone of voice in addition to words, while written English uses punctuation. These differences are mentioned and discussed throughout this book; for reading, the implication is clear—students must read a lot to be able to understand and use standard written English.

Some poor readers do not even realize that they have weak reading skills. After all, they know how to "read" the words, but they find it difficult to figure out the writer's main point or to detect tone, such as sarcasm and humour. Their vocabulary is limited, so they misunderstand what the writer is saying. They may read slowly and laboriously.

Reading skills, like all skills, are built slowly. The more you read, the easier it becomes. If you rarely open a book, it will be a chore when you do have to read something. With practice, you can increase your reading speed and level of comprehension. You will learn more words and be exposed to more new ideas. The more familiar you are with a subject, the easier it is to understand stories and articles on that topic.

Remember that reading is a skill that is developed gradually. It is better to read some easier materials, such as children's books and simplified ESL readers, than to struggle through newspaper articles for which you do not have the background knowledge or the vocabulary to understand. Start with easier texts and increase the level of difficulty as you get more comfortable. Of course, you do not always have the luxury of time to do this. If you are taking a course with required readings, you must work your way through them as well as you can, even if you find it a struggle. But try to find time for that extra reading that will build your skills.

How you read a text depends on why you are reading it. When you read a chapter of your textbook, you highlight important sections and make notes. When you read a novel for pleasure, you just read through it. You scan a newspaper, reading headlines, looking at pictures, and choosing interesting articles to read. You can skim a chapter in a textbook to get the gist of what is said. If you need to study a story or an article for school, you should do a more careful reading—making notes, highlighting important points, and looking up unfamiliar words in the dictionary.

This unit introduces some of the basics of reading. You can practise and build your skills with the actual readings in part 2 of this book.

Distinguishing Fiction and Non-fiction

When you walk into any bookstore or library, you will find that the main division between books is fiction and non-fiction. Even though this distinction becomes blurred when it comes to works such as autobiographical fiction, it is important to differentiate these two kinds of writing. Sometimes students get confused and talk about a character in an essay or about the author doing the actions in a short story.

Even in the "real world," outside school, this distinction becomes important. Theological experts and historians have argued about the theories presented in *The Da Vinci code*, even though it is a novel, a work of fiction. James Frey was censured in the media because he fabricated part of his memoirs (his life story).

Fiction is made-up stories. We use the terms *short story* and *novel* to refer to works of fiction. Short stories can be anywhere from 500 to 5,000 words. There are four short stories among the reading selections in this textbook. Novels are usually 300 to 1,000 pages. Sometimes books are made up of linked short stories. Autobiographical fiction tells the life story of the author, but it is told in a narrative style, events in the story are not exactly as they happened, and the dialogue does not represent the actual words the participants used. Movies are usually works of fiction, unless they are documentaries. Docudramas blur the line between fiction and non-fiction because actual events are dramatized, but they are not absolutely true because they are only an interpretation as to how things could have happened.

Fiction is more open to interpretation. We can use our imagination to picture characters and settings. And yet fiction can be more true than non-fiction because it can speak to us and stay with us. For instance, the novel *To kill a mockingbird* is a powerful story that can have more effect on readers than a textbook reading on racism. It has been shown that people learn facts better if they are delivered in the form of a story. This is not surprising because it was the way our ancestors learned and passed down knowledge. Readers of historical novels can get a good sense of the history of the period even though they are reading fiction.

Most of the readings in this text are non-fiction. You can call them *essays* or *articles*. Many of them were first published as columns in newspaper or magazines. In newspapers and magazines, news stories are written by reporters and relate the facts as objectively as possible. Columns are usually accompanied by a picture of the columnist in the newspaper or magazine. They give the columnist's opinion and are therefore more like essays.

If *I* appears in the piece of writing, the identity of that person depends on what kind of writing it is. An *I* in a work of non-fiction refers to the author himself or herself. Thus, for example, for the article "Free to drive," we can say, "Margaret Wente says she will not give up her SUV no matter how much gas costs." However, "Why my mother can't speak English" is a short story based on true events; in other words, it is autobiographical fiction. You cannot say, "Garry Engkent's mother blamed her husband." Because the mother and the son in the story have not been given names in the story, we have to refer to them as *the mother* and *the son*. They are characters, not real people. You can also refer to the son as *the narrator*.

Note that we can refer to characters by their first or last names, depending on what they are called in the short story or novel. When you are discussing a non-fiction reading, you should give the author's full name the first time you mention it but then use just the family name. For example, you can say, "In 'All grown up and still in tow,' Sherri Beattie talks about the overprotective parents she sees at university. Beattie is a graduate student from a different generation."

Identifying the Main Idea

Most essays have one main idea that the author is trying to communicate to his or her audience. Sometimes the idea is stated directly, and sometimes it is not. The reader may have to infer the thesis. If the thesis is not immediately obvious to you, look at the organization of the reading. Remember that you are looking for the most general idea that is supported in the essay.

One of the best ways to figure out the main idea of a non-fiction reading is to look at the title. This especially holds true for newspaper stories and columns because their titles are actually headlines, which are sentences with some of the function words (such as determiners) taken out. Take a look at the table of contents of this book and read the titles of the readings in part

2. The non-fiction articles are mostly from newspapers; the titles tell you very clearly what the thesis is. For example, Jim Coyle's piece is called "No point fearing terror attacks we can't stop," which is short for "There is no point in fearing terror attacks we can't stop." Compare these titles to the fiction pieces. It is not as obvious what "Soap and water" or "The open window" are about.

A common organizational pattern for non-fiction writing, especially in newspapers and magazines, is to start with an anecdote—a story of something that happened to the author or to someone he knows. This is an introduction that catches readers' attention because it is personal, something they can relate to. Then the author goes on to make general statements about the issue he or she is interested in. This is where you can find the thesis.

Remember that in an academic essay, the thesis comes at the end of the introduction. This pattern is often used in journalistic essays and articles, except that the introduction may be several paragraphs long instead of the one-paragraph introduction you are used to writing for your essays. (Keep in mind that newspaper and magazine articles have many short paragraphs because they are written in columns.)

In specific sentences, the main idea will be in the main clause. Look at the transitions the author uses. For example, expressions such as *however* and *it is vital to remember* point the way to main points.

Remember that the main idea will be supported by examples and explanations. When you read such specific statements, look for the point that is being made.

Distinguishing Writers' Opinions

When you read essays and columns in newspapers and magazines, you have to make sure you follow different people's arguments. Often authors mention some popular views before coming to their own. They will start relating these other views and then emphasize their own with a phrase like *the truth is . . .*

Here are some things to watch for:
- expressions like *people think*, which automatically distances that view from the author's view;
- words in quotation marks which show that the author does not agree with that term;
- transition signals such as *however* and *more importantly*;
- use of personal pronouns (*I*, *me*) to emphasize the author's point of view.

Here are some examples:

> "The tobacco industry and its supporters have long insisted that smoking is simply a matter of 'individual choice'." McQuaig, page 293. [Note that she is giving an argument she disagrees with.]

"But those same stupid choices don't strike me as being much of an argument in favour of governments (or, for that matter, individuals) suing tobacco companies for the cost of tobacco-related illnesses." Adamson, page 295.

"What a lot of unhelpful blather has been uttered lately by Public Safety Minister Anne McLellan." Coyle, page 298. [Notice how the author uses strong language to dismiss McLellan's speech.]

The reading selections in this text have comprehension and discussion questions that ask you about the author's viewpoint. As you read, look for the cues and discuss them in class.

Recognizing Writers' Techniques

Writing is a craft. Writers use a variety of techniques to get their message across to their readers. Each word they put down is chosen from a vast array of possibilities. The way they structure their paragraphs and sentences is part of their craft. They keep in mind their audience and purpose. They want to make sure that everything is clear to the readers. They try to entertain, inform, and convince readers.

As you read the selections in part 2, some of the authors' techniques will become clear. They will deal with essay structure, sentence structure, and word choice. As you read, consider the decisions the author made. Look at the connotation of words. Consider how the topic is introduced and concluded. Are you caught up in the story the author tells? Are you convinced by the arguments? Reading attentively will make you a better reader, but do not forget that sometimes you can just sit back and enjoy the ride the author takes you on.

Dealing with Unfamiliar Words

As you read, you will come across unfamiliar words. If you stopped to look each one up in the dictionary, reading would become tedious. Try to get by on guessing the meaning from the context. If you understand the gist of what is being said in the text, you do not have to go to your dictionary when you spot a difficult word. If, however, it is an important reading, such as your English homework, then you should read it the first time through without a dictionary but then go back over it again, highlighting important points, making notes, and looking up unfamiliar words to make sure you understand everything.

Children learn words by hearing them many times and gradually working out the meaning in their own minds. They use their knowledge of their language and of the world to help them. This type of learning continues as they learn to read and encounter a larger body of vocabulary items. The more they read, the more words they learn. This is why people who read little have weak vocabularies. Avid readers generally have a large vocabulary, but they may rarely consult dictionaries. They use them only when they need to be absolutely sure of the meaning of a word or when they are curious about the word. Remember that it is impossible for even the most educated speakers to know all the words of English.

Here are some examples of how context can help you understand words:

> As we passed the rotting garbage, we tried covering our noses to keep out the vile stench.

If you do not know what the words *vile* and *stench* mean, you can figure out from this sentence that they refer to the awful smell of the garbage. And, in fact, *vile* means "terrible, really bad" and *stench* means "bad smell".

> When his father asked, "And where do you think you're going?" the teenager looked back at him sullenly.

Sullenly is an adverb, describing the way the teenager looked at his father. The father is chastising his son, so chances are that the son is not too happy. From what you know about relationships between teenagers and their parents, you can guess that it is not a pleasant expression on his face. The adjective *sullen* means "resentful, unsociable, and sulky."

In addition to looking around the word to the context to figure out its meaning, you can look inside the word. You can look for familiar prefixes, suffixes, and roots. (Many of the common ones were introduced in unit 2.) For example, the word *indeterminate* has an *in–* prefix, which is probably negative. The root *determine* is recognizable as the verb meaning "to find out the facts about something," so indeterminate means "impossible to know exactly." Another example is the word *naysayer*, which can be easily divided into its three parts: *nay* (meaning "no"), *say*, and *–er* (a suffix showing someone who does something), so a naysayer is someone who says no.

When you come across an unfamiliar word, keep reading and see if the meaning of the sentence is clear enough. Use context clues and your knowledge of language to help you figure out the word. Go to the dictionary when you need to. You will have an opportunity to practise these vocabulary skills with the reading selections in the text and the accompanying exercises.

Exercise 8.1

Use context clues and word form to help you figure out the meaning of the underlined words:

1. It was <u>serendipity</u> that I came across that article. I wasn't even thinking of my research project when I found it, but it has just what I need.

2. They were <u>at loggerheads</u> over the proposal. In the end, they couldn't work together and had to submit separate proposals.

3. His <u>punctual</u> arrival was a relief since they were so used to waiting for him.

4. The leather sofa was comfortable, but it was <u>cumbersome</u> every time he had to move.

5. They were surprised at his decision to donate the proceeds of the sale because <u>altruism</u> had never been one of his qualities.

6. Simplified novels are <u>abridged</u> versions of the books that also have changes in vocabulary and sentence structure to make them easier to read.

7. I am <u>famished</u>. I only had a cup of yogurt for lunch.

8. The immigrant family was so happy to be here that they <u>assimilated</u> into Canadian society with ease.

9. I love to watch professional soccer because the players have such speed and <u>agility</u>.

10. It's important to eat a good breakfast to <u>fortify</u> yourself for the hard day ahead.

Exercise 8.2

Choose the right meaning of the underlined word, using context clues:

1. She thought that adults would behave better, but this class was as <u>obstreperous</u> as a bunch of preschoolers.
    a) well-motivated and on task
    b) noisy and difficult to control
    c) bored and sleepy

2. Ever since I started taking that medication I feel so <u>listless</u> that I don't get enough of my work done.
    a) without goals or a to-do list
    b) wide awake and alert
    c) without energy or enthusiasm

Exercise 8.2 – *continued*

3. Because cellphones are <u>ubiquitous</u>, people feel they have the right to use them any time they choose, just as everyone else is doing.
   a) everywhere
   b) useful
   c) expensive

4. Neighbours complained about the local teenagers using the <u>derelict</u> building as a hang-out and were relieved when it was destroyed by a fire.
   a) large, impressive
   b) abandoned, not cared for
   c) historical

5. She presented some <u>cogent</u> arguments and managed to get the opposition to back her plan.
   a) angry
   b) silly
   c) convincing

6. Ever since his girlfriend left him, he's been <u>in the doldrums</u>. His friends are worried and trying to get him to snap out of it.
   a) depressed
   b) bored
   c) happy

7. She found it disgusting when men would <u>expectorate</u> on the street, some barely missing her feet.
   a) spit
   b) sing
   c) smoke

8. Unlike his shy sisters, he is very <u>gregarious</u> and makes friends easily.
   a) selfish
   b) giving
   c) talkative

9. His friends like to tell him crazy, made-up stories because he is so <u>credulous</u>.
   a) too ready to believe things
   b) dramatic and fond of acting
   c) sad and depressed

10. Because the electricity supply can be quite <u>erratic</u>, people have a lot of battery-powered items as back-up in case the power goes.
    a) expensive
    b) not regular, not dependable
    c) has mistakes in it

Exercise 8.2 – *continued*

11. Tommy was definitely the <u>instigator</u> of the playground battle, but Amy and Khalid were also punished because they should have known better than to strike back. They should have gone to the teacher.
    a) victim, one who got hurt
    b) witness
    c) person who started something

12. His <u>vociferous</u> complaints angered the sales clerks and embarrassed the other customers all over the store.
    a) drunken
    b) loud
    c) illogical

Researching and Referencing

Some of your reading will be research for your writing. You may be doing just general background reading to help you understand a topic, or you may be doing specific research for a paper.

Like most students today, you probably rely on the Internet for all your research, but be sure not to overlook other sources. Most of the world's published material is not yet available on the Internet. Your school library and local public library will probably have a good selection of books on your topic. Do not be daunted by the size of a book. You can read just the section you need. The index will point you in the right direction. Skimming and scanning (quickly looking over the words) will also help you find the information you want.

Newspapers and magazines offer articles on many different topics. Many have been digitized but are not available through the standard web-pages. Some are open only to subscribers. Your school library has subscriptions to database services through which you can access these publications. Look at the library's website to learn more.

The most important thing to keep in mind is that published material generally goes through a review process and is checked by editors. (The exception is self-publication, also referred to as "vanity press.") What you read on the Internet does not go through that type of formal review. Anyone can start a website on any subject—he or she does not have to be an expert on the subject. Moreover, *Wikipedia*, an on-line encyclopedia, is open to editing by users and has had misinformation deliberately posted in its entries. Even sites from reputable organizations can be hacked. Misinformation from one site can be copied to another.

You should try to authenticate any information you get from the Internet. See if it fits what you already know. Take anything that sounds odd with a grain of salt. Look for independent sources that give the same information. Look at traditional print sources. Check where the websites are based. For instance, an *edu* at the end of the URL, or Internet address, usually denotes a school, and information on the official sites should be reliable—unless they are student project pages.

When you incorporate information from another writer into your essay, you need to reference (cite) it. General knowledge and historical facts do not have to be cited, but interpretation and analysis of the facts should be referenced. Any time you copy phrases and sentences from another writer, you must use quotation marks to show the copied words, and you must include a citation to show your reader where these words came from. Your essay should be essentially your ideas and words, with support from other writers' work.

There are different ways of referencing the material you have used in your research, but essentially in the body of your paper you show when you are quoting or paraphrasing someone's words. The citation you use refers the reader to the full bibliography in the back. The bibliography (also called "references" or "works consulted") gives the reader the information needed to locate that source. For example, after a quote you might have a reference that says "(Brown 24)" which tells the reader that the quote came from page 24 of the work by Brown. You can see examples of this in "Appearance: Its social meaning" on page 311.

There are three common styles of referencing. The Chicago style is often used in high schools; it uses footnotes for citations. The Modern Language Association (MLA) style is used for humanities subjects, such as English, in universities and colleges. The American Psychological Association (APA) style is used in the sciences and social sciences. Your school library will have information on the format of these styles, often with a style guide on its website. Your instructor will tell you which style you should use and may give you a hand-out to guide you.

Avoiding Plagiarizing

Plagiarism is copying someone else's words or ideas and claiming them as your own. It is considered cheating or academic dishonesty. Usually, the punishment gets worse with each offence. For example, a first offence may mean a grade of zero on the paper and a notation on the student record. A second time may mean failing the whole course, while the third may result in expulsion from the school.

Plagiarism is easy to spot. Instructors get to know their students' writing styles and know what they are capable of. Generally, there is a noticeable difference between a student's writing style and a published author's. With modern technology, it is easy to cut and paste from other writers' works, but the same technology also makes the original sources easy to find.

Be careful when you take notes. Make sure you mark quotes accurately and keep references clear. It is also helpful to write your paper without constant consultation of your notes and sources. Make your points and use your research to support those points. Quote only when necessary, and make sure you use quotation marks and include the reference. Follow the techniques for paraphrasing in the next section.

Paraphrasing

Paraphrasing is the art of reporting what is said in words other than those used in the original. You restate often in the course of a day because you rarely quote other people's words exactly. Teachers are calling upon you to paraphrase when they ask you to answer reading comprehension questions "in your own words." They are testing both your reading and writing skills. A reading comprehension question that consists of a sentence or two copied from the original article does not show that the student actually understands what he or she has copied down. You also use paraphrase when you write a summary or a research paper. A paraphrase is often shorter than the original.

To be able to paraphrase well, you need a strong vocabulary and a good understanding of the original text. Do not just substitute synonyms; you need to reword it entirely. Put the information in the words you would normally use. Use different sentence structure. Be sure to change pronouns. For example, you do not use *I* because it is not you who is speaking.

When told that they have to put something in their own words, students sometimes ask what words from the original they can use in their paraphrase. Avoid phrases particular to the author. You can use the same basic English words if they have no handy synonym. One test is that the words you use should be the ones you would normally use to say the same thing. For example, you cannot avoid words like *language* and *immigrant*. You can also use expressions if they are standard English, such as *supply and demand*.

Study the examples below to see how to paraphrase:

> Reading question: In the story "Why my mother can't speak English," what is the main reason the mother does not learn English?

> Original text: "For thirty-some years, my mother did not learn the English language, not because she was not smart enough, not because she was too old to learn, and not because my father forbade her, but because she feared that learning English would change her Chinese soul." (page 322)

Poor paraphrase: The mother did not learn English because she was afraid that it would change her Chinese soul. ["Chinese soul" is an expression unique to the author.]

Good paraphrase: The mother did not learn English because she was afraid that she would lose her identity as a Chinese woman. [does not repeat author's words and shows the meaning of "Chinese soul"]

Reading question: Paraphrase the following two passages from "Survive squalor and learn to tidy":

Original text: "I'd always been a messy person, from childhood clear on down. They often say youngest children are 'messies' and I guess with my parents not making me do chores, and not a scrap of self-discipline, I developed a mentality where I didn't even see it." (page 269)

Poor paraphrase: I was always an untidy person, since childhood. Youngest children are often "messies." My parents never made me do housework, and I had no self-discipline. I developed an attitude where I didn't even see it. [only minor changes to the original with synonyms substituted for some words; the pronoun *I* should be changed]

Good paraphrase: Pavlov blames her untidiness on her childhood since she was the youngest child and never had to do chores. She also says she lacked the discipline to clean and could not really see the mess.

Original text: "Needless to say, the shame associated with living such a life is not palatable. You cringe when the doorbell rings and peek out the window hoping they'll go away. When the landlord says he wants to take a look at the plumbing, you feel like you are going to throw up." (page 269)

Paraphrase: Pavlov says that it is so embarrassing to live in a messy apartment that she does not want to invite anyone in, even the landlord.

Exercise 8.3

Paraphrase these passages:

1. Appearance is everything. We are constantly being judged by the way we look—to our advantage or disadvantage. Unattractive people may be viewed as inconsequential or ill-favoured, while very attractive people may be thought of as all beauty and no brains.

2. Although some people argue that people today are ruder and less considerate of others, it is easy to find examples of how we are better behaved than our ancestors. For example, our society has made improvements in the way we treat those who have lesser status. We make fewer class distinctions, and overt racism is not socially accepted today. Women are no longer treated as being nothing more than the property of their husbands or relatives.

3. It's hard to say who is more addicted to lotteries—the people who play them or the governments who depend on the revenue they generate. The money goes to many facilities that should be funded by taxes, such as hospitals and recreation centres. However, taxpayers seem to prefer putting their money towards lottery tickets than towards tax increases.

4. Women's sports have always gotten short shrift. Women golfers and tennis players would play for peanuts compared to the men's prizes. Women's hockey teams have trouble getting ice time. The poor media coverage for women's teams means that even their victories are buried in a few paragraphs in the sports section of the newspaper while losing men's teams get front-page coverage.

5. Halloween has become such a big holiday in North America that spending on it is second to that of Christmas. Houses are elaborately decorated to resemble haunted houses with ghosts and skeletons. Adults wear costumes to scare and delight trick-or-treaters or for parties. An interest in the supernatural is reflected in the current popularity of vampire books and movies.

Exercise 8.4

Paraphrase each of these quotes from the readings:

1. "It's no accident that bus and subway riders are mostly young and poor. They take public transit not because it's the better way, but because they can't afford to drive. The moment they get a little older and a little better off, they move to the suburbs and buy a car." (Margaret Wente, page 287)

Exercise 8.4 – *continued*

2. "Throughout the week, we found ourselves pacing the resort, looking for members of the group. It felt as though we were circling each other, meeting up only by happenstance. We tried to make plans, and set up meeting points, but they were all half-baked, and rarely fulfilled. We kept meaning to play poker, to play a game of Monopoly, to do whatever, but we couldn't make it happen." (Christopher Hutsul, page 282)

3. "Too many baby-boomer parents are overly concerned with success. From grade-point averages and admission standards to academic programs and future graduate or professional schools, parents think they can control the process and that, in the end, it all reflects back on them." (Sherri Beattie, page 263)

4. "I'd simply have to move. And I like this place, I really do. It took me so long to get the furniture where it should be, and I went all over town to find drapes to match the carpets. And I've only just memorized the bus schedule. Moving is out of the question." (Sara McDonald, page 340) [Note that this is fiction, so you will have to identify the "I" as "the narrator" or "the woman."]

5. "She turns to the photograph of my father on the mantle. Daily, she burns incense, pours fresh cups of fragrant tea, and spreads dishes of his favourite fruits in front of the framed picture as is the custom. In memory of his passing, she treks two miles to the cemetery to place flowers by his headstone, to burn ceremonial paper money, and to talk to him. Regularly, rain or shine, or even snow, she does these things." (Garry Engkent, page 320)

Quoting and Using Reported Speech

When you report what someone says, you put that person's words between quotation marks, but only if you are quoting the exact words used. More frequently, instead of quoting directly, you use reported speech, also called indirect speech, to paraphrase what is said:

> Quote: Rhett Butler said, "Frankly, my dear, I don't give a damn."
>
> Reported speech: Rhett Butler said he didn't give a damn.
>
> Paraphrase: Rhett Butler exclaimed that he didn't care.

Notice the punctuation for a direct quote. The quotation marks curl around the quote and are found at the top of the line. A comma separates the quote from the rest of the sentence. The period of the sentence comes before the quotation mark.

In research papers, you use two kinds of quotations. In one, you incorporate the words of the speaker in your sentences and show the exact words with quotation marks. Longer quotes are set off separate from your paragraph and indented from your text. Both forms require a footnote or a parenthetical citation (putting the author's name and the page number in round brackets) to show where the reference comes from. The methods used for such referencing differ slightly (see the section "Research and referencing" earlier in this unit), and you should refer to the style guide you are using to format your quote and citation correctly.

Make sure you choose quotes wisely. Do not quote facts or straightforward, simple sentences. Choose quotes that express something in a unique manner. You should use quotes for impact, not to fill up space.

For reported speech, you must make several changes. Pay attention to pronouns. The speaker's reference to *I* becomes *he* or *she*. Time references may have to change. If the speaker says *today* or *tomorrow*, you may have to change it to *that day* or *the next day*. Verb tense is also tricky. Often you have to change the present tense verb to past tense. Here are some examples:

The director said, "Why isn't anyone listening to me?"

The director asked why no one was listening to him.

The actor said, "Why am I not getting more auditions?"

The actor wondered why he was not getting any more auditions.

Peter said, "You have to do that scene all over again."

Peter said we would have to do the scene again.

Peter told us to do the scene again.

John said, "Why don't you come with me to the game on Saturday?"

John invited me to the game on Saturday.

Ivana said, "Let's go to the 8 o'clock show and then we can go for dessert."

Ivana suggested going to the 8 o'clock show and going for dessert afterwards.

Exercise 8.5

Change these sentences from direct quotation to reported speech. You do not have to use all the words as long as you get the meaning across:

1. Susan said, "I'm going to work on that assignment tomorrow."

2. Ryan said, "I will help you with your painting this weekend."

3. "Why didn't you come to the party?" Mariko asked.

4. My sister asked, "What shall we get Mom for her birthday?"

5. Dave said, "Why don't we get tickets for the Great Big Sea concert?"

6. Lulu asked, "Will you help me prepare my oral presentation?"

7. Hans said, "I'm going to visit my cousins tonight."

8. "I'm sorry. I forgot to call you yesterday," said Amar.

9. Brad said, "I think we should take up curling. It looks like a sport I could handle."

10. Lindy said, "Tomas should buy a new car. His is a piece of junk."

11. Elena said, "I wouldn't do that if I were you. That chair doesn't look steady enough to stand on."

12. Abby said, "I think I failed that test."

13. Melissa said, "I wonder what the test will be like."

14. Pierre said, "Emily has to work tonight, so she can't come to the concert."

15. Marie said to the clerk in the Returns Department, "This DVD I bought last week won't play through the movie. It keeps skipping around."

Writing a Summary

Summarizing is a skill used every day. You summarize when you recount the plot of a movie or relate what happened to you in your day; summarizing textbook chapters is an excellent way to study for exams; journal articles are summarized in abstracts; and business reports often include an executive summary.

When you summarize, you give just the main ideas from a reading such as an article, story, or report. You do not include specific details, such as dates, figures, and biographical data, unless they are important. Minor examples should not be included, but if an article depends on the examples to tell the story, then these examples should be summarized.

These main ideas should be in the same order as in the original whenever possible. Sometimes, however, a different order might work better. For example, Sidney Katz does not tell the story of the Richard hockey riot chronologically, but following his order would be too confusing in a short summary.

The summary should be clear enough that someone who has not read the original text can still understand the summary and come away with the same basic information. Avoid vague statements such as "the author discusses the problem university students have with their parents" and "she talks about the service she receives when she goes shopping." Usually the word *about* signals such a vague statement. One way to check clarity is to ask a friend to read the summary on its own and see if he or she has any questions.

Conciseness is important because the main purpose is to make something shorter. For school assignments, you may be asked to write a summary that is one-tenth the length of the original so that a 100-word paragraph summarizes a 1,000-word article. When you have a strict word limit, it is often easier to write a first draft saying everything that you want to say and then cut this down with careful editing.

Paraphrase is an important part of summarizing. Use your own words to express the ideas of the author. Copying sentences from the original is not acceptable. One good way to avoid copying phrases from the text is to jot down your points without looking at the original. You can check later to make sure you have covered everything.

A summary should maintain good paragraph structure. The first sentence is the topic sentence; it should tell the reader that this is a summary. Usually, the author and title of the article are named, and the source information (the name of the newspaper, the date, and the page number, for example) may be given if necessary.

A summary by itself is objective. You do not give your opinion of what is said in the article or evaluate the author's writing.

Steps for writing a summary:

1. Read the entire article, story, or report, making sure you understand it all. You may have to read it a few times. Use a dictionary for unfamiliar words.
2. Put the article or story away and think about what it said. Without referring to the original, write a quick draft of your summary, using your own words. Your draft can be in the form of jot notes.
3. Go over the article again, making sure you've covered all the main points in your draft.
4. Rewrite your summary putting it in proper form.

5. Start a summary paragraph with a topic sentence that identifies the article (title, author's name, and source) and gives the main idea of the original reading.
6. Make sure your summary paraphrases the words of the author. Do not copy his or her specific expressions. Do not quote.
7. Check to see if your summary says enough to be clear to readers who have not read the original.
8. Edit your summary to meet the required word length.
9. Correct grammar, spelling, and punctuation for your final draft.

Sample summary

Here is a sample summary. You can see the original reading on page 304.

> "The strange forces behind the Richard hockey riot" by Sidney Katz tells of the events that led to the riot on 17 March 1955 in Montreal. In a game against the Boston Bruins, Montreal Canadien Maurice Richard was injured with a high stick and went after the offending player. Richard was penalized for the slashing and fighting. After a hearing on 16 March, National Hockey League president Clarence Campbell suspended Richard from the rest of the season's games. The citizens of Montreal were upset at the suspension of their beloved hockey hero. The ill-feeling was fuelled by racial tension between French and English-Canadians. The riot was touched off when someone exploded a tear gas bomb in the Montreal Forum during a game with the Detroit Red Wings. The people spilled out onto the streets and started on a path of destruction down Ste-Catherine Street, vandalizing cars and buildings for several blocks. Richard's public statement the next day forestalled any further violence. [161 words]

Note that the summary above has several specific details, such as dates, because these details are necessary for readers to follow the sequence of the story. Moreover, because the article is almost 2,000 words (about twice the length of most of the non-fiction essays in this text), the summary is longer than the 100 words often required.

Here is an example of a poorly written summary of the article on page 262:

> In the article "All grown up and still in tow" by Sherri Beattie, the author talks about baby-boomer parents today struggling with saying no and letting go. She sees a young man standing in line at the registrar's office. His father was taking charge. The woman at the counter was also embarrassed for

the young man. The father was no doubt well-intentioned but misguided. The son could barely lift his eyes. Sherri Beattie was angry and wanted to yell at the father to let his son grow up. At a lecture for teaching assistants, she learned that this was not unusual. For example, parents often complained about their children's marks. This was very different from how she started university in her undergraduate days. [124 words]

This summary is poor for several reasons: It is too detailed and wordy, it does not cover the whole article, it copies the wording of the original text, and it leaves the reader with a lack of information at the end (what was it like in her day?). Here is a better summary:

> In "All Grown up and still in tow," Sherri Beattie compares the attitudes toward child-raising of baby-boomer parents and her own parents. Beattie sees parents taking over for their children at university registration. They can't seem to give up control and let their children muddle through on their own. Twenty years earlier, her own parents had just dropped her off at school, letting her settle into campus life on her own. They considered her an adult, capable of making her own choices. Beattie thinks the boomer parents are making a mistake by not letting their children grow up. [100 words]

Exercise 8.6

Here is a 172-word summary of "Survive squalor and learn to tidy" (page 268). Eliminate unnecessary words and reduce wordiness to make the summary less than 100 words:

In the article "Survive squalor and learn to tidy" by Jo Pavlov, the author explains that she lives in an apartment that is a really messy environment. Because Jo Pavlov is unable to clean all the mess herself, she had to ask her mother and sister to come over to help her tidy up her place. The huge pile of clothing in her room was two feet deep and surrounded the bed. Jo Pavlov says she does not really understand tidiness. She wonders where dishes, clothes, and other things should be kept. She does not know where to put all her things. However, she does not want to live in squalor any more. She's tired of the mess. She wants a clean, tidy apartment. She wants to invite friends over without being embarrassed about the state of her apartment. She has found help on-line from an Internet support group for people just like her. With the help of the group, she is learning to tackle the mess one step at a time.

> **A good summary**
> - is clear to people who have not read the original;
> - gives only the main ideas of the original;
> - is a paraphrase, with no quotes from the original;
> - tells the reader it is a summary in the first sentence by identifying the original work;
> - is concise, meeting word limits.

Answering Reading Comprehension Questions

Open-ended reading comprehension questions are a good way for instructors to test your reading and writing skills. They are not perfect because it is difficult to test reading comprehension on its own: instructors cannot get into your head to figure out what you understand. An answer might be poor because you made writing, rather than reading, errors. However, since instructors are usually testing both your reading and writing skills, they like to give comprehension tests.

Understanding what a question is asking is key for academic success. This applies to essay questions as well as reading questions. Remember that language is communication. If your answer does not address what is being asked, then fundamental communication has failed. If you order a chicken dinner in a restaurant and get fish, it does not matter how well the fish is prepared.

One way to get your answer on the right track is to use a few words from the question. For example, if the question asks, "Why does the father encourage the waiters to learn English?" you can start by saying, "He encourages them because . . ."

Look for key words such as *describe*, *compare*, and *explain*. Make sure you understand what those terms are asking. If it is a two-part question, answer both parts. Check to see how many marks each question is worth. A three-mark question requires more than three words.

You can also succeed if you apply logic and knowledge of academic situations. For example, instructors are not likely to ask the same reading question twice, so if two of your answers say essentially the same thing, one of them is probably wrong. Get to know your instructors—the types of tests they like to give and the kind of answers they expect. Make sure you pay attention when tests are taken up so you can learn from your mistakes.

Instructors generally want you to answer a question in your own words, paraphrasing the original wording. If you copy the author's words directly, your instructor cannot tell how much you understand. Even a person with very little English could be lucky enough to find and copy the right sentence to answer the question.

You will need your instructor's help to practise answering comprehension questions. Many instructors give sample questions or tests before giving ones that count for marks. All the reading selections in this textbook are accompanied by comprehension questions that you will probably take up and discuss in class.

Here is an example for the reading on page 293:

> What does Linda McQuaig mean by the putting the expression "individual choice" in quotation marks? Explain her reasoning.

> It isn't meaningful to talk of "individual choice" with a product notorious for its addictiveness. [poor answer—copied from reading, doesn't explain]

> Smoking is very harmful and leads to many deaths. [poor answer—doesn't address the question]

> McQuaig doesn't think it's a choice at all. The quotation marks show she is using the term as others use it. When teenagers start smoking, it's not a rational choice because they are not mature enough to make one. Moreover, tobacco is highly addictive, and almost everyone would choose not to have started. [good answer]

Writing about Readings

You may be called upon to write a literary essay in which you analyze what a writer did in a short story, novel, or play. You may have to compare two literary works. What students find most difficult about this task is doing actual analysis and not just retelling the plot. You can keep on track if you remember what you learned about academic paragraphs—begin each paragraph with your main idea. Then you use examples from the text to support what you said.

This passage simply retells the plot—what you should *not* do:

> In "Why my mother can't speak English," the narrator begins with the old mother wanting to get her citizenship because she is afraid of being deported and of losing her old age pension. After a disappointing interview with a Citizenship clerk, the narrator recounts the reasons why his mother never learned the English language. While the father in the story encourages the Chinese waiters to learn English, he discourages his own wife from doing so because he is afraid of losing control over her. More interesting is the revelation that the mother does not want to learn because she thinks she may be changed. However, the story ends somewhat happily: The mother does get her citizenship, and she wants to show her achievement to her dead husband at the cemetery.

This is an analysis—what you should do:

> In "Why my mother can't speak English," the writer gives some complex reasons for the difficulty immigrant women have in learning a new language. First, learning English opens up the new world to women, and some men have trouble accepting that. For example, the husband does not permit his wife to learn English because he can control her if she cannot speak the language. Moreover, he is afraid that she will learn the ways of white women, something he cannot accept. Second, the wife is reluctant to become more than merely functionally literate in the restaurant because she is afraid that English may change her cultural identity. The writer underscores the point that language is more than a medium of communication.

Building Reading Skills

- Read as often as possible. Carry a paperback novel or magazine with you for the times when you have to wait, such as at the doctor's office or in a line-up for service.
- Read a variety of materials. Read both fiction and non-fiction. Read both short works like newspaper articles and long ones like novels.
- For readings assigned for school, read them more than once. Look up unfamiliar words in the dictionary. Summarize the readings in your notes.
- Read attentively, paying attention to the use of language.
- For non-fiction, read popular treatments of subjects you are interested in. Many science and social science books are written for a lay (non-professional) audience.
- Get in the newspaper habit. The daily newspaper offers articles of interest for everyone, and they are often available free on campus. The more you learn about a specific subject, the easier the readings will get.
- Read books at a level you are comfortable with. They should be challenging enough to allow you to build your skills but not too frustrating that they make the reading a chore.
- Give children's literature or books written for teenagers a chance. Some of the books are quite sophisticated. Moreover, the classic books are part of a shared culture and are often referred to. Learning this shared culture is especially important for ESL students.
- Check out simplified novels if you find other novels difficult. These are written at different reading levels and can be found in the public library.
- Try different kinds of literature. Give the book or article a fair chance, but if you decide it is not for you, try something else.
- Ask your instructors and librarians for advice and book recommendations.

Part 2

Reading Selections

Non-fiction Readings

All Grown up and Still in Tow

by Sherri Beattie

My heart went out to him. In fact, I cringed and looked away. How humiliating to be in a university registrar's office with your father taking charge.

As I stood in line, waiting for my own minor inquiry to be processed, I reflected on how times have changed.

I am a mature student, a softening euphemism indicating that I am as old, if not older, than most faculty members.

Nonetheless, I do remember what it was like to be an 18-year-old undergraduate. The experience is equal parts thrilling, liberating and terrifying, all rolled into one intense, first-year undertaking that catapults us from adolescence into adulthood. That is, if our parents don't come with us.

The young man at the counter had some sort of registrar problem. It is inevitable in first year. The woman behind the counter clearly felt, as I did, embarrassed for this young man, who was accompanied by his no doubt well-intentioned, but misguided, father.

Dad did the talking while his son struggled to lift his eyes and look at the woman trying to help them. I thought about those tiny morsels of self-confidence that are so painstakingly built in adolescence, and how they were being crushed at the counter. What I saw was a student who looked perfectly capable of asking a few questions and obtaining the information he needed.

I was infuriated. "Oh grow up, go home," I wanted to yell at Dad from my perch in the line.

I was equally shocked as I sat in a seminar for 500 first-year teaching assistants and was told what to do when Mom and/or Dad shows up in your office complaining about the marks or assignments that you have given to their children. It is a very real issue in universities these days.

Baby-boomer parents seem to struggle with two things: saying no and letting go. The teaching assistants massed together in the theatre were advised to send unhappy parents directly to professors, especially if they show up with legal counsel. I sat in disbelief, but yes, it happens.

Mom and Dad, your children are no longer children. Rather, they are desperately trying to be adults. So whatever are you doing in line with them at the registrar's office?

Twenty years ago, when I first entered university, parents did not follow their children into post-secondary institutions. My parents dropped me at the front door of St. Hilda's College at the University of Toronto and drove five hours back home.

I was not ready, prepared or sufficiently enlightened about what would happen over the course of the next four years, but I muddled through. From professors and teaching assistants to registrars and student-loan officers, I learned to navigate my way through the perils and pleasures of university life. Naturally, I made mistakes, but then I still do.

Were my parents indifferent, neglectful or uninterested? Not at all. What they were not was university-educated baby-boomers who believe all events must be choreographed and controlled and that everything I did was a direct reflection on them.

My parents did not intervene, or advise on course selection or academic results. They came from another generation. They never set foot in a university. They were pleased, and supportive, when I decided to attend but they considered me an adult at 18.

My mother married at 19, and my father had been helping to support his family since his early adolescence. In turn, their parents had not fussed over them.

I was not entering married life or taking on a full-time job and support responsibilities, I was just going to university. They did not struggle for perspective and neither did I. Sometimes I triumphed and at other times fell flat on my face.

The incident I witnessed in the registrar's office was not an anomaly. I wish it were. Rather, about six people behind me in line, I discovered another parent-child grouping. This time a son was pleading with his mother to stay put while he went to the counter and dealt with the problem himself. They were still negotiating when I departed.

Too many baby-boomer parents are overly concerned with success. From grade-point averages and admission standards to academic programs and future graduate or professional schools, parents think they can control the process and that, in the end, it all reflects back on them.

When I tell my mother that I have won a scholarship and will undertake graduate research in Europe this fall she says, "That's nice, dear."

My mother would argue that my success is my own. I would argue that my success is a result of being allowed the freedom to make mistakes and find my own way.

To parents whose children are attending first-year university, just remember they have all grown up now. It is time for you to do the same.

(*The Globe and Mail* 8 September 2004)
Sherri Beattie is a former journalist and currently a LLB candidate at Osgoode Hall Law School.

Notes

The term *baby boomer* refers to Canadians born between 1947 and 1966. Other Western countries also had a baby boom, or population explosion, after World War II. Because the generation is so large, it has social, economic, and political effects on the nation.

Comprehension

1. What prompted the author to write this essay?
2. What criticisms does Beattie make about the baby-boomer parents?
3. How were her parents different? How was their attitude different from boomers?
4. How does Beattie give credit to her parents for her success?
5. What advice does Beattie give baby-boomer parents?
6. Why does Beattie feel that it is important to let children do things on their own?
7. Explain the title in your own words.

Discussion

1. What do you think of this essay? Did you enjoy reading it? Do you agree with the author? Do you think she made her point effectively?
2. Are teenagers coddled in our society? Adolescence seems to be getting longer with each generation. In the past, 14-year-olds went off to work full-time. Now even 25-year-olds are treated (and behave) like kids.
3. Beattie says that baby-boomer parents "struggle with two things: saying no and letting go." She only discusses the latter. What do you think she means when she mentions the problem of "saying no"? Do you think this is a problem these parents have? Give examples.
4. Beattie says that boomer parents are "overly concerned with success" and that they think their children's success "reflects back on them." Discuss this statement. Do you agree or disagree? What are the effects of such an attitude?
5. Overprotective parents are sometimes referred to as "helicopter parents." Explain this expression. Is it apt? Can you think of another term to describe them?
6. Consider the other side: First-year college and university students are usually 18 years old. Is that old enough to handle the complexities of life? Have they been prepared for this? Consider that neurological and psychological studies have shown that teenage brains go through many changes, with the reasoning centres of their brains not fully developed until they are in their twenties. Do you think teenagers today are ready for the responsibilities of going away to school and living on their own? What support do they need from their parents?
7. Many young adults choose to live in their parents' home instead of seeking an independent lifestyle. Some are students or recent graduates who cannot afford their own place. Some are from ethnic cultures in

which parents expect adult children to stay home until, and maybe even after, they get married. Sometimes parents even move to live near where their child is attending school. Discuss these different lifestyles. What would you accept?

Assignments

Write an essay on one of the following topics:

1. How much help should parents give their children when they are going off to college or university? Explain and support your answer.
2. Should parents pay for their children's post-secondary education? How much financial support should parents be responsible for?
3. Many cultures favour more parental control over legally adult children than North American culture does. Discuss this statement with reference to a specific culture.
4. What is the best way to raise children so that they become responsible, well-adjusted adults?
5. How should people deal with overprotective parents?
6. What do the studies on teenage brain development mean for the way our society deals with young people? For example, since teenagers do not always understand the ramifications of their actions, should they be held legally responsible for their crimes?

(If you are practising paragraph writing, you can take one idea for one of these topics and write a paragraph instead of an essay.)

Paraphrasing and summarizing

1. In one or two sentences, describe the scene Beattie witnessed at the registrar's office.
2. Paraphrase: "I thought about those tiny morsels of self-confidence that are so painstakingly built in adolescence, and how they were being crushed at the counter."
3. Paraphrase: "The experience is equal parts thrilling, liberating and terrifying, all rolled into one intense, first-year undertaking that catapults us from adolescence into adulthood."

Vocabulary study
Vocabulary quiz

Identify the meaning of each word or expression:

1. cringe
   a) fight an injustice
   b) apologize for someone else
   c) move away in fear or embarrassment
   d) put something into a small ball

2. euphemism
   a) compliment
   b) more polite way of saying something
   c) registration officer
   d) when someone is publicly embarrassed
3. catapult
   a) throw suddenly
   b) hide from someone
   c) answer angrily
   d) wait patiently
4. inevitable
   a) unavoidable
   b) understandable
   c) able to work on one's own
   d) dangerous
5. morsel
   a) type of mushroom
   b) small piece
   c) shame
   d) registrar's assistant
6. painstakingly
   a) hurting badly
   b) hiding in shame
   c) worrying about the result
   d) taking care to do things right
7. infuriated
   a) confused, not understanding
   b) very angry
   c) very embarrassed
   d) calm, peaceful
8. enlightened
   a) feeling less of a burden
   b) having changed colour
   c) confused and lost
   d) having achieved understanding
9. navigate
   a) get lost
   b) shout at someone
   c) embarrass someone
   d) direct or find the way to something
10. peril
    a) effort, hard work
    b) beautiful and impressive
    c) afraid
    d) danger

11. indifferent
    a) not different, the same
    b) not caring about something
    c) looking the same but not really the same
    d) making a distinction clear
12. choreograph
    a) help someone do something
    b) determine movements, how something is done
    c) register for a course
    d) lead someone in a song
13. triumph
    a) win, defeat someone or something
    b) do again
    c) suggest
    d) wait for the right time to try something
14. anomaly
    a) natural existence
    b) display of anger
    c) unusual occurrence
    d) friendly help
15. negotiate
    a) avoid someone or something
    b) yell at someone
    c) try to reach an agreement
    d) want to quit something

Word families

Identify the part of speech for each of these words and explain any meaning or pronunciation differences. Write a sentence for each word:

adolescence, adolescent, adolescents
advice, advise
anomaly, anomalous
intervene, intervention
negotiate, negotiation
registrar, register, registration

Idioms and expressions

Discuss and define the following idioms and expressions from the text:

my heart went out to him
take charge
to muddle through
never set foot in
fuss over
fall flat on your face
stay put

Structure and technique

1. Notice the first sentence: "My heart went out to **him**." Beattie deliberately doesn't properly identify "him" until the fifth paragraph, although we get clues to who "he" is before then. (This is a technique used in journalistic writing and creative writing but not academic writing.) What is the effect on the reader?

2. Beattie is comparing baby-boomer parents and her own parents, using a block format (talking about one and then the other). Show where the essay is divided to make the comparison. Discuss how effective this structure is.

3. Beattie addresses the parents directly in two of the paragraphs. Which ones?

Sentence structure

1. Change this fragment to a full, grammatical sentence: "How humiliating to be in a university registrar's office with your father taking charge."

2. Note the structure "baby-boomer parents." Explain what it means and how it is formed and compare it to "baby boomer's parents" and "baby boomers' parents."

3. Identify the subject and verb in these sentences:
    a) "The incident I witnessed in the registrar's office was not an anomaly."
    b) "From grade-point averages and admission standards to academic programs and future graduate or professional schools, parents think they can control the process and that, in the end, it all reflects back on them."

Survive Squalor and Learn to Tidy

by Jo Pavlov

Once, when I was in my late twenties, I called my mom and sister in tears because the apartment had once again fallen into a state of disrepair and mess. I was despondent.

They came over and soothed my grief, wearing bandanas, rubber gloves and carrying industrial-sized garbage bags and cans of Lysol. We started in the bedroom where the layer of clothing strewn about the floor was about two feet deep and encircled the bed completely. The top of the pile was flush with the bedspread. Or where a bedspread would be if the bed wasn't piled high with clutter, too.

Mom and Sis whistled while they worked and made me laugh. Their kindness and compassion was overwhelming. We were calling the layers "strata" and likening the process to an archaeological dig. We would periodically find newspapers that dated when a given layer began. That made me laugh in a nearly unlaughable situation. At one point, we pulled out a crushed pair of jeans with legs cuffed up and crumbled autumn leaves fell from the cuffs. It was July; the pile hadn't been touched in nearly a year.

The kitchen was even worse. It was unspeakable.

I can't believe I just typed that. I can't believe I'm saying these things out loud. My dirty secret shame.

I remember my mom used the word "squalor" and it made me laugh. Nervous laughter, because it summed up the situation pretty succinctly. To admit you live in squalor is heady stuff. It's beyond the old, "Oh, I'm a little on the cluttered side" and way past, "I can't have you over until I tidy," because tidy is a word that makes sense to other people, not you, and tidy is a world away. "Tidy" is when you have a place to put stuff and you put it there. Squalor is when no such thing exists.

I'd always been a messy person, from childhood clear on down. They often say youngest children are "messies" and I guess with my parents not making me do chores, and not a scrap of self-discipline, I developed a men-tality where I didn't even see it. Mom would periodically tell me to clean my room and I didn't even know what that meant. Where does the stuff go? In drawers? Drawers were like the abyss . . . when stuff went in drawers, I never saw it again until such time as the drawer was packed so tightly with crap that I had to dump the whole thing in the middle of the floor and start fresh.

Piles were my organizational system of choice, because at least you could see everything. Paper piles, clothing piles, piles of shoes, piles of dishes, dirty and otherwise. "Squalorees" will often say how they can find exactly what they are looking for in their piles, as in some twisted way it makes sense to them. But some squalorees can't, and end up buying the same thing three times because they lost it in the pile the first two times.

I never liked living this way. I saw that other people lived differently, but like people who run marathons or concert pianists or British royalty, those lives were not mine and I didn't know how to get from where I was to that place. How do you become a concert pianist when you are starting from zero? What's a piano? Do you touch those white and black parts with your fingers or toes? Things that are obvious to the masses are not obvious to squalorees. (Or maybe it's the squalorous.)

Needless to say, the shame associated with living such a life is not palatable. You cringe when the doorbell rings and peek out the window hop-ing they'll go away. When the landlord says he wants to take a look at the plumbing, you feel like you are going to throw up. You bulldoze the contents of your house into the bedroom and shut the door. At work, you laugh politely at the water cooler as your co-workers regale the group with stories of how they had the in-laws over for supper, and you know you can't have anyone over. Ever. They even have an acronym for it: CHAOS – Can't Have Anyone Over Syndrome.

And then came the Internet.

You can be sure that if there are two people on the planet with some-thing in common, there is an Internet discussion group for those two people.

I remember the day I found a site for Squalor Survivors, I actually cried. Living in squalor is extremely isolating and you always feel that no one could possibly understand or have compassion.

But people do. Lots of people. There is a whole community devoted to making squalorees feel human again, and then holding their hand while they lift themselves up from the abyss. It's empowering and it's effective. No one understands an alcoholic like another alcoholic. There are no secrets on the board. People post pictures of their progress and pour out their souls to one another. When I found that website, I felt like I'd come home.

Two of the five rooms in my apartment are now in good condition and the other three are at least livable. A dishwasher was one big investment and donating more than half my clothes was another step forward. It's a long, uphill battle, and I still don't have people over because old habits die hard. That's an emotional battle that I'll have to wage another day. Battling that pile in the bedroom was effort enough for one day.

(*The Globe and Mail* 24 January 2006)
This essay first appeared on the Facts & Arguments page of *The Globe and Mail* in Toronto, Canada.

Comprehension

1. Is the author male or female? Why do you think so? Consider what the author says, not just the name.
2. How did the mother and sister make Pavlov feel better as they cleaned up the place?
3. What does Pavlov say to explain how the problem began? Is this a valid explanation?
4. What social problem does the author have because of the mess in the apartment?
5. How did Pavlov finally learn to cope with the mess? Explain what helped and why.
6. How did Pavlov start dealing with the mess on her own?
7. Pavlov focuses on the clutter of the apartment and says very little about actual dirt. Do you think the apartment is filthy? Why or why not? Why would Pavlov say little about the state of cleanliness? Notice that she describes the kitchen as "unspeakable."

Discussion

1. Do you feel sympathy for Pavlov? Why or why not?
2. Do men and women have different standards of cleanliness, or does it vary more from individual to individual?
3. The author equates living in squalor to an illness like alcoholism. Do you think this is a valid comparison? Why?
4. What would you do if you found out that someone you were dating lived in squalor like this? Would it affect your relationship? Why or why not?
5. How clean does a place need to be? Explain the dividing line between a mess and squalor.

6. How can self-help groups be effective? How has the Internet made it easier to help people with physical, psychological, or social problems?

Assignments

1. Write an essay explaining the problems that result from living in squalor.
2. Take one of the synonyms for *clean* or *dirty* (such as *neat, cluttered, squalid*) and write a paragraph defining the word.
3. Write a paragraph explaining the difference between *clean* and *cluttered* (or between *dirty* and *messy*).
4. Write a description of an apartment or house that is filthy and cluttered. If you have trouble picturing such a mess, look for pictures on self-help websites or watch television programs such as *Clean sweep, Neat,* or *How clean is your house?*
5. Use the Internet to research a self-help organization for a physical, psychological, or social problem. Write a report on how the group helps people.

Paraphrasing and summarizing

1. Write a sentence or two to explain the specific event Pavlov opens with.
2. Paraphrase: "Drawers were like the abyss . . . when stuff went in drawers, I never saw it again until such time as the drawer was packed so tightly with crap that I had to dump the whole thing in the middle of the floor and start fresh."

Vocabulary study
Squalor

The word *squalor* refers to dirty and unpleasant conditions. It is often associated with poverty. Note that *squalor* describes the state of a place. The adjective form is *squalid*, but there is no noun to refer to people who live in squalor. Pavlov tries to make one up, suggesting "squalorees" and "squalorous." She also uses the term "messies" to describe the people, but again this is a made-up term. The quotation marks show that these are not real words.

Note the grammatical difference between *squalorees* and *squalorous*. The former would be a noun, following the pattern of *employees* and *trainees*. The latter would be an adjective, following the pattern of *dangerous* and *serious*. Notice that she uses the article *the* with the adjective form and not with the noun: "not obvious to squalorees. (Or maybe it's the squalorous.)." This usage is an ellipsis, which means that a word or words are left out. In this case, the noun that would naturally follow the adjective is missing; the full expression would be *squalourous people* or *squalorous ones*. This is the same usage that you see in expressions such as *the rich* or *the poor*.

Based on how the word *squalor* is used in the article, cross out any sentences below that are incorrect:

1. The poor people lived in squalor in their huts on the outskirts of the city.
2. A squalor may have many health problems, such as respiratory ailments.
3. I couldn't believe the squalor I found in his apartment.
4. I hate squalors. I like everything in its place.
5. He doesn't mind living in a squalor, but his roommate can't stand it.
6. The squalor man was tired and depressed.
7. When she got upset, she squalored her apartment.
8. She was appalled at the poverty and squalor in the slums.

Acronyms

An *acronym* is a word made up from the initials of an expression. For example, NATO is the North Atlantic Treaty Organization, and the word scuba was formed from "self-contained underwater breathing apparatus." Some acronyms are a bit forced when words are chosen specifically so that the initials form an appropriate word. A good acronym should be memorable, appropriate, and useful. Is CHAOS (Can't Have Anyone Over Syndrome) a good acronym? Discuss other common acronyms.

Definitions

Look up these words and expressions in the dictionary. For each word, write down the part of speech and the meaning (the one that fits the way the word is used in the text):

1. despondent
2. strewn
3. flush (with)
4. strata
5. archaeological dig
6. cuff
7. succinctly
8. heady
9. abyss
10. palatable
11. cringe
12. empowering

Idioms and expressions

Discuss meaning and usage:

1. in tears
2. soothe one's grief
3. clear on down to something
4. not a scrap
5. regale someone with stories
6. holding someone's hand
7. pour out your soul to someone
8. to come home
9. long, uphill battle
10. to wage a battle

Word forms

Fill in the following chart:

Noun	Verb	Adjective	Adverb
cleanliness	to clean, to cleanse	clean	cleanly*
		cluttered	n/a
dirt			
	to mess (up)		
		neat	
		tidy	

*_Cleanly_ has a slightly different meaning. Check the definition in the dictionary.

Activity

In groups, make a list of synonyms for _clean_ and _dirty_. See which group can come up with the longest list, without using a thesaurus or dictionary. Then consult a thesaurus to add to your initial list. Write down the words that are more familiar to you. Discuss the differences of meaning.

Structure and technique

1. Note how the author starts the essay with a brief account of one particular event when she called on her sister and mother for help. Then she discusses the problem in general and ends with the solution she found. Is this opening effective? Why?

2. Pavlov uses very short sentences for emphasis. Note that near the end of paragraph 10, she uses a one-word sentence fragment: "Ever." Look over the essay to see how she uses both long and short sentences for effect. Discuss. Is the same effect achieved with the short paragraphs?

3. Note the use of verb tenses in the article. Paragraph 3 is about a specific past event and is mostly in the simple past. Two sentences are not in the simple past: "We were calling the layers 'strata' and likening the process to an archaeological dig" and "We would periodically find newspapers that dated when a given layer began." What do these verb forms show? Paragraph 10 is mostly in the simple present tense. Why?

4. Pavlov repeats the beginning in this pair of sentences: "I can't believe I just typed that. I can't believe I'm saying these things out loud." What is the effect?

5. Look at the words Pavlov puts in quotation marks. Explain the difference in usage. In other words, do the quotation marks around the word _strata_ mean the same as those around the word _Squalorees_?

Helpless

by Karen von Hahn

To the girl at Blockbuster who saw me searching through the foreign films: Thank you for noticing that I was having trouble finding a movie. It was sweet of you to come over and offer your assistance. But no, Fellini's *Amarcord* is not a new release. It is an old, famous foreign film by a major Italian director. And if you don't know that, then how is it that you feel you can be of any help to me whatsoever?

To the people at the checkout counter at Staples: Thank you for asking so politely whether I had found everything I was looking for. I must admit that I lied when I told you that yes, of course, I had found all I wanted. If I had confessed that I wasn't able to locate my favourite type of erasable gel pen, we both know what would have happened.

I would have been forced to wait by the cash desk like a demanding child for hours while you got on the speaker system to flag down the ballpoint-pen expert, who would have then checked the stockroom, the main warehouse ("What was that pen again?") and other outlets before telling me that if I didn't see it on the shelves, it wasn't available. So thanks for your concern, but isn't it quicker and easier for everybody if I just lie and leave?

To the man who tried to help me find the right computer cable at Future Shop: Thank you for taking the time to carefully read the packaging of all the cables on display right there in front of me. What with the rapid changes in technology, I'm sure it must be difficult keeping abreast of new products in your workplace. It was nice of you to make yourself available, but guess what? I, too, can read the information on the packages. In fact, I am an accomplished reader of the English language. And if you have no idea what cables you have in your store and what each one is for, then what exactly can you help me with?

To everybody who works in stores, restaurants, banks—anywhere in customer service: Clearly you have been instructed to be helpful, but please stop offering to help when you have no idea what that is.

Since you seem confused, let me help *you* with a few ideas of what is not helpful. First, help is not the same as friendliness. Startling us when we walk in to your establishment with loud toothy greetings, for instance, is not good. Telling us your name and that you will be our server when you don't know how anything is being prepared in the kitchen of the restaurant that you work in is of no assistance. Nor is introducing yourself so that we are forced to recall your name, as if on some test, at the cash desk when we've gone ahead and found the top in small all by ourselves at the Gap or Banana Republic.

Also, just because you have named something "Help" doesn't make it helpful. Staffing information kiosks and help desks with cute, semi-literate high-schoolers may look good, for instance, but it is not useful. Similarly, obscure troubleshooting lists, infuriating Help icons that lead nowhere and impossibly busy 1-800 lines merely pay lip service to the idea of assistance. And marketers: Spinning this by telling us in expensive ad campaigns that you are all about 'one customer at a time' only adds insult to injury.

If you are so hell-bent on being helpful, here is what would do the trick. It's your job to be there all day, right? Why not try learning about what you're selling during the downtime?

When you're unpacking the cables, how about trying to figure out which ones might work with Apple computers and older model printers? Next time you're in the kitchen, find out how the chef prepares the salmon. What makes the $500 lawn mower any different from the one for $250? Hey, you work in a video store—what are the names of some of the big foreign-film directors?

You might discover that working in a store or restaurant or bank can be interesting. And when you offer to help a customer, you'll be able to do it.

Until then, I hope you understand why I will be refusing all your offers of assistance—because there is nothing less helpful than this appalling trend of turning Help into an empty four-letter word.

(*The Globe and Mail* 11 June 2005)

Notes
Blockbuster is a video rental service. Staples sells office supplies. Future Shop sells electronics and appliances. The Gap and Banana Republic are two popular clothing stores.

Comprehension
1. What is the author's main point in this essay?
2. Explain what the author means when she says that help is not the same as friendliness.
3. What complaints does she have about help lines?
4. What does the author refer to when she says, "we are forced to recall your name, as if on some test, at the cash desk"?
5. What general advice does she give store clerks? How can this benefit them?
6. What does the author mean when she says, "this appalling trend of turning Help into an empty four-letter word"?

Discussion
1. Who is the intended audience of this article?
2. Do you agree with what the author is saying? Discuss some of your shopping experiences and what you like and dislike about dealing with clerks and servers.

3. Why do clerks and servers not know enough about the products they sell?
4. Talk about your experience in service jobs. What are some of the problems that clerks and servers have with customers?
5. Discuss the advantages and disadvantages of one of the following ways of shopping:
    • big-box stores (large stores that deal with one kind of product);
    • department stores (large stores that have a wide variety of products);
    • smaller, independent stores;
    • malls;
    • downtown stores;
    • on-line shopping.

Assignments

1. Write a one-paragraph narrative evaluating a recent shopping experience you had. What was good and what was bad about it? Why? How would it have been improved? Make sure you have one main point in the topic sentence and that your paragraph is more evaluation than narration.
2. Is shopping a good leisure activity? Explain why or why not in an essay.
3. Write an essay explaining three important facets of good customer service.
4. Write an essay from the opposite point of view—a clerk complaining about customers. You can either mimic von Hahn's tone and structure or write an academic essay.

Paraphrasing and summarizing

1. Summarize von Hahn's complaints about the service she receives.
2. Summarize in one short sentence what would have happened if von Hahn had told the clerk that she couldn't find the pen she wanted.
3. Paraphrase: "Startling us when we walk in to your establishment with loud toothy greetings, for instance, is not good." Try giving the same message in a positive way.
4. Paraphrase: "Nor is introducing yourself so that we are forced to recall your name, as if on some test, at the cash desk when we've gone ahead and found the top in small all by ourselves at the Gap or Banana Republic." Make the statement more general.
5. Paraphrase, putting the sentences in academic English, eliminating the use of *you* and the questions: "If you are so hell-bent on being helpful, here is what would do the trick. It's your job to be there all day, right? Why not try learning about what you're selling during the downtime?"

Vocabulary study

Fill in the vocabulary chart:

Noun	Verb	Adjective	Synonym	Antonym
	n/a	famous		
		erasable		
		accomplished		
friendliness				
		obscure		

Idioms and expressions

Explain the meaning and use of these expressions:

1. to flag down
2. to keep abreast of something
3. to pay lip service to something
4. to spin something
5. to be hell-bent on something
6. to do the trick
7. downtime
8. it adds insult to injury

Structure and technique

1. Karen von Hahn uses a one-sided conversation directed at clerks and servers to get her point across. How effective is this technique? How else could this essay have been structured?
2. What is the tone of this article? Is the author giving helpful advice? Is she being snarky and sarcastic? Is she just frustrated? How is this tone created? What effect is she creating with phrases such as "It was sweet of you" and "Thank you for asking so politely"? What other way could the author have gotten her point across? Write a few sentences to illustrate this.
3. The author has several sentences that are top-heavy—with much longer subjects than predicates. Find two such sentences. Are they unwieldy, or are they easy to follow?

Podless and Happy to Be that Way

by Mickey Vallee

Recently I'd made my decision. I was going to buy one. I was going to own one. I was going to throw caution to the wind, to be one of the people connected to their virtual universe by a little white appendage. I was going to buy an iPod.

It happened after a friend let me try hers. It was protected in a velvet pouch, and I was honoured at the opportunity to massage the sensitive wheel, which directed me through a bright catalogue of all the music I ever needed, from Beethoven to Radiohead.

Just to test the sound, I carefully selected a favourite, *Blonde Redhead*. I pressed play, and up came lyrics, notes, the album cover, all floating behind a crystal screen as serene as a pond.

And the sound? "Kryptonite subwoofer," was all I could think of.

My appetite whetted, I needed to get my fix. But, as a student on a limited budget, I couldn't possibly have rationalized buying one for what they cost. I decided to buy an iPod Shuffle, which is smaller in storage capacity but equal in quality.

I went to a downtown Edmonton mega-store for electronics and marched past advertisements for *The Incredibles*, past rows of cameras and microwaves, past stereos blasting Nickelback, straight to the iPod display case, where I stood gazing with acute concentration at the iPod Shuffle that would soon be mine.

And, of course, the salespeople slid out from under their doors and between the cracks in the walls.

One appeared before me: "Can I help you?"

"Yes, I'd like the iPod Shuffle, please."

"Absolutely, I'll get the manager," who apparently had the keys.

I was pleased so far. There was no pressure to upgrade to the mini iPod and no talk of useless appendages. Just an iPod Shuffle, so I could create a daily soundtrack for my life, walking around the university, walking to the store, to the bar. Everywhere, like everybody, walking every which way and walking with their iPod. Total music emancipation.

The manager came, unlocked the cabinet, and passed the Shuffle to the sales rep, who trotted to the till. What a well-oiled machine, I thought.

Pleased, I went to the till with cash in hand.

"So," the sales rep said. "One Shuffle. These things are great."

"Yeah, well, I love the sound and the convenience."

"Everybody does. Can I interest you in the one- or two-year warranty?"

I'd been pitched this in the past and, like every time before, said, "No thanks." I was already spending enough money as it was and didn't want to add to my tab. "I don't need it."

"Are you sure?" he persisted. "If you pay this flat rate, you're guaranteed repairs for the next year or two, depending on which warranty you opt for."

"I'll opt for none, thanks. I'm not going to toss it around or anything."

A sudden pause made me feel like a wrench in the well-oiled machine. I was blocking the production line. The salesman looked to the floor, then with boldness looked up at me and claimed, "You know, these are the most serviced products in the world."

Startled, I asked, "So what happens to them?"

OXFORD
UNIVERSITY PRESS

70 Wynford Drive, Don Mills, Ontario, Canada, M3C 1J9
Tel: (416)441-2941   Fax: (416)444-0427
SAN # 115-0731   G.S.T. No T.P.S.R122319775

Complimentary Copy /
Exemplaire gratuit

Ship-To / Destinataire

SCOTT-MORGAN STRAKER
39 KENNETH AVENUE
TORONTO ON   M6P 1J1
CANADA

Account / No de compte

135771

Invoice No / No de facture	DATE	Page No / No de page
90442693	23.03.2007	1 of / de 1

Shipped Via / Mode d'expédition   Canpar Promo

Delivery / Livraison   80396273

The following examination copies are sent to you compliments of your
Oxford University Press representative:

Votre représentant d'Oxford University Press a le plaisir de vous faire
parvenir les exemplaires gratuits suivants :

Jennifer Colt
Tel: 416-441-2941 ext 2523 email: Jennifer.colt@oup.com

Qty / Qté	ISBN ISBN-10	Title / Titre	Author / Auteur - Auteure
1	9780195423075 0195423070	SKILL SET PA: STRATEGIES FOR READING&WRI	LUCIA ENGKENT

We welcome your comments on our titles. Please e-mail us at customer.service.ca@oup.com, visit us on the Web at www.oup.com/ca/services/contact, or contact your local sales representative. A complete catalogue of OUP titles is available at www.oup.com/ca.

Vos commentaires sur nos titres sont les bienvenus. Veuillez nous envoyer un courriel à customer.service.ca@oup.com, nous visiter sur le Web à l'adresse www.oup.com/ca/services/contact, ou communiquer avec votre représentant des ventes local. Vous pouvez trouver un catalogue complet des titres de OUP à la page www.oup.com/ca.

He continued his claim: "Well, the buttons stick, the memory sometimes freezes, songs don't play fully. It's a new product so these things are all likely to go wrong in the first year."

I was surprised to hear myself say, "Then why don't I just wait for a few years until they're more affordable and reliable?"

Another pause. I had caught him in the headlights of my suggestion.

I continued innocently, "I mean, when portable CD players came out years ago they were expensive and used to skip like mad, but now they're reliable. If fact, I have one right now that works perfectly, so instead of putting 120 songs onto an iPod that you say is guaranteed to break, why don't I buy some CDs and continue to use my Discman?"

Another pause. I was suddenly so aware of my distaste for the whole transaction.

So I said, "I think that's what I'll do. I'll wait a few years to buy one."

I stood outside, no iPod, no music, silently thanking my intuition.

Listening to the sounds of the traffic I'd anticipated to avoid with my iPod, I experienced a momentary sense of triumph. I didn't want to be a part of the cycle, to be sold something by a company that obviously considered my initial purchase an opportunity to make more money.

Of course, I didn't believe the iPod would break, but since when did it become acceptable for businesses to guarantee the self-destruction of the products they sell? More so, why should they pin the responsibility on the consumer? I took my long walk home, listened to the sounds of traffic, to stereos cranked, people laughing and talking, a busker playing his guitar.

Feeling so much more connected, I walked past someone with the identifiable white earplugs that used to tease me, and I thought, he's missing so much.

(*The Globe and Mail* 30 September 2005: A24)

Reprinted by permission of the author. Mickey Vallee is working towards his PhD at the University of Alberta.

Comprehension

1. What does the author want the iPod for? What impresses him about the product?
2. What is significant about the fact that a velvet pouch protects the friend's iPod? What impression does the author give when he describes how he tried the iPod?
3. Why does he feel that the iPod will give him "total musical emancipation"?
4. How does the salesman's pitch backfire?
5. Why does Vallee not buy an iPod? How are the reasons he gives the salesman different from the ones he concludes with?
6. How does the author benefit from not having an iPod?

Discussion

1. Do you think Vallee made the right choice by refusing to buy the iPod?
2. What could the salesman have said to convince Vallee to buy the iPod?

3. How does the proliferation of personal music devices affect our society?
4. Is this article anti-technology? What aspects of new technology does it criticize?
5. What are the advantages of MP3 music players over CD players?
6. This article was written in September 2005. Do you think Vallee has an iPod now? Why or why not? What kind of player would he get?
7. The technology revolution of the late twentieth century started a trend in going against language conventions in naming products. For example, software with names like *WordPerfect* showed capital letters in the middle of words, a trend carried on in the name *iPod*. Discuss the names of currently popular products. Which ones are catchy? What kind of effect does the sound and the spelling of the words have? Are the names appropriate? Suggest alternatives.

Assignments

1. Research the additional warranties often offered by retailers and give a report or write an essay (depending on your instructor's specifications) as to whether purchasing them is a good idea or not.
2. Why do companies rush products to the market before all the bugs are worked out of them? Is this a good marketing strategy? How do the companies deal with problems? Write an essay.
3. Look up Mickey Vallee's webpage on the Internet. Is there anything here that surprises you about the author? Write a short paragraph explaining what impression you get from the article and from the website.

Paraphrasing and summarizing

1. Summarize Vallee's shopping experience.
2. Explain in your own words: "And, of course, the salespeople slid out from under their doors and between the cracks in the walls." What effect is the author creating with this sentence?
3. Paraphrase: "I was going to throw caution to the wind, to be one of the people connected to their virtual universe by a little white appendage."
4. Use indirect speech forms to relate the conversation between Vallee and the cashier. For example, you can start with "At first, the sales rep praised the iPod that Vallee was purchasing."

Vocabulary study
Words
Match the word to the meaning as it is used in the article:

1. appendage _____	a)	at a high volume
2. serene _____	b)	bill, total amount due
3. whet _____	c)	calm and peaceful
4. rationalize _____	d)	cash register
5. acute _____	e)	choose

6. till (n.) _____
7. pitch (v.) _____
8. tab _____
9. persist _____
10. opt for _____
11. startled _____
12. distaste _____
13. pin something on someone _____
14. cranked _____
15. busker _____

f) continue to try to do something
g) feeling that something is unpleasant or offensive
h) give reasons for behaviour
i) put blame or responsibility on someone
j) serious, strong, severe
k) sharpen or stimulate
l) something attached to something bigger or more important
m) street performer
n) surprised
o) try to persuade someone to buy or accept something

Idioms and expressions

Discuss the meaning:

1. throw caution to the wind
2. get a fix
3. throw a wrench into a machine (or "a spanner in the works," the British idiom)
4. caught in the headlights
5. like mad
6. pin something on someone

Structure and technique

1. Note that the author does not identify what he is buying until the last word of the first paragraph. At first, he refers to it as "one," and then he refers to "a little white appendage." What effect does this technique have on the reader?
2. This is a narrative essay that includes dialogue. The dialogue is reconstructed but probably not completely faithful. (Could you relate the exact words somebody said to you in a conversation?) The dialogue gives it the feel of a short story, so although this is an essay, it approaches the line between fiction and non-fiction. How does the author use dramatic techniques to relate what happened?

Sentence structure

Change the underlined phrases to clauses by adding words such as conjunctions:

1. Just to test the sound, I carefully selected a favourite, *Blonde Redhead*.
2. I pressed play, and up came lyrics, notes, the album cover, all floating behind a crystal screen as serene as a pond.

3. My appetite whetted, I needed to get my fix.
4. But, as a student on a limited budget, I couldn't possibly have rationalized buying one for what they cost.
5. Feeling so much more connected, I walked past someone with the identifiable white earplugs that used to tease me, and I thought, he's missing so much.

Disconnecting Hard to Do, Cellphone Generation Finds

by Christopher Hutsul

I was surprised and disappointed to see, when on vacation at an all-inclusive resort in the Dominican Republic, a vacationer yammering into a cellphone at poolside. I'd left mine at home. That my phone was ill-equipped to work in Puerto Plata was beside the point. Thirty of us, mostly late twentysomethings, had gathered at the handsome resort for a wedding, an event that would be enveloped by sun, surf and Scrabble. A cellphone, I figured, would detract from the weightlessness that I'd yearned for.

I approached the phone-talker, a fellow wedding guest, and questioned his choice of travel accoutrements.

He explained he was in the midst of launching a business, that he shouldn't even be on vacation right now, and that he was 60/40 for the week—that is, 60 per cent work, and 40 per cent vacation. I shrugged off a wave of guilt for being on a 100 per cent vacation, and proceeded to the bar for a Mai Tai. It's okay, I told myself, to not be so damn connected all the time.

I soon learned it's also not easy. It was unnerving. Without our phones, without being able to text each other, our group was lost.

The trip was like some kind of sociology experiment. Take 30 heavy users, remove their communication devices, and see how they fare. Will they be able to find each other, stick to a plan, adapt to a less connected environment? No, no, and no.

Throughout the week, we found ourselves pacing the resort, looking for members of the group. It felt as though we were circling each other, meeting up only by happenstance. We tried to make plans, and set up meeting points, but they were all half-baked, and rarely fulfilled. We kept meaning to play poker, to play a game of Monopoly, to do whatever, but we couldn't make it happen. Cellphones, I kept thinking, would have come in handy.

My girlfriend and I, for example, would have breakfast, then plan to meet up again after lunch, without setting an exact time or place to meet. A couple of hours later, it would dawn on me that not only did we not have a firm plan, but we also didn't have the means (cellphones) to make one. And so, more wandering.

We were behaving as though we still had our phones on us. As a matter of habit, we were making *cellular plans*, if you will. That is, malleable, non-specific plans made between heavy cellphone users that are prone to adaptation and cancellation via a last-minute phone call. At home and fully equipped, a plan to meet at a particular restaurant means, "If I get to the restaurant early, and see that it's busy, I might be at a restaurant across the street, but don't worry because I'll call you."

All this goes out the window when a user makes plans with a non-user. When, for example, my buddy Mike and I agree to meet for drinks at 10 p.m. at Sweaty Betty's, that plan, barring illness, is a lock, because I have no way to reach him to cancel or change the plan.

I assume that an elder generation would have handled things differently at the resort. People who didn't grow up with the cellphones would be used to limited connectivity, and have ways to deal with it. On such a trip, they might have set up a central meeting place, or make firmer plans.

For us, that's easier said than done. We have been using our phones through most of our youth, and have grown dependent. We're used to living in a warm bubble of cellular connectivity. Being able to know, on a whim, the emotional status and physical whereabouts of our friends has become a way of life. A cheap phone and a basic plan buys something that strikingly resembles telepathy. Take our sixth sense away from us, like on this recent trip, and we'll all be a little bit useless.

Not that we didn't adapt in the end. By the time the vacation was wrapping up, we were able to track each other down to play some poker, and at least half a game of Monopoly. Miraculously, we all made it to the wedding on time.

As for the pool-side phone-talker, his ambitious 60/40 plan turned out to be more like 60 per cent rum and 40 per cent vodka. He lost his phone on the resort grounds, and appeared to be having a tremendous time—at least, on the rare occasion we crossed paths.

(*The Toronto Star* 9 May 2005)
Reprinted with permission—Torstar Syndication Services.

Comprehension

1. Where did the author go? Why? Who else was there?
2. Who is the author criticizing? Why? What happens in the end to this person? Is there a moral to this story?
3. What did Hutsul expect to be doing on his trip?
4. What problem does the author find on his vacation? What causes this?
5. What is the author's thesis—the main point he is discussing in this article?
6. What point is Hutsul making when he mentions his friend Mike?

Discussion

1. Do you agree with Hutsul? Are you dependent on a cellphone for making and changing plans? Have you ever had problems like the ones he is describing?

2. We can now bring our work home thanks to technology such as computers, the Internet, cellphones, and PDAs. What are the advantages and disadvantages?
3. Explain different attitudes towards cellphones. For example, young people who are dependent on their phones are reluctant to turn them off in class or at social functions. Older people who grew up without phones often cannot understand this attitude.
4. Discuss proper use and misuse of cellphones.
5. "Destination weddings" are getting popular. The wedding may take place on a cruise or at a resort. Destination weddings are different from elopements, when a couple goes off to get married by themselves. At a destination wedding, guests generally pay for their own trip, but they are getting a vacation as well as attending a wedding. Destination weddings are smaller than in-town weddings. Only very close family and friends attend. Sometimes couples have a reception in their own town after they get married. What are the advantages and disadvantages of destination weddings and of elopements?

Assignments

1. Have you ever had a problem with a meeting because you didn't have a cellphone or because it didn't work? Describe what happened in a narrative paragraph.
2. Research places that are popular for destination weddings. Compare the facilities and services offered. Write a report explaining how resorts and cruise ships are trying to attract the wedding business.
3. How can technology be harmful to the balance in our everyday lives?

Paraphrasing and summarizing

1. Write a one-paragraph summary of this article. Do not exceed 100 words.
2. Paraphrase: "The trip was like some kind of sociology experiment. Take 30 heavy users, remove their communication devices, and see how they fare."
3. Paraphrase: "Being able to know, on a whim, the emotional status and physical whereabouts of our friends has become a way of life."
4. Paraphrase, changing the statements that Hutsul puts in quotation marks into indirect speech: "At home and fully equipped, a plan to meet at a particular restaurant means, 'If I get to the restaurant early, and see that it's busy, I might be at a restaurant across the street, but don't worry because I'll call you.'"

Vocabulary study

to yammer: What word would you use instead of *yammer* in an academic essay?
accoutrements: Which language is this word from? What does it mean?
to launch: What objects can you use with the verb *launch*?

to shrug off: What can you shrug off? Give possible objects.

unnerving: Explain the connection between *unnerving*, *nerves*, and *nervous*.

to fare: List the meanings of both *fare* and *fair*. Which meaning of *fare* is used in the text? What is the relationship between *fare* and *welfare*?

happenstance: Give a synonym that rhymes.

half-baked: What can be described as half-baked?

malleable: Find both the meaning and the etymology (the word history).

prone to: Explain the different meanings of *prone*. Which one is used in the article?

whereabouts: Give a synonym.

telepathy: Explain what this word means by giving the meaning of the Greek prefix *tele–* and the root *path–*. What is the adjective form?

Idioms and expressions

Replace the underlined idioms and expressions with words that mean the same thing:

1. Whether or not he started the fight <u>is beside the point</u> now.
2. I was <u>in the midst of</u> cleaning the house when you called.
3. Having a back-up computer would sure <u>come in handy</u>.
4. When she made that off-hand comment, <u>it dawned on me</u> that she'd been lying all along.
5. My hard work all <u>went out the window</u> when they did not accept the proposal.
6. We booked the trip and paid the deposit, so <u>it's all a lock</u>.
7. We tried to adopt a healthier lifestyle, but that was <u>easier said than done</u>.
8. He decided to fly to Montreal <u>on a whim</u>.
9. Whenever I go downtown, I seem to <u>cross paths</u> with one of my former classmates.
10. Mothers seem to have <u>a sixth sense</u> of when their children are in trouble.

Structure and technique

1. Note how Hutsul starts with the story of a particular person and then returns to the same person in his last paragraph. This is a favoured technique in both journalistic and academic writing—closing the circle, introducing and concluding with the same element.
2. Hutsul's writing style is conversational. Give examples of language that would not be proper for an academic essay.

Sentence structure

1. Hutsul's writing style includes many phrases or clauses in the middle of sentences. These are grammatical and properly set apart by commas, but they are not the usual sentence structure. What is the effect of such sentences? In the following examples, rearrange the sentence to a regular pattern:

Example: "A cellphone, I figured, would detract from the weightlessness that I'd yearned for."

I figured that a cellphone would detract from the weightlessness that I'd yearned for.

-

a) "I was surprised and disappointed to see, when on vacation at an all-inclusive resort in the Dominican Republic, a vacationer yammering into a cellphone at poolside."
b) "It's okay, I told myself, to not be so damn connected all the time."
c) "Cellphones, I kept thinking, would have come in handy."
d) "When, for example, my buddy Mike and I agree to meet for drinks at 10 p.m. at Sweaty Betty's, that plan, barring illness, is a lock, because I have no way to reach him to cancel or change the plan."

2. An overuse of commas is characteristic of conversational style. The commas make the reader pause, mimicking speech style. For example, in "We tried to make plans, and set up meeting points, but they were all half-baked, and rarely fulfilled," only the second comma is required. Find three other examples of unnecessary commas in the text.

Free to Drive

by Margaret Wente

The other day I stuck the nozzle in the tank of my dainty little SUV and paid for my first $50 fill. It was a shock, but I knew it was coming, and I know it's going to get worse. Gas prices in Toronto are about to hit a dollar a litre, and the outlook is not good. I have a feeling that one day I'll remember my $50 fill as fondly as a 25-cent Coke.

Not everyone is miserable about the price of gas. Environmentalists are happy because they think people might drive less. Public-transit boosters are happy because they think more people will take the subway. Hybrid-car salesmen are happy, and so are oil sheiks and Albertans (although, for reasons I don't grasp, Albertans pay even more for gas than we do).

Theoretically, I know my car dependency is bad (and my SUV dependency is even worse). It pollutes the air, undermines our cash-strapped transit system, contributes to wasteful land use and ugly urban sprawl, destroys the fabric of communities, and promotes obesity. And now, it's costing me fifty bucks a fill. I ought to kick the habit. And one day, I will—the day that someone wrests the car keys from my cold, dead fingers.

What might induce us to change our gas-guzzling ways? It sure won't be a $50 fill-up. We love to gripe about the price of gas. But we're rich. We drop more money on a night at the movies or an evening's worth of babysitting. Gas would have to hit $3 or $4 a litre to make a dent in people's driving habits, and even then we'd simply downsize.

In Toronto, we've had a 20-year debate about how to get people to give up their cars and switch to public transit. Last week, Conservative Leader Stephen Harper proposed tax breaks for transit users. His idea was loudly ridiculed by the experts, who scoffed that nobody is about to switch to public transit for a lousy 60 cents a day. According to them, the answer is to offer better service—more routes, with nicer buses that run on time.

The truth is that the experts are wrong, too. You can make the buses free, furnish them with widescreen TVs and run them every five minutes, and people will still drive. I know. I live right near the streetcar, which zips across town and lets me off four blocks from where I work. It doesn't get much better than that. How often do I take the streetcar? Every time my car is getting fixed.

No matter how good you make it, public transit will never be able to compete with cars. Cars are private. They're convenient. They're comfortable. They're fun. They're cooler in the summer and warmer In the winter. They hold groceries and kids and kitty litter and booze and all the other stuff you have to pick up on the way home. They go exactly where you need to go, whenever you want to go there, and you never have to smell a stranger's sweaty armpits.

Public transit also depends on population density. But Toronto, like most other cities, is increasingly spread out, and hundreds of thousands of people commute among the far-flung suburbs. For them, a car is a necessity.

It's no accident that bus and subway riders are mostly young and poor. They take public transit not because it's the better way, but because they can't afford to drive. The moment they get a little older and a little better off, they move to the suburbs and buy a car. The only cities where the middle-aged middle classes resort to public transit (London, New York) are places where driving and parking in the city core are nearly impossible.

People will pay a huge price for convenience and autonomy. In China, experts predicted that it would be years before average people would become rich enough to buy private cars. They were wrong. The Chinese are quite happy to fork over an astonishing amount of money for the privilege—at least five times more, relative to income, than we do—and to drive at a crawl on roads that are gridlocked.

Some day, we'll have to break our dependency on oil (the sooner the better, as far as I'm concerned, since I'm no fan of propping up corrupt thugs and sheiks and countries that believe in flogging unveiled women and homosexuals). But break our dependency on cars? Never. We may have to run them on electricity or wind power or moonshine. We may have to pay a fortune for the privilege. But pay we will. Cars mean freedom, and freedom's worth a lot.

(*The Globe and Mail* 9 August 2005)
Reprinted with permission from *The Globe and Mail*.

Notes

When this article was written, Stephen Harper was the leader of the Opposition and not yet prime minister.

The phrase "It's the better way" (paragraph 9) is a slogan used by the Toronto Transit Commission (TTC).

Follow-up: A year after Margaret Wente wrote this, she decided to give public transit a chance. She gave up her SUV for five days. Her trip to work took an hour longer, and she missed the convenience of being able to carry items in her car, which she referred to as a "giant purse." She did, however, appreciate the TTC, saying that it did a good job with its limited resources. ("Carless in Toronto: not a love story." *The Globe and Mail* 7 October: M1, M4)

Comprehension

1. What is Wente's thesis?
2. Why does she call her vehicle a "dainty little SUV"? What adjectives are usually used to describe SUVs?
3. How does Wente inject humour into the article?
4. What does she like about driving?
5. What does she dislike about public transit?
6. What point is she proving with her example of what is happening in China?

Discussion

1. What are the strong arguments Wente makes? Which of her arguments are weaker?
2. If transit was as convenient for you as it is for Wente, would you drive your own vehicle? What are the advantages of taking transit instead of driving?
3. Wente makes a strong statement about some oil-producing countries in the last paragraph. Discuss this statement with your classmates. How valid do you think her opinion is?
4. Forgoing the convenience of personal vehicles for public transit undoubtedly takes selflessness. What besides money could convince people to take transit?
5. People do not have to get rid of their personal vehicles, but they could cut down on their use. What kind of compromises could be made?

Summary and paraphrase

1. Paraphrase: "The Chinese are quite happy to fork over an astonishing amount of money for the privilege—at least five times more, relative to income, than we do—and to drive at a crawl on roads that are gridlocked."

2. Summarize in one sentence the advantages of cars (paragraph 7), making Wente's specific examples more of a general statement.
3. Write a one-paragraph summary, of no more than 100 words, of this article.

Vocabulary study

Replace the underlined words and phrases with synonyms:

1. Nothing will <u>induce</u> me to give up my motorcycle. I don't care about the danger.
2. They're always <u>griping about</u> something—the location, the date, the food.
3. Adam <u>scoffed at</u> my plans to all the way drive to Yellowknife.
4. She's hoping they can work through their problems with a separation; she doesn't want to <u>resort to</u> divorce.
5. Children need to have some <u>autonomy,</u> so I let them make decisions about their own rooms.
6. Clara has developed a <u>dependency on</u> sleeping pills.
7. The <u>corrupt</u> officials were accepting bribes.

Collocations

Write a sentence for each of these expressions:

1. remember fondly (OR fond memories)
2. grasp reasons/explanation
3. undermine a system
4. kick a habit
5. make a dent in something
6. fork over (OR fork out)
7. break [our] dependency on

Structure and technique

1. Although this is a journalistic essay, it is quite similar in structure to an academic essay in that most of the paragraphs have one main idea introduced in the topic sentence. For instance, note the general statements "Not everyone is miserable about the price of gas" and "Theoretically, I know my car dependency is bad." How are these topic sentences supported by specific statements? Find other examples of general topic sentences and their support.
2. The style of language is conversational. Make a list of slang words and conversational expressions that Wente uses.
3. Note how Wente acknowledges the arguments against driving her car: "Theoretically, I know my car dependency is bad (and my SUV dependency is even worse). It pollutes the air, undermines our cash-strapped transit system, contributes to wasteful land use and ugly urban sprawl, destroys the fabric of communities, and promotes obesity. And now, it's costing me fifty bucks a fill." How does she show that she is not swayed by these arguments?

Letters to the Editor

Margaret Wente's column hit a nerve with *Globe and Mail* readers. The newspaper received dozens of letters to the editor, publishing 16 of them. The first day there were nine letters arguing against Wente's stand; the next day there were seven supporting her view. Here are some of them:

Letters to the editor: Life at a buck a litre

Letter 1

Margaret Wente (Free to Drive—Aug. 9) asks: "What might induce us to change our gas-guzzling ways?" How about some wisdom and selflessness. But, as Ms. Wente illustrates, most of her car-dependent cohorts lack the requisite ability to act for anything other than their own comfort and needs. Perhaps she has unintentionally suggested a better solution herself when she says that "the only cities where the middle-aged middle classes resort to public transit (London, New York) are places where driving and parking in the city core are nearly impossible."

If short-sighted self-interested car owners are unable to regulate their behaviour in the interest of their own society and planet's health, then maybe it's time society regulates their behaviour for them.

Letter 2

Margaret Wente perfectly exemplifies the selfish attitude that is creating the massive traffic congestion in our cities, both at home and abroad: It is all about me, me, me.

Letter 3

I must thank Margaret Wente for her candour in admitting her lust for driving. One need only look at the clogged arteries of any major North American city to realize she is just one among millions of similarly narrow-minded individuals. But she's right about one thing: Oil is dwindling but not our precious dependence on it.

Letter 4

Margaret Wente says her SUV is private, convenient, comfortable, fun, and holds her bottles of booze. She says her SUV gives her freedom, and freedom is something she's willing to pay for. My bike does all these things, and I have the body fat of a professional athlete. How much would she pay for that?

Letter 5

I'm 58 years old. I've never learned to drive and, let's face it, I never will. So it was with some amusement that I read Margaret Wente's column and then the thought du jour (Social Studies) from Horace: "He is almost always a slave who cannot live on little." Life has its moments.

(*The Globe and Mail* 10 August 2005)

Letters to the editor: Honk if you like Wente

Letter 6

Based on yesterday's letters to the editor (Life At A Buck A Litre), one might conclude that Margaret Wente's views on driving her SUV in the face of rising gasoline prices are out to lunch. Imagine, nine letters in a row slamming her. But I'm certain this ratio is not representative of the views of your subscribers at large.

When will these people figure out that most of us don't live in the city core where public transit can be a reasonable alternative? When will they realize that most adults with real jobs don't consider a bicycle to be sensible transportation given our climate and distances?

In the Greater Toronto Area, the majority of people drive because it's the better way. What the letter writers self-righteously call "selfish" and "elitist" is simply considered pragmatic by more people than they could imagine.

Letter 7

Public transit is hell! When I take the bus, I have to endure a procession of foul-mouthed panhandlers while I wait for it. The bus is often packed, and there's no place to sit. Loud cellphone users are everywhere. There's no air conditioning. A smooth talker once tried to pick me up saying: "So, are you on welfare, too?" And I'd like to know how those sanctimonious bike riders would manage with two toddlers and five bags of groceries.

Letter 8

Margaret Wente (Free to Drive—Aug. 9) omitted an increasingly relevant reason to drive her car instead of taking public transit: The chances of a suicide bomber showing up beside her in the passenger seat are somewhat less than would be the case for the bus, streetcar or subway.

Letter 9

If we can buy bottled water at $2.88 a litre, why do we moan when we buy gas at a third of the price?

Letter 10

All the responses to Margaret Wente's column share a common thread: that people should put the collective good ahead of personal convenience. While I believe Canadians care about the environment and social cohesiveness, it's hard to place those relative abstractions front and centre when it's 35 or minus 25 outside and you're running late for work. This is the conundrum of affluent societies that sanctimonious lecturing won't solve.

Perhaps the marketplace will address this issue, but not the way your letter writers would prefer: Someone will invent a cheap zero-emission car, and people will keep on driving.

(*The Globe and Mail* 11 August 2005)

Notes

Newspapers generally have a "Letters to the editor" section giving readers a chance to comment on news stories or columns. Check out the letters section in your local newspaper. Letters have to make a point in very few words. Newspaper editors sometimes print only part of a letter.

Letter 5 refers to another section of *The Globe and Mail*, "Social studies," which has a quote in the "Thought du jour" section. "Du jour" is French for "of the day."

Comprehension

1. Give the main point of each letter in your own words.
2. What does letter 1 suggest?
3. On what grounds do the letter writers disagree with Wente? What is the common argument?
4. What common complaint do the "pro" letter writers have?
5. Which letters are the most strongly worded? Which are in a more academic style? Which are more conversational?

Discussion

1. Did these letters make you reconsider Wente's essay? How?
2. Evaluate the arguments used by each of the letter writers. Which letters do you consider the most effective? Which ones do you agree with?
3. Discuss the quote from Horace: "He is almost always a slave who cannot live on little." What does it mean? Do you agree or disagree?
4. If you have read Jim Coyle's "No point fearing terror attacks we can't stop," consider the comment in letter 8. Do you think the letter writer is serious?

Assignments

1. Write your own letter to the editor about Wente's column. Or choose a column that you find interesting from your local paper and write a letter to the editor. You can even send it in to see if it gets published.
2. Research other ways to combat urban sprawl. Write an essay in support of one of these ways.
3. Are SUV drivers the most selfish on the road? Are they deluded about the safety of SUVs? Research this topic and write an essay either defending or attacking SUVs.

Paraphrasing and summarizing

1. Write a sentence summarizing each letter. For example, "Letter 9 says the price is not high compared to other liquids."
2. Paraphrase: "All the responses to Margaret Wente's column share a common thread: that people should put the collective good ahead of personal convenience. While I believe Canadians care about the environment and

social cohesiveness, it's hard to place those relative abstractions front and centre when it's 35 or minus 25 outside and you're running late for work. This is the conundrum of affluent societies that sanctimonious lecturing won't solve."

Vocabulary study

Give a word or expression that means the opposite of these words. Make sure you keep the same part of speech:

1. selflessness
2. requisite
3. unintentionally
4. short-sighted
5. self-interested
6. massive
7. candour
8. narrow-minded
9. dwindling
10. perilous
11. convenient
12. pragmatic
13. increasingly
14. relevant
15. affluent

Structure and technique

Review the uses of punctuation found in the letters. Look at the quotation marks, colons, parentheses, hyphens, and commas. Discuss the examples of usage.

Was Court Right to Back Suits against Big Tobacco?

Pro: Ruling Rightly Blames Adults for Teen Addictions

by Linda McQuaig

The tobacco industry and its supporters have long insisted that smoking is simply a matter of "individual choice."

They note that the dangers of smoking are well-known, and yet people choose to smoke anyway—just like people choose to drive cars even though they realize many die in car accidents, and people eat junk food even though they know that can cause heart problems.

But cigarettes are in a class by themselves when it comes to their sheer killing power. Fully half the people who take up smoking on a long-term basis will die from it. This can't be said of driving cars or eating potato chips.

Furthermore, is it meaningful to talk of "individual choice" with a product notorious for its addictiveness?

Many a child made the "choice" to become a lifelong smoker at the age of 13 or even younger, when offered a cigarette in a schoolyard or hanging out at a mall, long before he or she could possibly appreciate the consequences to be faced 30 or 40 years later.

A recent Canadian study showed more than 90 per cent of adult smokers say they regret their decision to start smoking.

Getting young people hooked on smoking has long been the bread and butter of the tobacco industry.

Companies have gone to great lengths to present smoking as the symbol of coolness and rebellion—something highly seductive to teenagers. When governments have blocked marketing and selling to teenagers, the industry has figured out other ways to get their logos in front of young eyes, like sponsoring music and sports events.

Internal tobacco company documents have shown that targeting teens has been a key industry strategy.

So the notion of "individual choice" in becoming a lifelong cigarette addict is dubious.

Even more dubious is the notion of "individual choice" when it comes to paying the $4 billion heath-care bill of smoking-related diseases, which kill 47,000 Canadians a year.

Clearly this financial burden isn't shouldered just by individual smokers, but by all Canadians, whose taxes pay for our public health-care system.

So, it's encouraging that the Supreme Court of Canada has unanimously upheld a B.C. law allowing the province to sue cigarette makers to recover smoking-related health care costs. The court saw evidence that for decades the tobacco industry actively covered up its own research showing how lethal smoking is.

The ruling could direct some badly needed cash into our health-care system.

More importantly, it could pave the way for far-reaching reforms that would make it difficult for cigarette manufacturers to profit from hooking young smokers. One option urged by Non-Smokers' Rights Association would be to penalize tobacco companies based on the number of customers under the age of 19.

Ultimately, the court ruling clarifies that the blame for the nation's overflowing cancer wards belongs not on uninformed 13-year-olds, but on the well-informed adults mapping out marketing strategies in the boardrooms of the tobacco industry.

Con: Do We Really Want Private Decisions Regulated?

by Rondi Adamson

I do not smoke. But I accept, as part of living in a country with taxpayer-subsidized health care, that I have to pay for other people's stupid choices, as well as their misfortunes. And likewise. That people make stupid choices may well be at least one argument in favour of privatized health care. But those same stupid choices don't strike me as being much of an argument in favour of governments (or, for that matter, individuals) suing tobacco companies for the cost of tobacco-related illnesses.

A choice is just that. For more than 40 years the perils of smoking have been known to us. An emphasis on personal responsibility in this country would be refreshing.

How far would we like to take things? It is indisputable that smoking causes illness.

It is also true that all kinds of illnesses could be avoided—the cost of them, as well—if people would control their weight. Cirrhosis of the liver could be avoided if people wouldn't drink, high blood pressure if one exercised more and stayed away from aggravating situations.

Careful use of condoms can prevent all manner of disease and unwanted babies, the former causing pain and costing money now, the latter sure to cost a bundle right now, and to develop bad, pricey habits of their own down the line.

But just how much do you want your private decisions regulated by others, snitched-on by your neighbours or used by your government so they can make some money?

It is not inconceivable that junk food will be next.

A report released this week by the Ontario Medical Association found obesity rates in Canadian children had nearly doubled between 1981 and 1996. Thirty years from now, those kids will be making us pay through the nose for stomach staplings. Will the government tax their chips, and sue Ruffles?

The Supreme Court's ruling doesn't just set a dangerous precedent. It represents an utterly transparent double standard. Our governments continue to allow tobacco to be sold, and collect taxes on cigarettes. They also sell liquor and promote gambling. Should Canadian citizens sue them, then, for encouraging and profiting from such deadly endeavours?

Or perhaps tobacco should simply be banned. That would be less hypocritical than suing a tobacco company whose product you tax.

But banning tobacco would be a mistake, depending on the kind of society you want to live in. I want one where adults are free to take risks and indulge in their own selection of vices, within reason.

Adults, in turn, should then be held responsible for whatever those vices bring about. And a government that taxes cigarettes to high heaven, and then claims tobacco companies owe it money to cover treatment for emphysema and lung cancer, is not being held responsible for its own policies.

But that would suit them fine, since, while they decry smoking, the last thing any government that taxes cigarettes wants, is for its citizens to stop the deadly puffing.

("Faceoff: Seeking compensation." *The Toronto Star* 9 October 2005: A16)

Linda McQuaig is a Canadian author and journalist.

Rondi Adamson is an award–winning Canadian journalist.

Notes

On 29 September 2005, the Supreme Court of Canada ruled that British Columbia could sue tobacco companies to recover health care costs for illnesses caused by smoking.

Comprehension

1. Explain what prompted the writing of these two essays.
2. What does McQuaig mean by the putting the expression "individual choice" in quotation marks? Explain her reasoning.
3. Why does McQuaig consider smoking to be different from other dangerous behaviours people engage in?
4. Why is it significant that tobacco companies deliberately target teenagers?
5. What is the effect of Adamson's first sentence?
6. Explain what Adamson means about personal responsibility.
7. Explain what Adamson fears in her reference in paragraph 6.
8. Both writers say that people make stupid choices. What is the difference, however, in their points of view on this?

Discussion

1. Who do you think makes the stronger argument—McQuaig or Adamson?
2. Whose side do you tend to agree with? Why?
3. Do you think the comparisons of cigarette smoking with alcohol use and with overeating are valid? What are some important differences?
4. What do you think of current smoking rules and regulations? Over the past few years, smoking in public places has been more and more restricted. For instance, smoking in restaurants moved from being unrestricted, to restricted to a certain area, to restricted to an enclosed space, to being totally banned. Summarize the arguments used by both sides in the debate.

Assignments

1. Do you agree with McQuaig or Adamson? Explain why in a paragraph.
2. In an essay, explain the reasons that young people take up smoking.
3. Should tobacco be more strictly controlled and eventually banned? Write an essay giving your reasons.
4. As we learn more about human biology, we find that many of the things that we blame people for (mental illnesses, addictions, obesity, and homosexuality) actually are determined more by genes than by poor choices. What implication does this have for our society?
5. Research the 29 September 2005 Supreme Court ruling against tobacco companies and similar judgments. Write a report.
6. Watch one of the films dealing with the tobacco industry, such as *The insider* (1999) and *Thank you for smoking* (2005). Write a review.

Summarizing and paraphrasing

1. In two or three sentences, summarize the arguments given by each author.
2. Paraphrase: "Companies have gone to great lengths to present smoking as the symbol of coolness and rebellion—something highly seductive to teenagers. When governments have blocked marketing and selling to teenagers, the industry has figured out other ways to get their logos in front of young eyes, like sponsoring music and sports events." (McQuaig)
3. Paraphrase: "I want one where adults are free to take risks and indulge in their own selection of vices, within reason." (Adamson)
4. Paraphrase: "Careful use of condoms can prevent all manner of disease and unwanted babies, the former causing pain and costing money now, the latter sure to cost a bundle right now, and to develop bad, pricey habits of their own down the line." (Adamson)

Vocabulary study

Fill in the chart for the other parts of speech, showing important patterns (such as whether a verb is transitive or whether a certain preposition is often used with the noun or verb):

Noun	Verb	Adjective	Meaning
supporter [person]			
support			
danger			
	choose [transitive]		
		meaningful	
addictiveness			
addiction			
decision			
		seductive	
argument			
peril			
	prevent [transitive]		
	indulge in		
		responsible	

Collocations

Discuss the meaning and usage of these expressions and write a sentence for each:

1. a matter of choice
2. in a class by themselves
3. take up smoking
4. bread and butter
5. go to great lengths
6. shoulder a burden
7. pave the way for something
8. map out strategy
9. set a precedent
10. double standard

Structure and technique

1. Discuss how the writers make their opinions clear and their arguments effective. Find statements in which they are giving opinions they do not agree with, and show how they distinguish those statements from their own opinions.
2. The authors use both long and short sentences. Where are the short sentences particularly effective?
3. Note the sentences that begin with co-ordinate conjunctions (*and, but, or, so*). What is the effect?

Sentence structure

Identify the grammatical subject in these sentences:

1. "A recent Canadian study showed more than 90 per cent of adult smokers say they regret their decision to start smoking."
2. "Getting young people hooked on smoking has long been the bread and butter of the tobacco industry."
3. "Even more dubious is the notion of 'individual choice' when it comes to paying the $4 billion heath-care bill of smoking-related diseases, which kill 47,000 Canadians a year."
4. "That people make stupid choices may well be at least one argument in favour of privatized health care."
5. "For more than 40 years the perils of smoking have been known to us."

No Point Fearing Terror Attacks We Can't Stop

by Jim Coyle

What a lot of unhelpful blather has been uttered lately by Public Safety Minister Anne McLellan. Canadians are not as "psychologically prepared" for a terror attack here as they should be, she says. Canada is "not immune" from the mayhem wrought elsewhere in the world, she warns. "I think we have, for too long, thought that these are things that happen somewhere else."

None of this does very much to enhance the safety of Canadians. None of it provides any practical guidance for citizens, or much insight into the security and emergency plans of government. None of it, on reflection, even makes much sense.

Perhaps Canadians have tended to regard such attacks as things that "happen somewhere else" for the perfectly logical reason that, so far at least, they have.

Perhaps it's not, as McLellan suggests, that Canadians think they're immune to terrorist attack—global events make the vulnerability of large cosmopolitan cities like Toronto, with their easy targets of packed and accessible public places, fairly clear. Perhaps it's the case that, either by instinct or conscious calculation, Canadians have merely reached certain conclusions about what they can and can't do to prevent it.

Perhaps Canadians simply understand that there is no way to be "psychologically prepared" for events that are, by definition, sudden, shocking and beyond anything in most people's personal experience.

Could it be that Canadians are not living in a fool's paradise but, rather, have simply paid attention to world events and come to the only rational conclusion available?

That being that since there is no such thing as immunity, since there is no reliable way of knowing when evil will strike, since mere chance determines who's in harm's way and who's not, the best course of action is an alert business-as-usual, the worst a lapse into paranoia and paralysis.

If the investigation into last week's terror attack in London makes anything clear, it is how little can be done to prevent those bound on murder from murdering if they are willing to spend their own lives in the process.

In London, they'd long expected such an attack. Leaders had said so publicly. It was not if, they warned, but when. Yet they could not stop it.

The British capital is a city with just about the highest level of camera surveillance in the world. But it turns out those cameras were chiefly of benefit not in deterrence—consequences are of little concern to those intent on suicide—but only in investigation after the fact.

Even then, what the cameras make clear more than anything is how easily those who would destroy society can fit in and travel through it. What did police ultimately find on the screens? The image of four men meeting at King's Cross subway station carrying backpacks. And what did it look like?

"You would think they were going on a hiking holiday," a security source reportedly told Sky News. And what could be more English than that?

That's what it must have looked like—if they noticed at all—to the throngs bustling through the station that morning, their minds on work, or a marital spat, or holiday plans, or rumoured premiership transfers, or the pint (or several) waiting at day's end.

In the busyness of a metropolitan centre—where the range of normal is wide—much is inevitably missed. In the avert-the-gaze culture of big-city life much is judiciously ignored. In traumatic events like this, the import of what was seen is often significant only in retrospect.

As it happens, a man who got off the bombed bus just before the blast would later tell Associated Press he had noticed another passenger, a man, fiddling anxiously with a bag.

"This young guy kept diving into this bag or whatever he had in front of his feet," the man said.

But what did he think that morning? Probably just that the chap was checking to make sure he hadn't forgot his squash racquet. Or that he was a run-of-the-mill urban oddball. Nothing, apparently, that prompted an emergency call to police.

Maybe McLellan sells Canadians short. Maybe they've simply—as people do daily in all kinds of ways—done their private sums, their risk assessments, their cost-benefit analysis about where they must be and how best to get there.

After all, this is an age famous for fearing the wrong things. We're terrified of crime, when rates are actually dropping. We obsess about teen violence, and ignore the victims of poverty. We warn against creepy strangers, when most harm done to children is carried out by those they know. It might be, however, that on the terrorism front Canadians have kept things in just about the right perspective.

As horrifying as the prospect is, terror attacks rank well down the list of things likely to kill them. They're more likely, statistically speaking, to die in a car crash on a trip to the cottage. They're more likely to die of stroke or heart disease, or prostate or breast cancer. They're probably more likely to be hit by lightning.

As always, fear itself is one of today's bigger hazards.

McLellan should take pains not to spread it.

(*The Toronto Star* 14 July 2005: B2)
Reprinted with permission—Torstar Syndication Services

Comprehension

1. Sum up Jim Coyle's opinion of Anne McLellan's announcement.
2. What does Coyle suggest is a reasonable course of action for people considering the threat of terrorism?
3. Why does Coyle say our fears are misplaced?
4. What are the lessons learned from the London subway bombing?

Discussion

1. What do you think of Anne McLellan's statements? Is Coyle's criticism justified?
2. Do you agree with Coyle's arguments? Why or why not?
3. What should Canada do to guard against terrorist attacks?

4. This article was written in 2005. Discuss recent terrorist actions. Do you think the situation is different? Would Coyle's arguments still apply?

Assignments

1. In a paragraph, define "irrational fear."
2. Should Canadian streets and public spaces have more surveillance cameras? Explain why or why not in an essay.
3. The fear of crime has risen even though the crime rate has dropped. Find out more about the arguments about crime and policing in your area. For example, are politicians campaigning on a get-tough-on-crime platform? Write a report on the political situation or an essay giving your point of view.
4. Research the 2005 London bombing. Write a report summarizing what happened and the consequences.

Paraphrasing and summarizing

1. Summarize Coyle's arguments.
2. Paraphrase: "That being that since there is no such thing as immunity, since there is no reliable way of knowing when evil will strike, since mere chance determines who's in harm's way and who's not, the best course of action is an alert business-as-usual, the worst a lapse into paranoia and paralysis."
3. Paraphrase: "As always, fear itself is one of today's bigger hazards. McLellan should take pains not to spread it."

Vocabulary study

Using your dictionary, give the definition of each of the following words and answer the accompanying questions:

1. blather [n.]:
   What is the verb form? What is the connotation (i.e., positive, negative, or neutral)?

2. utter [v.]:
   What is the noun form?
   Identify the correct collocations:
   > utter a word, utter a question, utter a threat, utter a sound, utter a language

3. mayhem:
   What is the part of speech? Write a sentence using this word.

4. wrought:
   This is the past form of what verb?
   The most common use of *wrought* is to describe a certain kind of fence. What is the term for this fence?

5. immune [adj.]:
   What is the noun form?
   What is the verb form?

6. vulnerability [n.]:
   What are the adjective form and its opposite?

7. accessible [adj.]:
   What is the opposite of this adjective?
   Complete this sentence with the verb form (is another word needed after the verb?):
   > He couldn't _____ the files on the hard drive.

   Give the noun form and the preposition to complete this sentence:
   > The tenants also have _____ _____ the laundry room in the basement.

8. rational [adj.]:
   What is the opposite of this adjective?
   What is the verb form (meaning "to make rational")?

9. lapse:
   Lapse can be both a noun and a verb. How is it used in the article? Noun or verb?

10. paranoia [n.]:
    What is the adjective form? How are these words used?

11. paralysis [n.]:
    What is the verb form? Write a sentence using it.

12. surveillance [n.]:
    Choose the correct collocations:
    > surveillance camera, surveillance guard, surveillance survey, surveillance report
    > in surveillance, under surveillance, at surveillance

13. deterrence [n.]:
    What is another noun form?
    What is the verb form?

14. ultimately:
    What is the part of speech?

15. bustling [adj.]:
    What is the verb form? Write a sentence with this verb.
    What is the noun form?

16. marital [adj.]:
    What are the related noun and verb?
    A word close in spelling is *martial*. What does *martial* mean?

17. spat [n.]:
    Give synonyms for this word.

18. avert:
    What is the part of speech?
    What is the noun form? Write a sentence using the noun.

19. gaze [n.]:
    Give synonyms for both the noun and the verb form.
    Use the verb form and any necessary preposition in this sentence:
    > He liked to daydream and _____ _____ his girlfriend across the room.

20. retrospect [n.]:
    Identify the correct collocation:
    > at retrospect, by retrospect, in retrospect, of retrospect

Idioms and expressions

Define these expressions and use them in a sentence:

1. a fool's paradise
2. mere chance
3. in harm's way
4. course of action
5. business as usual
6. run of the mill
7. sell someone short
8. cost–benefit analysis
9. keep something in the right perspective
10. take pains to do something

Structure and technique

1. Note how Coyle distances himself from what McLellan said. He is making it very clear that he does not agree with her. First, he refers to it as "unhelpful blather." Then in the second paragraph, he quotes her words and says both "she says" and "she warns." This repetition is saying, in effect, that he does not share her views.

2. Newspaper articles have headlines rather than titles. They pretty much give the main idea of the piece, but they are usually written in short form—some words are eliminated and short forms are used. Short words are sought out. Restore the headline for this article to a proper sentence. Discuss other possible headlines for the article.

3. Coyle uses many parenthetical dashes. Review the usage on page 115, and discuss the examples in this reading. Can you think of other ways the same function could have been fulfilled?

4. Look at the way Coyle uses the word *perhaps* (and its synonym *maybe*). What effect does the repetition have?

The Strange Forces behind the Richard Hockey Riot

by Sidney Katz

On March 17, 1955, at 9:11 p.m. a tear-gas bomb exploded in the Montreal Forum where 16,000 people had gathered to watch a hockey match between the Montreal Canadiens and the Detroit Red Wings. The acrid yellowish fumes that filled the stadium sent the crowd rushing to the exits, crying, shrieking, coughing and retching. But it did more. It touched off the most destructive and frenzied riot in the history of Canadian sport.

The explosion of the bomb was the last straw in a long series of provocative incidents that swept away the last remnant of the crowd's restraint and decency. Many of the hockey fans had come to the game in an ugly mood. The day before, Clarence Campbell, president of the National Hockey League, had banished Maurice (The Rocket) Richard, the star of the Canadiens and the idol of the Montreal fans, from hockey for the remainder of the season. The suspension couldn't have come at a worse time for the Canadiens. They were leading Detroit by just two points. Richard's award for individual high scoring was at stake, too—he was only two points ahead of his teammate Bernie (Boom-Boom) Geoffrion.

At one time there were as many as 10,000 people packed around the outside of the Forum. For a time it looked as if a lynching might even be attempted: groups of rioters were savagely chanting in unison, "Kill Campbell! Kill Campbell!" The windows of passing streetcars were smashed and, for no apparent reason, cab drivers were hauled from their vehicles and pummelled. The mob smashed hundreds of windows in the Forum by throwing bricks and bottles of beer. They pulled down signs and tore doors off their hinges. They toppled corner newsstands and telephone booths, doused them in oil and left them burning.

When the mob grew weary of the Forum, they moved eastward down Ste-Catherine Street, Montreal's main shopping district. For 15 blocks, they left in their path a swath of destruction. It looked like the aftermath of a wartime blitz in London. Hardly a store was spared. Display windows were smashed and looters carried away everything portable.

The cost of the riot was added up later: an estimated $30,000 worth of damage; 12 policemen and 25 civilians injured; eight police cars and several streetcars, taxis and private automobiles damaged.

But the greatest damage done was not physical. Montrealers awoke ashamed and stunned after their emotional binge. Canadian hockey was given a black name on the front pages of newspapers as far apart as Los Angeles and London, England. "Ice hockey is rough," observed the London News Chronicle, "but it is now a matter of grim record that Canadian players are spring lambs compared to those who support them."

The newspapers and radio were blamed for whipping up public opinion against Campbell before the riot. Frank Hanley, of the Montreal city council, said that Mayor Jean Drapeau must accept at least some of the responsibility. Drapeau, in turn, blamed the riot on Campbell, who "provoked it" by his presence at the game. Frank D. Corbett, a citizen of Westmount, expressed an opinion about the riot which many people thought about but few discussed publicly. In a letter to the editor of a local paper, he said bluntly that the outbreak was symptomatic of racial ill-feeling. "French and English relationships have deteriorated badly over the past 10 years and they have never been worse," he wrote. "The basic unrest is nationalism, which is ever-present in Quebec. Let's face it . . . the French-Canadians want the English expelled from the province."

All of these observations contained some germ of truth, but no single one of them explains satisfactorily what happened in Montreal on St. Patrick's Night.

In the case history of the Richard riot, the night of March 13, four nights before the Montreal outburst, is important. The Montreal Canadiens were playing against the Boston Bruins in Boston. Six minutes before the end of the game, Boston was leading 4–2, playing one man short because of a penalty. In a desperate effort to score, the Canadiens had removed their goalie and sent six men up the ice. Richard was skating across the Boston blue line past Boston defenceman Hal Laycoe when the latter put his stick up and caught Richard on the side of his head. It made a nasty gash which later required five stitches. Frank Udvari, the referee, signalled a penalty to Laycoe.

Richard skated behind the Boston net and had returned to the blue line when the whistle blew. He rubbed his head, then suddenly skated over to Laycoe. Lifting his stick high over his head with both hands Richard pounded Laycoe over the face and shoulders with all his strength. Laycoe dropped his gloves and stick and motioned to Richard to come and fight with his fists.

A linesman, Cliff Thompson, grabbed Richard and took his stick away from him. Richard broke away, picked up a loose stick on the ice and again slashed away at Laycoe, this time breaking the stick on him. Again Thompson got hold of Richard, but again Richard escaped and with another stick slashed at the man who had injured him. Thompson subdued Richard for the third time, forcing him down to the ice. With the help of a teammate, Richard regained his feet and sprang at Thompson, bruising his face and blackening his eye. Thompson finally got Richard under control and sent him to the first-aid room for medical attention.

Richard was penalized for the remainder of the game and fined $100. Laycoe, who suffered body bruises and face wounds, was penalized five minutes for high-sticking and was given a further 10-minute penalty for tossing a blood-stained towel at the referee as he entered the penalty box.

Many observers feel that the Richard riot was merely another example of how lawlessness can spread from players to spectators. Team owners, coaches and trainers have promoted disrespect for law and authority in hockey by their attitude. They complain bitterly when referees apply the rules strictly. In this new brand of hockey which permits rough play and often ignores the rules, the most harassed player in the NHL is Richard. Thirty-four years old, five foot nine, he weighs 180 pounds and is handsome in a sullen kind of way. His intense, penetrating eyes seem to perceive everything in microscopic detail. It's possible that Richard is the greatest hockey player who ever lived. Canadiens were once offered $135,000 for him—the highest value ever placed on a player. Frank Selke, Canadiens managing director, refused, saying, "I'd sooner sell half the Forum."

Opposing teams recognize Richard's talents and use rugged methods to stop him. Sometimes two players are specifically detailed to nettle him. They regularly hang on to him, put hockey sticks between his legs, body-check him and board him harder than necessary. Once he skated 20 feet with two men on his shoulders to score a goal. His opponents also employ psychological warfare to unnerve him. Inspector William Minogue, who, as police officer in charge of the Forum, is regularly at the rink side during games, frequently hears opposing players calling Richard "French pea soup" or "dirty French bastard" as they skate past.

Because of these tactics, Richard frequently explodes. But he is a rarity among men as well as among hockey players. He is an artist. He is completely dedicated to playing good hockey and scoring goals. "It's the most important thing in my life," he told me.

On the night of the Boston fracas, Clarence Campbell was travelling from Montreal to New York by train to attend a meeting of the NHL board of governors where plans for the Stanley Cup playoffs were to be made. In Grand Central station next morning he read about the rumpus in the *New York Times*. Hurrying to his hotel, he phoned referee Frank Udvari and linesmen Sam Babcock and Cliff Thompson to get a verbal report. Disturbed by what he heard, he set a hearing in Montreal to ascertain all the facts and decide on what punishment should be given to the players involved. The time set was two days later—March 16 at 10:30 a.m.

The hearing lasted for three hours. The attacks on Laycoe and Thompson were deliberate and persistent, Campbell found. The room was completely silent as Campbell then pronounced the punishment. "Richard is suspended from playing in the remaining league and playoff games."

No sports decision ever hit the Montreal public with such impact. It seemed to strike at the very heart and soul of the city. A bus driver became so upset by the news that he ignored a flashing railway-level-crossing signal and almost killed his passengers.

There were portents of what was to happen on the night of March 17 in the phone calls received by Campbell. Many of them were taken by Campbell's secretary, Phyllis King. "They were nearly all abusive and they seemed to grow worse as the day wore on," says Miss King. One of the first callers said, "Tell Campbell I'm an undertaker and he'll be needing me in a few days."

The strong racial feelings engendered by the decision should have sounded an ominous warning. One of the letters that Campbell received said, "If Richard's name was Richardson, you would have given a different verdict."

Many prominent people added fuel to the fire. One French weekly published a cartoon of Campbell's head on a platter, dripping blood, with the caption: "This is how we would like to see him."

A few minutes after the Canadien–Detroit game started, Richard slipped into the Forum unnoticed and took a seat near the south end of the rink. He gazed intently at the ice, a look of distress on his face: the Canadiens were playing sloppy hockey. At the 11th minute of the first period, Detroit scored a second goal and the Canadiens saw their hopes of a league championship go up in smoke. It was at this minute that Clarence Campbell entered the arena. He couldn't have chosen a worse time.

As soon as Campbell sat down the crowd recognized him and pandemonium broke loose.

Richard was still asleep when reporters knocked on the door of his home at 8 o'clock. It was answered by his six-year-old son who said, "I hope you didn't come to talk to him about hockey." When the reporters returned later, Richard was attired in a white T-shirt and a pair of slacks. His face was lined with fatigue. "This certainly isn't the time for me to say anything," he said. "It might start something again." By 3 o'clock he changed his mind. He showed up in Frank Selke's office and said that he wanted to make a public statement. At 7 o'clock, seated in front of a battery of microphones, he made the following short speech in French:

"Because I always try so hard to win and had my troubles in Boston, I was suspended. At playoff time it hurts not to be in the game with the boys. However, I want to do what is good for the people of Montreal and the team. So that no further harm will be done, I would like to ask everyone to get behind the team and to help the boys win from the Rangers and Detroit. I will take my punishment and come back next year to help the club and younger players to win the cup."

As he repeated the speech in English, Richard appeared restless and upset. He rubbed his eyes, tugged at his tie and scratched his left ear. His words seemed to have a settling effect on the city. The question of his suspension was laid aside, at least for the time being. Mayor Drapeau and other leaders followed Richard with strong pleas for law and order. There was to be no further violence for the remainder of the season, despite the fact that the Canadiens lost the championship.

(*Maclean's* 17 September 1955; reprinted 10 October 2005)

Notes

Note that "Maurice Richard" is a French name, so his surname is not pronounced the same as the English first name "Richard." Also, note that the spelling of his team's name is with an *e*, the French spelling—Canadiens, not Canadians.

This article was written 50 years ago. Some of the language sounds quaintly old-fashioned today. For example, a sportswriter today would be unlikely to use words such as *rugged* and *nettle* (paragraph 14). The writing style is more formal and more like academic style.

Comprehension

1. What was significant about this riot?
2. Who were the rioters angry at? Why?
3. Why was Maurice Richard suspended?
4. Why was Richard such a great player?
5. How did Richard help defuse the situation?

Timeline

You may find this article difficult to follow because of the shifts in time. Look for transition signals to figure out the sequence. Most paragraphs deal mainly with one time period, but a few span two dates. Fill in this chart with corresponding paragraph numbers. One paragraph can fit more than one category. Some have been done to help you:

	Paragraphs:
13 March 1955	9
16 March 1955	2
17 March 1955	2
18 March 1955	
Unidentified later time	5
Background information/explanation	13

Discussion

1. Why would people be reluctant to talk about racism in regard to the riot? Why are people reluctant to talk about racism in general?
2. Is the author overly sympathetic to Richard? Does he imply that Richard's violent attack was somehow justified, that he was provoked, that it was the straw that broke the camel's back?
3. How is trash talk used in sports today?
4. Why is hockey such a popular sport in Canada? Do Canadians take hockey too seriously?

5. Is hockey too violent? How does it compare to other sports?
6. Do sports fans still get worked up so much that they could run riot in the streets? Why?

Assignments

1. There is an expression in French *plus ça change, plus c'est la même chose,* which means the more things change, the more they remain the same. One reason to read older pieces is to find out the truth of this statement. Obviously, we still have hockey violence, hooliganism, and rioting in the streets. Write an essay comparing something from the Richard story with a recent event, such as soccer hooliganism. Or write a paragraph comparing Richard's attack on Laycoe with similar famous incidents, such as Todd Bertuzzi's sucker punch to Steve Moore in 2004.

2. Write a review of one of the films about Maurice Richard, such as *The Rocket* (2005) or the documentary *Fire and ice: The Rocket Richard riot* (2000).

3. Research athletes' salaries. Find out what $135,000 in 1955 would be worth today. Find out more about free agency and the increase in salaries. Do athletes deserve this much money? Write an essay explaining, criticizing, or defending athlete salaries.

4. Katz says, "Many observers feel that the Richard riot was merely another example of how lawlessness can spread from players to spectators" (paragraph 13). Write an essay explaining crowd behaviour using the Richard hockey riot and other similar events as examples.

5. Choose a current famous NHLer and compare him to Richard in a paragraph.

6. Find another famous public apology and compare it to Richard's.

Paraphrasing and summarizing

1. Summarize what Richard did to get suspended.
2. Summarize the actions that led to the riot.
3. Paraphrase: "Opposing teams recognize Richard's talent and use rugged methods to stop him. Sometimes two players are specifically detailed to nettle him." (paragraph 14)
4. Paraphrase: "The strong racial feelings engendered by the decision should have sounded an ominous warning." (paragraph 20)

Vocabulary study

Use the context to help you choose the correct definition. The paragraph number is given in parentheses.

1. acrid (1) _____   a) beaten with the fists
2. provocative (2) _____   b) cause a particular feeling or situation
3. remnant (2) _____   c) confusion, lots of noise and activity
4. pummelled (3) _____   from people
5. binge (6) _____   d) dressed

6. bluntly (7) _____

7. symptomatic (7) _____

8. subdue (11) _____

9. unnerve (14) _____

10. ascertain (16) _____

11. engender (20) _____

12. ominous (20) _____

13. prominent (21) _____

14. pandemonium (23) _____

15. attired (24) _____

e) harsh, stinging

f) important or well-known

g) intentionally causing anger

h) make not as loud or bright as usual

i) make someone lose confidence

j) make sure

k) period of uncontrolled eating or drinking

l) remaining piece

m) showing signs of an illness or problem

n) suggesting that something bad is going to happen

o) without softening, directly, honestly

Idioms and collocations

Discuss the meaning and write a sentence for each expression (paragraph numbers in parentheses):

1. touch off (1)
2. the last straw (2)
3. swept away (2)
4. at stake (2)
5. in unison (3)
6. a swath of destruction (4)
7. contain a germ of truth (8)
8. be dedicated to something (15)
9. strike at the very heart and soul of something (18)
10. go up in smoke (22)

Structure and technique

1. Katz starts the article with the thick of the riot to give a dramatic opening to his article. He then has to go back to explain what led up to the riot. You can also see this done in movies and TV shows. Look at the cues Katz gives to help readers follow the time sequence. Are there paragraphs that could be better marked for time? Discuss.

2. Notice the journalistic style of giving the person's full name the first time he or she is mentioned and then just using a surname to refer to the person. What different techniques and grammatical structures are used to give additional information about the person?

3. Look at the use of quotation in this article, including the punctuation. What does the ellipsis (the . . .) mean in paragraph 7?

Appearance: Its Social Meaning

by Lorne Tepperman

In his classic sociological work *Asylums*, Erving Goffman (1958) notes that the first step taken by a total institution, such as a prison or mental hospital is to re-socialize an inmate, by separating the inmate from old identities and identifiers. Interestingly, this process begins by changing the inmate's appearance—for example, by forcing the inmate to wear an institutional uniform, while removing all individual identifiers such as jewellery or personal assets. Often the inmate is forced to wear a generic hairstyle, which is another way of regimenting the body and eliminating individuality. The loss of one's own clothing signifies the loss of an old identity and social status. The adoption of an institutional uniform represents entry into a low-status community of identical inmates or subjects. In this real sense, the old maxim is true that "clothes make the man" (or woman). Humble clothes make humble people.

Consider the humble uniforms worn by members of the Salvation Army—a religious organization devoted to urban good works, originally involving the moral uplift of fallen people. Winston (2003) notes that the popular image of Salvation Army women changed during the period 1880–1918, due in part to their adoption of plain, unfashionable clothing, which enabled them to enter public places such as saloons to do their work without criticism. So dressed, Salvation Army women practised spiritual warfare on establishments that promoted sin and vice. Their uniform, dramatically severe, came to represent traditional service and old-fashioned virtue.

The connection between appearance, clothing, and self has been known and commented on for a long time. The nineteenth-century Scottish novelist and essayist Thomas Carlyle wrote about clothing metaphorically in his comic work *Sartor Resartus*. There he used clothing to stand in for all symbols of self. People use clothing and other items related to their appearance to construct, confirm, and modify their personal identities within the context of their daily lives. However, personal identities are linked to social identities. Clothes define our place, role, and position in the social order. Carlyle believed that "clothes present us to ourselves and to the world" as we negotiate our freedom of dressed self-expression.

In turn, society affects both what we reveal and conceal of our bodies (Keenan, 2001). Social pressures constantly undermine our realm of choice and reduce the basic right of self-expression. As a result, clothes never reveal the whole self, since they may be imposed on us or we may use clothes to conceal ourselves. However, given some modicum of choice in how we dress, the choices we make tell the world who we think we are, and who we want to be.

Not surprisingly, appearance norms are gendered—like many other social norms. Not only are men and women judged by different appearance standards; they also wear different kinds of clothing, connoting their different social roles and statuses. Take pockets: historically, pockets on women's clothing have been smaller and fewer than pockets on men's clothing. For women, pockets have been decorative, for men practical. Even today, men and women use their pockets differently (that's why women carry purses), and pockets play a part in the construction of gender.

Underwear is also gendered, though usually unseen except by their wearers and intimate acquaintances. Men's underwear tends to be sturdy and plain. Women's underwear tends to be flimsy and decorative, as though it was on display as part of the mating game. When middle-class women began to wear underpants in the early 1800s, their "drawers" were feminized by fabric, ornamentation, and an open crotch (Fields, 2002). Such open drawers on respectable, supposedly passionless women presented female sexuality as both erotic and modest. In the twentieth century, however, women demanded crotches in their drawers, to establish their sexual propriety. Women increasingly chose to wear closed drawers during a period of women's greater public presence and feminist activism. This change symbolically closed the gap between men and women.

Even today, the type of underwear known as "lingerie" is particularly invested with meanings of femininity, sexuality, and pleasure (Storr, 2002). Mass-market lingerie, sex toys, and other "personal" products are sold to women through the use of particular strategies and images. The processes of choosing and buying lingerie involve identifications of gender, sexuality, and sensuality, even though the garments themselves are rarely if ever worn in public. Moreover, they hold implications of class (and classiness). The class connotations of mass-market lingerie are used by working- and lower-middle-class women to distinguish themselves from higher-class women who are thereby defined as pretentious, boring, or tasteless.

Fashions, then, declare a person's gender and class, and they also declare ethnic origins. In multi-cultural urban areas, women's fashion choices are closely tied to issues of self-definition. For example, young Asian and white women living in urban, "multi-cultural" areas in the United Kingdom express their differently sexualized and racialized female identities through styles of appearance and tastes in clothing, hairstyles, and cosmetics (Malson, Marshall, and Woollett, 2002). In doing so, they are making statements about who they are and how they differ from conventional United Kingdom style and culture.

As we saw with degradation ceremonies in total institutions, when people in authority want to control people, they try to control their modes of dress. This has been evident in the history of fashion in fascist countries, and it is true of dress codes for schoolchildren in our own society. Paulicelli (2002) notes that Italy under the fascist dictator Mussolini used fashion to discipline the social body—especially women's bodies—and to create an identifiable national style. The issue of school uniforms in our society—a practice of imposing dress codes to regiment people's self-expression—brings up a variety of issues that include safety, egalitarianism, social inclusion, and marketing that encourages students to dress competitively (Bodine, 2003).

Left on their own, and unless required to wear uniforms, young people develop clothing aspirations very early in life. Even before adolescence, at ages 8 to 12, children begin making product decisions and building knowledge about different products and brands (Meyer and Anderson, 2000). A desire to conform to appearance norms influences their shopping behaviour, especially with regard to clothing purchase criteria and shopping independence. As preadolescents age, they acquire more of the norms and information needed to make informed clothing decisions. Conformity concerns influence how children shop, whom they shop with, and what they purchase.

Clothing is an expression of both individual and collective identity even among 10 to 11 year olds (Swain, 2002). Relaxing the enforcement of school appearance norms (i.e., a dress code) allows pupils to use clothing to gain recognition, forge common bonds, and share interests within peer group cultures. It also, however, serves to distinguish and separate those who fit in with social expectations of dressing in popular fashions, and those who do not. Certain items and brand names—for example, Doc Martens—acquire a specific, symbolic value for purposes of conformity or rebellion. Pupils who conform to the school dress rules may satisfy the formal requirements of their institution but run a high risk of being stigmatized and excluded by their peers.

Our tendency to conform to appearance norms, learned from childhood onward, largely continues throughout life. This results in a widespread interest in "fashion."

References

Bodine, Ann. 2003. "School Uniforms and Discourses on Childhood," *Childhood*, 10 (1):43–63.

Fields, Jill. 2002. "Erotic Modesty: (Ad)dressing Female Sexuality and Propriety in Open and Closed Drawers, USA, 1800–1930," Gender & History, 14 (3):492–515.

Goffman, Irving. 1961. *Asylums: Essays on the Social Situation of Mental Patients and Other Inmates*. Garden City, NY: Doubleday Anchor.

Keenan, William J.R., ed. 2001. *Dressed to Impress: Looking the Part*. Oxford: Berg.

Malson, Helen, Hariette Marshall, and Anne Woollett. 2002. "Talking of Taste: A Discourse Analytic Exploration of Young Women's Gendered and Racialized Subjectivities in British Urban, Multicultural Contexts," *Feminism & Psychology*, 12 (4): 469–90.

Meyer, Deborah J.C., and Heather C. Anderson. 2000. "Preadolescents and Apparel Purchasing: Conformity to Parents and Peers in the Consumer Socialization Process," *Journal of Social Behaviour and Personality*, 15 (2): 243–57.

Paulicelli, Eugenia. 2002. "Fashion, the Politics of Style and National Identity in Pre-Fascist and Fascist Italy," *Gender & History*, 14 (3): 537–59.

Storr, Merl. 2002. "Classy Lingerie," *Feminist Review*, 71: 18–36.

Swain, Jon. 2002. "The Right Stuff: Fashioning and Identity through Clothing in a Junior School," *Gender and Education*, 14 (1): 53–69.

Winston, Diane. 2002. "Living in the Material World: The Changing Role of Salvation Army Women, 1880–1918," *Journal of Urban History*, 28 (4): 466–87.

from *Deviance, crime, and control: Beyond the straight and narrow*

Notes

This is an excerpt from a sociology textbook. Note the academic style of language and the use of references. The referencing is done according to APA style, the one commonly used in the sciences and social sciences. After each quote or reference to another author's work, Tepperman cites the work by giving the name of the author and the year of the work in round brackets. These references point the reader to the full information in the references section at the end of the book. This information allows readers to find the original article or book and read it for themselves.

The term "total institution" is used by Goffman to denote a place where people live in a group cut off from the regular society.

Comprehension

Choose the best answer according to what is directly said in the reading:

1. Which method of re-socializing inmates is not mentioned?
   a) wearing uniforms
   b) having common haircuts
   c) tattooing ID numbers on forearms
   d) removing jewellery
2. The Salvation Army had its female members change clothing in order to:
   a) look like poor people.
   b) show that they were different from authoritarian figures like the police.
   c) protect them from being beaten by those they wish to help.
   d) be able to enter bars and brothels and do their good works.
3. According to Thomas Carlyle, appearance and clothing are important because:
   a) they reveal personal identity and social status.
   b) they keep people happy.
   c) they played an important role in the novel he wrote.
   d) people want to attract the opposite sex.

4. What does social pressure do?
   a) It makes us reveal our whole self.
   b) It limits our choice of clothing.
   c) It makes us choose unflattering clothes.
   d) It restricts our modicum.
5. Pockets on women's clothes:
   a) don't show social norms.
   b) are mainly ornamental.
   c) are a substitute for a purse.
   d) serve a practical purpose.
6. How did closed drawers reduce the gap between men and women?
   a) It let them both show their underwear.
   b) It made lingerie more erotic.
   c) The underwear made women seem less like sex objects.
   d) The underwear wasn't worn in the 1800s.
7. According to the reading passage, which statement is correct?
   a) Mussolini started Italian high fashion.
   b) Dress codes in schools tend to liberate rather than to restrict.
   c) Controlling dress is one way of controlling people.
   d) Regimenting people's self-expression is not a good way to run a society.
8. When young people choose their clothing:
   a) they have no fashion sense at all.
   b) they would prefer to wear school uniforms.
   c) they are not concerned with conformity.
   d) they try to follow the fashion for their group.
9. Students who follow the school dress code:
   a) may be unpopular.
   b) are rebelling against the norms of their society.
   c) become mature faster.
   d) cannot afford designer clothes and expensive brand names.
10. The main idea of this reading selection is:
    a) clothing can be racially motivated.
    b) underwear is sexy.
    c) conformity in appearance is important.
    d) fashion is based on illogical conclusions.

Discussion

1. What does Tepperman mean when he says, "clothes never reveal the whole self, since they may be imposed on us or we may use clothes to conceal ourselves"? Give examples.
2. What was the dress code in your high school? Do you think it was fair? Should there be dress codes?
3. How important are designer labels in your clothing?

4. Consider different forms of self-expression through appearance: hair-styles, make-up, jewellery, tattoos, and piercings. Discuss these elements and specific styles such as goth, punk, jock, and prep. What and how is the image portrayed?

5. Clothing for babies and toddlers has become more gendered. It used to be possible to dress a small child in plain T-shirts and sweatshirts that would suit either gender. Today, however, baby clothing is either feminine (pink and frilly) or masculine (decorated with pictures of trucks and racing cars). Why has the clothing industry moved in this direction? What does this say about our society?

6. Although traditionally underwear is supposed to remain hidden, recent fashions have exposed underwear. For instance, young men have the top of their boxer shorts showing at the top of their low-slung pants. Young women wear lacy camisoles that can be seen under jackets and show bra straps along with the thin straps of tank tops. What does this trend say about society and fashion?

Assignments

1. Write a paragraph arguing that men should use purses (or that women should use pockets).
2. Research the use of uniforms by the Salvation Army and write a brief report.
3. Write an essay for or against school uniforms.
4. Tepperman says, "when people in authority want to control people, they try to control their modes of dress." In an essay, discuss one example of clothing used in this way. For example, you can discuss the burqa in Afghanistan or the Mao suit in China.
5. Choose an item of clothing that has significance in a religion. Discuss this significance and any controversy. For example, you can explore the wearing of head coverings such as the turban, the yarmulke, or the hijab. You could discuss nuns' habits or monks' robes. Instead of clothing, you could discuss the way the hair is worn, such as the long hair that is part of Sikhism.

Paraphrasing and summarizing

1. Paraphrase: "A desire to conform to appearance norms influences their shopping behaviour, especially with regard to clothing purchase criteria and shopping independence. As preadolescents age, they acquire more of the norms and information needed to make informed clothing decisions. Conformity concerns influence how children shop, whom they shop with, and what they purchase." (paragraph 10)
2. Paraphrase: "Certain items and brand names—for example, Doc Martens—acquire a specific, symbolic value for purposes of conformity or rebellion. Pupils who conform to the school dress rules may

satisfy the formal requirements of their institution but run a high risk of being stigmatized and excluded by their peers." (paragraph 11)

3. Read paragraph 3 carefully and reword the ending: "as we negotiate our freedom of dressed self-expression."

4. Summarize this article in no more than 120 words.

Vocabulary study

1. What kind of places can you call an institution? What does the verb *institute* mean? What is the verb that means "to put someone in an institution"?

2. The nouns *identity*, *identifier*, and *identification* and the adjectives *identical* and *identifiable* are all related to the verb *identify*. What are the differences in meaning?

3. The word *generic* is often used to talk about product names. What is the opposite of a generic name?

4. From the reading passage, find 10 adjectives ending in *–al* (a common adjective ending). Give the related adverbs, nouns, and verbs. For example, related to the adjective *individual* are the adverb *individually*, the noun *individuality*, and the verb *individualize*. Explain any meaning differences. Look for common patterns in your completed list, such as the *–ity* ending in nouns.

5. What are the verb and noun related to the adjective *humble*?

6. In the second paragraph, find two words that mean the opposite of each other and start with the same letter.

7. Use a dictionary to find the different meanings of *drawer* and *drawers*.

8. Use a dictionary to find the pronunciation and origin of *lingerie*.

9. What word does *pretentious* look like? What do you think it means? Look at the context (the last sentence of paragraph 7). What clues does the sentence give you? Check the dictionary definition to see if your guess is correct.

10. The suffix *–ism* denotes a belief in something (*racism, feminism, capitalism*), and the *–ist* ending is the person who believes in that "ism" (*racist, feminist, capitalist*). Paragraph 9 contains the word *egalitarianism*. Use the context to help you figure out the meaning. A knowledge of French can also help you. Check the meaning in the dictionary.

Structure and technique

1. In the first paragraph, the author uses a singular form—"the inmate"—but avoids the sticky he/she pronoun problem. What techniques does he use to do this?

2. Unlike the short paragraphs used in journalistic style, this reading has longer, developed paragraphs. Using the topic sentences, identify the main idea of each paragraph.

3. Which words are italicized in the text? Why?

Fiction Readings

Why My Mother Can't Speak English

by Garry Engkent

My mother is 70 years old. Widowed for five years now, she lives alone in her own house except for the occasions when I come home to tidy her household affairs. She has been in *gum san* for the past 30 years. She clings to the old-country ways so much so that today she astonishes me with this announcement:

"I want to get my citizenship," she says as she slaps down the *Dai Pao*, "before they come and take away my house."

"Nobody's going to do that. This is Canada."

"So everyone says," she retorts, "but did you read what the *Dai Pao* said? Ah, you can't read Chinese. The government is cutting back on old age pensions. Anybody who hasn't got citizenship will lose everything. Or worse."

"The *Dai Pao* can't even typeset accurately," I tell her. Sometimes I worry about the information Mother receives from that bi-weekly community newspaper. "Don't worry—the Ministry of Immigration won't send you back to China."

"Little you know," she snaps back. "I am old, helpless, and without citizenship. Reasons enough. Now get me citizenship. Hurry!"

"Mother, getting citizenship papers is not like going to the bank to cash in your pension cheque. First, you have to—"

"Excuses, my son, excuses. When your father was alive—"

"Oh, Mother, not again! You throw that at me every—"

"—made excuses, too." Her jaw tightens. "If you can't do this little thing for your own mother, well, I will just have to go and beg your cousin to . . ."

Every time I try to explain about the ways of the *fan gwei* she thinks I do not want to help her.

"I'll do it, okay? Just give me some time."

"That's easy for you," Mother snorts. "You're not 70 years old. You're not going to lose your pension. You're not going to lose your house. Now, how much *lai-shi* will this take?"

After all these years in *gum san* she cannot understand that you don't give government officials *lai-shi*, the traditional Chinese money-gift given to persons who do things for you.

"That won't be necessary," I tell her. "And you needn't go to my cousin."

Mother picks up the *Dai Pao* again and says: "Why should I beg at the door of a village cousin when I have a son who is a university graduate?"

I wish my father were alive. Then he would be doing this. But he is not here, and as a dutiful son, I am responsible for the welfare of my widowed mother. So I take her to the Citizenship Court.

There are several people from the Chinese community waiting there. Mother knows a few of the Chinese women and she chats with them. My cousin is there, too.

"I thought your mother already got her citizenship," he says to me. "Didn't your father—"

"No, he didn't."

He shakes his head sadly. "Still, better now than never. That's why I'm getting these people through."

"So they've been reading the *Dai Pao*."

He gives me a quizzical look, so I explain to him, and he laughs.

"You are the new generation," he says. "You didn't live long enough in *hon san*, the sweet land, to understand the fears of the old. You can't expect the elderly to renounce all attachments to China for the ways of the *fan gwei*, white devils. How old is she, 70 now? Much harder."

"She woke me up this morning at six and Citizenship Court doesn't open until ten."

The doors of the Court finally open, and Mother motions me to hurry. We wait in line for a while.

The clerk distributes applications and tells me the requirements. Mother wants to know what the clerk is saying so half the time I translate for her.

The clerk suggests that we see one of the liaison officers.

"Your mother has been living in Canada for the past 30 years and she still can't speak English?"

"It happens," I tell the liaison officer.

"I find it hard to believe that—not one word?"

"Well, she understands some restaurant English," I tell her. "You know, French fries, pork chops, soup, and so on. And she can say a few words."

"But will she be able to understand the judge's questions? The interview with the judge, as you know, is a very important part of the citizenship procedure. Can she read the booklet? What does she know about Canada?"

"So you don't think my mother has a chance?"

"The requirements are that the candidate must be able to speak either French or English, the two official languages of Canada. The candidate must be able to pass an oral interview with the citizenship judge, and then he or she must be able to recite the oath of allegiance—"

"My mother needs to speak English," I conclude for her.

"Look, I don't mean to be rude, but why didn't your mother learn English when she first came over?"

I have not been translating this conversation, and Mother, annoyed and agitated, asks me what is going on. I tell her there is a slight problem.

"What problem?" mother opens her purse, and I see her taking a small red envelope—*lai-shi*—I quickly cover her hand.

"What is going on?" the liaison officer demands.

"Nothing," I say hurriedly. "Just a cultural misunderstanding, I assure you."

My mother rattles off some indignant words and I snap back in Chinese: "Put that away! The woman won't understand, and we'll be in a lot of trouble."

The officer looks confused and I realize an explanation is needed.

"My mother was about to give you a money-gift as a token of appreciation for what you are doing for us. I was afraid you might misconstrue it as a bribe. We have no intention of doing that."

"I'm relieved to hear that."

We conclude the interview, and I take Mother home. Still clutching the application, Mother scowls at me.

"I didn't get my citizenship papers. Now I will lose my old age pension. The government will ship me back to China. My old bones will lie there while your father's will be here. What will happen to me?"

How can I teach her to speak the language when she is too old to learn, too old to want to learn? She resists anything that is *fan gwei*. She does everything the Chinese way. Mother spends much time staring blankly at the four walls of her house. She does not cry. She sighs and shakes her head. Sometimes she goes about the house touching her favourite things.

"This is all your dead father's fault," she says quietly. She turns to the photograph of my father on the mantle. Daily, she burns incense, pours fresh cups of fragrant tea, and spreads dishes of his favourite fruits in front of the framed picture as is the custom. In memory of his passing, she treks two miles to the cemetery to place flowers by his headstone, to burn ceremonial paper money, and to talk to him. Regularly, rain or shine, or even snow, she does these things. Such love, such devotion, now such vehemence. Mother curses my father, her husband, in his grave.

When my mother and I emigrated from China, she was 40 years old, and I, five. My father was already a well-established restaurant owner. He put me in school and Mother in the restaurant kitchen, washing dishes and cooking strange foods like hot dogs, hamburgers, and French fries. She worked seven days a week from six in the morning until eleven at night. This lasted for 25 years, almost to the day of my father's death.

The years were hard on her. The black-and-white photographs show a robust woman; now I see a withered, frail, white-haired old woman, angry, frustrated with the years, and scared of losing what little material wealth she has to show for the toil in *gum san*, the golden mountain.

"I begged him," Mother says. "But he would either ignore my pleas or say: 'What do you need to know English for? You're better off here in the kitchen. Here you can talk to the others in our own tongue. English is far too complicated for you. How old are you now? Too old to learn a new language. Let the young speak *fan gwei*. All you need is to understand the orders from the waitresses. Anyway, if you need to know something, the men will translate for you. I am here; I can do your talking for you.'"

As a conscientious boss of the young male immigrants, my father would force them out of the kitchen and into the dining room. "The kitchen is no place for you to learn English. All you do is speak Chinese in here. To survive in gum san, you have to speak English, and the only way you can do that is to wait on tables and force yourselves to speak English with the customers. How can you get your families over here if you can't talk to the Immigration officers in English?"

A few of the husbands who had the good fortune to bring their wives over to Canada hired a retired school teacher to teach a bit of English to their wives. Father discouraged Mother from going to those once-a-week sessions.

"That old woman will get rich, doing nothing. What have these women learned? *Fan gwei* ways—make-up, lipstick, smelly perfumes, fancy clothes —like whores. Once she gets through with them, they won't be Chinese women any more—and they certainly won't be white, either."

Some of the husbands heeded the words of the boss, for he was older than they, and had been in the white devils' land longer. These wives stayed at home and tended the children, or they worked in the restaurant kitchen, washing dishes and cooking *fan gwei* foods, and talking in Chinese about the land and the life they were forced to leave behind.

"He was afraid that I would leave him. I depended on him for everything. I could not go anywhere by myself. He drove me to work and he drove me home. He only taught me to print my name so that I could sign anything he wanted me to, bank cheques, legal documents . . ."

Perhaps I am not Chinese enough any more to understand why my mother would want to take in the sorrow, the pain, and the anguish and then to recount them every so often.

Once I was presumptuous enough to ask her why she would want to remember in such detail. She said the memories didn't hurt any more. I did not tell her that her reminiscences cut me to the quick. Her only solace now is to be listened to.

My father wanted more sons, but she was too old to give him more. One son was not enough security he needed for old age. "You smell of stale perfume," she would say to him after he had driven the waitresses home. Or, to me, she would say: "A second mother will not treat you so well, you know," and, "Would you like another mother at home?" Even at that tender age, I knew that in China a husband could take a second wife. I told her that I didn't need another mother, and she would nod her head.

When my father died five years ago, she cried and cried. "Don't leave me in this world. Let me die with you."

Grief-stricken, she would not eat for days. She was so weak from hunger that I feared she wouldn't be able to attend the funeral. At his grave side, she chanted over and over a dirge, commending his spirit to the next world and begging the goddess of mercy to be kind to him. By custom, she set his picture on the mantel and burned incense in front of it daily. And we would go to the cemetery often. There she would arrange fresh flowers and talk to him in the gentlest way.

Often she would warn me: "The world of the golden mountain is so strange, *fan gwei* improprieties, and customs. The white devils will have you abandon your own aged mother to some old age home to rot away and die unmourned. If you are here long enough, they will turn your head until you don't know who you are, what you are—Chinese."

My mother would convert the months and the days into the Chinese lunar calendar. She would tell me about the seasons and the harvests and festivals in China. We did not celebrate any *fan gwei* holidays.

My mother sits here at the table, fingering the booklet from the Citizenship Court. For thirty-some years, my mother did not learn the English language, not because she was not smart enough, not because she was too old to learn, and not because my father forbade her, but because she feared that learning English would change her Chinese soul. She only learned enough English to survive in the restaurant kitchen.

Now, Mother wants *gum san* citizenship.

"Is there no hope that I will be given it?" she asks.

"There is always a chance," I tell her. "I'll hand in the application."

"I should have given that person the *lai-shi*," Mother says obstinately.

"Maybe I should teach you some English," I retort. "You have about six months before the oral interview."

"I am 70 years old," she says. "*Lai-shi* is definitely much easier."

My brief glimpse into mother's heart is over, and it has taken so long to come about. I do not know whether I understand my aged mother any better now. Despite my mother's constant instruction, there is too much *fan gwei* in me.

The booklet from the Citizenship Court lies, unmoved, on the table, gathering dust for weeks. She has not mentioned citizenship again with the urgency of that particular time. Once in a while, she would say: "They have forgotten me. I told you they don't want old Chinese women as citizens."

Finally, her interview date is set. I try to teach her some ready made phrases, but she forgets them.

"You should not sigh so much. It is bad for your health," Mother observes.

On the day of her examination, I accompany her into the judge's chamber. I am more nervous than my mother.

Staring at the judge, my mother remarks: "*Noi yren.*" The judge shows interest in what my mother says, and I translate it: "She says you're a woman."

The judge smiles "Yes. Is that strange?"

"If she is going to examine me," Mother tells me, "I might as well start packing for China. Sell my house. Dig up your father's bones, I'll take them back with me."

Without knowing what my mother said, the judge reassures her. "This is just a formality. Really. We know that you obviously want to be part of our Canadian society. Why else would you have gone through all this trouble? We want to welcome you as a new citizen, no matter what race, nationality, religion or age. And we want you to be proud—as a new Canadian."

Six weeks have passed since the interview with the judge. Mother receives a registered letter telling her to come in three weeks time to take part in the oath of allegiance ceremony.

With patient help from the same judge, my mother recites the oath and becomes a Canadian citizen after 30 years in *gum san*.

"How does it feel to be Canadian?" I ask.

"In China, this is the eighth month, the season of harvest." Then she adds: "The *Dai Pao* says that old age pension cheques will be increased by nine dollars next month."

As we walk home on this bright autumn morning, my mother clutches her piece of paper. Citizenship. She says she will go up to the cemetery and talk to my father this afternoon. She has something to tell him.

1985

Notes

This story is autobiographical fiction. It is based on true events, but these events have been dramatized in the story-telling.

Second-generation immigrants are those born or raised in Canada, like the son in the story. Many have a first language that is different from their mother tongue. (*Mother tongue* refers to the language first learned and still understood, usually their parents' native language. *First language* means the language the person is most comfortable speaking.) Most second-generation immigrants become very comfortable in English or French, especially as they progress through their schooling in that language. They do not develop their ability to speak their mother tongue in the same way. For example, they might be able to talk about history and do math in English but only talk about household concerns in their native language. A common situation is that the immigrant parents speak the mother tongue to their children, but the children answer back in English or French. In this story, the son cannot read Chinese but does speak to his mother in Chinese.

Unlike other ethnic groups, the Chinese were not encouraged to establish families in Canada. While the men were welcome as workers, Canadian immigration policies such as the Head Tax (1885–1923) and the Chinese Exclusion Act (1923–1947) prevented them from bringing over family members. This is why the father in the story was in Canada before his wife and son.

Comprehension

1. Why does the mother want to get her citizenship?
2. Describe the process by which the mother gained her citizenship.
3. Why did the mother want to use *lai-shi*? Why did the son not want to do that?
4. What is the father's attitude towards immigrants learning English? What is the double standard he has?
5. What reasons contribute to the mother's not learning English? What is the most important reason she does not learn?
6. Explain the author's reference to the mother's "Chinese soul."
7. What is ironic about the last bit of dialogue in the story—the last exchange between the mother and son?
8. How does the writer make the story humorous?

Discussion

1. How realistic is the portrayal of the mother? Do you know any immigrants like her?
2. Are the mother's fears justified? Why or why not?
3. What is the most important factor in learning a second language? Could the mother have overcome her age and her husband's disapproval had she really wanted to?
4. What are some of the problems faced by immigrant women learning English?
5. What kind of conflicts are common between first and second-generation immigrants?
6. Discuss the immigration and citizenship procedures in Canada. Use examples of the experience of friends, family, or yourself.

Assignments

1. What factors determine how well an immigrant assimilates? Explain these factors in an essay.
2. What factors determine how much a second-generation immigrant will keep his or her mother tongue? Explain these factors in an essay.
3. Research the history of the Chinese in Canada or of another immigrant group. Write a report on the factors that played a part in their settlement. Or write an essay comparing two immigrant groups.
4. Write an essay explaining the process of becoming a Canadian citizen.
5. Take a stand on one of the controversial issues concerning Canadian immigration, and write an essay supporting your position. For example,

what kind of immigrants should Canada seek? Should there be amnesty for illegal immigrants?

Paraphrasing and summarizing

1. Paraphrase: "Perhaps I am not Chinese enough any more to understand why my mother would want to take in the sorrow, the pain, and the anguish and then to recount them every so often."
2. Paraphrase: "Once I was presumptuous enough to ask her why she would want to remember in such detail. She said the memories didn't hurt any more. I did not tell her that her reminiscences cut me to the quick. Her only solace now is to be listened to."
3. Paraphrase: "She turns to the photograph of my father on the mantle. Daily, she burns incense, pours fresh cups of fragrant tea, and spreads dishes of his favourite fruits in front of the framed picture as is the custom. In memory of his passing, she treks two miles to the cemetery to place flowers by his headstone, to burn ceremonial paper money, and to talk to him. Regularly, rain or shine, or even snow, she does these things."
4. Write a 200-word summary of the story.

Vocabulary study

Use the context to match the meaning with these words (paragraph placement is given in brackets):

1. astonish (1) _____
2. welfare (17) _____
3. quizzical (23) _____
4. agitated (38) _____
5. misconstrue (44) _____
6. clutch (46) _____
7. trek (49) _____
8. vehemence (49) _____
9. robust (51) _____
10. conscientious (53) _____
11. heed (56) _____
12. anguish (58) _____
13. presumptuous (59) _____
14. reminiscences (59) _____
15. solace (59) _____
16. dirge (62) _____
17. improprieties (63) _____
18. obstinately (69) _____
19. retort (70) _____
20. glimpse (72) _____

a) answer back angrily
b) anxious, nervous
c) attend to, take notice of, follow
d) behaviour that is morally wrong
e) emotional comfort
f) funeral chant
g) hold tight
h) memories
i) misunderstand
j) questioning
k) severe misery or mental suffering
l) showing strong feelings, usually anger
m) small look
n) state of health and happiness
o) strong and healthy
p) stubbornly
q) surprise
r) take a long walk
s) taking care to do a good job
t) too confident of one's position, showing lack of respect

Idioms and collocations

Explain the meaning of the following expressions:

1. cut back on (4)
2. renounce attachments (24)
3. have a chance (34)
4. rattle off (42)
5. ignore pleas (52)
6. to be better off (52)
7. cut me to the quick (59)
8. grief-stricken (62)
9. recite an oath (82)

Structure and technique
First person, unnamed narrator

This story is told in first person narration: *I*. The narrator's name is not given. Note that this story is fiction, so the *I* is a character, and you cannot refer to him as "Garry Engkent." Instead, you can call him "the son" or "the narrator."

In first person narration, the *I* tells the story from the *I* perspective, not from a general one. The reader gets only the narrator's way of seeing or interpreting an action and must trust that what the narrator says is valid and true. Often, the reader identifies with the narrator.

Present tense narration

Although most stories are told in the simple past tense, the use of the present tense brings a sense of immediacy. The reader follows the story-telling at the same time that the narrator says anything. The present tense creates the illusion that everything is happening right at that moment.

Dialogue

Notice that much of this story is told in dialogue. Look at the punctuation used and the wording that sets up the speech. When a new speaker begins, there is a new paragraph.

Use of foreign words

Words from a foreign language that are not a standard part of English are generally printed in italics. Engkent uses words in Chinese to add flavour to the story. The author knows that his audience will not know what these words mean; even Chinese-speaking readers would be unlikely to know this particular dialect. Therefore, he gives the readers many clues to help them figure out the meaning.

The most common technique is to put the translation in apposition. This means it is set off by commas. For example, in "for the toil in *gum san*, the golden mountain", Engkent shows that the translation of *gum san* is "golden mountain," which is the way the Chinese referred to Canada and the United States. (The term reflects the fact that the first Chinese came to North America as part of the gold rush.)

Context is also important for understanding the meaning of the words. Note how the meaning of *Dai Pao* gradually becomes clearer, as something the mother slaps down and reads. Look at all the Chinese words in the text and find the clues the author gives you. Figure out what each word means. Sometimes the translation or definition does not come with the first use of the word in the story.

The Open Window

by Saki (H.H. Munro)

"My aunt will be down presently, Mr. Nuttel," said a very self-possessed young lady of fifteen; "in the meantime you must try and put up with me."

Framton Nuttel endeavored to say the correct something which should duly flatter the niece of the moment without unduly discounting the aunt that was to come. Privately he doubted more than ever whether these formal visits on a succession of total strangers would do much towards helping the nerve cure which he was supposed to be undergoing.

"I know how it will be," his sister had said when he was preparing to migrate to this rural retreat; "you will bury yourself down there and not speak to a living soul, and your nerves will be worse than ever from moping. I shall just give you letters of introduction to all the people I know there. Some of them, as far as I can remember, were quite nice."

Framton wondered whether Mrs. Sappleton, the lady to whom he was presenting one of the letters of introduction, came into the nice division.

"Do you know many of the people round here?" asked the niece, when she judged that they had had sufficient silent communion.

"Hardly a soul," said Framton. "My sister was staying here, at the rectory, you know, some four years ago, and she gave me letters of introduction to some of the people here."

He made the last statement in a tone of distinct regret.

"Then you know practically nothing about my aunt?" pursued the self-possessed young lady.

"Only her name and address," admitted the caller. He was wondering whether Mrs. Sappleton was in the married or widowed state. An undefinable something about the room seemed to suggest masculine habitation.

"Her great tragedy happened just three years ago," said the child; "that would be since your sister's time."

"Her tragedy?" asked Framton; somehow in this restful country spot tragedies seemed out of place.

"You may wonder why we keep that window wide open on an October afternoon," said the niece, indicating a large French window that opened on to a lawn.

"It is quite warm for the time of the year," said Framton, "but has that window got anything to do with the tragedy?"

"Out through that window, three years ago to a day, her husband and her two young brothers went off for their day's shooting. They never came back. In crossing the moor to their favorite snipe-shooting ground they were all three engulfed in a treacherous piece of bog. It had been that dreadful wet summer, you know, and places that were safe in other years gave way suddenly without warning. Their bodies were never recovered. That was the dreadful part of it." Here the child's voice lost its self-possessed note and became falteringly human. "Poor aunt always thinks that they will come back some day, they and the little brown spaniel that was lost with them, and walk in at that window just as they used to do. That is why the window is kept open every evening till it is quite dusk. Poor dear aunt, she has often told me how they went out, her husband with his white waterproof coat over his arm, and Ronnie, her youngest brother, singing 'Bertie, why do you bound?' as he always did to tease her, because she said it got on her nerves. Do you know, sometimes on still, quiet evenings like this, I almost get a creepy feeling that they will all walk in through that window—"

She broke off with a little shudder. It was a relief to Framton when the aunt bustled into the room with a whirl of apologies for being late in making her appearance.

"I hope Vera has been amusing you?" she said.

"She has been very interesting," said Framton.

"I hope you don't mind the open window," said Mrs. Sappleton briskly; "my husband and brothers will be home directly from shooting, and they always come in this way. They've been out for snipe in the marshes today, so they'll make a fine mess over my poor carpets. So like you menfolk, isn't it?"

She rattled on cheerfully about the shooting and the scarcity of birds, and the prospects for duck in the winter. To Framton it was all purely horrible. He made a desperate but only partially successful effort to turn the talk on to a less ghastly topic, he was conscious that his hostess was giving him only a fragment of her attention, and her eyes were constantly straying past him to the open window and the lawn beyond. It was certainly an unfortunate coincidence that he should have paid his visit on this tragic anniversary.

"The doctors agree in ordering me complete rest, an absence of mental excitement, and avoidance of anything in the nature of violent physical exercise," announced Framton, who labored under the tolerably wide-spread delusion that total strangers and chance acquaintances are hungry for the least detail of one's ailments and infirmities, their cause and cure. "On the matter of diet they are not so much in agreement," he continued.

"No?" said Mrs. Sappleton, in a voice which only replaced a yawn at the last moment. Then she suddenly brightened into alert attention—but not to what Framton was saying.

"Here they are at last!" she cried. "Just in time for tea, and don't they look as if they were muddy up to the eyes!"

Framton shivered slightly and turned towards the niece with a look intended to convey sympathetic comprehension. The child was staring out through the open window with dazed horror in her eyes. In a chill shock of nameless fear Framton swung round in his seat and looked in the same direction.

In the deepening twilight three figures were walking across the lawn towards the window; they all carried guns under their arms, and one of them was additionally burdened with a white coat hung over his shoulders. A tired brown spaniel kept close at their heels. Noiselessly they neared the house, and then a hoarse young voice chanted out of the dusk: "I said, Bertie, why do you bound?"

Framton grabbed wildly at his stick and hat; the hall door, the gravel drive, and the front gate were dimly noted stages in his headlong retreat. A cyclist coming along the road had to run into the hedge to avoid imminent collision.

"Here we are, my dear," said the bearer of the white mackintosh, coming in through the window, "fairly muddy, but most of it's dry. Who was that who bolted out as we came up?"

"A most extraordinary man, a Mr. Nuttel," said Mrs. Sappleton; "could only talk about his illnesses, and dashed off without a word of good-bye or apology when you arrived. One would think he had seen a ghost."

"I expect it was the spaniel," said the niece calmly; "he told me he had a horror of dogs. He was once hunted into a cemetery somewhere on the banks of the Ganges by a pack of pariah dogs, and had to spend the night in a newly dug grave with the creatures snarling and grinning and foaming just above him. Enough to make anyone lose their nerve."

Romance at short notice was her speciality.

1914

Notes

By reading older readings, such as this story, you can get an idea of how language and society changes. This story was published in 1914, but its sensibilities are very much of the Victorian era of the previous century. Making calls with letters of introduction, for example, is not a modern practice.

The use of the adverb *presently* shows a shift in meaning. It means both *currently* and *in a short time*, with the meaning shifting towards the former. In the story, it obviously means *in a short time*, but this usage is more British and more old-fashioned. It also depends on where the adverb appears in the sentence. If it appears before the verb (e.g., "he's presently reviewing the notes"), it means *currently* or *at this time*.

Another change in vocabulary is the term *French window*, which we would call *French doors* today.

The word *romance* today refers to love stories, but it had a broader meaning before, referring to any fiction.

Older literature is also challenging because many of the references are meaningless to us today. For example, Ronnie's singing, "Bertie, why do you bound?" does not mean much to us today, but it probably would to contemporary readers.

Comprehension
1.   Why has Framton come to the area?
2.   Why is he calling on the Sappletons?
3.   Who is entertaining him while he waits?
4.   What is the story Vera tells Framton?
5.   What happens after Mrs Sappleton arrives?
6.   How does Vera react to the return of the men?
7.   How does Framton react? What does he do?
8.   How does Vera explain Framton's departure?
9.   What does the last line of the story mean?

Discussion
1.   Do you admire Vera or not? Why do you think she tells such tales?
2.   Is Framton an admirable character?
3.   What impression do you get of the aunt?
4.   Do you find the story funny? Why or why not?
5.   What do you think a person like Vera would grow up to be?

Assignments
1.   Why are horror stories such popular entertainment? Explain the appeal in an essay.
2.   Compare this story to another one by Saki or one by O. Henry or Stephen Leacock.

Paraphrasing and summarizing
1.   Paraphrase: "Framton Nuttel endeavored to say the correct something which should duly flatter the niece of the moment without unduly discounting the aunt that was to come."
2.   Paraphrase: "The doctors agree in ordering me complete rest, an absence of mental excitement, and avoidance of anything in the nature of violent physical exercise,' announced Framton, who labored under the tolerably wide-spread delusion that total strangers and chance acquaintances are hungry for the least detail of one's ailments and infirmities, their cause and cure."
3.   Paraphrase: "Framton grabbed wildly at his stick and hat; the hall door, the gravel drive, and the front gate were dimly noted stages in his head

long retreat. A cyclist coming along the road had to run into the hedge to avoid imminent collision."

4. Summarize the story in a paragraph of no more than 100 words.

Vocabulary study

Fill in the following chart:

Noun	Verb	Adjective	Definition
	flatter		
	doubt		
	migrate		
	bury		
division			
	judge		
regret			
tragedy	n/a		
	n/a	treacherous	
scarcity	n/a		
avoidance			
delusion			
ailment			
	replace		
		sympathetic	
comprehension			
collision			
apology			
	arrive		
speciality			

Idioms and collocations

Discuss the meaning of these expressions:

1. put up with someone
2. bury oneself
3. worse than ever

4. hardly a soul
5. get on someone's nerves
6. break off
7. not mind something
8. rattle on
9. unfortunate coincidence
10. labour under a delusion
11. dash off
12. [as if] someone had seen a ghost
13. lose one's nerve

Structure and technique

In story-telling, the names can help establish the character. "Framton Nuttel" is not a strong name; it points to a weak character. The name "Vera" means truth, which is ironic.

Discuss the way Saki lets the story unfold. For instance, when does the reader figure out that Vera is lying? What clues does Saki give?

Soap and Water

by Urs Frei

The other day a man walked into the store, carrying a cat. I don't know which I noticed first, the cat, or how the man was crying. The cat was his, I guess. Its legs were mangled and blood was dripping through his fingers. He was crying so hard he didn't notice that this wasn't a vet hospital anymore.

"I need you to put my cat to sleep," he said.

There he stood, dripping onto the carpet. We had three customers in the store. Of course they were staring.

"The vet moved out last month, sir," I said. I came around the counter to show my concern. But also to move him out of there. You have to understand, we'd only been open a month. "We sell computers."

The man was silent. The cat was crying low, strange cries.

"Where's the vet?" he said.

"Where'd that vet go?" I said. Robert, one of my sales reps, was staring back at me. It was a pointless question, actually, because I knew the vet hadn't moved anywhere near. I was pretty sure there was no vet within a mile. "Have a look in the phone book," I told him.

The man was sobbing again. I couldn't decide if the best thing to do would be to ask him to step outside, or if this would antagonize the customers. I had a closer look at him. He had earrings in both ears. His hair was shaved on the sides of his head. He was wearing a leather jacket, and it was hard to say for sure, but he seemed handsome, the kind of man who would talk about his successes with women. What was he doing crying about a cat?

The stock boy had heard the cat and come in from the stock room. He wasn't supposed to be in the store.

Robert said, "There's a vet over on K- road."

K- road was the other side of town.

"Should I call them?" he said. "They have a pet ambulance, it says here."

"Call the pet ambulance," I said. "Get that pet ambulance over here."

The stock boy wasn't a boy at all. He was a Mexican man, about forty years old, named Ricardo, who spoke almost no English. He was wearing dirty blue-jeans and a blue work shirt. Also, he wasn't legal. He was taking off his shirt. I thought, Lord in heaven—Lord in heaven. There was that cat, dripping on my new carpet, and there was the stock boy, taking off his shirt.

He walked up to the man, spreading the shirt on his palms, and took the cat, and wrapped it in the shirt. The man said nothing. Ricardo turned his back so that no one could see, but everyone heard the snap as he broke the cat's neck. The cat went silent. One of the customers, a lady, made a horrified sound. Then Ricardo, with his head bowed, handed the cat back, along with his shirt.

I was glad I'd got that in about the pet ambulance. You have to understand that this was before I learned that blood comes out easily with just soap and water. It was that lady customer who told me.

1997

Reprinted by permission of the author.

Notes

The stock boy "wasn't legal", which means he didn't have proper status from the Immigration Department.

Comprehension

1. Describe the narrator: male or female? young or old? personality? skills? weaknesses? occupation? admirable or not?
2. What is the stereotype of someone who works with computers?
3. What is the setting for the story? Why is this significant? Could this story happen somewhere else with the same impact?
4. Why did the man with the cat come into the store?
5. How did the various characters react to this?
6. What is the narrator concerned about?
7. What is the narrator apologizing for in the last paragraph?
8. Compare the narrator and the stock boy. How do their different backgrounds explain their reactions?
9. What is the significance of the title?

Discussion

1. What would you do in this situation?
2. How far would you go to save the life of a pet? Would you pay thousands of dollars for surgery, for example?

3. Do Canadians care too much about their pets? Consider, for example, people who have severe allergies and yet refuse to get rid of their pets.
4. Could you kill an animal if necessary? Could you, for example, kill a chicken, clean it, and prepare it for dinner? Could your parents do it? Could your grandparents? What has changed? Does this matter?
5. What is this story saying about modern society? Is this a valid criticism?
6. Canadians use the terms *illegal immigrant* and *landed immigrant*, while Americans say *illegal alien* and *resident alien*. What does the difference in terminology say about the two countries?

Assignments

1. Have Canadians become too urbanized? Have we lost touch with nature? Write an essay explaining the problems this causes. Or write an essay arguing that it does not matter.
2. Take one of the controversial issues surrounding animal rights and discuss it in an essay. For example, how should farming practices be changed to be more humane? Or are vegans going too far?
3. Consider the problems of illegal immigrants. Canadians rely on them for cheap labour, but Canadian immigration favours educated immigrants, many of whom have trouble getting jobs that suit their education level. Some people argue that illegal immigrants should be given amnesty since they have established themselves here, often having children born in Canada and therefore Canadian citizens. Yet they live in an underground economy and cannot avail themselves of simple services such as health care and education. Suggest a possible solution and discuss it in an essay.

Paraphrasing and summarizing

1. In one short paragraph, summarize what happens in the story.
2. Write a one-sentence description of each character, paraphrasing what the narrator says.

Vocabulary study
Connotation
Explain the meaning of these terms and the differences:

1. put an animal to sleep
2. put an animal down
3. euthanasia
4. mercy killing
5. kill
6. murder
7. die
8. pass away
9. to be six feet under
10. a visit from the grim reaper

Make a list of other idioms and expressions that describe death. You can also discuss cultural differences. For example, why are euphemisms used? We prefer to say "my grandmother passed away" instead of "my grandmother died," and we would never say "my grandmother kicked the bucket."

Structure and technique

1. The author has decided to use first person narration. The narrator is unnamed. What is the effect of this type of narration in this story?
2. The author gives us the narrator's internal dialogue. How does this reveal the narrator's personality?
3. The story hinges on an implied contrast between the narrator and the stock boy. Should this contrast have been made more explicit?

Tempest in the School Teapot

Excerpt from chapter xv, *Anne of Green Gables*

by L. M. Montgomery

Mr. Phillips was back in the corner explaining a problem in algebra to Prissy Andrews and the rest of the scholars were doing pretty much as they pleased, eating green apples, whispering, drawing pictures on their slates, and driving crickets, harnessed to strings, up and down the aisle. Gilbert Blythe was trying to make Anne Shirley look at him and failing utterly, because Anne was at that moment totally oblivious, not only of the very existence of Gilbert Blythe, but of every other scholar in Avonlea school and of Avonlea school itself. With her chin propped on her hands and her eyes fixed on the blue glimpse of the Lake of Shining Waters that the west window afforded, she was far away in a gorgeous dreamland, hearing and seeing nothing save her own wonderful visions.

Gilbert Blythe wasn't used to putting himself out to make a girl look at him and meeting with failure. She *should* look at him, that red-haired Shirley girl with the little pointed chin and the big eyes that weren't like the eyes of any other girl in Avonlea school.

Gilbert reached across the aisle, picked up the end of Anne's long red braid, held it out at arm's length and said in a piercing whisper:

"Carrots! Carrots!"

Then Anne looked at him with a vengeance!

She did more than look. She sprang to her feet, her bright fancies fallen into cureless ruin. She flashed one indignant glance at Gilbert from eyes whose angry sparkle was swiftly quenched in equally angry tears.

"You mean, hateful boy!" she exclaimed passionately. "How dare you!"

And then—Thwack! Anne had brought her slate down on Gilbert's head and cracked it—slate not head—clear across.

Avonlea school always enjoyed a scene. This was an especially enjoyable one. Everybody said, "Oh" in horrified delight. Diana gasped. Ruby Gillis, who was inclined to be hysterical, began to cry. Tommy Sloane let his team of crickets escape him altogether while he stared open-mouthed at the tableau.

Mr. Phillips stalked down the aisle and laid his hand heavily on Anne's shoulder.

"Anne Shirley, what does this mean?" he said angrily.

Anne returned no answer. It was asking too much of flesh and blood to expect her to tell before the whole school that she had been called "carrots." Gilbert it was who spoke up stoutly.

"It was my fault Mr. Phillips. I teased her."

Mr. Phillips paid no heed to Gilbert.

"I am sorry to see a pupil of mine displaying such a temper and such a vindictive spirit," he said in a solemn tone, as if the mere fact of being a pupil of his ought to root out all evil passions from the hearts of small imperfect mortals. "Anne, go and stand on the platform in front of the blackboard for the rest of the afternoon."

Anne would have infinitely preferred a whipping to this punishment, under which her sensitive spirit quivered as from a whiplash. With a white, set face, she obeyed. Mr. Phillips took a chalk crayon and wrote on the blackboard above her head.

"Ann Shirley has a very bad temper. Ann Shirley must learn to control her temper," and then read it out loud so that even the primer class, who couldn't read writing, should understand it.

Anne stood there the rest of the afternoon with that legend above her. She did not cry or hang her head. Anger was still too hot in her heart for that and it sustained her amid all her agony of humiliation. With resentful eyes and passion-red cheeks she confronted alike Diana's sympathetic gaze and Charlie Sloane's indignant nods and Josie Pye's malicious smiles. As for Gilbert Blythe, she would not even look at him. She would never look at him again! She would never speak to him!

1908

Notes

Unlike most of the other reading selections in this textbook, this is an excerpt from a longer work. Excerpts are often harder to understand because the context is missing. Some of the context is usually explained in notes.

The most famous Canadian book in the world is undoubtedly *Anne of Green Gables* by Lucy Maud Montgomery. It was first published in 1908 and is the first in a series of books about Anne Shirley. When the book begins, Anne, who is then 11 years old, comes from an orphanage in Nova Scotia to live with Matthew and Marilla Cuthbert, an elderly brother and sister who need help on their family farm in Prince Edward Island. Anne has red hair (which she is very sensitive about), a lively imagination, a keen intelligence, a tendency to daydream, and a talent for getting into trouble. Her best friend is Diana.

Avonlea school was a one-room rural school, typical of that day. Children from six to 16 studied in the same classroom. Students wrote on slates (small, individual blackboards). Girls often wore their hair in long braids, which were irresistible to boys; a typical prank was to dip the braid in an ink bottle. This scene takes place early in the school year, on the first day Gilbert is at school.

Note that Mr. Phillips misspells Anne's name on the blackboard—another thing that Anne is sensitive about.

Comprehension

1. Why was Anne punished in class? What was her punishment?
2. How had Gilbert provoked her? Why had he done so?
3. Explain what was going on in the class as Mr. Phillips worked with one student.

Discussion

1. Who was most at fault in this incident?
2. Is Anne's anger at Gilbert justified? What do you think happens to them?
3. How is this school scene different from what one would expect today? Do you find this kind of school life appealing?
4. What would modern students do if their teacher was preoccupied or out of the classroom?
5. What kind of teasing went on in school when you were a child?
6. What were common methods of punishment in your school? How effective were they?

Assignments

1. Write a narrative retelling the basic story but updating it to modern times. For instance, the students could be using laptops instead of slates.
2. Read more of the book. It can easily be found in the library or on-line. Write a book report.
3. Watch the TV miniseries from 1985, starring Megan Follows. Write a review of the film.
4. Research the book's fame and position in Canadian literature. Find out about the role of the story in the tourist industry of Prince Edward Island. Do you find this interest surprising, or is the book's fame justified? Write an essay.
5. In small groups, act out the scene in class. Do not read or memorize the text; feel free to interpret it. Compare your version to the one in the 1985 miniseries.

Paraphrasing and summarizing

1. In less than 60 words, summarize the main action of the story.
2. Paraphrase: "Anne returned no answer. It was asking too much of flesh and blood to expect her to tell before the whole school that she had been called 'carrots.'"
3. Paraphrase: "Anger was still too hot in her heart for that and it sustained her amid all her agony of humiliation. With resentful eyes and passion-red cheeks she confronted alike Diana's sympathetic gaze and Charlie Sloane's indignant nods and Josie Pye's malicious smiles."
4. Paraphrase: ". . . Anne was at that moment totally oblivious, not only of the very existence of Gilbert Blythe, but of every other scholar in Avonlea school and of Avonlea school itself. With her chin propped on her hands and her eyes fixed on the blue glimpse of the Lake of Shining Waters that the west window afforded, she was far away in a gorgeous dreamland, hearing and seeing nothing save her own wonderful visions."

Vocabulary study

Fill in the following chart:

Noun	Verb	Adjective	Meaning
		oblivious	
vengeance			
	n/a	indignant	
		enjoyable	
	n/a	hysterical	
		solemn	
agony			
humiliation			
		resentful	
		sympathetic	

Idioms and collocations

Discuss the meaning and usage of the following expression:

1. do as one pleases
2. put oneself out to do something
3. with a vengeance
4. be inclined to be something
5. ask too much of somebody
6. to speak up

7. pay no heed to someone/something
8. to have a bad temper, to control one's temper

Structure and technique

Change the sentence structure of "Gilbert it was who spoke up stoutly" to one that would be commonly used today. What effect does the original sentence have? In other words, why does Montgomery start her sentence with "Gilbert"?

Explain Montgomery's technique in this sentence: "And then—Thwack! Anne had brought her slate down on Gilbert's head and cracked it—slate not head—clear across." Does the word "thwack" give a good idea of the sound? Why is the verb ("had brought") in the past perfect tense? Is the use of parenthetical dashes effective? Is it humorous? Would it be as effective if Montgomery had chosen the more grammatically correct phrase "her slate and not his head"?

The Squatter

by Sara McDonald

I woke up and there was a naked man sleeping beside me. I turned on the light to have a look at him. Not bad, but he wasn't anybody I knew. And certainly not someone I knew well enough to give an apartment key. If he'd broken in, surely I would've heard him. Mind you, he did manage to sneak into bed without waking me, and this isn't a very big bed.

Hello, I said. Nothing. His eyelids didn't even flicker. I prodded him in the ribs. He murmured and turned, throwing his leg over mine. Hey you, I shouted in his ear. Hello darling, he said. Then he kissed me and rolled back over, snuggling deeper into the pillows.

I got out of bed and looked for something to put on. I couldn't see his clothes anywhere and began to wonder if he had arrived naked. I pulled on jeans and a t-shirt and went to see how he'd gotten in. The windows were all closed and the deadbolt was on the door. There were no signs that anything was wrong.

A drink, I said aloud. What I need is a drink. There wasn't anything in the cupboard but a bottle of Peppermint Schnapps. It had been there so long I couldn't remember where it came from. So I poured myself a tall glass.

It tasted like mouthwash, but it seemed to help me think more clearly.

I could have phoned the police, but the problem there was my neighbours. I live in this townhouse complex where everybody can see what everybody else is up to. And if the police were to pull in here on a Saturday night, everybody would be out on their balconies in no time. They'd all be real casual about it, mind you. That's the sort of neighbourhood this is.

They'd make like they were having a midnight barbeque, or just wanted to look at the moon. Anyway, if the police escorted a naked man out of my place, that would be it. I'd simply have to move. And I like this place, I really do. It took me so long to get the furniture where it should be, and I went all over town to find drapes to match the carpets. And I've only just memorized the bus schedule. Moving is out of the question.

Darling, he called from the bedroom. Come back to bed.

———————

1988

Notes

This is a complete short story from a collection called *Open window: Canadian short short stories*, edited by Kent Thompson. A short short story can be as few as 50 words. This one is 402 words.

Comprehension

1. What is happening to the narrator?
2. What is her reaction? Why is this strange?
3. Describe the narrator. What kind of person do you think she is?
4. What is Peppermint Schnapps? What do you think it says about a person who would have it in his or her cupboard?

Discussion

1. What do you think is going on? Can you explain this story?
2. Did you enjoy this story? Why or why not?

Assignments

1. Write a brief continuation of the story. Keep it in the same style.
2. Write your own short short story. Do not go over 400 words.

Paraphrasing and summarizing

1. Summarize the story in less than 50 words.
2. Paraphrase: "And if the police were to pull in here on a Saturday night, everybody would be out on their balconies in no time. They'd all be real casual about it, mind you. That's the sort of neighbourhood this is. They'd make like they were having a midnight barbeque, or just wanted to look at the moon."

Vocabulary study

Mind you is an expression like *you know*. It does not really mean much.

Check out the verbs in the story and determine what kind of verb they are:

Find five transitive verbs.
Find five intransitive verbs.

Find five phrasal verbs. Be careful not to confuse phrasal verbs with verbs followed by a prepositional phrase. Compare:

I like to <u>sleep in</u> whenever I can. [phrasal verb]

I <u>sleep</u> in a double bed. [verb + prepositional phrase]

Structure and technique

Notice how the first sentence gets the reader's attention right away. Explain why it is effective.

The author does not use quotation marks around the words said by the characters. What effect does this have?

Appendix A

Following Format Guidelines

Presenting your work properly is important whether you are in elementary school, college, or the workforce. The two most important criteria for school assignments are that the work is easy to read and that it leaves the marker with plenty of room for comments and corrections. Instructors with specific format guidelines generally make them clear with assignment instructions. Here are some common format guidelines:

- Type your assignments on a computer. The printout should be black ink (not faded) on medium-weight 8½-by-11-inch white paper.
- Use a plain typeface in a size that is easy to read, such as Times New Roman 12 point. Do not use typefaces that look like printing or handwriting.
- Double space your essay. (Set paragraph line spacing at 2.)
- Leave a one-inch margin on all sides of the page.
- Number your pages, often in the bottom centre or bottom right. Start your numbering with the first page of the essay, not the cover page.
- Use only one side of the paper.
- Indent your paragraphs with five spaces, the default tab setting.
- Use left justification and a ragged right margin. (Full justification often makes large gaps between words.)
- Make sure your sentences are clearly shown with a capital letter at the beginning and a period at the end.
- Use one space after a period. Do not put spaces before periods or commas.
- Include a cover page that gives the title of the assignment, your name and student identification number, the course code including section number, the date, and the professor's name.
- Avoid unnecessary artwork. Include illustrations only when necessary.
- Staple the pages together in the top left corner. Do not use a cover or folder unless your instructor has specifically asked for one.

Appendix B

Writing E-mail

Most students use e-mail to communicate with their professors, and it is important to write messages that communicate effectively. Here are some guidelines:

Using a subject heading

You should always give your e-mail a brief, descriptive subject heading. "Hi this is Jung" is not an appropriate subject heading. Be as specific as possible. Here are some examples: "question about midterm," "course outline inquiry," and "assignment due date."

Identifying yourself

Make sure that any e-mail from you includes your full name. The recipient should be able to tell immediately whom the message is from. This should be evident from your e-mail address.

Do not start your message with "Hi, my name is May Novak. I'm one of your students," and do not put your name in your subject heading. Instead, give your full name at the bottom of the e-mail as a signature. You can also use an automatic signature with information about yourself, such as your title, address, and phone number.

You will generally be given a school e-mail address; use it for correspondence with your instructor. It is not professional to send out e-mail with an address like "sexyguy@hotmail.com," and the messages may end up in the trash as suspected spam. If you use a web-based e-mail service, you can set up separate accounts for social contacts and more professional uses.

Including a salutation

Letters generally start with a salutation, such as "Dear Professor Brown," but memos do not have salutations since the information at the top of the page gives the addressee's name. An e-mail message is more like a memo since there is "to," "from," and subject information with the message. Therefore, salutations are considered optional in e-mail. They are a good idea when you initiate an e-mail conversation but unnecessary once you get into a back-and-forth exchange of information.

You can use a letter-like salutation with *Dear* and the person's name. You can use the last name with a title (Mrs Bhatia) or the first name (Anita) depending on how well you know the person.

Using correct, standard English

You can use abbreviations such as "U R" in chat messages or in e-mail to your friends, but your mail to your instructor should be written in correct, standard English—especially for an English course and especially if you are asking for something such as an extension on an assignment or an opportunity to write a supplemental test. Use a spell checker and proofread carefully before you send your message.

Making your message clear and concise

Like all writing, e-mail messages should be clear and concise. No one wants to read a long, rambling message only to come to the end with no clear idea of what the sender wants.

Write an e-mail message like a business letter. State right away what the purpose of your message is.

Being prudent

Before you hit the "send" button, rethink your message. Remember that e-mail is recorded forever. Keep in mind that e-mail is legally the property of the institution, so your supervisor is entitled to read any message you send from company computers. If you are sending an emotional message, such as a response to an insult, save your message and read it again the next day before you send it.

Reducing e-mail traffic

Do not hit "reply all" unless your information must actually go to every recipient on the list. For example, if someone is setting up a meeting, you probably do not have to tell everybody on that mailing list whether you will attend or not.

Do not request a "received receipt" unless it is absolutely necessary.

Do not let messages get longer and longer as the back-and-forth correspondence goes on. Delete any of the copied information from previous messages unless it is important reference information.

Attachments

Your instructor will probably have definite preferences on whether or not work can be submitted electronically, so ask if your instructor does not tell you this in the course information. Some instructors prefer to get essays by e-mail, while others are wary of opening attachments. Many instructors prefer hard copy of assignments so that they do not have to print out your work (especially if they do not have access to school facilities to do this). If you have questions about your draft, you can cut and paste the text into the body of the message.

School policies

Your institution may have official etiquette policies for appropriate use of e-mail. Check these policies for further information.

Appendix C

Making Oral Presentations

You may be asked to make an oral presentation as part of your English course. A good presentation is similar to a good essay—both have an introduction and conclusion, both have a clear thesis, both have information organized in blocks (or paragraphs), and both have support for the points made. The main difference is presentation: You should not read a presentation as if you were reading an essay out loud. Here are a few tips:

Preparation
- Understand your topic, and write down your thoughts about it.
- Ask yourself what you can do to make your ideas interesting to your listeners.
- Organize your main points. Make sure you support them.
- Make notes to guide you. Print or enlarge the notes so that your eyes can catch the points at a glance. Keep cards or pieces of paper to a minimum.
- Know your topic thoroughly enough that you can deliver it without notes.
- If you are using handouts, overheads, or PowerPoint, do not write down your presentation exactly as you plan to deliver it. Use the documents for main points or headings and key details, such as names and dates.
- Practise your delivery in front of a full-length mirror.
- Time your presentation and adjust where necessary so that it fits time requirements.
- Rehearse in front of a small group of friends or family and get feedback.
- If possible, record and listen to your own speech so you can catch the tone, rhythm, and volume.
- Avoid wearing clothing that may prove a distraction to your delivery, such as a baseball hat that covers your face or necklaces that you fiddle with.

Delivery
- Open with a salutation, such as "Good afternoon, ladies and gentlemen . . ."
- Look at your audience. Try to keep eye contact at least once with everyone in the audience. Talk *to* them, not *at* them.
- Pay attention to your body language. Avoid needless movements that may distract your listeners.
- Strive for a confident look because when you exude confidence, your audience will be more receptive.
- Note the facial and body language of your audience to gauge reaction. Adjust accordingly when facial nuances reveal that the listeners do not understand, do not hear, or do not agree.
- Do not read your speech. This is very important. Instead, talk with a normal rhythm.

- If the opportunity arises, ad lib but do not stray too far or too long from your set speech.
- Be loud enough so that the back-row listeners need not strain to hear you.
- If you are using PowerPoint, slides, or overheads, do not merely read the information on the screen.
- With technology, be prepared for unforeseen glitches and soldier on with your delivery. You may want to have back-ups, such as transparencies or handouts, for important information from your PowerPoint slides, but try to keep them to a minimum.
- Conclude by summarizing the main points quickly.
- Ask whether there are any questions.
- Thank the audience for their attention.

Answer Key

Exercise 1.1
1. Driving on the highway has fewer distractions. The traffic is all travelling in the same direction, so it is only necessary to watch out for lane changers and the occasional traffic jam.
2. Tattoos are often a mistake. People regret them when they get older. They may no longer have the same interests, and the tattoo may not look as good later when the ink fades and skin changes with age.
3. Large batches of food can be cooked on the weekend and then frozen in order to cut down on food preparation time. Chili, stews, spaghetti sauce, and some soups freeze well.
4. Showers are preferable to baths. The running water feels invigorating. Showers are a refreshing way to start the day.
5. Children should not have TVs and computers in their bedrooms because they are too distracting. Children would not do their homework if they could play electronic games instead. They would just stay in their room and never talk to parents and siblings.

Exercise 1.3
1. The smallest problem with a luxury car costs more money because the parts are harder to find and labour is so expensive.
2. All the road rules and signs in the driver's handbook must be memorized for the test.
3. College students can be successful if they attend class, pay attention to the instructor, and do their homework.
4. Spring cleaning and de-cluttering is important and should include getting rid of clothes no longer worn.
5. Teenagers can be seen hanging around the mall with nothing to do.

Exercise 2.2
1. competence; 2. enrichment; 3. speech; 4. wealth; 5. success; 6. reality; 7. invitation; 8. willingness; 9. denial; 10. contribution

Exercise 2.5
1. describe; 2. evade; 3. inspire; 4. facilitate; 5. whiten; 6. threaten; 7. authorize; 8. defy; 9. pursue; 10. expand

Exercise 2.6
1. misty; 2. comic, comical, comedic; 3. operational, operative; 4. forceful; 5. experimental; 6. acceptable; 7. stressful; 8. disastrous; 9. scientific; 10. public

Exercise 2.7
1. secret ballot; 2. brute force; 3. frantic haste; 4. jagged hole; 5. masked intruder; 6. tempting offer; 7. tough opponent; 8. heartfelt sympathy; 9. limited visibility; 10. extensive vocabulary

Exercise 2.9
1. simply; 2. really; 3. truly; 4. significantly; 5. uneasily; 6. brutally; 7. hazily; 8. absurdly; 9. frequently; 10. evidently

Exercise 2.12
1. courageous; 2. advice; 3. angered; 4. envisioned; 5. pitiful; 6. legal; 7. excessive, risky; 8. soft, wise/angry; 9. advised/agreed, risky, performed; 10. excessively/highly

Exercise 2.13
1. smiling; 2. tiled; 3. requirement; 4. fades; 5. wading; 6. completed; 7. comprising; 8. shades; 9. settled; 10. eroding

Exercise 2.14
1. wedding; 2. waited; 3. dreamless; 4. dipped; 5. controlled; 6. chugging; 7. occurrence; 8. keeping; 9. grunted; 10. dripping

Exercise 2.15
1. Whose; 2. women's; 3. does, choose; 4. You're, thought, compliment; 5. loose; 6. affects, whether; 7. patience; 8. Were, scene; 9. to, two; 10. passed, there

Exercise 2.17
unable/disabled, inability/disability, inactive, non-addictive, moral, counter-argument, unappetizing, inaudible, unbelievable, misbehave, unclassified/non-classified, incompetent, discontinue, colour, indivisible, inexcusable, unfavourable, infinite, inflexible, unforgettable, informal, malfunction, ungrateful, anti-hero, plausible, uninformed/ill-informed, uninteresting, unjustified, illiterate, nutrition, mismanage, impatient, malpractice, misquote, unreadable, irregular, non-renewable, misrepresent, unsuccessful, non-toxic, worthy, unusable, invisible, unwise

Exercise 2.18
1. a; 2. k; 3. g; 4. h; 5. n; 6. d; 7. e; 8. f; 9. b; 10. l; 11. o; 12. c; 13. j; 14. m; 15. i

Exercise 2.19
1. j; 2. a; 3. o; 4. e; 5. d; 6. h; 7. m; 8. n; 9. k; 10. b; 11. f; 12. c; 13. g; 14. i; 15. l

Exercise 2.20
1. take a test; 2. make a request, grant a request; 3. conduct research, carry out research; 4. drop a hint, take a hint; 5. lack experience, acquire experience; 6. run up a debt, settle a debt; 7. adopt a method, follow a method; 8. give a reason; 9. run a risk; 10. gain support, provide support

Exercise 2.21
1. border patrol; 2. calculated risk; 3. daring attack; 4. hazardous material; 5. momentary hesitation; 6. reasonable request; 7. subtle reminder; 8. torrential rain; 9. urgent matter; 10. weak tea

Exercise 2.23
1. medicine; 2. law; 3. computer science; 4. real estate; 5. police work

Exercise 3.1
1. Peter/whistled/tune; 2. team/won/game; 3. we/went; 4. she/can indulge/tastes; 5. one/has decided; 6. friend/is throwing/party; 7. I/lost/book, I/can borrow/yours; 8. neighbour/signed, forgot; 9. flight/leaves, he/has packed; 10. I/know

Exercise 3.2
1. brought, behaved; 2. saw, avoided, had warned; 3. ate; 4. leaves, have; 5. play; 6. will meet; 7. did not sleep; 8. enjoyed; 9. did you buy, bought; 10. has already seen, will go, will meet

Exercise 3.3
1. been, have; 2. waiting; 3. written; 4. be, contact; 5. solved; 6. have, been; 7. take; 8. be; 9. follow, been; 10. read

Exercise 3.5
1. slam brakes, door; 2. pronounce name, word; 3. install alarm, locks, software; 4. throw ball, party, pottery; 5. review account, notes; 6. watch children, television, time; 7. drive ball, truck; 8. elevate leg, position; 9. expect honesty, promotion, person, reward; 10. skip class, meal, rope; 11. access information, room; 12. bear burden, fruit; 13. wipe counter, glasses, tears, window; 14. make date, dinner, mistake; 15. report accident, crime, person

Exercise 3.7
1. cars; 2. apple, is; 3. is, has; 4. members, are; 5. dogs, leashes; 6. posters, market; 7. takes, dance, lessons, Tuesday; 8. errors; 9. pieces, is; 10. mistakes, ones

Exercise 3.8
1. Peter's; 2. Her, Tim's; 3. children's, their; 4. Megan's; 5. Murphy's; 6. boys', their; 7. students'; 9. our; 10. Ian's, our

Exercise 3.9

Here are the places where articles or other determiners are required:

1. on my/the trip, A student, the University of Ottawa, her French, a tutor, an asset
2. a picnic for the park's anniversary, The neighbourhood high school band, the band shell, the afternoon
3. a wonderful trip, the museum, at the pier, to their final destinations, the name of the ship that my family, a trip on the Bluenose, a tall ship was a real thrill, the display about the Titanic at the Maritime Museum of the Atlantic, the Titanic victims, The story of the 1917 Halifax explosion, A munitions ship, in the harbour, the entire downtown area
4. an apartment, near the university, the bus when the weather, a two-bedroom apartment, my cousin, a high-rise building, on the seventh floor, The living room, a picture window with a view of the river, a few pieces, the thrift shop, my own place
5. the most important factor, a student succeeds, a wish, a/the student, A/The motivated student, the student

Exercise 3.11

1. in the summer, for his regular games on ice in the winter; 2. on Friday night, in the highest part of the stadium in the nosebleed section; 3. near my sister's house, to/for work, with my nephews, to the park, on the monkey bars; 4. on the couch on Sunday afternoons, on television; 5. out of the park for his second home run of the game; 6. in the early morning at the cottage, off the end of the dock, across the bay to the small beach; 7. on the bookshelf by the door, on the top shelf near/next to/by the other dictionaries; 8. in the park after class on Wednesday afternoons, By the time; 9. at a resort on the island; 10. on the hook, in my purse, on the desk, in the junk drawer, under the desk

Exercise 3.13

1. Peter had to get the transmission and the brakes fixed.
2. Zach thought he passed his driver's test, but he had to book another one.
3. Kate plays the piano and guitar.
4. My uncle was killed in a motorcycle accident, so my mother won't allow me to get a motorcycle.
5. Erin's brother and her brother-in-law are engineers.
6. Melissa could go to the University of Calgary or the University of Alberta.
7. Ben thought he had a job on the oil rig, but the job fell through.
8. We thought of holding my parents' anniversary party on a dinner cruise boat or in the revolving restaurant.
9. Christine was supposed to pick Jim up at the train station, but she forgot.
10. Suji couldn't understand the formula, so she read the chapter again.

Exercise 3.16

1. to rake the leaves, plant some bulbs, and spread the mulch; 2. canoeing, sailing, and waterskiing; 3. reasonable financial compensation, a good work environment, and friendly co-workers; 4. coloured, cut, and straightened; 5. excessive violence, swearing, and nudity.

Exercise 3.21

1. While Tim Horton had a hand in starting the business that bears his name, Laura Secord had nothing to do with the candy-making business.
2. The candy store was named after Laura Secord because the founder wanted a Canadian heroine as a trademark.
3. Although the Canadian flag is such a recognized symbol today, it did not have an easy road to design and official acceptance in 1965.
4. While the first explorers came to Canada seeking a route to the Orient, they came back for the valuable fish and furs.
5. British Columbia agreed to join Canada if a railroad would be built to connect it with the eastern provinces.
6. The Canadian Pacific Railway took many years to complete because it was so difficult to build through the rock of the Canadian Shield in Central Canada and the mountain ranges in British Columbia.
7. The United Empire Loyalists came north to Canada after the American Revolution because they wanted to remain British subjects.
8. Even though lacrosse is one of Canada's national sports, it is not very popular, especially when compared to hockey.
9. When Tommy Douglas became a member of Parliament, he wanted to introduce the same reforms to Canada that he brought to Saskatchewan.
10. After the Acadians were expelled from Nova Scotia, they settled in Louisiana.

Exercise 3.23

1. Touring the house; 2. located in a prime downtown area; 3. tucked under the stairway; 4. Having worked for his father's construction company; 6. Marc's wife Elena, not wanting to live in a construction zone for years; 7. Although handy with power tools and a paint brush; 9. Doing the work themselves; 10. After weighing all the pros and cons

Exercise 3.26

Cleaning out my grandmother's cluttered, musty old house after she died was a monumental task. Like many old people who had lived through unspeakable war and famine, she was an incurable hoarder. She kept old newspapers, plastic bags, and cardboard boxes. She didn't trash out-of-date calendars; she just tacked up a new one in a different spot on the wall. We found new clothes that had been saved for a special occasion and never used. Her husband's clothes still hung in the closet even though he had passed away a dozen years earlier. In the cold cellar were jars of pickled food that must have been 20 years old. Two full-size freezers were crammed with food. Some of the packages were many years old. She felt safe with all her possessions and never wanted to let anything go.

Exercise 3.27

1. Susan's brother, grandfather's house, He's missed, he's planning, university's; 2. Let's go, Johnsons' cottage, We've, I'll just give, it's okay, It'll, don't go, we'll be; 3. his teachers' instructions; 4. he's willing, father's business; 5. students' work, I don't

Exercise 3.28

1. Jillian decided to take a psychology course from the Continuing Education Department.
2. Do you want to order Chinese food or pizza? I have a coupon from Marco's Pizza.
3. Sir John A. Macdonald was Canada's first prime minister. His picture is on the ten-dollar bill.
4. John McCrae wrote the poem "In Flanders fields," which is on the back of the bill.
5. Remembrance Day honours Canada's war dead. A minute of silence commemorates the end of World War I at 11 a.m. on November 11.

Exercise 3.29

1. Mr Peterson requested the review of the department because of its poor performance. The manager thought it was unnecessary.
2. Shakespeare's play *Romeo and Juliet* tells the story of two teenagers in love in sixteenth-century Italy. It's a tragic tale because the lovers are from two feuding families.
3. I don't know what to buy as a gift for Joanne's baby shower. She's having twin boys.
4. If you're worried about fitting the course into your schedule, why don't you take it on-line?
5. Let's take the train to Montreal so we don't have to worry about driving and parking. The city's subway system, which is called the metro, is an efficient way to get around town.
6. A man who grew up not having to do housework is less likely to help his wife out around the house.
7. To bake a cake, you need to assemble the following ingredients: butter, sugar, eggs, flour, baking powder, salt, buttermilk, baking soda, and vanilla.
8. I asked him to leave me a copy of the report, but he forgot. He finally e-mailed it to me, and I had to print out a copy.
9. We went over every word of the report; however, we missed several errors, so it didn't look very good when we gave it to the supervisor.

10. She asked whether I could take over her shift on Saturday night.
I wanted to go to Jack's party, so I said no.

Exercise 4.3
1. a; 2. c; 3. b; 4. d; 5. b

Exercise 4.4
1. b; 2. d; 3. b; 4. c; 5. a

Exercise 4.5
b, d, g

Exercise 4.6
1. c; 2. b; 3. b

Exercise 4.7
1. a; 2. c; 3. c

Exercise 4.8
1. b; 2. b; 3. b; 4. a; 5. c

Exercise 4.9
Pairs of sentences where the second is an example of the first: 1, 3, 5

Exercise 4.13
Modern novels are also good reading practice because students have to follow a complex plot with a variety of characters.
Andersen was a Dane who had an unhappy childhood but gained a measure of fame with the stories he wrote.

Exercise 4.14
Sentences 1, 4, 5, 7, 9, 10

Exercise 4.15
Only one transition signal for each blank is given here, but you can use a different one if it has the same meaning.
1. for example; 2. in addition; 3. for example; 4. at the same time; 5. consequently; 6. however; 7. therefore; 8. for instance; 9. however; 10. in addition; 11. then; 12. nevertheless; 13. for instance; 14. specifically; 15. however

Exercise 4.16
College students moving into an apartment or a house should just use a cellphone and not bother with a land line. First, the cost of a cellphone is comparable. Monthly fees are similar, and students can get the plan that suits their usage level. Since students may move more than once a year, they can

avoid the high cost of getting new land-line hook-ups each time. Secondly, convenience is an important consideration. Students can keep the phone with them at all times, which is especially important since students are rarely at home. Instead of changing their phone numbers each time they move, cellphone users can keep their own individual numbers. Finally, with students having individual phones, potential roommate problems can be avoided. For example, there will be no arguing over how to split the phone bill and which long-distance charges belong to which person. Cellphone users can have their own voice mail and not depend on their roommates to pass on messages. Even though there are disadvantages such as poor reception, cellphones are a better choice for most students.

Exercise 5.2

1. Despite the evidence that shows fast food is unhealthy, people keep eating it because it's cheap, tasty, and convenient.
2. People get tattoos to decorate their bodies, to show belonging to a specific group, and to show what is important to them.
3. The QWERTY keyboard is illogically designed because it makes the left hand work harder, hampers faster typing, and is more difficult to learn.
4. Leasing a car means lower monthly payments, access to new cars, and warranty coverage.
5. Students at a loss during a teachers' strike can read their textbook and notes, complete their assignments, and do extra reading.
6. The basic types of TV commercial include lifestyle ads, humorous commercials, and straight information.
7. Transportation in big cities can be fixed by improving public transit system, shipping more goods by rail, and controlling the use of personal vehicles.

Exercise 5.3

1. The government should encourage young people to vote by teaching them about politics in schools, showing political news on television shows geared to them, and demonstrating how easy voting is.
2. With a reduced workweek, the employment rate would be lower, productivity would go up, and employees would have more time for families.
3. Parents can help their children go off to college by giving them money, helping them choose a program, and encouraging them.
4. When shopping on-line, buyers can choose from a wide array of items, shop in the convenience of their own home, and compare goods before they buy.
5. My choice of job would be determined by potential happiness, challenge, and variety.

Exercise 7.1 Word choice

1. transition; 2. sales clerks; 3. outstanding; 4. incinerated; 5. piqued; 6. tried; 7. difficult or not easy; 8. strive; 9. committing; 10. told; 11. unenjoyable; 12. process; 13. sanitation; 14. sensible; 15. implying; 16. wealth; 17. problem; 18. stressed out; 19. appearance; 20. habits

Exercise 7.2 Word differences

1. famous; 2. disturb; 3. Finally; 4. ashamed; 5. graciously; 6. intolerant; 7. shortcomings; 8. respectful; 9. disprove; 10. adapting; 11. desire; 12. popular; 13. continually; 14. donate; 15. studied

Exercise 7.3 Word choice

1. curfew; 2. widower; 3. edible; 4. punctuality; 5. tantrums; 6. my sister-in-law; 7. tuition; 8. pension plan; 9. orphans; 10. drought; 11. bigamist; 12. decade; 13. chauffeur; 14. stationary; 15. shoplifting

Exercise 7.4 Collocation

1. practise my English; 2. to support themselves; 3. feel like I have accomplished something; 4. or stolen; 5. illness will be worse; 6. make a good choice; 7. pan; 8. volume; 9. spoon-fed; 10. robbing

Exercise 7.5 Parts of speech

1. safe, crime, worried, dangers; 2. extreme; 3. lost, absence; 4. beautify, important; 5. respond, worth; 6. valuable; 7. easily; 8. succeed, carefully; 9. recent, study; 10. beliefs, culture; 11. definite; 12. comprehension, practising, confident; 13. certain, offer; 14. dead; 15. immigrants' country, gradually

Exercise 7.6 Spelling

1. through, highlighted, studying; 2. environment, pollution; 3. There, salad; 4. recklessly, night, jail; 5. idolized, wore, capes; 6. write-off; 7. whether, adapt; 8. severe, maybe, lights; 9. Clothes, wear; 10. nutritious, well-balanced, definitely

Exercise 7.7 One word or two?

1. any more; 2. alike; 3. in front; 4. a part; 5. ahead; 6. a lot; 7. aloud; 8. a while, aside; 9. at all, Even though, voice mail; 10. another; 12. alone, other hand, along; 13. Nevertheless; 14. Furthermore, a way, back up; 15. all ready; 16. about; 17. outside; 18. Nowadays; 19. In spite, up to

Exercise 7.8 Troublesome words

1. afford to buy; 2. concerned; 3. Compared; 4. People spend too much money on clothes, toys, or cars. 5. was supposed to; 6. used to be; 7. be concerned; 8. Even if; 9. Having a laptop is very convenient; 10. make it easy; 11. are concerned; 12. We cannot afford; 13. worked hard; 14. She used to live; 15. even when

Exercise 7.9 Determiners

1. the first person, across Lake Ontario; 2. the Internet; 3. Many of the students, at a time; 4. the University of British Columbia; 5. the most popular; 6. The meaning, a relationship; 7. a success, the program; 8. Honesty, one of the most important; 9. a doctor

Exercise 7.10 Countable and uncountable nouns

1. gave him advice, the furniture on delayed payment; 2. the information; 3. much homework, my vocabulary; 4. new luggage; 5. used it; 7. to alcohol; 8. and hope; 9. another project (or more work); 11. have trouble; 12. and jewellery; 13. a loaf of bread, a jug of milk, some cheese; 14. much research

Exercise 7.11 Verb tense and form

1. could be, I had, After I found several articles; 2. employees have, loosen up, make themselves; 3. I went; 4. are not taught, they might not pay attention; 5. never attended; 6. are used to spending, it is time; 7. people work, amount accomplished; 8. would not have, make sure I do, I will not pass; 9. do not take, hate; 10. to go camping, like; 11. students have; 12. used to, will help management pinpoint problems; 13. I decided, I arrived, I had forgotten; 14. has danced, she saw; 15. I would still want, I would still need

Exercise 7.12 Active and passive voice

1. happened; 3. get misled, they regret; 4. People fear, people suffer; 5. he would take; 6. I hurried; 7. It rained; 8. could appear; 9. will improve; 10. be assigned, to be shared; 11. can also benefit, games improve; 12. should be bought, to keep up with; 13. family is only allowed; 14. were built; 15. are exchanged

Exercise 7.13

1. confused; 2. frightened; 3. pleased; 4. disappointing, misleading; 5. offended; 6. disgusting, bothered; 7. interesting, shocked; 8. annoying, relieved; 9. flattered; 10. satisfying, encouraging

Exercise 7.14

1. was pleased; 2. confusing; 4. exciting part; 6. felt worried, seems satisfied; 8. an interesting person; 9. annoying; 10. flattering

Exercise 7.15 Gerunds or infinitives

1. taking; 2. to wait, seeing; 3. to fire; 4. taking; 5. to see, to join; 6. repainting; 7. to return; 8. telling, to take; 9. to take, redoing; 10. to try, to keep

Exercise 7.16 Gerunds and infinitives

1. seeing; 2. hope to get, start studying; 4. expected to see; 5. suggest trying, pretend to agree; 8. waiting; 9. to fire more staff; 10. answering

Exercise 7.17 Prepositions

1. for winter conditions, with something; 2. for you, for the test; 3. earphones on, listens to, oblivious to; 4. capable of, in class; 5. at the airport, for the plane, wait for; 6. with that brand, known for; 7. grateful for, confused by; 8. adjacent to, from my window; 9. talk to; 10. depend on, argue with

Exercise 7.18 Prepositions

1. on her own; 2. to/for the problem; 3. on my laptop computer, at my convenience; 4. at the dinner table; 5. to the behaviour; 6. for a luxury car; 7. in the textbook every week; 8. on the Internet; 9. by choosing; 10. get downtown

Exercise 7.19 Prepositions and different parts of speech

1. fears terrorist attacks; 3. understanding of; 4. emphasizes basic first aid treatments; 6. affect the results; 7. describes the difficulties, mentions the misunderstandings; 8. expects Zach; 11. desire for privacy; 12. gained a new division; 13. increase charity programs

Exercise 7.20 Possessive forms

1. whose keys, Security Department; 2. storage rooms, misplaced mine; 3. nowadays; 5. children's babysitter; 6. Johnsons' house; Their whole place; 7. Whose dog; 8. their backpacks; 9. Sally's car; 10. your textbook, Elizabeth's

Exercise 7.21 Subject/verb and pronoun agreement

1. is from Australia, plays the trumpet; 2. was a pleasure; 3. It takes; 6. It has; 7. cameras do; They only help; 8. has risen; 9. they can be found, is stored; 10. It will

Exercise 7.22 Fragments and run-ons

1. She's pretending to work, but she's just playing solitaire on the computer, with the time running out.
3. She lets Jake use the car whenever he asks even though he's a terrible driver.
4. We studied all the readings in class; however, many of the students had trouble remembering the material for the test.
5. It's not hard to see what the problem is. The machine won't start because this piece is jamming it.
6. Because he had accumulated so much stuff in residence, he borrowed his parents' van when he was moving out.
7. In most cases, the advantages of self-employment are being your own boss and not having to answer to anyone.
9. He lets his employees have a say in the decision-making process; therefore, their job satisfaction is high. Few of them move on to other jobs.
10. Because of his success with the last project, he was promoted to assistant manager. After a while, he was making much more money, so he asked his girlfriend to marry him.

Exercise 7.23 Sentence Structure

1. that she was late; 3. that everyone wants; 4. where the national language; 5. Going to a fast food restaurant will save time; 6. and more willing; 7. he broke the nib; 8. International students in Canada face difficulties with daily life; 9. Because of the fast development; 10. The manager cut the staff, reorganized the filing system, and got everything to run more smoothly.

Exercise 7.24 Apostrophes

1. Jill's brother couldn't; 2. extra practices; 3. lets, icons; 4. doesn't, Marshalls', it's; 5. always, she's; 6. Who's, it's too late; 7. Let's, knows, It's; 8. likes, superheroes; buys; 9. We're, shipments, suppliers; 10. It's, I've, Martin's abilities, lets; 11. checks; 12. Today's, DVDs; 13. Tuesdays, seniors/seniors'; 14. buses; 15. concerns, signs

Exercise 7.25 Mechanics

1. If I hadn't been paying attention, I would have been hit by that ball.
2. The Japanese garden at UBC is a beautiful, restful place. I like to visit there on Sunday afternoons.
3. Allison loves horror movies, but I hate being scared. My favourite movie is *Gone with the wind*.
4. Tailgating is a traffic violation. Moreover, it is dangerous. Not only can the tailgater easily hit the car ahead, but drivers behind the tailgater get frustrated seeing brake lights because they do not know whether there is an actual traffic slowdown.
5. Like a drill sergeant, Steven shouted, "Do not panic! Walk! Don't run!"
6. On my trip to Europe, I visited Paris, Monaco, Florence, Rome, Venice, Munich, and Amsterdam. I met a lot of students from different countries who were travelling on the same tour bus.
7. The people's response is predictable. They won't support the new party because of its stand on social justice issues.
8. I can't say who's coming to the wedding because I haven't seen the latest list.
9. The women's washroom was closed for maintenance, so Frances and Lee took over the men's room.
10. Charles's mother used to play for a ladies softball team. She held a few pitching records.

Index